CAN DEMOCRACY SURVIVE GLOBAL CAPITALISM?

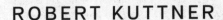

ROBERT KUTTNER

W. W. NORTON & COMPANY

Independent Publishers Since 1923

New York | London

Copyright © 2018 by Robert Kuttner

For information about permission to reproduce selections from this book,
write to Permissions, W. W. Norton & Company, Inc.,
500 Fifth Avenue, New York, NY 10110

For information about special discounts for bulk purchases, please contact
W. W. Norton Special Sales at specialsales@wwnorton.com or 800-233-4830

Manufacturing by LSC Communications, Harrisonburg
Book design by Chris Welch
Production manager: Lauren Abbate

Library of Congress Cataloging-in-Publication Data

Names: Kuttner, Robert, author.
Title: Can democracy survive global capitalism? / by Robert Kuttner.
Description: First Edition. | New York : W. W. Norton & Company, [2018] |
Includes bibliographical references and index.
Identifiers: LCCN 2017053895 | ISBN 9780393609936 (hardcover)
Subjects: LCSH: Economic policy. | Democracy. | Corporate state.
| Taxation.| Globalization.
Classification: LCC HD87 .K88 2018 | DDC 320.9182/1—dc23
LC record available at https://lccn.loc.gov/2017053895

ISBN 978-0-393-35689-2 pbk.

W. W. Norton & Company, Inc., 500 Fifth Avenue, New York, N.Y. 10110
www.wwnorton.com

W. W. Norton & Company Ltd., 15 Carlisle Street, London W1D 3BS

1 2 3 4 5 6 7 8 9 0

For Gabriel, Jessica, and Shelly

"A timely polemic against globalization and marketization. . . . [Robert Kuttner is]. . . something of a national treasure. . . . Kuttner has tirelessly poked holes in dominant economic narratives and consistently espoused a social-democratic populism that is looking much better than some of the alternatives these days."
—*New York Times Book Review*

"Using historical synthesis and reporting, [Kuttner] explores how [unfettered global finance's] resurgence captured the political process and cut off policy approaches that could have protected the interests of workers and nations, leading to disillusionment with political institutions and the rise of ideological extremes. Kuttner's call to recognize and fight this status quo doesn't come with easy solutions, but it will inspire readers to think deeply about our complex and troubling times."
—*Booklist*

"[A] vigorous critique. . . . Capitalism as we know it today is antidemocratic—and not likely to relinquish power without a fight. A useful resource for setting agendas."　　　—*Kirkus Reviews*

"Illuminating. . . . [A]ccessible to lay readers. . . . [T]hought-provoking."
—*Publishers' Weekly*

"Democracies govern nations, while global capitalism runs the world. Robert Kuttner provides a clear-eyed, intellectually riveting account of how the inevitable tensions between the two have fueled neo-fascist nationalism here and abroad, and why the response must be a new progressive populism rooted in democracy and social justice. Timely and compelling."　　　—Robert B. Reich, Chancellor's Professor of Public Policy, University of California, Berkeley

"Robert Kuttner combines economic acumen, a gift for narrative, and genuine passion in his persuasive new book. In his telling, the issue isn't whether national economies should be open to foreign trade or

finance. It's whether the rules of the global economy are set up to benefit ordinary citizens or merely economic elites."

—Jacob S. Hacker, Yale University, and coauthor of
Winner-Take-All Politics

"Kuttner brilliantly brings together two strands of thought: explaining both the economics and politics of global capitalism and how our society has abandoned core principles of fairness and equality. The rise of inequality helped pave the way for Donald Trump—a figure out of step with basic American values. Kuttner reminds us of the urgency with which we need to get back to a more just society."

—Joseph E. Stiglitz, Columbia University, winner of
the Nobel Prize in Economics, and best-selling author of
The Price of Inequality

"Standing on the shoulders of Karl Polanyi, Bob Kuttner revives the lost art of political economy in this absorbing and important analysis of wild markets, assaults on labor, and profound changes to institutional rules."

—Ira Katznelson, Columbia University, and author of
the Bancroft Prize–winning *Fear Itself:
The New Deal and the Origins of Our Time*

"Conventional wisdom has it that our income disparities and dysfunctional politics are the consequence of inexorable and uncontrollable developments in technology, market competition, and globalization. As Robert Kuttner argues in this superb book, they are instead the result of our own policy choices."

—Dani Rodrik, Harvard University, and author of
Straight Talk on Trade and *The Globalization Paradox*

CAN
DEMOCRACY
SURVIVE
GLOBAL
CAPITALISM?

Debtors' Prison:
The Politics of Austerity Versus Possibility

A Presidency in Peril:
The Inside Story of Obama's Promise, Wall Street's Power, and the Struggle
to Control Our Economic Future

Obama's Challenge:
America's Economic Crisis and the Power of a Transformative Presidency

The Squandering of America:
How the Failure of Our Politics Undermines Our Prosperity

Family Reunion:
Reconnecting Parents and Children in Adulthood (with Sharland Trotter)

Everything for Sale:
The Virtues and Limits of Markets

The End of Laissez-Faire:
National Purpose and the Global Economy after the Cold War

The Life of the Party:
Democratic Prospects in 1988 and Beyond

The Economic Illusion:
False Choices Between Prosperity and Social Justice

Revolt of the Haves:
Tax Rebellions and Hard Times

Misery generates hate.

– CHARLOTTE BRONTË

A polity with extremes of wealth and poverty is a city not of free persons but of slaves and masters, the ones consumed by envy, the others by contempt.

– ARISTOTLE

The victory of fascism was made practically unavoidable by the liberals' obstruction of any reform involving planning, regulation, or control.

– KARL POLANYI

Ideas, knowledge, art, hospitality, travel–these are the things which should of their nature be international. But let goods be homespun whenever it is reasonably and conveniently possible; and, above all, let finance be primarily national.

– JOHN MAYNARD KEYNES

Democracy, national sovereignty and global economic integration are mutually incompatible.

– DANI RODRIK

CONTENTS

PREFACE

A quarter century ago in the glow of postcommunist triumphalism, many were predicting that globalization would link democracy with capitalism in a splendid convergence. Instead, we are witnessing a primitive backlash against both the global market and liberal democracy.

In the United States, the rise of Donald Trump revealed broad disaffection with both economics and politics. The British vote to exit the EU reflects a comparable spasm of right-wing populism. Ultranationalists who reject both the EU and the doctrine of liberal trade are now the second or third largest party in much of Europe, and some are in government. Democracy itself is under siege.

This upheaval is occurring not just in nations with weak democratic roots such as Turkey, Hungary, Egypt, and the Philippines, but in the democratic heartland—western Europe and the United States. Autocrats are using the forms of democracy to destroy the substance. As a whole other model, China's state-led semi-capitalism shows no signs of evolving into liberal democracy. Nor is China embracing anything like free markets.

This ultranationalist reaction is compounded by resentment of immigrants and refugees, as well as resurgent racism. But the fundamental driver of these trends is the resurrection of heedless, globalized capitalism that serves the few, damages the many, and breeds antisystem politics. Though the turn was abrupt and extreme, the mass frustrations have been brewing for decades, under the noses of elites.

THE ARGUMENT OF THIS BOOK

My purpose in writing this book is to connect the dots between the rise of right-wing populism and the fall of a social contract that once served the broad citizenry in Western democracies. The story has five key elements.

First, the postwar era was exceptional in the history of capitalism. It was the result of a fortuitous convergence of events that constrained finance and shifted power to organized workers and democratic governments. In the aftermath of World War II, having learned the bitter lessons of the 1930s, enlightened leaders built a mixed economy whose broad prosperity would reinforce support for liberal democracy and reduce the risk of war.

The postwar social contract, with national variations, demonstrated that a social form of contained capitalism could be successful economics. In that era, the economy grew at record rates even as it became more equal. This was true throughout the West, suggesting that common, systemic dynamics were at work. But that era has given way to one alarmingly like the 1920s, and with similar repercussions. A decent political economy is still possible, but it will again require an exceptional politics.

Second, contrary to a lot of commentary blaming the loss of secure livelihoods on such factors as trade, technology, and the shift from manufacturing to services, nothing in the structure of the late-twentieth-century economy compelled a reversion to an unregulated nineteenth-century market. This was a political shift. The economic turbulence of the 1970s opened space for elites to weaken democratic counterweights to capital, substantially using globalization as their instrument. The resulting policies were perverse for efficiency as well as for equality.

Third, the dominant role of the US during and after World War II is central both to the creation and the destruction of a decent economy. In the early 1940s, America was in a rare progressive mood. The global institutions created in 1944, when American power was preeminent, were intended to allow both the US and its allies in Europe to build mixed economies in the spirit of the New Deal, insulated from the speculative power of private finance. When American government turned back into an ally of finance beginning in the 1970s and continuing emphatically in the 1980s, its goals for the global system also reversed.

Fourth, today's version of globalization is profoundly antidemocratic. On one flank, global trade agreements narrow the space for national policy and weaken government's ability to housebreak capitalism. On the other flank, the popular revulsion against the results of globalization is elevating antidemocratic leaders, parties, and ultranationalist sentiments. The rise in terrorism and in fear of aliens, in a parallel dialectic, promotes domestic support for antiforeign strongmen. Radical Islam and right-wing populism in the West are in symbiosis.

The fifth and final observation concerns the collapse of the democratic left. Anger against market excess can go right, toward fascism, or can energize a progressive left that anchors a decent economy. By the 1990s, center-left parties (led by Bill Clinton in the US and Tony Blair in the UK) had joined the neoliberal globalist consensus, undermining their own credibility when ordinary people decided they'd had enough. Social democratic parties across Europe have lost support as much of their working-class base has defected to the far right. The global regime produced such tight constraints on national policy (enforced by financial markets) that even when further-left parties such as Greece's Syriza coalition managed to get elected, they found themselves shackled by the system's rules.

All of this muddled politics. Today, large numbers of citizens throughout the West are angry that the good life is being stolen from them. They are not quite sure whom to be angry at—immigrants, corporations, the government, politically correct liberals, the rich, the poor? The anger is both unfocused and inchoate, but increasingly articulated by a neofascist right. The election of Donald Trump and the British vote to exit the European Union, neither of which will remedy the pocketbook grievances, are emblematic of this muddle.

After the attacks of September 11, 2001, some commentators declared a "clash of civilizations," as Samuel P. Huntington famously termed it—the democratic West against a barbaric form of radical Islam. Well before 9/11, fellow political scientist Benjamin Barber's book title *Jihad versus McWorld* summed it up: the commercial, often tawdry norms of the globalizing West promoting primitive reaction rather than spreading liberal democracy.

But recent events signal something worse. The threat to democracy is increasingly *within* the West.

THE DANCE OF DEMOCRACY AND THE MARKET

Our deeper story is about the fraught relationship between socially bearable capitalism and robust democracy. When the system is in balance, strong democracy tempers market forces for the general good, in turn reinforcing democratic legitimacy. Democracy must be national because the polity is national. As a citizen of the United States, I can vote for my leaders. My government has certain rules and procedures that are relatively transparent and can be contested.

But there is no global government and no global citizenship. To the extent that democracy requires taming of the market, globalization weakens that endeavor. Today's globalization undermines national regulatory authority. There is no global lender of last resort, no global financial supervisor, no global antitrust authority, no global tax collector, no global labor relations board, no global entity to enforce democratic rights or broker social contracts. Quasi-governmental global organizations, like the International Monetary Fund and the World Trade Organization, are far less transparent and less accountable than their domestic public counterparts, and easier for corporate elites to capture and dominate. Globalization tends to alter the political distribution of power domestically, and to increase the influence of elites who favor more laissez-faire and more globalization, so the process feeds on itself.

A key aspect of the postwar system was the very tight regulation of finance, which remained mostly private but was turned into something close to a public utility. Uniquely in the history of industrial capitalism, the ability of private finance to operate globally was tightly limited. The system constrained international movements of capital. Banks, for the most part, could not do business outside the borders of their home countries. There was no speculation in currencies because exchange rates were fixed. Entire categories of financial products that operate globally today and thus add to the system's ungovernability and instability, such as credit default swaps, did not exist.

The tight national controls on financial capital had significant consequences for the broader political economy of the era. In the real economy, finance was the servant, not the master. Interest rates could be kept low, providing cheap capital to the real economy, without the worry that easy money would fuel speculation, instability, and investment bubbles. With strict limits on what finance could do, the wealth and power of financial elites were also constrained, reinforcing the power shift that undergirded the entire social compact.

The unraveling of the several elements of the postwar social settlement had multiple sources. "Globalization" in the current usage—meaning deregulation of constraints on transnational movements of money, products, services, and labor—was not the only element. But it was clearly a driver and an intensifier. Globalization was a key vector in the transmission of neoliberal policies and values.* New global rules not only restored the ability of finance to operate speculatively across national borders, but undermined the capacity of national governments to regulate it. Globalization helped to restore the temporarily suppressed political power of corporate and financial elites, as well as their wealth. Globalization of capital created a reality, even for left-of-center governments, in which there seemed to be no alternative, as Margaret Thatcher famously put it, to even more laissez-faire, because of the need to reassure markets. The process was cumulative, both politically and economically.

The fact that the far-right backlash is occurring in nearly all Western nations at the same time is no coincidence, nor is it accidental contagion. It is a common reaction against the impact of globalization on the livelihoods of ordinary people. The resulting sentiments produce a politics that is sullen, resentful, and perverse, further undermining democracy. Elites have won the policy debates but have lost the citizenry.

---

*Some critics use "neoliberal" as an epithet. I find it to be a useful, neutral term meaning simply a reversion to the verities of classical liberal economics, which mistakenly assumed the efficiency of unregulated and self-correcting markets.

Far-right sentiments are always lurking around the fringes of society, but when democracy does a good job of managing capitalism, they remain at the fringe. When capitalism overwhelms democracy, we get the alt-right with a friend in the White House. We get Breitbart News, Stephen Bannon, and Donald Trump.

Globalized capitalism, increasingly deregulated and unmoored from national restraints, undermines a balanced economy in multiple, complex, and cumulative ways. With global markets and no global standards, domestic workers are thrown into direct competition with more desperate overseas workers. A century's worth of democratic struggles to regulate labor standards are hosed away. At the other end of the wealth spectrum, the worldwide liberation of finance creates astronomical incomes for the elite. The developing world gains access to world markets but, for the most part, becomes an even more extreme case of wealth and poverty. Money becomes more powerful than citizenship, corrupting both the polity and the economy.

Globalization also accelerates cross-border movements of people. Corporate leaders and their political allies have promoted international flows of cheap labor. Remittances have become an important source of income for much of the third world. The European Union requires free cross-border movements of workers as a condition of membership. Immigrants are also refugees from wars or dictators. A few national leaders, from Sweden to Germany to Canada, have idealistically opened their doors to political and economic refugees. Migrants, often poor and often scorned, are outside national social contracts; they are nonparticipants in national democratic deliberation, and vulnerable to both exploitation and retribution. Even before recent terrorist attacks, their presence undermined settled social compromises.

In the democracies, government and politics are hobbled by a seemingly opposite but complementary problem—paralysis in the face of escalating problems. In the US, three decades of cynical Republican and corporate blockage of economic remedies discredited government and politics, and paved the way for Donald Trump. In the EU, neoliberal rules have constrained policy options for member governments. The rise of far-right antisystem parties has narrowed the parliamentary space of the mainstream, necessitating weak coalition governments of center-right and center-left parties, leading to feeble compromise policies at a time when economic stagnation requires stronger remedies. This blockage, also reminiscent of the 1920s, discredits government and invites Caesarism.

Some have argued that capitalism promotes democracy, because of common norms of transparency, rule of law, and free competition—for markets, for ideas, for votes. In some idealized world, capitalism may enhance democracy, but in the history of the West, democracy has expanded by *limiting* the power of capitalists. When that project fails, dark forces are often unleashed. In the twentieth century, capitalism coexisted nicely with dictatorships, which conveniently create friendly business climates and repress independent worker organizations. Western capitalists have enriched and propped up third-world despots who crush local democracy. Hitler had a nice understanding with German corporations and bankers, who thrived until the unfortunate miscalculation of World War II. Communist China works hand in glove with its capitalist business partners to destroy free trade unions and to preserve the political monopoly of the Party. Vladimir Putin presides over a rigged brand of capitalism and governs in harmony with kleptocrats.

When push comes to shove, the story that capitalism and democracy are natural complements is a myth. Corporations are happy to make a separate peace with dictators—and short of that, to narrow the domain of civic deliberation even in democracies. After Trump's election, we saw corporations standing up for immigrants and saluting the happy rainbow of identity politics, but lining up to back Trump's program of gutting taxes and regulation. Some individual executives belatedly broke with Trump over his racist comments, but not a single large company has resisted the broad right-wing assault on democracy that began long before Trump, and all have been happy with the dismantling of regulation. If democracy is revived, the movement will come from empowered citizens, not from corporations.

A line attributed to Mark Twain holds that history doesn't repeat, but sometimes it rhymes. The current rhyme is a discordant one, with echoes that should be treated as ominous warnings.

A POLANYI MOMENT

We have seen this movie before. During the period between the two world wars, free-market liberals governing Britain, France, and the US tried to restore the pre–World War I laissez-faire system. They put debt collection ahead of economic recovery. It was an era of rampant speculation and no controls on private capital. All this was supposed to promote prosperity and peace. Instead, it produced a decade of economic insecurity combined with heights of inequality, a discrediting of democracy, fascist backlash, and deeper depression. Right up until the German election of July 1932, in which the Nazis became the largest party, the pre-Hitler governing coalition was practicing the economic austerity commended by Germany's creditors and by orthodox financial opinion throughout Europe.

The great prophet of how market forces taken to an extreme destroy both democracy and a functioning economy was less Karl Marx than Karl Polanyi. As Polanyi demonstrated in his 1944 masterwork, *The Great Transformation*, the disembedding of markets from their societies and resulting inattention to social consequences inevitably triggers a reaction. The reaction is more often chaotic and fascistic than politely democratic. "The fascist solution to the impasse of liberal capitalism," Polanyi wrote, is containment of the market "achieved at the price of extirpation of all democratic institutions."

Polanyi saw the catastrophe of World War I, the interwar period, the Great Depression, fascism, and World War II as the logical culmination of market forces overwhelming society. "The origins of the cataclysm," he wrote, "lay in the utopian endeavor of economic liberalism to set up a self-regulating market system."

Rereading Polanyi at a time when events vindicate his vision, one is struck by the eerie present-day ring. Polanyi, like his great contemporary John Maynard Keynes, the architect of Bretton Woods, was an optimist. With the right politics and the right mobilization of democracy, both men believed markets could be harnessed for the common good. They recognized the propensity of capitalism to create calamity but did not believe that outcome to be inevitable. Polanyi lived to see the postwar system confirm his hopes.

The great pessimist, of course, was Marx. In the mid-twentieth century, history failed to follow Marx's script. At the apex of the postwar boom in the United States and Europe, Marx's bleak prediction of capitalist self-destruction seemed ludicrous. A contented bourgeoisie was huge and growing. The proletariat enjoyed steady income gains, thanks to strong trade unions and public regulation. The political energy of aroused workers that Marx imagined as revolutionary instead went to support social democratic and progressive parliamentary parties. These built a welfare state, to temper but not supplant capitalism. Nations that celebrated Marx, meanwhile, were bleak economic failures that repressed their own working classes.

Half a century later, working people are beleaguered and insecure. A global reserve army of the unemployed batters down wages and marginalizes labor's political power. A *Lumpenproletariat* of homeless vagrants and stateless migrants rends the social fabric. Even elite professions are becoming proletarianized. The globalized market weakens the reach of the democratic polity, undermining the protections of the mixed economy.

Ideologically, the neoliberal view that markets are good and states are bad is close to hegemonic, another Marxian concept that once seemed far-fetched, referring to the tyranny of unquestioned, self-serving ideas. With finance still supreme despite the disgrace of the 2008 collapse, it is no longer risible to use "capital," Marx-style, as a collective noun. Goldman Sachs alums provided five of the last six US secretaries of the treasury, Democrats as well as Republicans, even under the alleged populist Donald Trump. If the state is not quite the Marxian executive committee of the ruling class, it is doing a pretty fair imitation.

But Marx got several big things wrong. In countries where rulers invoked his name, there was no "dictatorship of the proletariat," just plain totalitarianism. Most important for our purposes, Marx—in his conjuring of a global proletariat—left out nationalism. He left out the fact that the reaction against a predatory capitalism that annihilates social institutions more typically ended in fascism.

I still believe, with Polanyi and Keynes, that economies can be democratically harnessed for the general good. However, in order to achieve a democratically constrained mixed economy, almost everything has to break right. Success requires fortuitous historical circumstances, movements that mobilize citizens against elites, inspired democratic leaders, and a good dose of luck.

These moments tend not to last. The institutions often turn out to be more fragile than they first appear, and they require continual renewal. In a basically capitalist economy, financial elites, even when constrained, retain an immense amount of residual power. That can be contained only by countervailing democratic power.

The Bretton Woods era suggests that a more benign form of globalization is possible. But the postwar brand of globalization, balancing citizenship and market, above all required a *politics*. Today, a few thinkers could sit in a seminar room and design a thinner globalization and a stronger democratic national polity. Keynes and his generation did just that after World War II. But they had the political winds at their backs. Today's architects of democratic capitalism face political headwinds. Though ideas do matter, they are no substitute for political movements.

Can we reclaim a decent economy that works for most people, and in turn restore democracy? Perhaps. But once again, it will take leadership, power, and luck. First we need a deeper understanding of how things went off the rails.

CAN
DEMOCRACY
SURVIVE
GLOBAL
CAPITALISM?

1

A SONG OF ANGRY MEN

n January 2017, as Donald Trump was taking the oath of office, the world's elite gathered for their annual Davos meetings at the famed Swiss ski resort, to contemplate the populist upsurge against people like themselves. One British economist, Ian Goldin, who teaches globalization and development at Oxford, seemed genuinely puzzled. Speaking at an opening session, defending globalism, Professor Goldin said, "There's never been a better time to be alive, and yet we feel so glum. . . . The idea that somehow we can forge our future in an insular way, even for the biggest countries like the US, is a fantasy."

But for most working people, it wasn't such a great time to be alive. Living standards were precarious and declining. As Tonto said to the Lone Ranger in a famous joke, "What you mean, we?" The vast majority of humanity was not part of the Davos we.

The rise of the Tea Parties and the election of Donald Trump et al. set off debates about what had occurred. Were the grievances that led working-class voters, especially white men, to abandon the Democrats in favor of a faux-populist billionaire mainly economic? Racial? Cultural?

All of the above played a role, but the elements are complex and worth unpacking. Trump's appeals to Make America Great Again resonated with so many voters because the economy of recent decades, supercharged by the new rules of globalization, had left too many working people behind. The America they remembered was a more stable and secure place. Trump's bashing of immigrants was effective because terrorist attacks, though rare, were real; and because some migrant workers do, in fact, take certain jobs at lower-than-prevailing wages, at a time of general economic distress. The criticisms of trade rang true because corporate elites had promoted a version of trade that displaced millions of workers.

The Democrats' drift into becoming a party of aggressive cultural liberalism compounded the alienation. Giving illegal migrants a path to citizenship while largely ignoring the plight of the domestic working class seemed disrespectful to hardworking Americans who obeyed the law. It is admirable that the Democrats took seriously the grievances of newly conscious cultural minorities. Yet any party that wants to vocally champion the rights of transgender people to choose their own bathrooms had better also redouble its efforts on behalf of wage-earning people generally, or it will be entrusted by the voters to do neither.

ECONOMIC COLLAPSE AND POLITICAL CONDESCENSION

In the past four decades, the economy has been turned viciously against ordinary working people. The combination of strong unions and economic regulations that once defended good wages, benefits, and job security has been largely dismantled. Many jobs that could be regular payroll positions are now structured as temp and freelance work. None of this just happened spontaneously. These vanishing labor protections were the deliberate work of a politically resurgent business class. The same broad patterns operated on both sides of the Atlantic, as this book will recount in Chapters 4–7. A common driver of these trends was intensified globalization.

Domestically, we do not allow child labor, or unsafe labor, or labor that pays less than a minimum wage. Those policy choices reflect a century of domestic political struggle. To allow the fruits of such labor to enter via the back door of trade was a conscious political choice by elites. The orthodox view is that these shifts resulted from changes in the nature of the economy. The market, naturally, rewarded those with more advanced skills and education, while routine workers whose jobs could be done by machines or by cheaper labor offshore lost out. The basic problem with this story is that the postwar blue-collar middle class did not have college degrees, and most semiskilled factory workers had not graduated from high school. Yet the social contract of that era called for paying them decently. For a century, markets have often been wrong, and good social policy has overridden their verdicts. The US, on average, is more than twice as rich as it was in the postwar era. But those riches are being shared very differently today.

The message that worker skills were no longer competitive and that the cure was more education conveyed a deeply political and insulting subtext: If your economic life has gone to hell, *it's your fault*. As Thomas Frank wrote in a scathing 2016 book faulting centrist liberals for their political tin ears, "Technological innovation is not what is hammering down working people's share of what the country earns. Technological innovation is the excuse for this development."

People had worked hard at jobs that were often hot and dirty. Someone had not only changed the game and taken away the jobs, but looked down on them for being losers. This was the injury that Trump understood and the message that he so effectively countered. It was not just about economics, but about dignity.

The collapse of a decent working-class economy shows up vividly in the declining health of large numbers of Americans and in the increasing epidemic of opiate addiction. Princeton economists Anne Case and her husband, Angus Deaton (the 2015 Nobel laureate in economics), demonstrated that for the first time since the Great Depression, the life expectancy of midlife working-class whites began declining in the late 1990s, mainly because of "deaths of despair," from increasing alcoholism, drug dependence, and suicide. This increased mortality, in turn, reflects the collapse of stable economic life.

When a local factory and its supplier industries shut down, it isn't just the immediate good jobs that vanish, but downtowns, retailers, bars and social clubs, churches, schools—an entire way of life. The values that working-class men had lived by—laboring diligently at mostly unpleasant jobs, being a good provider, valuing the traditional family and church, cherishing patriotism—were being dishonored by the global governing class. The capricious worldwide relocation of factories by corporate chieftains signaled their belief that patriotism was for suckers.

The fact that new claimants were getting respect from Democrats such as Hillary Clinton—gays, lesbians, and transgender people with

a very different conception of family, immigrants in the country illegally, racial groups who benefited from affirmative action—rubbed
salt in the wounds. It didn't mean that the white working class was
simply racist. Something more complex was at work.

Polls showed that working people who flocked to Donald Trump
were attracted not by his policy pronouncements, but by the chance to
give the governing and economic elite a big middle-finger salute. Only
29 percent reported that they liked his program. Fully half said they
wanted to "shake up the political establishment."

THE COLLAPSE OF WORKING-CLASS
SUPPORT FOR DEMOCRATS

You could read Hillary Clinton's shocking loss to Donald Trump as
a perfect storm that included a bungled campaign, serial misjudg-
ments about email servers, Russian hacking, FBI meddling, sexism,
and more. Even her ability to call out Donald Trump's grotesque
treatment of women was compromised by memories of Bill Clinton's
womanizing and the sick sexting of Anthony Weiner, husband of the
candidate's closest aide. All of that was true—but a far deeper erosion was at work.

The statistics of political disaffection of working people from the
party of Roosevelt are astonishing. Working-class white voters,
defined as those without college degrees, supported Trump by a margin 67 to 28, a gap of 39 percent. Among working-class white men, the
margin was an even larger: 72 to 23, or a chasm of 49 percent. Clinton, counting on the feminist symbolism of a shattered glass ceiling to
make up the loss, even lost a majority of white women, by 10 points.

As recently as the 1996 presidential election, if you compared the
political leanings of counties that were at least 85 percent white and
had household incomes below the national median, they split about
evenly in their support for that year's presidential nominees, Republican Bob Dole and Democrat Bill Clinton. In 2016, Donald Trump carried 658 of those beleaguered counties. Hillary Clinton carried just 2.

The electoral successes of Bill Clinton and Barack Obama had an
element of luck and political crisis deferred. Bob Dole was far from
a populist Republican, and Clinton did a pretty good imitation of

Bubba. Obama was likewise fortunate in that he ran against two traditional Republicans, John McCain and Mitt Romney, neither of whom offered a shred of populism. But after a while, if Democrats court Wall Street and do little for the economically crushed parts of America, the working class stops believing in them. If the right Republican comes along, the perfect storm strikes.

The white working class declined as a percentage of the total electorate—from 83 percent in 1960, to 70 percent in 1980, to just 34 percent by 2016. Yet that's still more than one-third of the electorate—and white working-class voters happen to be distributed with great geographic and electoral efficiency. Politicians ignore that reality at their peril. In 2016, all of the key states in the Midwest had voting populations that were at least 50 percent white working class. In Ohio, Indiana, Iowa, Missouri, and Wisconsin, the share exceeded 60 percent. In key counties of western Pennsylvania, Ohio, Michigan, and Wisconsin, where support for the Democrats collapsed, the white working-class percentage of voters exceeded 80 percent.

The regional tilt of recent economic growth played into Trump's hands. The recovery that had begun in 2010 was highly concentrated, mainly in the largest metro areas. Small cities and areas outside high-tech America, which had seen their economies weaken over time and then collapse after 2008, did not share in the recovery. Just twenty counties, with only 2 percent of the US population, accounted for half of all the new business growth in the recovery.

The geography of economic collapse had political repercussions. Among the states where new business growth lagged far behind the national rate were Pennsylvania, Ohio, Michigan, Indiana, Iowa, West Virginia, and Wisconsin—the states where Trump exceeded expectations and won the election. This pattern was the opposite of the economy of 1992–96, in which benefits of the recovery were broadly shared. In that recovery, 58 percent of Americans lived in counties where job creation equaled or exceeded the national average. In the 2010–14 recovery, that number fell to 28 percent.

A Brookings Institution study found that every one of America's wealthiest 493 counties, most of them urban or metropolitan, supported Clinton. Those 493 Clinton counties, Brookings reported, produced about two-thirds of the national GDP. The remaining 2,623 counties mostly went for Trump. Something similar happened in

Britain, where voters in Greater London opted to stay in the EU by a margin of two to one, but the rest of the UK voted to leave by an even larger spread.

The Democrats, pollster and strategist Stanley Greenberg concluded, "embraced the liberal values of America's dynamic and best-educated metropolitan areas, while seeming not to respect the values or economic stress of older voters in small town and rural America" and working-class voters generally. There was a time when Democrats did pay attention to the economic aspirations of non-metro America. Franklin Roosevelt not only empowered unions and built a welfare state, the New Deal used public capital to help depressed regions, with large-scale programs such as the TVA in the Southeast and the major western hydroelectric dams that not only brought electricity, but promoted regional development.

But as globalized corporations shifted economic activity away from once prosperous regions and governments largely failed to respond, the same pattern of working-class backlash operated, with national variations, in much of Europe. In Britain, the support for the anti-immigrant and anti-Europe UK Independence Party (UKIP) was heavily concentrated in regions that had not shared Greater London's prosperity. In France, a map of Marine Le Pen's support tracks regions in economic decline. Even in Denmark, with low average unemployment, the rise in support for the right-populist Danish People's Party was concentrated in regions like Jutland, where good jobs were scarce. Mogens Madsen, editor of the *Vejle Amts Folkeblad*, the local newspaper, observed, "In areas like Jutland, people got tired of hearing [Social Democratic prime minister] Helle Thorning-Schmidt saying that Denmark was out of the crisis, creating good jobs again. People couldn't see those jobs around here. Maybe it's happening in Copenhagen, but not here. It's impossible to sell your house for a decent price because people don't want to move here. People were sick of this dream picture from Helle."

Substitute Michigan for Jutland and Hillary for Helle, and it's the same story.

DUELING INJURIES OF CLASS,
RACE, GENDER, CULTURE

The sociologist Arlie Hochschild, in a five-year foray into Tea Party territory, tried to gain a deeper understanding of why rural working- and middle-class people apparently voted against their own self-interests. Interviewing citizens of Lake Charles, Louisiana, a once-pristine area ruined by the petrochemical industry, Hochschild found that local Tea Party supporters trusted government even less than they trusted industry. She quotes a seventy-seven-year-old man named Harold Areno, whose pristine environment has been destroyed by the nearby chemical plants.

> The state always seems to come down on the little guy. Take
> this bayou. If your motorboat leaks a little gas into the water,
> the warden'll write you up. But if companies leak thousands
> of gallons of it and kill all the life here? The state lets them
> go. If you shoot an endangered brown pelican, they'll put you
> in jail. But if a company kills the brown pelican by poisoning
> the fish he eats? They let it go. I think they over-regulate the
> bottom because it's harder to regulate the top.

This sounds almost like something Bernie Sanders or Ralph Nader might say, but it leads to an opposite brand of populism—a sense of both resignation and deep resentment against a government that is distant and ineffectual yet intrusive, a feeling that all we can rely on is our own grit. Hochschild found that Areno and his neighbors mostly supported the Tea Parties and Donald Trump.

The journalist John Judis makes an important distinction between left-wing populism and right-wing populism. Left-wing populism is binary—leaders rallying masses against economic elites to achieve overdue reforms. Franklin Roosevelt was the classic progressive populist. He baited the bankers, rallied the people, and delivered reforms that rescued the economy and changed lives for the better.

Right-wing populism, by contrast, is a triad. It typically entails a leader, often demagogic, who rallies masses against elites—but also against some despised "others" who are allegedly coddled by those elites at the expense of the true people. In the US those others were blacks, feminists, illegal immigrants, welfare cheats, Muslims who might be potential terrorists, and transgender people transgressing traditional bathrooms—the entire multicultural stew paraded at the 2016 Democratic National Convention by Hillary Clinton. That embrace, denounced by Trump, Fox News, and the so-called alt right as "politically correct," might have proved less toxic, had Democrats also made a big issue of how the economy was deserting the working class. But Clinton was better known for her large speaking fees from Goldman Sachs.

In Europe, "others" included immigrants and refugees from Africa and the Middle East, who not only were culturally alien, but also depressed local wages. Except for Germany, nearly all of Europe had prolonged unemployment rates of more than 10 percent, heavily concentrated among workers bypassed by the new economy. For the locals, the EU signaled a brand of globalism that worsened their lives. In western Europe, "others" also meant economic migrants from eastern Europe with good skills who had been free since 1993 under EU rules to seek work in the West. On both sides of the Atlantic the result was similar—a culturally and economically displaced working and middle class, increasingly attracted to strong, nationalist leaders who were less concerned about democratic niceties than about Making America (or France, Britain, Norway, Poland, Hungary—fill in the blank) Great Again.

It speaks volumes about where the real power in America lies that Democrats found it easier to move to the left on an array of identity issues than to move left on pocketbook issues and challenge the dominance of finance. This is not to say that Democrats were wrong to embrace rights of women, immigrants, and various sexual minorities—only that they were in trouble when they abandoned the politics of class uplift and the calling out of class elites. When FDR declared in 1936, after the greatest landslide reelection in American history, "They hate me and I welcome their hatred," he was not speaking of bigots. He was speaking of bankers.

Democrats were stymied by what I have called "dueling injuries" of class, race, gender, and culture. Among people with traditional values about household roles, men felt displaced from the position of honor as breadwinners that they had once enjoyed. Many women felt displaced from their ability to feel like competent homemakers and mothers. A middle-class income now required two full-time wage earners. Men were deprived of the traditional services of wives at the same time that women were deprived of their capacity to focus on children and the household. Juggling jobs and kids and keeping a family together required an everyday struggle and heroism that cultural elites seemed to dishonor. The rich solved the problem with nannies. Society was caught between the traditional, patriarchal family structure and a new egalitarian family structure long sought by feminists that was largely blocked by a lack of social supports. Neither model worked well for most people.

Some whites felt displaced by blacks, but that was far from the whole story. If the US had continued to generate large numbers of well-paying jobs, the entry of blacks and of women into the labor force would not have had the same devastating effect on white men. Racial progress during World War II, though limited, was somewhat easier for society to accommodate because there were shortages of workers and plenty of good jobs to go around. Despite persistent racism, the war and the postwar boom promoted racial progress. Remarkably, in the two decades *before* the civil rights revolution of the 1960s, black workers actually gained income at a slightly higher rate than white workers. Why? Because nearly all blacks in the labor force were working-class, and the war and postwar were supremely an era of class uplift.

In the 1970s, as laws on nondiscrimination and affirmative-action programs were just beginning to bite, good jobs and secure career paths started becoming scarce. Yet, while the 1960s civil rights revolution displaced the white-male monopoly on good jobs and careers, it was also incomplete. Though educated blacks could now get into good colleges in token numbers and pursue success in the professions, police brutalization of blacks persisted. So did racially tainted stop-and-frisks, the disproportionate incarceration of blacks, as well as discrimination in the rental and sale of housing.

Even blacks with college degrees were at risk of life and limb if they found themselves in the wrong place at the wrong time. As President Obama put it, commenting on the killing of Trayvon Martin, "If I had a son, he'd look like Trayvon." As Harvard professor Henry Louis Gates learned, when police arrested him at home in Cambridge, exalted status was no protection against lingering racism. In Ta-Nehisi Coates's best-selling book *Between the World and Me*, one of the most moving passages describes the police killing of an exemplary Howard University student who did everything right, in a case of pure mistaken identity for which the murderer was never charged.

So, as the Black Lives Matter movement heated up, multiple senses of injury clashed. Whites, especially white men, felt displaced and dishonored, while blacks continued to feel disrespected. Feminist women, too, felt a deepening sense of grievance. Though male and female earnings were very slowly converging, women in comparable jobs still earned 30 percent less than men, and glass ceilings persisted. The gap between male and female professional earnings increased with age, as working women paid a career price, not paid by men, for having children. Everything from the porn industry to the online dating system to hookup norms, sexual harassment, and the coarsened media culture seemed to leave women with less respect, not more—despite half a century of legal progress. Both feminists and women with traditional values felt aggrieved, albeit in different ways.

By the time Donald Trump appeared on the scene, the US was a cauldron of dueling grievances, each legitimate in its own way. Middle America, struggling with its own downward economic mobility, felt something of compassion fatigue; and Donald Trump had a perfect ear for how to turn that into a winning politics.

CHECK YOUR PRIVILEGE—AND YOUR PREMISE

The mainstream press, elite universities, and well-meaning white liberals all tried to treat the new demands with respect, even with kid gloves. Blacks and other nonwhites were now to be called people of color, a full-circle reversion to the polite term of a century ago. In its revived construction, *people of color* was also a political usage, intended to signal a still wishful solidarity among all nonwhites. Illegal aliens were prettified as *undocumented workers*, a linguistic evasion that bespoke a political dodge (was the speaker thus implying that all people who entered the country illegally had a right to stay?).

Trump's scorn for political correctness deftly combined a signal to crudely racist whites with a softer appeal to a much larger segment of the electorate fed up with arguments about toilets. Try demanding, "Check your privilege!" to white workers facing collapsed communities, declining earnings, and fading prospects in West Virginia or Michigan or Ohio. You can make a case that white men are privileged, on average, relative to blacks. But that misses the political point. Non-elite white men are getting economically clobbered. There is plenty of privilege in the economy, but it mainly resides in the top few percent—whose extreme privileges were not much part of the 2016 debate once Bernie Sanders was eliminated.

Hillary Clinton made the fatal blunder of thinking that the so-called rising electorate of various ethnic and sexual minorities, professionals, politicized women, and the young added up to an automatic electoral majority. Where Barack Obama had spoken passionately about bridging differences, Clinton had a penchant for *spotlighting* differences, evidently in the hope that this strategy would energize each separate element of the coalition. The one group largely left out of this coalition was white men. Clinton's speeches often pointed to people seeded in the audience, who were Muslim, or transgender, or disabled, or immigrants without papers, or victims of racial oppression, or members of some other group defined by its identity—as opposed to defined by common interests as Americans.

Speaking in Henderson, Nevada, on the eve of that state's Democratic caucuses, Clinton led a call-and-response with a friendly audience:

> "If we broke up the big banks tomorrow—and I will, if they deserve it, if they pose a systemic risk, I will—would that end racism?"
>
> "No!" [responded the crowd]
>
> "Would that end sexism?"
>
> "No."
>
> "Would that end discrimination against the LGBT community?"
>
> "No."
>
> "Would that make people feel more welcoming to immigrants overnight?"
>
> "No."

This speech simultaneously issued a backhanded defense of the big banks, while trying to change the subject to identity politics rather than class.

On the last day of the 2016 Democratic National Convention in Philadelphia, there were twenty-five podium speakers in a row, each chosen to represent some presumably oppressed group, but not one of them was a straight, white male. The soundtrack of the campaign relentlessly blared the feminist anthem of the moment, "This Is My Fight Song," assuming that an overwhelming gender gap in favor of Clinton would carry her over the top. Yet her general appeal to working Americans was so blunted that she did lose a majority of white women. The assumption that Bill Clinton's genuine popularity among blacks would carry over to Hillary Clinton, especially with the letdown of Obama's presidency coming to a close, also proved faulty. Even with the palpable threat of Trump planning to roll back civil rights, black turnout actually fell.

Despite the elements of racism in Trump's victory, which was surely part of the story, Barack Obama actually did better among white working-class voters in 2008 than Hillary Clinton did in 2016. Exit polls showed that he gained the vote of about 40 percent of working-class whites nationally. Obama, as a barely known forty-six-year-old African American, could wrest the nomination from Clinton partly because he sounded like the more populist of the two. He was the outsider, and the public was getting sick of insiders. Obama carried a surprisingly impressive share of the white working-class vote, both in the primaries and in the general election. In North Carolina, fully 35 percent of white people, including more than 55 percent of those with incomes under $50,000, voted for Obama against McCain. Obama represented change. In 2008, Sean Quinn of the website FiveThirty-Eight reported the story, possibly apocryphal but believable, of the white voter in a depressed area of western Pennsylvania who told a canvasser, "We're voting for the nigger."

As the AFL-CIO's chief economist, William Spriggs, has observed, the argument about why Democrats lost the white working class ducks the larger issue. In fact, about 45 percent of the working class is nonwhite. In the 2016 election, Clinton lost ground *among the entire working class*—white, black, Hispanic, Asian—relative to the Obama vote and the vote that was normal for Democrats of an earlier era. The white working-class vote for Obama in both 2008 and 2012 fell by about one-fourth in 2016.

The missing ingredient of Clinton's campaign was class. The one subject largely absent was a serious attack on the one group whose excesses potentially united all of the aggrieved Americans—the very rich, whose share of the total pie and whose power to make the rules had been relentlessly increasing. The fact that Bernie Sanders, a seventy-four-year-old self-declared socialist transplant from Brooklyn to Vermont came within an ace of denying Clinton the nomination should have been a warning. The Democratic base plus millions of swing voters were disgusted with politics as usual—of which there was no better emblem than Hillary Clinton. Yet Clinton addressed class only reluctantly, mainly to counter Sanders. In the general election, once Sanders was dispatched, her campaign largely disdained any kind of progressive populism, leaving the field to the faux-populist Trump.

Much of the right-wing populist message is a contradictory mélange of nationalism, racism, and purely symbolic economic outreach to the white working class. But one strategist who attempted something more coherent and strategic was Stephen Bannon, the head of the far-right website Breitbart.com. For almost exactly one year, Bannon was Trump's chief political strategist, first during the campaign and then at the White House, until his ouster in August 2017.

At Breitbart, Bannon had grasped that alienated people at the fringes of society could be politicized as white nationalists and mobilized into shock troops for Donald Trump. Breitbart connected the existing far right that followed Fox News and right-wing talk shows to an even more extremist "alt right." Bannon promoted this grand design to Trump, who had previously been popular with blacks in his role as a reality TV host who went out of his way to feature black contestants. In the campaign and at the White House, Bannon was the architect of Trump's immigrant-bashing, racist, anti-Semitic, and economic nationalist messages.

Unlike much of the Trump administration, however, Bannon sought to connect an energized racist and nativist backlash to a program of economic nationalism that would actually deliver benefits to a frustrated white working class. He hoped that the racism would bait Democrats into defending minorities while Republicans attracted white workers with economic benefits. "The Democrats," he told me in an interview that helped produce his dismissal, "the longer they talk about identity politics, I got 'em. I want them to talk about racism every day. If the left is focused on race and identity, and we go with economic nationalism, we can crush the Democrats."

Bannon favored a large program of public infrastructure, tax increases for the rich, and a get-tough program with China intended to bring home industrial jobs. Trump intermittently channeled the positive part of the Bannon strategy, but mainly at the level of rhetoric. The actual tax, trade, and investment policies reflected the more substantial influence of the corporate wing of the administration, and did nothing for the working class. After his ouster, Bannon ran far-right challengers against incumbent Republicans. Bannon's more strategic view of reactionary economic nationalism suggested a possible majority politics—but this coherence was precluded both by Trump's personal instability and by the corporate lock on the Republican Party.

In the wings was a more progressive brand of economic nationalism: extensive public investments, promotion of domestic industry, regulation of wage standards and worker rights, a more balanced trade policy, and rejection of pro–Wall Street trade deals that were really deregulation deals. This was also potentially a winning politics, but it was far from the theme of the Clinton campaign—which fell into Bannon's trap.

DEMOCRATIC DECAY

If a slow assault on the livelihoods of working people was one key aspect of the long road to Trumpism, the slow decline of democracy itself was the other. Strong democracy is both a bulwark against totalitarianism and a shield against economic concentration. When democracy is weak, lower-income people have no defense against the wealthy rigging the rules and taking too large a share of the pie. Sooner or later, people of modest means, who tend to be cynical about government to begin with, give up on the idea that democratic participation and affirmative government can improve their lives. For more than forty years, voter turnout has been on a steady decline. States governed by Republicans have sought to deliberately depress turnout, especially among people likely to vote for Democrats. Extreme gerrymandering has compounded the sense that voting is futile, since incumbents can usually count on getting reelected. But the best-off 20 percent still vote at historic levels, while the decline has been steepest among the poor. When the bottom half turns away from government, people oscillate between not voting at all and embracing the magical promises of demagogues.

One key avenue of democratic decay was financial. Campaign money increasingly crowded out civic participation, creating a vicious circle that granted the wealthy and their corporate allies increasing influence and energy, and left ordinary voters cynical and disconnected. In 2010, a right-wing Supreme Court supercharged the trend in the *Citizens United* ruling, literally defining money as speech and overturning the remaining constraints on unlimited political donations.

This shift whipsaws Democrats far more than Republicans. On pocketbook issues, wealthy donors, in effect, pay Democrats to abandon their normal instincts to defend workaday voters—to become less like Democrats. For Republicans, reliance on big money reinforces a natural affinity of conservatives, corporations, and laissez-faire economics.

Democratic fund-raising operations have often sacrificed progressive politics in order to enlist big donors. The head of the Democratic Congressional Campaign Committee, the fund-raising arm of the House Democratic Caucus, frequently looks for center-right Democrats to contest House seats, because they can self-fund or raise money from their personal wealthy contacts.

In 1981, at the dawn of the Reagan presidency, the head of the DCCC was an obscure California congressman named Tony Coelho. He began aggressively courting business donations to Democrats. Reagan's efforts to promote a big tax cut soon became a "bidding war" between the two parties, with each seeking to outdo the other in providing special-interest favors. Coelho dramatically increased the Democrats' funds but reinforced the conventional wisdom that Democrats should move to the right and distance the party from the working class.

Things have only worsened since Coelho's day. In 2006, the head of the DCCC was then-congressman Rahm Emanuel, who had moved between the Clinton White House and Wall Street, and then to Congress. Like Coelho, he prized center-right candidates who could raise scads of business money. Emanuel intervened to enlarge the size of the House Financial Services Committee, which was coveted by conservative Democrats as a venue to do favors for Wall Street allies and raise campaign funds in return. When the progressive committee chairman, Barney Frank, began holding hearings to fashion the reform legislation that eventually became the Dodd-Frank Act, Frank was furious that Emanuel had loaded his committee with so many center-right Democrats that Frank often lacked a working majority of his own committee.

These second- and third-order consequences of the rule of big money distanced many Democrats from their own natural pocketbook issues. It was much easier for Democrats to bond with Wall Street allies on social issues such as identity politics, and to steer clear of progressive populism. With these maneuvers, Democrats do manage to stay financially "competitive" with Republicans—but at grave cost to their role as tribunes of ordinary people. In 2016, Hillary Clinton raised more money than Trump. But the money couldn't buy her love.

PARTICIPATORY INEQUALITY

On any given day in Washington, DC, the city's luxury hotels are teeming with civic activity. Trade associations, lobbies, corporations seeking government contracts, power lawyers looking to influence agency rules, all form a beehive of action—at strategy meetings, fund-raisers, seminars, and conventions. Of the top-spending trade associations or issue organizations, the US Chamber of Commerce leads the list with a budget of more than $1.35 billion. Only one quasi-liberal group, the AARP, is even in the top twenty.

This is the vision of Alexis de Tocqueville made flesh—with one notable difference: nearly everyone in this associational paradise is in the top 1 or 2 percent of the income distribution. Tocqueville, in *Democracy in America*, famously identified "the art of association" as an essential complement to American constitutional democracy. The franchise was only the beginning of an effective republic. Political associations, to Tocqueville, were "great free schools" of democracy. They breathed civic life into formally democratic institutions of government. To engage with public issues, people did so more effectively in groups, not as isolated individuals. "Americans of all ages, all stations of life, are forever forming associations," he wrote, admiringly. And he added this warning: "If men are to remain civilized or to become so, the art of associating together must grow and improve in the same ratio in which the equality of conditions is increased."

In the past four decades, Tocqueville's hope has gone into reverse. As "equality of conditions" has declined, so has "the art of associating together." Tocqueville's celebration of the participatory habits of "all stations of life" no longer applies. Civic and political association and the organized exercise of influence have all but collapsed for the bottom half, dwindled for the bottom three-quarters, and intensified for the elite.

This trend has not only reduced political influence for the nonrich. More ominously, it has increased the slide into what sociologists call "mass society." In a mass society, there is a loss of institutions of representation or of political voice that connect people to one another. This atomization, in turn, leaves people alienated and primed to embrace dictators. As William Kornhauser wrote, in his classic *Politics of Mass Society*, Caesarism thrives when people are drawn to totalitarian leaders and "there is a paucity of intervening groups to channelize and filter popular participation in the larger society." In these circumstances, "mass participation tends to be irrational and unrestrained."

Thus, while inequalities of campaign finance have garnered most of the attention and indignation of reformers, participatory inequality is just as important. In fact, it is even more important, since the only antidote to the narrow, concentrated power of wealth is the broad power of organized people.

In their authoritative 1995 work, *Voice and Equality*, political scientists Sidney Verba, Kay Lehman Schlozman, and Henry E. Brady demonstrated that political activity varied by class. Their study found that 86 percent of high-income people reported having voted, but only 52 percent of low-income people said they voted. And 73 percent of high-income people were involved with a political organization, compared to 29 percent of low-income people. A 2012 sequel by the same authors showed a widening of these patterns, as institutions of working-class participation such as trade unions continued to decline, while the influence of the wealthy concentrated.

The affluent go to meetings, are active members of groups concerned with public issues, and develop "civic skills" far more than the poor do—and that disparity has been widening. The iconic Norman Rockwell painting of an ordinary working fellow standing up to speak his mind at a town meeting, meant to depict one of FDR's Four Freedoms, belongs to another era. And yet, in the Trump rebellion, regular working people who had little regard for civic norms abruptly recovered their voices in a fashion characteristic of mass society—disaffected people sharing not always rational rage with an irrational leader. They even formed new, Tocqueville-style associations, the Tea Parties.

Voice and Equality concluded that lower-income people participate at lower rates for three reasons: "they can't" (because they lack the time or money); "they don't want to" (because they don't believe that politics will make a positive difference in their lives); and "nobody asked them" (the political system has few avenues of recruitment for lower-income people). In a survey of why so many people avoided politics, one key reason was that politics felt irrelevant. This view, of course, was also correlated by social class. Nobody in large corporations believes that politics is irrelevant.

Trust in government—and in all major institutions—has been falling for half a century. When the American National Election Study first asked the question in 1958, 73 percent of Americans said they trusted the federal government to do the right thing "just about always" or "most of the time." That sense of trust peaked in 1964, at 78 percent, and has been steadily dropping ever since. By 2015, it was down to just 19 percent. The same rising distrust applies to the media, the courts, schools, the health system, and all large institutions. The military retains the highest degree of trust, at 73 percent, and corporations and Congress are at the bottom, at 18 percent and 9 percent, respectively. The distrust for corporations suggests a latent popular politics that seldom gets fully realized, because of the concentrated, quiet corporate power and the abuse that progressive critics of corporate power take as populist rabble-rousers.

The political scientist Walter Dean Burnham terms this dynamic "the politics of excluded alternatives." Whether voters cast their ballots for Clinton, Bush, Obama, or Trump, they somehow get Goldman Sachs. Distrust of government, in turn, leads to further desertion from civic life, and to deeper asymmetry in the power between the very rich and everybody else. Social scientists Roberto Foa and Yascha Mounk find declining confidence in democracy throughout the West.

Complementary research by the political scientist Martin Gilens demonstrates the policy payoff to the rich and well-connected. The title of his 2013 book says it all: *Affluence and Influence*. Gilens documents that the policy preferences of the rich are at odds with those of most people. In the populace, there is broad support for preschool, paid parental leave, universal medical coverage, and affordable higher education. These public benefits never arrive, while the rules sought and created by the rich tend to dictate actual policy. Gilens found that the policy preferences of the rich are fifteen times more likely to become public policy as those of non-elites. The rules, you might say, are rigged.

THE DECLINE OF POPULAR INSTITUTIONS

There was a time when America was characterized by greater, though not fully symmetrical, equality of participation. Tocqueville's observations in 1835 were not wishful.

In addition to the impact of growing income gaps, three trends over the past half century have intensified participatory inequality. First, large mass-membership organizations that once engaged lower- and middle-class Americans in civic and political life have atrophied. Second, an entire habitat of mutual self-help organizations, ranging from unions to local building and loan societies, which also served as a civic training ground and an avenue of influence for the nonrich, have been substantially depleted as well. Finally, the mass entry of women into the labor force without a proportional reduction in the hours worked by most men has deprived localities of civic capital.

Many of the large social reform organizations of a century ago were women's groups or were staffed mainly by stay-at-home wives and widows. To the extent that it was predominantly women who organized and attended PTA meetings, volunteered with the League of Women Voters, and attended zoning and tax-override meetings, the fabric of nonrich community and civic life has been weakened by the time squeeze on the two-income family.

As Harvard's Theda Skocpol demonstrated in her work on large, democratically governed federations, a century ago there were dozens of cross-class membership organizations, organized into local chapters, each with total memberships of at least a million. Some were fraternal and service organizations such as the Elks. Others had explicit reform goals, such as the National Congress of Mothers, the General Federation of Women's Clubs, or any of several labor unions. Still others combined fraternal, vocational, and political objectives, such as the Grange. A majority included working-class as well as professional-class members. They were "schools for democracy," in precisely Tocqueville's sense.

At their peak, according to Skocpol, there were fifty-nine national federations of local groups with at least a million card-carrying, dues-paying members. Local groups elected leaders who, in turn, were the constituents of state and finally national organizations. They held meetings, took positions, testified before local and national legislative bodies, used Robert's Rules of Order, and became training and recruiting grounds for regular people to engage in civic and political life. This is not an observation made after the fact; the connections were well understood at the time. A poster from the early 1920s, cited by Skocpol, calls for an eight-hour workday, and adds:

8 HOURS FOR WORK!
8 HOURS FOR SLEEP!
8 HOURS FOR HOME AND CITIZENSHIP!

By the 1980s, most of these groups either had petered out or had converted into Washington-based advocacy groups. These were mostly mailing-list organizations, with no chapters or mass members, typically foundation-supported with small professional staffs. Some were pseudo-mass-membership organizations, such as the AARP, which sells insurance products to the elderly, does some issue advocacy on the side, and has a self-perpetuating board and no direct accountability to its "members." Two exceptions to this trend were authentic grassroots groups that helped the right wing: the NRA and the political network of evangelical churches, which in turn energized the Tea Parties.

In addition to mass-membership civic organizations, the US once had a profusion of cooperative and mutual self-help groups that recruited ordinary working people into civic and political activity. These have also become nearly extinct. Beginning in 1831, building and loan societies (later called savings and loans) pooled capital so that people of modest means could finance home ownership. According to David L. Mason's authoritative history, building and loan leaders and members understood their enterprise "as a movement, not an industry." Credit unions likewise were organized to serve people who could not get bank loans. Volunteer fire brigades grew into mutual fire insurance associations. Many of the first group health insurance plans in the 1930s and 1940s were organized as co-ops.

In the western states, the cooperative movement was one of the core constituencies of local Democratic Party politics and also a training ground for civic participation. Jerry Voorhis, the liberal California congressman who was defeated by Richard Nixon in 1946, was an activist and president of the Cooperative League of the USA. When the Group Health Cooperative of Puget Sound, one of the pioneering prepaid group health plans, was organized in the late 1930s, its founders included activists in trade unions and producer co-ops. Because health co-ops were fiercely opposed by organized medicine, their leaders and members necessarily had to become active in progressive politics.

Government played a supportive role by providing funding, supplying expertise, and enabling legislation so that farmers' co-ops, rural electric co-ops, nonprofit savings and loan associations, and credit unions could gain an economic foothold. Here, too, ordinary citizens served on boards and became involved in politics in order to defend and advance the interests of institutions that were insurgent in the context of conventional capitalist enterprise.

By the 1980s, this world, too, had mostly been destroyed or absorbed by conventional American capitalism. Not-for-profit savings and loans, nonprofit health plans and hospitals, and mutual life insurance companies all had hundreds of billions of dollars in reserves that corporate executives coveted. When a mutual institution converted to a stock institution, executives could vote themselves stock options, take the company public at a low price, and then personally cash in as the value of the stock rose. In the anything-goes atmosphere of the 1980s, business successfully lobbied Washington and state legislatures for rule changes to enable these conversions. Reagan's regulators changed the rules so that federally chartered S&Ls could be owned by one person, abolishing the old requirement of at least 400 shareholders, of which 125 had to be from the local community. Beginning with California, states changed the rules to make for-profit S&Ls the norm. A side effect was the weakening of social and civic capital for the nonrich.

LABOR LOST

The most potent mass-membership organization of political recruitment, representation, and education for working people, the trade union movement, has been the object of relentless attack by business elites. Union membership has been cut from about one-third of the private-sector workforce in the 1940s and 1950s to less than 7 percent today. For many working-class Americans, literally their only organized connection to civic and political life is their union. The remaining trade unions continue to be schools for democracy, venues for cross-race collaboration, as well as advocates of good wages and working conditions. But fewer and fewer Americans are members.

The labor movement did not dwindle because more Americans were now middle class and no longer felt they needed unions, as some accounts claimed. That contention became increasingly preposterous as more and more workers fell out of the middle class. Polls regularly show that about half of nonsupervisory workers report that they would like to join a union. Fear prevents that. Union activists in non-union workplaces regularly get fired, with management impunity. Unions lost membership because of relentless attacks by corporations, the outsourcing of jobs heavily concentrated in unionized sectors, deregulation and privatization, and the shift in the federal government's role from benign neutrality under Roosevelt and Truman to full-scale assault under Reagan and the Bushes.

One of President Reagan's first acts was to break the strike of air traffic controllers and to hire striker replacements, violating a norm that government had respected since FDR. Reagan's action, using the power of government to destroy a public-sector union, was also a signal to private industry that it was open season on their unions.

Here again, the asymmetry between a ferociously strategic, corporate Republican Party and a compromised Democratic Party is telling. Ever since the Carter administration, the top priority of the labor movement has been to reform the Wagner Act so that workers could freely choose to join a union without fear of management harassment or deprivation of their livelihood. The most recent version of reform is the idea of "card check": as soon as a majority of workers at a facility sign union cards, the union is officially recognized, as opposed to the current practice of a long period between the time the cards are certified and the time a formal election is held—a delay during which pro-union workers are sitting ducks.

But the presidential Democratic Party, whipsawed between a liberal/labor wing and a Wall Street/New Democrat wing, has not been willing to make it a priority to help working people exercise their rights under the Wagner Act. Even when Democrats had a working majority in Congress, as they did for four years under President Carter, two under Clinton, and two under Obama, the White House refused to spend serious political capital on labor reform.

THE MYTH OF LEGISLATIVE GRIDLOCK

One of the convenient myths of recent years has been the fable of partisan gridlock. You know the story; you can hardly read a newspaper or watch a newscast without encountering it.

Congress is hopelessly "deadlocked," as both parties have "moved to the extremes" and the political center has vanished. Instead of doing the people's business, legislators are consumed with "partisan bickering." Search these phrases online, and you will find millions of examples. This narrative has become a media cliché. The problem is that it's entirely wrong.

The ideological gap between the parties has indeed widened, and party discipline has increased. But the source of the widening gap is that Democrats have moved moderately to the center, while Republicans have moved to the far right. And the main source of deadlock is that Republicans have decided to refuse to compromise with Democrats, the better to destroy both Democrats and effective government.

Consider almost any public issue. Today's Democratic Party and its legislators, with a few notable individual exceptions, is well to the right of counterparts from the New Deal and Great Society eras. In the time of Lyndon Johnson, the average Democrat in Congress was for single-payer national health insurance. In 1971, Congress overwhelmingly passed the Comprehensive Child Development Act, for universal, public, tax-supported, high-quality day care and pre-kindergarten. Nixon vetoed the bill in 1972, but even Nixon was for a guaranteed annual income, and his version of health reform, "play or pay," in which employers would have to provide good health insurance or pay a tax to purchase it, was well to the left of either Bill or Hillary Clinton's version, or Barack Obama's.

The Medicare and Medicaid laws of 1965 were not byzantine mash-ups of public and private like Obamacare. They were public. Infrastructure investments were also public. There was no bipartisan drive for either privatization or deregulation. The late 1960s and early 1970s (with Nixon in the White House!) were the heyday of landmark health, safety, environmental, and financial regulation. To name just three out of several dozen, Nixon signed the 1970 Clean Air Act, the 1970 Occupational Safety and Health Act, and the 1973 Consumer Product Safety Act.

Why did Democrats move toward the center and Republicans to the far right? Several things occurred. Money became more important in politics. The Democratic Leadership Council, formed by business-friendly and Southern Democrats after Walter Mondale's epic 1984 defeat, believed that in order to be more competitive electorally, Democrats had to be more centrist on both economic and social issues. As old-fashioned progressive Democrats retired, some were replaced by corporate Democrats. Others were replaced by right-wing Republicans, as the Democratic Solid South gradually became the Republican Solid South, fueled by racial and regional resentment.

Republicans, meanwhile, moved from moderate right to far right, beginning with Barry Goldwater and Ronald Reagan. By the time Newt Gingrich became House Speaker in 1994, the Republican strategy was to deny Democrats successes on any issue. Under Obama, Republican legislators vowed to vote against the Affordable Care Act, sight unseen. Democrats, meanwhile, viewed themselves as the party of government, "the grown-ups in the room," and were more inclined to compromise in order to keep government functioning. This asymmetry enabled Republicans to roll Democrats, time after time. The tactic reached an apotheosis under Obama, a leader with a personal affinity for compromise, of which Republicans took full advantage.

So, the true gridlock of Washington was extreme Republican hardball, and a take-no-prisoners approach to politics. This politics of deliberate blockage served Republicans in multiple, mutually reinforcing respects. It denied the Democrats successes, even when Democrats held the White House. It seriously hurt both the prestige and the efficacy of government. Since Democrats represent the proposition that affirmative government is needed to serve the people, this was a double setback for them, and a win for the Republican ideology that government is a waste of money.

Because working-class people need affirmative government far more than affluent people do, Republican success in creating deadlock undermined politics and government as a balancing mechanism. The cynical Republican strategy of deadlock strengthened the Republican story that government is a hopeless mess. The perceived failures of government served to recruit aggrieved working people first to the Republican Party, then to the Tea Party, and then to Trump.

In the disconnect between grievance and remedy, there is an astonishing muddle. Angry people vote for a seeming populist, and they get an autocrat whose policies and appointees make the economy even more tilted to the very rich. Trump's populism turns out to be a blend of spite, entertainment, jingoism—and alliance with corporations when it comes to actual policy. Yet in the absence of government policies to lean against the predations of the market, Trumpism fills the vacuum.

It has been a long road from Franklin Roosevelt to Donald Trump. Some of that story is purely domestic. Much of it has to do with the resurgence of the power of finance and resulting changes in the rules of the global economy.

2

A VULNERABLE MIRACLE

To fully appreciate what we've lost, we need to begin with a deeper understanding of the egalitarian capitalism that the West once had—and how it eroded. The system created at the end of World War II was, of course, incomplete. Women were not equal citizens, nor were blacks. Much of the West still had colonies. But compared to any version of capitalism before or since, the three decades after World War II were remarkable.

The postwar system squared a circle. It achieved the improbable feat of combining dynamic capitalism with near-full employment, increasing income equality based on rising wages, and expanding social benefits. Such a convergence was unprecedented in the history of capitalism. Core elements of the system were the tight regulation of private finance, the offsetting empowerment of organized labor, and the activist role of government. The reign of finance in the 1920s had proved both deflationary and destabilizing—promoting speculation during booms and austerity during busts, and creating protracted unemployment. Joblessness, in turn, fed fascism and pan-European war. This was the fate the postwar architects were determined to avoid.

The new conception of the economy rested not just on drastic shifts in policy and new theoretical insights, but on altered power dynamics that made the policies possible. Yet the success of the postwar system was also the result of some happy accidents.

An anomaly of the postwar era was the temporary hegemony of the United States—in three respects. First, the US temporarily enjoyed towering economic supremacy, enough to be the flywheel of the system. America provided the capital, the currency, and the mass market for other nations' exports. This could not continue forever.

Second, because of the common threat of the Cold War, the US was prepared to use its power magnanimously in western Europe. In drastic contrast to the period after World War I, most Americans were now internationalists, thanks to Hitler and then Stalin—even most of the once-isolationist right. Public capital—the Marshall Plan— was central and reliable, in contrast to the volatile and speculative private-capital flows after World War I. For a time, the postwar brand of internationalism contained rather than liberated private capital.

Third, the US had a rare, effective left-wing government after twelve years of the Roosevelt administration. So, Washington became a partner of western Europe's managed capitalism rather than an obstacle. All of these elements would weaken and then reverse over time. America did remain internationalist and the leader of the Western alliance, but economically, the internationalism increasingly took the form of promoting the global laissez-faire that had been emphatically rejected in the reconstruction of the 1940s.

On the European side of the bargain, a generation of farsighted postwar leaders whose nations were recent enemies shared a common vision. They concluded from the ruinous events of the previous decade that fascism grew in the soil of human misery; that laissez-faire capitalism generated depression; that Europe must never again suffer a civil war; and that to fuse these several goals, Europe needed to move in the direction of both a managed form of capitalism and a federation. Thus was born an egalitarian system, unique in the history of international commerce. The roots of these events began more than a decade earlier in the United States, under Roosevelt's New Deal.

In the late 1940s, after a few years of uncertainty about postwar geopolitical alignments and confusion about economic goals and means, just about everything seemed to come round right. The United States, once isolationist, exercised unprecedented peacetime leadership. The Soviet Union was contained. Europe was soon on the road to reconstruction, embracing a new democratic Germany. The founders of the postwar order evidently found a recipe that combined growth with equity, showing the world that democratic capitalism was far superior to totalitarian communism. The postwar mixed economy enjoyed broad popular support. What could possibly go wrong?

In the final third of the twentieth century, the economy went wrong first, beginning in the 1970s—sacrificing both growth and equity, and then becoming mired in austerity. That story is told in succeeding chapters.

The global security order, which appeared so solid after the collapse of communism in 1989, faced new unsettling threats from terrorists early in the twenty-first century. Citizens rebelled against both economic and political insecurity, putting parliamentary democracy itself at risk.

This chapter begins an inquest. The basic finding: the postwar bargain was built more on a convergence of circumstances than on durable, permanent changes. The bargain proved surprisingly fragile, once capitalists regained their normal, temporarily suppressed powers in a still-capitalist economy. This shift occurred both in national politics and in the new globalization.

Yet, other roads were possible. As a matter of economics, the inflationary turmoil of the 1970s did not have to destroy the postwar social compact. Alternative, superior policies were available that might have continued the containment of finance and the commitment to empowered labor and full employment. However, the accident of inflation combined with rising unemployment gave an opening to the corporate and ideological right wing to pursue deflationary and deregulatory policies that fed on themselves and intensified the power shift, undermining the democratic and egalitarian nation-state.

THE RADICALISM OF ROOSEVELT

Literally thousands of books have been written on Franklin Roosevelt. My purpose here is not to repeat well-worked material, but to succinctly remind us how both the New Deal and then Roosevelt's structuring of the wartime economy contoured the postwar social settlement. The historian Jefferson Cowie has termed the New Deal "the great exception." However, it was not only the New Deal that was exceptional, but the entire era from 1933 to the mid-1970s, in Europe and America.

The crash of 1929 discredited laissez-faire ideology and the Republican Party, yet it was far from a foregone conclusion that Roosevelt would use the economic crisis to offer such a radical program. Some historians have argued that because the Great Depression had been deepening for three full years by the time of FDR's election in November 1932, his radicalism was almost inevitable. But a different president might well have been far less transformative. Roosevelt was famously a class traitor, comfortable enough in his own patrician skin to call out other patricians as economic royalists.

History is a blend of deep structural forces and contingent events that can be lucky or unlucky. To imagine that something like the New Deal was inevitable, one need only consider what might have occurred if Giuseppe Zangara, the assassin who fired five bullets at FDR while the president-elect was giving a speech in February 1933 in Miami, and who killed the mayor of Chicago instead, had hit his intended target. Rep. John Nance ("Cactus Jack") Garner, the vice-president-elect, a mediocrity from Texas added for ticket-balancing purposes, was no FDR.

The deeper radicalism of the New Deal was less in FDR's program of public investment and social insurance—strategies used by conservatives such as Otto von Bismarck as well as liberals—than in the collective empowerment of organized labor and the drastic regulation of private capital. Roosevelt, after dithering, also decided to delink the domestic economy from the international constraints of the gold standard, the better to pursue recovery at home—a radical decision early in his presidency that prefigured the design for the postwar system and contained private finance in yet another respect.

It is close to an iron law of American politics that the party of a new president loses seats in that president's first midterm election. In FDR's first midterm, however, the Democrats—uniquely in modern political history—picked up seats. The gains in 1934, subsequently reinforced by Roosevelt's own landslide reelection in 1936, made possible the so-called Second New Deal, which went even further than the first. FDR was emphatically on the side of the people, and the people reciprocated.

The empowering of organized labor came in several stages. In 1932, unionized workers were just 7 percent of the American labor force (about the same as their share of private-sector unionism today). Most of them were in relatively conservative craft unions that were closer to guilds. Except in New York and a few other cities that had left-wing unions in the needle trades, the labor movement was weak and not much of a progressive force. That would change drastically. Even before Roosevelt's inauguration, the majority-Democratic Congress elected in 1930 enacted the 1932 Norris-LaGuardia Act (sponsored by two progressive Republicans) barring courts from issuing injunctions in nonviolent labor disputes, effectively overturning earlier Supreme Court decisions holding that unions were "conspiracies in restraint of trade" that violated antitrust laws. Norris-LaGuardia also prohibited employers from requiring workers to be non-union as a condition of employment ("yellow-dog contracts").

The right to unionize was explicitly recognized in the 1933 National Industrial Recovery Act, Roosevelt's flawed attempt at corporatist industry codes, which was soon declared unconstitutional by the Supreme Court. Collective bargaining was explicitly legalized in the Wagner Act of 1935, which for the first time put government on the side of trade unionism. The word "collective" is key and worth a moment's reflection. So much of American liberalism, before and since, has been about individual rights. For a brief moment in the 1930s, however, American progressivism was about collective empowerment and class advancement—the stuff of mass movements. The Wagner Act also created a jurisprudence to make sure that the right to unionize would be enforced.

Radical unionism, meanwhile, was advancing on the ground. In another fortuitous coincidence, the stage of industrialization prevalent in the 1930s utilized immense factories. With a shift in worker consciousness and a friendly national government, these giant plants could be organized—and they were. The Committee for Industrial Organization, created in 1935 to organize the semiskilled assembly workers previously disdained by the American Federation of Labor (AFL), soon became the Congress of Industrial Organizations (CIO). The militants in these unions were a broad spectrum of the left— communists, socialists, left-wing Democrats. Organizing tactics such as sit-down strikes that occupied auto factories sometimes broke the law. But in contrast to the era of mass union busting in the late nineteenth century, labor after 1933 had a rare alliance with the state that, though far from consistent, allowed these tactics to succeed more often than they failed.

In 1937, Roosevelt followed bad fiscal advice and cut spending to narrow the budget deficit as recommended by orthodox economists who considered the Great Depression all but over. Deep recession ensued, raising unemployment rates, and the 1938 midterm election was a rout for the Democrats. The so-called Roosevelt Recession weakened the nascent labor movement, as hundreds of thousands of newly unionized workers were laid off in steel, automobile, rubber, and electrical manufacturing. Organizing efforts stalled as industrial giants such as the Ford Motor Company and Bethlehem Steel successfully resisted unionism, despite the guarantees of the Wagner Act.

But then, fortuitously, came the war. World War II strengthened worker bargaining power and reinforced labor's role as institutional social partner. In 1941, Roosevelt named Sidney Hillman, head of the Amalgamated Clothing Workers of America, a senior CIO leader and a longtime FDR confidante, as codirector of the Office of Production Management, an early wartime planning agency later replaced by the War Production Board. To get labor fully behind the war mobilization and reduce strike activity, which had burgeoned as the economy recovered in the defense buildup of 1940 and 1941, Roosevelt created a National Mediation Board, and then a War Labor Board, with a formal tripartite structure of business, government, and labor. All of this helped elevate the labor movement to the role of a full social partner.

THE GOOD WAR, FULL EMPLOYMENT, AND LABOR POWER

In 1942, the Roosevelt administration guaranteed union recognition in war production. In exchange for a no-strike pledge by labor, all defense contractors had to accept unions as collective-bargaining agents if a majority of workers signed up. Senior corporate executives were prosecuted for violating this strong enforcement of the Wagner Act and barred from receiving military contracts; and during the war, virtually every corporation of any size had defense contracts. In 1944, Sewell Avery, head of Montgomery Ward, defied Roosevelt's request to settle a strike with his 7,000 union workers. Many trade unionists still have on their walls an iconic photo of Avery being arrested in his Chicago office and carried out by National Guardsmen. The war even gave unions a foothold in the South, because of its defense contracts. The closed shop, later to be outlawed by the 1947 Taft-Hartley Act, allowed unions to insist that only union members be considered for jobs in factories with union contracts.

The combination of a war-driven full-employment economy plus the government guarantee of organizing rights massively increased union membership, especially in the new unions affiliated with the CIO. The United Auto Workers' membership rose from 165,000 in 1939 to over a million by 1944. The United Steelworkers' membership nearly tripled, from 225,000 in 1939 to 708,000 in 1944. Organized electrical, rubber, and packinghouse workers achieved similar gains.

Yet the war's official recognition of unions was double-edged. With war profiteering by corporations, and the cost of living often outstripping wages until price controls became fully effective in 1942, the union rank and file chafed under the no-strike pledge and the efforts of union officials to enforce it. There was also great tension between the membership and leadership as leaders loyal to FDR sought to carry out his efforts to hold down overtime pay.

On balance, the formal labor partnership gave labor an institutional role but sapped labor militancy as a social movement. When labor was again under siege in the late twentieth century, that militancy would not be there to draw on. Historian Nelson Lichtenstein, in his authoritative history of labor during World War II, writes, "The home-front pressures for social order and political orthodoxy during World War II did much to weaken the independence and shop-floor power that the industrial union movement had won in the 1930s." True enough, but this was still a rare moment when organized labor enjoyed substantial institutional power in the American system, while the power of private capital was contained.

The brief twelve-year period between 1935, when a Democratic Congress passed the Wagner Act, and 1947, when a Republican Congress crippled its key provisions via the Taft-Hartley Act, was literally the only time in American history when the immense power of government helped build and solidify a labor movement. That movement, in turn, provided a powerful constituency for progressive government. Taft-Hartley removed some of labor's strongest weapons, by barring the closed shop, prohibiting sympathy strikes and boycotts, and allowing states to destroy union shops by passing so-called right-to-work laws. Taft-Hartley also weakened union control over pensions. The Act, which Truman—no radical—termed the "Slave Labor Act," began the slow erosion of institutional labor power.

But at the apex of labor influence, unions represented about one-third of American workers, and their influence extended to other employers, many of whom matched union wages and benefits as union-avoidance medicine. Unionists also provided the foot soldiers of the New Deal electoral machine. When Harry Truman surprised nearly everyone by his come-from-behind win in 1948, his alliance with labor was key.

The practical experience of labor solidarity offset the social conservatism of much of the working class. The labor movement gives working people a political understanding of class. To this day, union members and their families vote far more progressively than do people with identical demographic and occupational characteristics who are not in unions. But there are far fewer unionists today, and they have fewer legal protections in the face of a business counterattack that began in 1947 with Taft-Hartley and only intensified over time.

The war did extend the New Deal system for several more years in other respects. The New Deal had used public capital on a number of fronts. Public power efforts, from TVA to the great western dams to local rural electrification co-ops promoted by the New Deal, demonstrated that public power was often more efficient than private power. These projects also provided what Roosevelt liked to call "benchmark competition" to restrain price gouging by private competitors. All of these broadly beneficial measures, not incidentally, increased the credibility and prestige of the state over the market.

The Reconstruction Finance Corporation provided $50 billion—an immense sum in the 1930s—in public funds to recapitalize industry at a time when the stock market was still traumatized and bank lending was unreliable. With RFC financing came public-interest quid pro quos. RFC representatives sat on corporate boards. They demanded arrangements that limited the pay and perks of senior executives.

The war was an accidental full-employment program, which disproved the claims of many economists who argued in the late 1930s that capitalism had settled into a stage of technological unemployment where there were just not enough human jobs to go around. The quick return to full employment vindicated Keynes's argument that in the aftermath of a depression—when trauma to the banking system coupled with a shortfall in consumer demand can lock the economy into a subpar equilibrium far below its productive potential—only public outlay and public investment can get the economy back on track.

The war gave the Roosevelt administration not just the massive jolt of demand that had eluded even FDR's several public works programs, but also greater control of capital and public planning and investment. An elaborate war-planning bureaucracy directed the operation and gained unprecedented powers over the private sector in requisitioning materials and orchestrating the conversion of peacetime production to military uses.

As the US mobilized for war, government provision of capital became far larger and more explicit. The RFC moved into war finance. Its subsidiary, the Defense Plan Corporation, spent $9.2 billion to capitalize some 2,300 war production factories in forty-six states. During World War I, by contrast, the government spent only $600 million on industrial plants for defense production, 90 percent of which were financed privately. In the first six months of 1942, the government entered about $100 billion of war production orders, more than the entire GDP of 1939. Most of the RFC-financed plants were leased to industry for a dollar a year, and then privatized after the war—a stunning government gift to private commerce.

There was widespread concern that as soon as the war ended, with over 12 million GIs being demobilized, the economy would sink back into depression. In 1944, Senators Robert Wagner of New York (sponsor of the 1935 Wagner Act) and James Murray of Montana drafted the Wagner-Murray Full Employment Act, creating a detailed system modeled on wartime planning for keeping the peacetime economy at full employment. The president was to transmit an annual National Production and Employment Budget to Congress. This budget would include estimates of the size of the labor force, total national production needed to provide jobs for the labor force, and the total projected production without special measures by the federal government. But if anticipated production was insufficient, the federal government was to encourage enough additional nonfederal investment to stimulate the creation of private-sector jobs, and if necessary, federal expenditures were to close the remaining gap to ensure full employment.

The bill passed the Senate overwhelmingly but was killed in the more conservative House in late 1945, after the Democrats lost dozens of seats in the 1944 election to a war-weary electorate. The eventual Employment Act of 1946 was substantially weakened into a set of goals rather than a concrete planning document. Indeed, the House bill was known as the Whittington-Taft bill, cosponsored by the same Robert Taft who in 1947 would be the lead author of the antilabor Taft-Hartley Act. Whittington-Taft ended the explicit planning system and was a harbinger of reversals to come.

However, the Cold War soon served as a partial proxy for public investment and planning. Spending on the Cold War played a tacit Keynesian role on both sides of the Atlantic. US defense spending continued at high and relatively stable levels, independent of the ups and downs of the private economy. Investment in military technologies allowed significant government-funded scientific innovation with both military and commercial uses. Even though planning was now ideologically verboten, the Pentagon played a de facto role as a kind of planning ministry for major segments of the industrial economy. Yet because this role was tacit and inconsistent with resurgent free-market ideology, the use of the military as a proxy Keynesian planning state was also vulnerable.

ROOSEVELT AND RACISM

Another fault line and source of deferred crisis in the New Deal system was race. Roosevelt was able to expand labor regulation, social insurance, and public investment only by guaranteeing the Dixie members of his coalition that nothing in his program would alter the Southern Jim Crow system of white supremacy. Indeed, some of the New Deal actually extended state-mandated segregation to the North, into neighborhoods that had previously been integrated. When the federal government began building large-scale social housing for the first time under the WPA, Southern congressmen initially demanded that it be for whites only. Harold Ickes, former chairman of the Chicago NAACP and one of the most left wing of Roosevelt's senior advisers, was able to broker a compromise under which public housing did get built for blacks, but it was rigidly segregated. Public works projects were also racially segregated, with the better jobs reserved for whites. Thus did the New Deal reinforce—and in many cases, *introduce*—not just racial segregation but white supremacy. Even so, FDR won increased black support because at least he was providing some practical help.

Under Southern pressure, new programs such as Social Security and protections for workers under the Wagner Act also preserved and reinforced the Jim Crow system. Occupations such as domestic worker and farm laborer, held predominantly by blacks or Hispanics, were explicitly excluded from Social Security and unemployment insurance, lest African Americans gain increased economic independence or bargaining power. Agriculture was deliberately not covered by the Wagner Act. Some blacks, in more mainstream occupations, did qualify for Social Security. Black workers, in integrated CIO unions or in segregated ones like the Brotherhood of Sleeping Car Porters, did benefit from the Wagner Act, but not enough to alter the racial system. Though Dixiecrats reluctantly went along with Social Security, the companion drive for national health insurance was blocked, partly because Southern leaders feared that it would bring integrated hospitals.

Thus, with minor exceptions, Roosevelt was able to construct an American quasi social democracy only by limiting it to whites; or at most, by providing that any benefits extended to blacks maintain or expand strict segregation. Working-class unity (among whites) was also somewhat easier to maintain because the immigration restrictions enacted by Congress in 1924 drastically reduced the number of foreign-born workers.

The settlement with segregation weakened working-class solidarity in several respects. It meant a narrower class coalition, since a third of the working class was not fully participating, as voters or as beneficiaries. Though cross-race class solidarity had been attempted since the early days of Reconstruction, racism invariably trumped efforts at transracial coalition. As late as the 1890s, there were multiracial governing coalitions in a number of Southern cities, such as Wilmington, North Carolina, where white violence literally destroyed the city government in a coup. Earlier, cross-race coalitions had governed in dozens of Southern cities, from Mobile to Memphis. But these were gradually crushed, as black voting rights were wiped out.

By 1901, the last post-Reconstruction members of both the House and the Senate were gone, and biracial class coalitions were dead.

Martin Luther King appreciated the political consequences. "The Southern aristocracy took the world and gave the poor white man Jim Crow," King said from the steps of the Alabama capitol following the 1965 march from Selma to Montgomery. "And when his wrinkled stomach cried out for the food that his empty pockets could not provide, he ate Jim Crow, a psychological bird that told him that no matter how bad off he was, at least he was a white man, better than a black man."

The deferral of racial justice would come back to haunt the Democratic Party class coalition in the 1960s, when the landmark civil rights acts and executive orders finally prohibited discrimination in education, lodging, dining, transportation, voting, housing, and employment, and companion executive orders required employers and unions to take "affirmative action" to overcome current effects of past discrimination. Those reforms drove many white workers into the arms of George Wallace and Richard Nixon in 1968. In subsequent decades, in the absence of robust policies to help the entire working class, the continuing sense of white displacement and grievance prefigured the rise of the Tea Parties and Donald Trump.

Yet, for the time being anyway, the New Deal gave labor an important place at the table (even if organized labor was mostly white), and its power did serve to counterbalance that of industry. Wartime full employment, coupled with the recognition of unions, both dramatically increased worker earnings and equalized the income distribution. Every bit as important for the political economy of the era was the suppression of the power of private capital—a revolution that also proved temporary and reversible.

SUPPRESSING SPECULATIVE FINANCE

The New Deal shackled private finance in a fashion that has not been equaled before or since. The 1933 Glass-Steagall Act removed one entire category of speculation and conflict of interest from the financial system by requiring stock brokerages and investment-banking houses to be divorced from commercial banking. The commercial banks were invited to accept federal deposit insurance (nearly all did) and were subjected to a far more rigorous system of regular examination. The interest rates they could charge borrowers and pay depositors were also tightly regulated, to discourage forms of competition for customers that could damage solvency—reckless behavior that recurred after regulation was weakened in the 1970s and 1980s.

Though it remained privately owned, retail banking was converted into something close to a public utility. Nationwide banking was prohibited, and branch banking limited. What was sacrificed in the arguable efficiency of larger-scale banks was more than offset by the purging of speculation, conflict of interest, and corruption. It was the behemoth banking conglomerates, liberated from the New Deal restraints, that engaged in complex speculation and excess leverage, reaped immense speculative profits, and then crashed the system in 2007–8.

The New Deal also created a national system of housing finance from scratch, and invented the modern, long-term self-amortizing mortgage. FDR's set of policies included a kind of central bank for housing lenders via the Federal Home Loan Bank System, modeled on the Federal Reserve. It added the Federal National Mortgage Association to purchase mortgages from savings banks and savings and loan associations. These were mostly local nonprofits, mutually owned. Government insured the mortgages. The original FNMA, in contrast to its post-1969 namesake, was a public institution. It used direct Treasury borrowing to finance its operations, and there was no complex private securitization of the sort introduced in the 1980s to add layers of opaque risk.

In addition, the New Deal created a Home Owners Loan Corporation, to help struggling homeowners refinance underwater mortgages resulting from collapsing property values in the Depression. At its peak, one mortgage in five was written by the HOLC. Rather than going through private bankers, the HOLC was a true public institution, with tens of thousands of government employees working in direct retail branches.

In this system, nobody got extremely rich, and nobody had any incentive to complicate transactions for the sake of speculative profiteering. Credit evaluation was not delegated to third parties, but was performed directly by loan officers. There were no layers of middlemen adding costs and complexity. Despite the hard times of the Depression, the system—purged of its speculative elements—worked like a Swiss watch. Mortgage defaults were soon as rare as bank failures. Once the Depression ended, home ownership rates rose dramatically, from less than 40 percent in the 1930s to about 64 percent by the 1960s.

The entire system of underwriting and marketing stocks, meanwhile, was subjected to a rigorous system of regulation and disclosure, via the Securities Act of 1933, the Securities Exchange Act of 1934, and finally the Investment Company Act and the Investment Advisers Act, both of 1940. In this structure, investment banking was simplified and made transparent. The system allowed no complex private securitization of mortgage loans, no leveraged buyouts, no private-equity or hedge fund firms taking advantage of loopholes. FDR wanted to go even further, to prohibit brokerages from both trading for their own accounts and trading for customers, a potential conflict of interest that became increasingly abusive after the 1980s. This reform he did not get from Congress. But the New Deal went far enough to render finance the servant rather than master of the real economy. Despite the slow recovery from the Depression, there were no significant bank failures after 1934.

The political preconditions of the New Deal system of financial regulation began eroding right after Roosevelt's death and the Republican takeover of Congress in 1946. But the system had a long half-life. Strictly regulated finance underwrote the great postwar economic boom. Even if it deprived financiers of the opportunity to become very rich, the system was salutary for the real economy—in many respects *because* it constrained private financiers. Not until the economic slowdown of the 1970s, which brought the resurgence of business influence, laissez-faire ideology, and right-wing politicians, did both political parties begin working to dismantle much of New Deal financial regulation—with calamitous results.

It's worth drawing an important distinction here. In a capitalist economy, enterprises need capital, and the provision of investment capital is the job of well-regulated private-capital markets. All investment is in a sense speculative, since the investor or banker does not know in advance how well the investment will pay off. If the enterprise thrives, so does the investor, and the banker gets repaid. Importantly, however, investments directly connected to the real economy are less of a gamble. It is possible for a loan officer to assess the business plan and the competence of the entrepreneur, and determine how much of the entrepreneur's own money is in the deal. The risk to the bank can be roughly calculated and priced accordingly. The additional risk is assumed by the entrepreneur.

But there is a whole other category of capital that is *purely* speculative, and often damaging to the real economy. This kind of financial play invents and uses complex financial instruments, often at several removes from the underlying asset. These instruments are known as derivatives. It's an insiders' game, in which financial entrepreneurs can profit whether or not the real economy does, by making bets on bets and ensuring that the house is better informed than the rubes who are gulled into playing. Often the insiders profit by betting *against* the success of the underlying enterprise—the essence of the subprime scam. This was the kind of speculative game that contributed to the crash of 1929—that was shut down by the New Deal–postwar regulatory system, and then clawed its way back in the 1980s and 1990s to crash the economy again in 2008. These plays operate at so many removes from the real economy that the securities and risks were opaque both to regulators and to customers, and even to the so-called credit-rating agencies, private companies like Moody's or Standard & Poor's that blessed such deals with triple-A ratings in exchange for fees.

CONFISCATION OF CAPITAL WITH NEGATIVE INTEREST RATES

In the system that prevailed between the 1930s and the 1970s, finance was suppressed in one other notable respect that has largely escaped general attention. The real interest rate was negative for much of the postwar boom, making the capital costs of the real economy very low. The negative interest rate did impose some costs on the wealth-owning class, contributing to the unprecedented compression of the income structure during this era, but that shift did little economic damage and was a net gain for both the income distribution and the real economy.

In both the United States and Britain, the rate of inflation tended to exceed the interest rate on public debt for three decades after World War II. This meant that the real value of the debt gradually dwindled. If you hold a bond worth $100,000 and the inflation rate is 10 percent, after a year the real value of the bond is now about $90,000 (more or less, depending on the prevailing interest rate and the bond's maturity). Even if the bond pays 5 percent interest, you are still out something like $5,000 in real money. The flip side of your loss is the government's gain: the burden of public debt declines over time. For the US and the UK during the postwar period, Harvard economist Carmen Reinhart calculated, "the annual liquidation of debt via negative real interest rates amounted on average from 3 to 4 percent of GDP a year."

Various public policies can be used to keep real interest rates low or negative, and these policies converged in the postwar era. Government can require its central bank to finance public debt at very low interest rates. This is just what the US government did between 1941 and 1951. And government can also put ceilings on rates paid and charged by banks, as federal policy did from the 1930s until the 1970s, and as state government did via usury laws until the 1980s. (Taken to an extreme, these policies can reduce the supply of capital, but within limits they are salutary for the real economy.) Government can promote high rates of growth, so that the cost of past debt fades relative to GDP. And it can tolerate moderate inflation to reduce the real value of the legacy debt. All of these policies are abhorrent to private financiers but tonic for the rest of the economy. The fact that government could pursue these policies reflects the temporarily suppressed *political* power of private capital. The fact that the real economy thrived despite the pain to private bondholders defies a lot of standard economic theory and blows away a core premise of supply-side economics.

If private markets had set interest rates on government bonds during the period of very high public debt after World War II, debt-financing costs would have been much higher, reduction of the debt overhang far lower, and the drag on the real economy more substantial. But thanks to the tight regulatory policies, real interest rates were significantly lower from 1945 to 1980 than in the freer capital markets in the period before World War II and after financial liberalization in the 1980s.

The negative real interest rate on government bonds was yet another legacy of the war. When the United States entered World War II in December 1941, the government immediately faced the challenge of how to finance it. Government massively increased direct spending on the military and entered into huge war production contracts. The war ended up costing just under $300 billion—about one-third of total GDP for four years once full mobilization was reached in 1942.

Government financed the war both with surtaxes on the wealthy, at rates as high as 94 percent, and with massive sales of bonds. War bond sales totaled about $167.2 billion. Bonds were purchased as patriotic acts by the general public, and were also bought by banks, pension funds, corporations, and most important, by the Federal Reserve. Usually in wartime, government is dependent on commercial and investment banks to underwrite and sell bonds, and bankers make a lot of money. Interest rates are high because it's hard to find enough bond buyers. This was the case in World War I. But World War II, as a total mobilization, was different. The Federal Reserve was directed to peg interest rates on government debt at three-eighths of 1 percent on short-term ninety-day debt and 2.5 percent on long-term debt. How did the Fed achieve that goal? It simply bought bonds in large enough quantity to maintain those low rates. Whatever the public did not buy, the Fed did. The policy was formalized in a memorandum between the Treasury and the Fed, pursuant to an order from President Roosevelt. Had private money markets set rates, the costs of the war would have been prohibitive, and economic recovery slower. A total war, of course, is not a model for a normal economy. But the containment of private finance can be constructive in peacetime as well.

The combination of demand stimulated by massive deficit financing, plus pegged interest rates and virtually unlimited bond buying by the Fed, was initially not inflationary for two reasons. The ultra-Keynesian policy promoted rapid growth of the real economy—almost 50 percent over the four war years—and the economy had temporary wage and price controls, as well as rationing. Once price controls took effect in 1942, the inflation rate for the remainder of the war was less than 3 percent per year. In other words, buyers of 2.5 percent war bonds were earning no interest and losing a sliver of principal.

Once the war ended, however, inflation did break out, because of suppressed demand both for products and for wage increases. It was 8.3 percent in 1946, 14.4 percent in 1947, and 7.7 percent in 1948—enough to inflate away a lot of 2.5 percent war debt in those three years alone. Inflation did not settle down to a range of 1–3 percent until after the Korean War. Even though price controls and rationing ended with demobilization and all controls were lifted by 1946 at the insistence of Congress, the Fed-Treasury agreement to peg interest rates on government debt continued until 1951. The policy persisted out of concern that letting private markets dictate rates on the large debt overhang would be a huge burden on government and on taxpayers. Interest rates on corporate bonds tended to be influenced by safer government bonds, and were suppressed as well. With low interest costs, high growth rates, and modest inflation, the debt-to-GDP ratio in the United States fell from 113 percent in 1945 to 51 percent in 1955. For Britain, the ratio dropped from 240 percent to 138 percent during the same period, because of the same dynamics.

In sum, the three-decade postwar period was great for the real economy, while investors in bonds had negative rates of return. Stocks were a better investment, thanks to the low or negative interest rates and the strong economic growth.

So, finance was repressed in multiple respects—through the strict limits on what the banking industry was permitted to do, in the debt-financing policy of the government, and in the negative real returns for the *rentier* class. Those constraints, in turn, limited both the wealth and the political power of financiers. Keynes had famously called for "the euthanasia of the rentier," meaning that a modern economy relying on public credit and low interest rates could innovate and achieve full employment without being at the mercy of the whims of stockholders, bondholders, and speculators. The postwar suppression of finance partly (and felicitously) carried out Keynes's wish.

The industrial structure of that era was concentrated, which meant that large companies were able to extract monopoly or oligopoly profits. But because of the institutionalized labor power, these profits were shared with workers. Today's economy, by contrast, is a blend of some companies with immense market power (Apple, Google, Amazon) and others that are hypercompetitive—some of which cash in big in an initial stock sale. But in neither case are windfalls shared with ordinary workers, because of the shift in the rules of the game and the distribution of power.

With stock and bond prices depressed, how did industry finance its impressive growth in the postwar era? Partly with public capital via defense contracts, mainly with retained earnings, later with issues of stock. Purely financial returns were low or negative, but corporate profits were solid, thanks to rising consumer demand, corporate concentration, and the low real capital costs. Policy tolerated no financial engineering, no funny-money securities, no leveraged buyouts in which speculators took over corporations with borrowed money collateralized by the target company's own stock. All that came later. It was a very different way to run an economy.

A JOLLY GOOD FELLOW

While the wartime system of pegged interest rates on government borrowing was an emergency expedient, it also reflected the Roosevelt administration's own eight-year peacetime experience containing the abuses of the banking industry and FDR's own mistrust of the power and destructive potential of private finance. The same sensibility pervaded the assumptions of the Bretton Woods system, which proposed an architecture for global finance unlike any the world had ever seen. Yet the actual Bretton Woods system that materialized in the late 1940s only partly realized the goals of its architects, and it eroded over time.

On July 22, 1944, as allied troops were racing across Normandy to liberate Paris, representatives of forty-four nations met at the Mount Washington resort in Bretton Woods, New Hampshire, to plan the postwar monetary and financial structure. The idea was to create a global currency system that would insulate domestic full-employment economies from the deflationary pressures of private finance—a global counterpart to the economic and financial assumptions of the New Deal. The conference took three weeks of exhausting diplomacy. At the closing banquet, the assembled delegates rose and sang "For He's a Jolly Good Fellow." The fellow in question was the chairman of the conference, John Maynard Keynes, leader of the British delegation and intellectual inspiration of the Bretton Woods design.

Keynes's core insight was that market economies tended to get stuck at levels of output and employment well below their capacity for growth. The international correlate was the tendency of global finance to produce systemic austerity by placing fiscal balance, currency stability, and debt repayment ahead of economic growth. This bias was "pro-cyclical," producing euphoric booms as finance chased fads, followed by crashes and then recessions or depressions.

Even in the gold-standard era, monetary stability came at the price of regular panics, crashes, and depressions, as economies regularly lost and struggled to regain the confidence of international private creditors. Keynes's idea was to create an international financial and monetary structure that permitted nations to run high-employment economies at home without being constrained by the pressure of private global finance.

As a young man, Keynes had been the leading critic of the austerity and reparations imposed at the Versailles Peace Conference in 1919, the gathering of the victorious Allied powers to set the terms of the peace. The Treaty of Versailles can be understood as a blunder on several levels. The best-known mistake was the attempt by Britain and France to punish Germany by imagining that a defeated and economically shrunken German economy was capable of paying war reparations far beyond its capacity, and doing nothing to help Germany to recover. But this folly was only one part of the broader deflationary effort by elites to set back the clock and restore the financial assumptions of the nineteenth century. Britain tried to revert to the prewar value of the pound, condemning its citizens to an era of high interest rates and permanent recession for the two decades between the wars. In the interwar period prior to the New Deal, all of the Allied powers supported a laissez-faire global financial system, in which the fates of real economies were tied to the fads and whims of private investors and speculators.

Unlike the period following World War II, the inter-ally loans after 1919 were underwritten mainly by commercial banks. Thus the credit system was also pro-cyclical, exaggerating the ups and downs of business cycles. When times were tough, credit was hard to come by. When times were booming, credit flowed too freely and created bubbles. The intermittent efforts of governments to contain the damage, with periodic ad hoc conferences to reschedule debt, were futile because they accepted these fundamental premises.

Now, a quarter century later, Keynes wanted to be certain that this would never happen again. He did not prevail on the details of what became the Bretton Woods system, but he did inspire the basic economic assumptions. The architects of the post–World War II economy rejected both the folly of permanent punishment for Germany and the assumption that laissez-faire needed to be restored. Instead, they combined a program of economic recovery with a global financial system that allowed each nation to pursue a managed form of capitalism domestically.

In Keynes's design, a new "clearing union" would provide loans to help tide nations over during shortfalls so that private speculation would not generate austerity, while a new global public bank would be a source of investment capital for recovery and development based on solid investments, not faddish bubbles. Exchange rates would be fixed, but periodically adjustable if fundamental misalignments arose. Keynes also proposed a global currency, which he named "bancor." He wanted debtor nations to be able to borrow money in the new currency virtually at will, to prevent temporary national financial crises from aggregating to general austerity. He also wanted to put pressure on creditor nations to expand their economies rather than having a system that achieved balance by causing debtors to contract. Keynes's proposed mechanism was a provision that fined chronic creditors and allowed other nations to "discriminate" (his word) against the exports of creditor nations. In the context of 1944, the only such creditor nation was the United States.

But in 1944, it was never in the cards for the US to assent to a scheme that allowed discrimination against its exports. Nor were the Americans, who held 80 percent of the world's reserves and the sole viable currency, going to embrace an untested form of global money beyond American control.

There was to be a third institution, the International Trade Organization, whose job was to reconcile relatively liberal trade with decent labor standards and full employment. To that end, discrimination against imports was expressly permitted when necessary to keep down domestic joblessness, and in the draft charter the ITO's members made a commitment to domestic policies to promote high labor standards. When politics in the US moved to the right after Roosevelt's death in 1945 and Republicans took back Congress in 1946, the ITO went unratified. In its place, a General Agreement on Tariffs and Trade, later expanded into the World Trade Organization, would promote the traditional form of laissez-faire trade.

Here is the key point. While the Bretton Woods meeting did create an International Monetary Fund and a World Bank, the actual postwar system did not carry out Keynes's explicit design. The system was only incidentally and temporarily Keynesian. It did boost demand, it did constrain finance, and it did create a system of fixed exchange rates, which also proved temporary. But none of these took the forms that Keynes had proposed. All relied on the anomaly of American economic supremacy. Thus, the entire system was weakly anchored—politically, institutionally, and ideologically.

In theory, the IMF was supposed to provide advances that would allow nations to defend currencies against private speculation. In practice, the actual IMF did little of this, and it later became a leading instrument of the very austerity it was intended to contain. Capital controls were maintained for a time, mainly as a by-product of the financial disruptions of the war, and not as a systemic principle. The World Bank provided only a tiny fraction of the reconstruction aid and aggregate demand that was needed. That responsibility would fall mainly to the Marshall Plan. Currency parities were volatile and chaotic through the end of the 1940s. They finally stabilized, more than four years after the Bretton Woods meetings, thanks to the anchor of the dollar and the muscle of the US Treasury, not the interventions of the IMF.

At the Bretton Woods meetings, the rival proposal by Keynes's American counterpart, Harry Dexter White, prevailed. White, a left-wing New Dealer serving as number two man at the Treasury, shared Keynes's basic views on money and expansionary fiscal policy. But the White plan provided a much more modest fund and bank. In practice, these entities turned out to be far more limited than even White's design dictated, and White was bitterly disappointed at the truncated institutions.

Nonetheless, the early postwar system was a vast improvement over both the rigid gold standard of pre-1914 and the monetary anarchy and deflationary bias of the interwar period. The key features that helped nations pursue recovery programs, free from the deflationary pressure of speculative finance, were capital controls and fixed exchange rates, plus the temporary role of the US as residual market and source of capital. But its success, like so much else about the postwar exception to predatory capitalism, was a happy convergence of accidents. New York bankers had lobbied mightily against the Bretton Woods system, and in favor of free movements of capital. Their political power, however, was temporarily suppressed. When it revived in the 1970s, their influence was a key factor in the shift back to laissez-faire global finance.

The Bretton Woods system survived less than three decades. Its successor system restored the primacy of speculative private finance, and with familiar results.

Some economic historians contend that the imperatives of recovery and rebuilding were the core explanation for the stunning revival of postwar Europe. In his comprehensive study *The European Economy since 1945*, Barry Eichengreen writes, "Initially, Europe could grow rapidly simply by repairing wartime damage, rebuilding its capital stock, and redeploying men drafted into the wartime task of destroying output and productive capacity into the normal peacetime job of rebuilding them." Eichengreen's description of the opportunity is accurate. Yet as Eichengreen has recognized in his other work, market systems do not automatically deliver such results. The same imperatives existed after World War I, but the system failed. Nor did the egalitarian path that postwar recovery took happen automatically. It required the convergence described in these pages—one that was both fortuitous and ideological.

As capitalism reverted to its more normal power structure, the splendid anomaly of broadly egalitarian capitalism common to the West was living on borrowed time. An intriguing question is whether events might have played out differently. Was managed capitalism destined to be a historical blip, or might the shift have been more durable, given different patterns of leadership and luck, policy, and power?

3

THE RISE AND FALL OF DEMOCRATIC GLOBALISM

n 1945 and 1946, as diplomats tried to sort out Europe's political future, the immediate challenge was sheer survival. The mass bombing by both sides was unprecedented. By war's end, at least 20 million *civilians* had died, more than the 15 million who lost their lives in the war's military casualties. Entire economies were in ruins. Tens of millions of people were homeless. As negotiations dragged on about Europe's postwar borders, millions of refugees were stateless.

Major cities like Berlin and Rotterdam had been reduced to rubble. London, never invaded, had lost a million homes from the Blitz. Food was in short supply. In German cities for three years after the war, the circulating currency was a mix of nearly worthless Hitler-era reichsmarks and various forms of scrip. Der Führer's face was gone from all public places but weirdly lived on the banknotes. Barter was a prime form of exchange. Not until 1948 did West Germany get a new currency.

In 1945 there were still hopes that the wartime alliance between the US and the USSR would continue into peacetime. The Soviet Union was invited to join the IMF and World Bank. The United Nations, whose charter was ratified in San Francisco in October 1945, had at its core a Security Council based on the assumption that the peace would be kept by a concert of great powers.

As the war was ending, it was far from clear whether postwar Europe was to be a staunch Western partner in an anticommunist alliance, or some kind of buffer between the US and the Soviet Union. Nor was it clear that Germany would be reindustrialized, rearmed, and welcomed (with what some felt was undue haste) back into the family of democratic nations. The realities of a sharply divided Europe emerged only in 1947 and 1948 with the hardening of the Cold War.

In the meantime, the promised new financial architecture of Bretton Woods had yet to reach the ruined real economy. Europe did not yet have a rebuilt economy with which to feed its people, much less to promote export earnings; its scarce gold and dollars were rapidly exhausted importing food. As a whole, Europe was running a trade deficit equal to 5 percent of its war-shrunken GDP, most of it with the United States. In the severe winter of 1946–47, thousands of Europeans died of starvation.

Had the Cold War not intervened, Europe might well have sunk back into something like the economic crisis of the 1920s—and under far more depleted conditions. But Stalin's designs on Europe, combined with the electoral strength of local communist parties in France, Italy, Belgium, and Greece, belatedly got Washington's attention. In early 1947, William Clayton, the new undersecretary of the Treasury, returned from a firsthand look at Europe's deepening economic disaster and warned of the need for much deeper US involvement. In March, President Truman announced the Truman Doctrine of supporting nations resisting Soviet advances, backed by $400 million of emergency economic aid for Greece and Turkey. Clayton wrote, "Europe is steadily deteriorating. The political position reflects the economic. One political crisis after another merely denotes the existence of grave economic distress. Millions of people in the cities are slowly starving."

In May, Dean Acheson, the new undersecretary of state, issued urgent warnings both about Stalin's design and about the vulnerability of Europe to communism. US policy toward Germany rapidly reversed, from one of punishment to one of nurturing and reviving a needed ally. "De-Nazification" was accelerated and then substantially abandoned. And in June, Secretary of State George Marshall gave his famous commencement address at Harvard, proposing what would become the Marshall Plan. George Kennan's "long telegram," calling for a policy of containment, privately sent to the secretary of state and the president in February 1946, was published in 1947 in *Foreign Affairs* magazine under the byline "X."

EARLY SEEDS OF A RETURN
TO LAISSEZ-FAIRE

The ideological views and diplomatic goals and actions of the anchor nation, the United States, drastically shifted between 1945 and 1948. At the time of the Bretton Woods meetings in July 1944, there was good reason to believe that the White version of the global monetary system, though not as radical as that of Keynes, would actually be carried out.

After Roosevelt's death in April 1945, not only did the Cold War gradually intrude, but left-wing New Dealers like White were quickly replaced by far more orthodox officials, especially on the subject of international finance. White himself was in line to be the first executive director of the IMF. He was duly appointed by Truman but served for barely a month. In March 1947 he resigned under fire, both from conservatives in the Truman administration and from FBI director J. Edgar Hoover, whose investigation confirmed allegations that White had been passing sensitive information to the Soviets before and during the war. The Republican takeover of Congress in November 1946 pushed American financial policy further back in the direction of laissez-faire orthodoxy. A quarter century before the Bretton Woods system collapsed in the early 1970s, and a half century before the full resurrection of laissez-faire, the seeds of a return to orthodoxy were being sown.

After a quite anomalous period in which left-wingers held key positions at the Treasury Department, Treasury reverted to type as guardian of the orthodoxy. Undersecretary Clayton, White's successor as Treasury's top official on international economic affairs, was a financially conservative millionaire former cotton broker and strong supporter of free trade and free markets. The new Treasury secretary was Fred Vinson, a former federal judge and crony of Harry Truman from Vinson's years in Congress. Vinson, later named as chief justice of the Supreme Court, was far from a New Dealer. This ideological shift ensured that the postwar financial arrangements would be treated as regrettable, temporary emergency expedients, not as the permanent shift into managed financial markets that Keynes and

White envisioned. At times, national security policy—which indulged western Europe's planning heresies for the sake of the alliance—was at odds with orthodox economic policy, which pressured Europe to abandon wartime controls and embrace markets.

As Europe struggled to stabilize its monetary system and kick its recovery into high gear, US policy sought to push Europe to liberalize flows of both trade and finance, sometimes prematurely. For example, American officials, using the leverage of the $3.75 billion loan to Britain and Marshall Plan aid, pressed the British to make the pound a fully convertible currency, meaning that holders of pounds could freely exchange them for dollars or gold. The British acceded to American demands and made the pound convertible on July 15, 1947, but the action triggered a run on the pound and had to be reversed in a matter of weeks.

In the system's chaotic first years, despite the design at Bretton Woods for pegged exchange rates, currencies were far from stable. The weakened IMF passively accepted most of the initial currency values set by member nations in 1947. These proved to be too high, making European exports uncompetitive with a United States whose industrial plant had grown far more productive during the war. And then, as massive trade imbalances with the United States persisted, the IMF was mostly a bystander in a wave of devaluations orchestrated by the US Treasury in 1949. The United States, further marginalizing the IMF, insisted that no currency advances from the fund were needed, because of the role of Marshall Plan aid, and total drawings from IMF members fell from more than $400 million (still a small sum) in 1947 to zero in 1950.

Between 1948 and 1952, the Marshall Plan would spend some $13 billion, about 5 percent of America's GDP. In Europe, the IMF never played more than a token version of its proposed role, and with the Marshall Plan delivering grants in aid that dwarfed the World Bank's resources, the World Bank soon shifted its activities from European reconstruction to third-world development.

US officials, for the time being, balanced their desire for an early return to multilateral principles of free trade and free movements of currency and capital with their appreciation of Europe's practical condition. The need to allow Europe to recover, as a bulwark against communism, sometimes trumped or at least delayed America's resurgent romance with laissez-faire. Because of the logic of the Cold War, Washington sponsored and blessed a movement that it ordinarily might have challenged—the evolution of continental Europe into its own preferential trading bloc.

The emergent system—a stunted cousin to what had been proposed by Keynes and White—did create shelter from the pressures of international finance, in which a full-employment welfare state could temporarily flourish. Marshall Plan aid was public, and the need to allocate it created a legitimate role for a proactive planning state. The European Coal and Steel Community, precursor to the Common Market, was a deliberate cartel aimed at allocating scarce coal and iron ore—a measure antithetical to free-market economics and multilateral trade. The Europeans created the ECSC, mindful of the role played by national rivalry for coal and iron supplies in the bitter divisions after World War I; and despite ideological qualms, the US supported it because of the need for western European unity against communism.

LEFT AND RIGHT IN THE EARLY POSTWAR PERIOD

Though the social bargain common to nations of the postwar West was in some respects convergent, its roots could hardly have been more different. Most observers tend to view western Europe, with its more generous welfare state, higher taxes, and stronger unions, as somewhere left of the United States. But in the first years of the recovery, that picture was reversed. In the US, the democratic left had governed for more than a decade; democracy, as well as labor influence, had been strengthened. In Europe, the Depression had created political chaos, while the Nazi occupation had destroyed democratic politics on most of the continent. Leaders of democratic parties and trade unions had been murdered or were in exile.

It took some time for the political complexion of postwar Europe to emerge. In Britain, under its first majority-Labour government in 1945, and in Scandinavia, where the democratic left had governed since the 1930s, the welfare state developed under explicitly social democratic auspices. Unions played a particularly strong role in the

Nordic states, where nearly every wage earner was a union member and the unions were the soul and strength of the parliamentary social democratic parties. In the rest of the continent, the story was more complex. The left initially had strength, but this was quickly diluted by the exigencies of the Cold War.

Socialists and communists together made up a majority of voters in the first wave of postwar elections and served in the early provisional governments in France, Italy, and Belgium between 1944 and 1947. But with the hardening Cold War, domestic communists, whether or not explicit agents of Stalin's expansionary designs, were soon seen by the US as unsuitable for governing coalitions.

The role of domestic communists tends to be omitted from the usual story. The received wisdom about postwar geopolitics and reconstruction is almost Manichean. Christian Democrats and anti-communist Social Democrats were doing their best with American help to reconstruct a democratic Europe while the barbarians were literally at the gates. The reality on the ground was more fluid and complex. Not only did communists serve in coalition governments and win the largest or second-largest number of seats in several parliaments. Communist-affiliated trade unions were part of the pressure on governments and employers to deliver wage gains and comprehensive welfare benefits. Communists had been a key part of the antifascist resistance. They were more than just a fifth column for the Red Army. But the ostracism of communists, once Stalin's designs became clear, had the effect of pushing mainstream politics more to the center. So did the success of the postwar reconstruction program and the popularity of the Marshall Plan.

Thus, the pressure from the left on what became Europe's postwar welfare state came mainly from outside the centrist coalition governments that dominated continental politics for two decades after 1947. One major influence was via trade unions, the most important of which were communist in France and Italy. An anomaly of the era was that while parliamentary communist parties were ostracized as antisystem, communist unions were active players in Europe's evolving structure of collective bargaining. Their militancy helped ensure that a decent share of Europe's returning prosperity went to workers. Socialist and social democratic parties, though mostly not in government, were also a pressure on more centrist governments to deliver a substantial welfare state. The fear of Stalin compelled the democracies to show that they, too, could deliver for the working class.

Once Germany hardened into two states and West Germany soon became Europe's largest economy, left influence declined further. Communists were effectively banned from the new Federal Republic. (If you fancied communism, there was always East Germany.) Social Democrats (the SPD), who were more left-wing then than they are today and who favored a neutral Germany brokering between the USSR and the US, narrowly lost West Germany's first postwar election in 1949, and they did not enter government even as a junior coalition partner until 1965.

With the left divided and the largest left party effectively barred from office by 1948, most of the key figures in western European governments were not socialists or even social democrats, but Christian Democrats. As left Catholics and veterans of an era of laissez-faire run amok, they shared with social democrats the concern that market excess destroyed society and that citizens needed economic security. But where socialists and social democrats saw a conflict between labor and capital, Christian Democrats sought consensus.

Three of the most important practical visionaries who led postwar Europe, all left Catholics, were Robert Schuman, the architect of the European Coal and Steel Community, early precursor of the European Union; Alcide de Gasperi, the Italian prime minister during the first crucial years of recovery planning; and Konrad Adenauer, the first chancellor of West Germany, beginning in 1949. The ECSC represented explicit economic planning, in contrast to free-market allocation of coal and steel. All six of the foreign ministers who signed the ECSC treaty (the Treaty of Paris) in 1951 were also Christian Democrats.

The governing philosophy of much of postwar Europe, reflecting both Catholic and trade union influence, is often called neo-corporatism. The word "corporate" in this usage derives from *corpus*, the Latin word for "body," not from "corporate" as in the corporation. The Catholic Church brought a perspective that viewed the entire society as an organic whole with constituent parts. The social encyclicals of Pope Leo XIII in 1891 and Pope Pius XI in 1931 added the idea that society, the church, and the state had an economic obligation to workers and the poor.

Fascism used a totalitarian form of corporatism, in which the state created organizations representing workers, farmers, youth, mothers, veterans, professionals, and other groups who represented mediating institutions between *Volk* and *Führer*, but without elections or the other elements of democracy. By contrast, democratic corporatism of the sort prevalent in postwar Europe complemented parliamentary democracy with state recognition of leaders of peak associations—of industrialists, farmers, trade unions, and in some cases, the church. It was a modern, democratic sequel to the estates of the Middle Ages. Roosevelt had flirted with corporatism in the National Recovery Administration (which was overturned by the Supreme Court), and elements of corporatism lingered in tripartite wartime institutions. The continental version involved a larger role for the state; the Scandinavian variant looked more to consensual bargaining by unions and employer associations with the state as honest broker.

The form of trade unionism prevalent in Europe after the war was also neo-corporatist. In much of western Europe, unions were formally recognized as social partners, and a great deal of collective bargaining was centralized. Key contracts set the national pattern for wage settlements as a whole. Both because of the need for investment capital to finance recovery and because of concerns about national competitiveness, unionists of that era understood the importance of not pricing themselves out of the market with excessive wage demands. This was known as wage restraint. Factory-level settlements more generous than national norms were frowned upon as destabilizing of the larger social bargain. Despite some strike activity, unions—even communist ones—generally adapted to their roles as constructive social partners, because they welcomed the legitimacy; wages did, in fact, grow with rising productivity, allowing real gains for workers and increasing income equality. Scandinavia had the most explicit version of this model, and Germany a good deal of it. In France and Italy, by contrast, the state played more of a role in upholding wages and benefits via elaborate regulations and labor codes.

Throughout Europe and America, the postwar recovery was strikingly similar in its egalitarian trajectory, despite different national political histories, constitutional structures, labor policies, and parliamentary governing coalitions. The explanation of this surprising convergence has to be systemic. The postwar system as a whole had a few key common factors, which promoted the anomaly of egalitarian capitalism for as long as the system lasted. Because financial capital was constrained, creditors could not require their usual macroeconomic drag. High growth and tight labor markets produced worker bargaining power, which was reinforced by the strength and institutional role of trade unions. The public capital and consumer market provided by the US were also key. In Europe, because of the staying power of institutions, especially strong unions and a more expansive welfare state, the bargain and the fact of greater income equality continued into the late twentieth century, even as their systemic footings eroded.

The Americans could live with a somewhat statist form of capitalism, as long as it served the grand design of containing communism, and as long as its administration was safely in anticommunist hands. By the time political life in most of the continent had again normalized in the early 1950s, democracy was hearteningly robust and the economy more egalitarian than ever, but except in Scandinavia and briefly in Britain, the political footings were not exactly left-wing.

For a generation, the most important legacy of the Bretton Woods system was fixed exchange rates and constraints on speculative movements of cross-border capital, not monetary advances from the IMF or the World Bank. Keynes himself, describing the role of the new IMF to the House of Lords in 1944, touchingly explained, "Not merely as a feature of the transition but as a permanent arrangement, the plan accords to every member government the right to control all capital movements. What used to be a heresy is now endorsed as orthodoxy." But that triumphalism proved premature. Controls on capital lasted only as long as the transition back to capitalism as usual.

Thanks to this shelter, Europe's mixed economy was able to thrive for a generation. There were notable differences among European brands of managed capitalism, but all prospered and all were stunningly egalitarian, reflecting the suppression of finance, the empowerment of labor and the larger-than-usual role of the state.

In the academic literature, one of the most oft-quoted descriptions of the postwar bargain is a phrase coined in 1982 by John Girard Ruggie, invoking Karl Polanyi. The core insight of Polanyi was that, since the mid-nineteenth century, market forces had become increasingly "disembedded" from society. The liberal free market became paramount, creating social dislocation and, ultimately, economic and political catastrophe. Ruggie, with a salute to Polanyi, termed the postwar settlement an oxymoron of "embedded liberalism." The newly created institutions, in contrast to either laissez-faire or socialism, allowed some role for the market—classical economic *liberalism*—but *re-embedded* the market in society, via regulations, a welfare state, and a full-employment economy. "Governments would be permitted—indeed, were expected—to maintain capital controls," Ruggie later wrote.

But Ruggie's characterization did not turn out to be a permanent shift. Embedded liberalism (academic language for a tightly regulated global market) was the *aspiration*—of Keynes, White, Roosevelt, and many of the early postwar European leaders. However, the actual institutions fell well short of the intent. As political power and ideology reverted to normal—to capitalist normal—the actual system was built more on temporary accommodations to the immediate recovery and the strategy of containing communism. The broadly prosperous mixed economy that ensued still had decades of half-life, but its days were numbered.

MANAGED CAPITALISM AND THE THIRTY-YEAR BOOM

By the early 1950s, the broad outline of the postwar economic miracle began to emerge. Marshall Plan aid got Europe out of the self-deepening slump of 1946 and 1947. The vicious circle of the immediate postwar years turned virtuous. As Europe's productive capacity recovered, so did its exports. The deficit with the US declined and turned into a surplus. When Marshall Plan aid ended in 1952, rising military spending took over, to play both a capital-supply and a Keynesian role. American military aid to NATO countries increased from $211 million in 1949 to $4.2 billion in 1953—more than the annual level of Marshall Plan aid at its peak.

Private-capital investment resumed, but it was mostly direct investment, not financial speculation. US private investment increased from $1.7 billion in 1950 to $21.5 billion by 1969. European banks, still substantially nationalized, resumed their normal role of providing capital to industry. These banks served as sources of long-term ("patient") capital, not short-term speculation. Workers enjoying decent earnings could resume setting aside private savings, complemented by public and private pension systems. Restored consumer demand also powered the recovery, in good Keynesian fashion.

The devaluations of 1949 were imperfect, but good enough. With minor adjustments in the 1950s and 1960s, currency values roughly stabilized for nearly a generation. This was also a virtuous circle. Because parities were fixed, there was no private financial speculation in currencies, of the sort that later proved so destabilizing of the system. Because capital controls lingered and the US Treasury and Federal Reserve worked with the IMF and their counterparts in other nations to maintain those parities, European nations were spared the need to raise interest rates and deflate their economy in order to win the confidence of international investors. That would come later.

While the European economy was plainly strengthening, its monetary system was still too weak to survive anything like economic liberalism. If French citizens had been free to move their francs to dollars or to gold, a run on the franc would have ensued, leading the Bank of France to deplete its reserves of dollars and gold in a hapless effort to prop up its currency. The same was true for most of Europe's money. Thus, the controls on currency and capital continued through the 1950s and beyond in some countries. And so did relatively high tariffs against external products, coexisting with an internal preferential free-trade area of the emerging common market. The right to regulate cross-border movements of capital, especially short-term capital, was codified in the IMF's 1945 Articles of Agreement and the 1957 Treaty of Rome, and even as late as the 1961 OECD Code of Liberalisation of Capital Movements. But this delicate bargain would soon tilt back toward laissez-faire.

In the 1950s and 1960s, western Europe enjoyed a balance between nationalism and a form of regulated internationalism that allowed each nation to build its own version of managed capitalism. Thanks to the creation of a European Payments Union in 1950, currencies that had been strictly controlled in the late 1940s were again convertible inside Europe, and trade within Europe became multilateral. Yet Washington, recognizing that Europe's recovery was still fragile, allowed European economies to discriminate as necessary against dollar imports. An accommodation that had been rejected as a foundation of Keynes's proposed Bretton Woods order was discreetly allowed in practice. Trade within Europe continued to increase, as did the consensus in favor of a customs union. In 1957, the Treaty of Rome created a tariff-free Common Market initially with six member nations. But unlike the successor European Union, it did not interfere with domestic policies. Each European nation was free to build its own welfare state, to have its own industrial policies, its own labor arrangements, and its own tax policies. These were seen as not the business of the nascent European Economic Community.

Trade expanded, but tariffs were still high until the Kennedy round of tariff reductions in the mid-1960s, to allow each nation to rebuild its domestic industry. Because of tight national banking regulations, the gradual removal of capital controls was not yet destabilizing. Moderate inflation reduced the burden of the war debt, gradually decreasing the debt-to-GDP ratio. In Germany, virtually all of the Hitler-era debt was written off by the Allies in 1953, as part of the postwar recovery program. Most domestic German debt was canceled as worthless. Banks were given special treatment, and remaining debt from the Weimar era was substantially forgiven, with repayment stretched out into the twenty-first century.

SOURCES OF GROWTH
AND INCREASING EQUALITY

The growth rates of the era were prodigious. In one generation after 1945, real per capita income in Europe increased as much as it had in the previous 150 years. This success was emphatically not the natural consequence of rebuilding after war damage. Every European country had already surpassed its 1938 levels of production by the early 1950s, and the great postwar boom still had twenty years more to run. The reality is that the era displayed an equipoise balancing tightly regulated finance, labor power, strong states, and a dynamic, innovative private sector—a brand of capitalism unlike anything the world had ever seen.

Both the economic-growth and income-distribution results were stunning. In Britain and the US, the income compression had begun during the war, as a result of the return of full employment, the strength of unions, and the policies of levying high taxes on the top. On the continent, the income distribution steadily became more equal throughout the postwar boom. The trend was weaker and more abbreviated in the United States, which had a less fully developed welfare state and relatively weaker trade unions and was among the first to deregulate capital. Even so, the share of US income going to the top 1 percent fell from 36 percent of total income in the 1920s to about 24 percent in the 1950s. On the continent, the share going to the top 1 percent fell to less than 15 percent in several nations, and the Gini coefficient, a standard measure of overall income inequality, kept declining in all of Europe through the 1970s. Unemployment was below 2 percent in most of the continent for two full decades.

It is simplistic to attribute the increased equality simply to the high growth. Though high growth, other things being equal, facilitates equality because of tight labor markets and plentiful fiscal resources, other things are, in fact, not equal. There have been periods of decent average GDP growth, such as the 1980s in the US, when public policy intentionally increased inequality. The egalitarian growth of the postwar boom was the product of deliberate policies anchored in a successful politics.

In his authoritative 2015 study of inequality, the economist Anthony Atkinson ascribes the improving income equality of the postwar era to three factors: an increased share of total income going to wages, a more equal distribution of wage and salary income, and greater equality of capital income. Full employment promoted all of this, by increasing labor bargaining power, both individually and via unions. With primary income (wages and salaries) enjoying greater equality, the system of taxes and transfers did not have to work so hard. With full employment, welfare-state outlays could underwrite valued and productivity-enhancing new social benefits such as health and education, rather than being wasted on unemployment compensation and basic income support—an insight suggested by the great architect of the British welfare state, William Beveridge, in his landmark 1944 blueprint, *Full Employment in a Free Society.*

All of this would change dramatically in the 1970s. As a laissez-faire financial system and global monetary disorder returned after 1973, unemployment rose and wages came under pressure. The welfare state could preserve the relatively equal income distribution of the early postwar period for a time—using second bests. It could increase taxes and benefits. As women entered the labor force in large numbers, household income continued to grow more equal for a few more years, even as individual wage and salary incomes began widening.

But as capital was deregulated, incomes at the top took off again. As supply-side theories gained ground, taxes were cut, especially for the well-off. As neoliberal labor market theories came back into fashion, labor protections were reduced. By the 1980s in several countries, the income distribution was already reverting to a pattern that looked more like that of the 1920s. The Scandinavian countries, with stronger unions and more explicit welfare states, held out longer. But by the new century, they, too, were hit by their exposure to a liberalized global financial system, and income inequality in Scandinavia began widening too.

Thomas Piketty's celebrated book *Capital in the Twenty-First Century* gets the statistics right and the politics mostly wrong. Piketty correctly points to something close to an iron law of capitalism: the return on invested capital tends to exceed the rate of economic growth. Thus, it logically follows that wealth becomes more concentrated over time. However, Piketty is intrigued by the one exception to this two-century pattern—the middle of the twentieth century, when economies became more equal. His main explanation for the more equal structure of that golden era is that a lot of wealth was wiped out in two wars. And since wealth is owned by the wealthy, that destruction, arithmetically, led to a more equal wealth distribution.

But Piketty's story is incomplete. Not only is it too general, but the timing is off. The national experiences of the major Western powers diverged in the two major world wars and their aftermaths. Britain, France, and Germany did suffer wealth destruction in both wars, but the United States did not. On the contrary, both wars helped energize US productive activity and wealth creation. But in the aftermath of World War I, America became far more unequal, while after World

War II, it became more equal. And despite dramatically divergent patterns of wealth destruction during and after World War II, the nations of Europe became more equal after World War II as well. The postwar experience needed to be understood as a system of political economy, whose rules were drastically different from the usual rules of capitalism. That's what explains the greater equality of wealth and income.

Piketty, for all his brilliance as a historian of economic statistics, mostly leaves out the politics. A more egalitarian brand of capitalism was possible in the middle third of the twentieth century primarily *because the distribution of power was different*, making possible different political coalitions, and thus radically more egalitarian policies than those of the 1920s. As the power of capital has reverted to normal, so has the distribution of income and wealth.

The social contract of the postwar era was less durable than it seemed, on several counts. Hence the post-1973 shift back to normal capitalist patterns of extreme inequality in wealth, income, and power. The destruction of wealth in wartime has little to do with the real story.

THE DOLLAR DILEMMA

A core aspect of the postwar system was a financial time bomb— its dependence on the US dollar. Keynes was right: the dollar was no permanent substitute for a global elastic currency, though it was more than good enough for a quarter century. During the Bretton Woods era, the dollar was the only currency freely convertible into gold, but because the dollar was so strong (and dollar investments, unlike gold, paid interest), few bothered with gold.

The value of gold, at $35 an ounce, anchored the currency values of the rest of the system. As Europe recovered and US dollars flowed outward in the form of military aid and tourism, the large US current-account surplus turned into a deficit. It grew to about $1 billion a year in the early 1950s, and $3 billion or more by the late 1950s. As dollars piled up outside the US, a so-called Eurodollar market grew, made up of offshore dollars that could be lent out to finance the growth of Europe's economy. Eurodollar loans, less highly regulated than other currencies, also became an engine of deregulation for the wider financial system.

As early as 1947 and more formally in 1957, the Belgian-born American economist Robert Triffin warned that it was not possible for the dollar to serve as both America's domestic currency and the monetary base of the world without courting inflation. If the US continued to supply the dollars that a growing world economy needed, America's outflow would eventually lead to dollar devaluation. Conversely, if the US defended its national currency by contracting its money supply, the world economy would be starved for liquidity. This contradiction was dubbed the "Triffin dilemma."

Triffin himself proposed a much stronger IMF and a toned-down global currency in the spirit of Keynes. Nations would be required to hold at least 20 percent of their reserves in the form of IMF currency. Absent that, he warned, nations that were worried about inflation and the fear of dollar devaluation eventually would begin cashing in dollars for gold. In a self-fulfilling prophecy, dollar devaluation would become inevitable. And this is exactly what occurred.

By the late 1950s, the United States was running an annual balance-of-payments deficit with Europe in the range of $3–$4 billion. The US still had a healthy positive balance from exports of goods. But this plus side was more than offset by transfers of dollars for military aid, tourism, and capital investment. By 1960, the value of dollars held offshore exceeded the total value of America's gold holdings at Fort Knox by $19 billion. If nations began exercising their right to exchange dollars for gold, the US would be insolvent. In 1963, the French under General Charles de Gaulle, who resented the dollar's "exorbitant privilege" (a phrase coined by then finance minister Valéry Giscard d'Estaing) as anchor currency of the system, began doing exactly that, exchanging dollars for gold at the rate of about thirty tons of gold per month.

The cat was out of the bag. Where fixed exchange rates and capital controls had once prevented speculation against currencies, partial liberalization inexorably led to more liberalization. The dollar itself was the prime target of currency speculators, including foreign sovereigns. Something would have to give.

Throughout the 1960s, the US resorted to a variety of expedients. The Kennedy administration organized a "gold pool," in which central bankers agreed to collectively intervene in markets to hold the line on the dollar price of gold. The New York Federal Reserve, as agent for the Treasury, devised reciprocal lines of credit ("swap lines") to help central banks lean against the wind by purchasing dollars. Despite the general US aversion to capital controls, the Johnson administration in 1964 persuaded Congress to enact an "interest equalization tax," to tax away any benefit that a US investor might gain by purchasing foreign bonds. The tax, ironically, only stimulated more activity in the Eurodollar market, which was not subject to the tax. Through this period, the US rejected calls for anything like an international currency. Eventually, in 1967, the Johnson administration agreed to the creation of Special Drawing Rights, a token version of Triffin's idea. But the US allowed only a very modest scale, and SDRs could be held only by central banks.

By 1968, the escalation of the Vietnam War had exacerbated the strain in two respects. Military spending overseas increased the outflow of US dollars, adding to the US current-account deficit. And the stimulus of war spiked the rate of inflation. After the new Nixon administration took office in 1969, the economy entered a mild recession in 1970, which temporarily reduced the payments imbalance by cutting US imports. But at Nixon's behest, the new Federal Reserve chair, Arthur Burns, a close Nixon ally, cut interest rates in the hope of stimulating a recovery in time for the 1972 election. Fiscal policy was also loosened, with a fiscal-year-1971 budget deficit of $23 billion. The payments deficit soared to an annual rate of almost $30 billion. A renewed bout of inflation proved the last straw, and the US could no longer defend the gold price of $35 an ounce.

What followed was a stunning reversal of US policy and stated ideology. The United States temporarily abandoned its role as benign hegemon of the system in favor of guarding its own short-term economic self-interest. That self-interest was expressed in an incoherent, ad hoc policy mix of free markets and economic nationalism. Facing a domestic crisis of rising prices and a run on the dollar, Nixon and his economic team repaired to the presidential retreat at Camp David in mid-August 1971. After two days of discussion, they announced a 10 percent tax on imports, as well as emergency wage and price controls, an expedient that Nixon had detested since his wartime service as a low-level clerk in the Office of Price Administration (headed by John

Kenneth Galbraith!). But exchange rates were now left to markets, as Nixon's administration would no longer intervene to defend the $35-an-ounce peg.

Other governments were not consulted. They were informed just before the public announcement. The director general of the IMF, Pierre-Paul Schweitzer, was summoned to the office of Treasury Secretary John Connally to view Nixon's announcement on TV. It was news to Schweitzer.

In December, after letting markets test the value of the dollar, the major nations agreed to try a new peg, of $38. This peg did not hold either, and after floating for a time, the dollar was devalued again in 1973, by another 11 percent. The Fed and Treasury stopped aggressively intervening to hold the peg, and the system entered a chaotic period of floating rates, reminiscent of the interwar period of monetary disorder. A variety of approaches were attempted, all aimed at stabilizing currency values within a relatively narrow band. But the Bretton Woods era was over. The termination of fixed rates and controls on currency opened the door to a return of much more aggressive financial deregulation, domestically and globally, which in turn undermined other footings of managed capitalism.

If you had to assign a watershed year to the beginning of the end of the postwar social contract, it was 1973. That year began the period of rising inflation and deepening monetary instability. It was the year when workers' wages began diverging from productivity growth. As the 1970s wore on, the wave of factory imports from state-subsidized and lower-wage countries began undermining stable working-class communities—especially in the US, where there was little government inclination to slow the pace of imports or pursue economic planning measures to help communities adjust or redevelop. The early seeds of twenty-first-century populist revolt were sown in the industrial dislocations of the 1970s, which only worsened over time.

Nixon's preoccupation with his Watergate woes was another of those accidental factors that added to the economic distress and hastily improvised policies. A scrap of tape from Nixon's secret Oval Office recordings gives a sense of the role played by his Watergate distraction. The tape from June 23, 1973, as the financial system was

descending into chaos, records the following exchange with the president's chief of staff, H. R. (Bob) Haldeman:

HALDEMAN: Did you get the report that the British floated the pound?
NIXON: No, I don't think so.
HALDEMAN: They did.
NIXON: That's devaluation?
HALDEMAN: Yeah. Flanigan's got a report on it here.
NIXON: I don't care about it. Nothing we can do about it.
HALDEMAN: You want a rundown?
NIXON: No, I don't.
HALDEMAN: He argues it shows the wisdom of our refusal to consider
    convertibility until we get a new monetary system.
NIXON: Good. I think he's right. It's too complicated for me to get into.
HALDEMAN: [Fed chairman] Burns expects a 5 percent devaluation
    against the dollar.
NIXON: Yeah, OK. Fine.
HALDEMAN: Burns is concerned about speculation about the lira.
NIXON: Well, I don't give a shit about the lira.

In yet another of those accidents of history, the dollar devaluations
coincided with one of the more brutal wars in the series of Arab-
Israeli conflicts. Since exports of crude oil are denominated in dollars, the devaluations of 1971–73 cost OPEC member states money.
The Arab states, moreover, were furious at the West for underwriting
Israel's victory in the October 1973 Yom Kippur War, which ended
with Israel crossing the Suez Canal and occupying the Sinai Penin-
sula. The Israeli offensive had relied on American arms and had the
express approval of Secretary of State Henry Kissinger.

In retaliation, OPEC announced an oil embargo, followed by a pun-
ishing increase in the price of crude oil far larger than necessary
merely to offset the modest dollar devaluation. The price was qua-
drupled, from $3 to $12 a barrel. From 1947 to 1967, the dollar price
of oil had risen by less than 2 percent per year. The 1973–74 price
hikes were the first of several. When Kissinger negotiated an Israeli
withdrawal from most of the Golan Heights and the Sinai, the oil
embargo was lifted, but the price hikes stuck. By early 1974, Nixon

was fighting for his political life. The Arabs gambled, correctly, that the West would not go to war over the price of oil.

BACK TO MONETARY DISORDER

As the Bretton Woods system was tottering, both Japanese and European leaders had pressed Washington to support cooperative capital controls to damp down destabilizing speculation but the Nixon Administration refused except as a temporary, emergency expedient to support the dollar. In place of the old Bretton Woods system of pegged but adjustable exchange rates, the Europeans devised a European Monetary System, with the strong German deutschmark as anchor currency. Instead of having fixed rates, currencies were permitted to float within a relatively narrow range. Central banks and finance ministries were supposed to collaborate to keep currencies within those bands. This coordinated effort was known as the Exchange Rate Mechanism. The system was makeshift; the terms were modified at several points between 1973, when Bretton Woods finally collapsed, and 2002, when most of Europe adopted the euro. By the early 1990s, currencies were supposed to stay within plus or minus 6 percent of their target rate relative to the deutschmark. This improvised system never jelled.

The problem was that even a managed float lets speculators back in. Once again, as in the interwar period, governments needed to run their economies less in service of steady growth, decent distribution, and full employment—and more to keep the trust of financial speculators, who tended to prize high interest rates, limited social outlays, low taxes on capital, and balanced budgets. Before creation of the euro, deficit countries at least had the expedient of devaluation, but the whole system now returned to the deflationary bias against which Keynes had warned, with pressure on deficit countries to shrink their economies rather than pressure on surplus countries to expand.

Even Britain under the fiscally obsessive Tories, in what some might call poetic justice, suffered this fate when George Soros (in his role as international speculator rather than international philanthropist) crashed the pound. The year was 1992. Britain had joined the Exchange Rate Mechanism at the urging of Thatcher's successor, John Major, hoping to stabilize the pound's value relative to the deutschmark. But Britain's inflation rate was higher than Germany's. The Bank of England was torn between promoting low interest rates to stimulate the economy and high ones to protect the exchange rate. The government tried to defend the value of its currency, but Soros and other traders began betting against the pound, ultimately wagering $15 billion that it would have to be devalued. Soros pocketed an estimated $1.4 billion when the pound crashed. Britain ignominiously quit the Exchange Rate Mechanism and let the pound float.

As it happened, a few weeks later Soros found himself in Cambridge, for a long-scheduled lecture. His host was John Eatwell, later Baron Eatwell, then a fellow of Trinity College and the senior economic adviser to the Labour Party. "Ladies and gentlemen," Eatwell began his introduction, "here is the man who cost Her Majesty's government a billion pounds." Soros blanched. Eatwell continued, to smiles and applause, "And the only thing I can say in his defense is that he will spend the money better than Her Majesty's government."

Thus, several convergent events from the late 1950s to the mid-1970s demolished the postwar financial system and its domestic social compacts. The collapse of fixed exchange rates and capital controls invited a return to financial speculation. The increased inflation, resulting from the breakdown of Bretton Woods and the oil price increases, undercut the system of consensual wage bargaining. The perverse tight-money response by conservative finance ministers and central bankers to price increases (that were, in fact, more sectoral than macroeconomic) helped create the anomaly of simultaneous high unemployment and inflation, known as "stagflation." All of these shifts tilted the balance between labor and capital decisively back to capital, especially to finance. By the late 1970s, these economic reversals and policy challenges discredited the governing parties, which at the time were mostly center-left.

Throughout the West, the system succumbed to stagnant real wages, rising public-sector costs, and increased government deficits. All of this discredited not only governments, but the supposed reigning gospel of Keynesianism, most of which had long since been abandoned in any meaningful sense. Thus the door was opened to a resurrection of laissez-faire ideology, radically conservative free-market governments in Britain and America, and a repositioning of left parties toward the center.

All this ruptured a supposed post-ideological consensus that anchored the mixed economy. When nominally conservative governing parties in Europe and the US had first returned to power in the 1950s, they basically accepted the mixed economy and the welfare state. In the United States, the Eisenhower administration did not seek to repeal the New Deal. In Britain, the Conservatives who were returned to office in 1951 did not try to dismantle Labour's welfare state. French Gaullists assumed a strong role for the state, and German Christian Democrats saw themselves as guardians of an inclusive social compact. It was an era when commentators could proclaim an end of ideology.

But Margaret Thatcher and Ronald Reagan soon offered a far more fundamentalist reversion to free markets, cheered on by resurgent financial leaders and newly influential laissez-faire economists. Each nation, of course, has its own political particulars. But it is more than accidental that politics throughout the West followed the same deeper rhythms. Unmistakably, international systemic characteristics had facilitated the convergence of high-growth, full-employment, egalitarian national economies nearly everywhere in the 1950s and 1960s—just as the destruction of that more highly managed system in the early 1970s ushered in another cycle of laissez-faire everywhere. The return to market fundamentalism was supposed to energize economic growth. It did not. It did restore both inequality and instability, with political repercussions to follow.

ROADS NOT TAKEN

A key question is whether this economic and political reversal was inevitable. The monetary and economic crisis of the 1970s, as noted, opened the door to right-wing leaders who used the occasion to further dismantle the postwar system. Even before the elections of Thatcher and Reagan, Federal Reserve Chair Paul Volcker—later something of a hero after the financial collapse of 2008—relied on perverse, tight-money policies to crush inflation by breaking worker bargaining power and deflating the economy. Very high interest rates in the US reverberated throughout the system, doing further damage to the postwar economic system, its political footings, and the security of working people, and creating catastrophic losses in Latin America.

Many Marxian scholars have insisted that because a crisis of capitalism is always inevitable, the collapse of the postwar order was only a matter of time. Looking through a Marxian lens, the inflation of the 1970s can be viewed as a renewed case of class conflict over the economic surplus, in the face of a Marxian falling rate of profit. The ultra-financialization that created the economic bubble and collapse of the early twenty-first century can be understood in Marxian terms, as the response of finance capital to the system's tendency to overproduce goods, which "immiserated" workers lack the income to consume.

But this story is too formulaic. In fact, a variety of alternative policy courses were available in the 1970s, to tame inflation and restore monetary order without destroying other, broadly valued and highly functional elements of the system. But the policy experts who proposed remedies more consistent with managed capitalism no longer had the ears of the dominant politicians, because of a shift in the balance of political power.

As Robert Triffin urged, a stronger IMF and a more expansive use of Special Drawing Rights as a quasi-global currency could have increased liquidity and relieved the pressure on deficit nations to shrink their economies. In the Nixon administration, Commerce Secretary Peter G. Peterson, later a private-equity billionaire and lobbyist for budgetary austerity, had been pushing for a more laissez-faire monetary system with a shift to floating rates and an abandonment of capital controls. The monetary crisis of August 1971 gave him his opening. But this view was far from universal. Expanded SDRs could have preserved fixed exchange rates and reduced financial speculation.

As early as 1972, in response to the collapsing Bretton Woods system, the future Nobel laureate, Yale economist James Tobin, proposed a tax on foreign currency transactions, to discourage speculators from betting against weak currencies and compelling targeted countries to deflate their economies. Violating one of the most sacred premises of classical economics—the supposed efficiency of frictionless markets—Tobin called for throwing "sand in the wheels of international finance." Two decades later, after successive currency crises in Mexico, East Asia, Russia, and elsewhere demonstrated the costs of monetary speculation, Tobin renewed his call for such a tax in 1991.

"Speculators," he explained, "invest their money in foreign exchange on a very short-term basis. If this money is suddenly withdrawn, countries have to drastically increase interest rates for their currency to still be attractive. But high interest is often disastrous for a national economy." Earlier in the postwar era, capital controls and fixed exchange rates blocked speculation outright, but no longer. A tax on short-term currency speculation would allow cross-border movements of investment capital but diminish the purely speculative damage. Needless to say, the resurgent power of private finance has been such that the Tobin tax has never been taken seriously by policy makers, much less enacted.

And in the inflationary 1970s, a number of economists proposed superior alternatives to Paul Volcker's strategy of very high interest rates as a way of damping down price pressures by creating a general recession. In orthodox economic theory, inflation is, by definition, macroeconomic—the result of too much purchasing power chasing too few goods, causing prices to rise. In Milton Friedman's even more fundamentalist variation, inflation was "always and everywhere a monetary phenomenon"—the consequence of governments creating too much money. The trouble with both theories was that they did not aptly describe the sectoral inflation of the 1970s.

Crude oil, the lifeblood of a modern economy, abruptly became more expensive—not because of increasing demand for oil, but because the OPEC cartel jacked up prices. Those prices cycled through the economy. In another unfortunate coincidence, the 1970s was a decade of bad harvests, increasing food prices. In the US, high inflation caused consumers to defensively stash wealth in real property, raising housing prices. And the delayed impact of Medicare, whose compromise with medical and hospital industries compelled the government to pay whatever doctors and hospitals billed, spiked prices in the health care sector as well. The convergence of these sectoral sources of inflation with cost-of-living clauses in many union contracts led wages to increase, creating what economists termed a wage-price spiral.

If you unpack these several sources of price increase, raising interest rates was a needlessly blunt tool for reducing price pressures by depressing the economy generally. (And it notably failed in the case of oil.) It would have been far better policy to address the problem sector by sector, as a number of economists recommended at the time, with specific policies for energy, housing, medical care, and food security. To the extent that automatic cost-of-living adjustments exacerbated the problem, strategies known as incomes policies—rewarding unions for wage restraint and resorting to sectoral controls in some cases—could have broken that cycle. Unions in Scandinavia, which enjoy more legitimacy and take more responsibility for the economy as a whole, pursued exactly that approach. Elsewhere, however, the inflationary crisis of the 1970s was used as a political windfall for resurgent conservatism. As an indication of just how thoroughly the social contract of the postwar era and the relative power of capital and labor had been upended, consider this: In the 1950s and 1960s, inflation reduced the returns of owners of wealth, whose bonds had fixed interest rates, while unionized workers enjoyed cost-of-living adjustments in their wages. By the 1980s, worker pay was lagging behind inflation, and owners of capital were enjoying supernormal windfalls.

The shift back to radical laissez-faire—neoliberalism—was not required by the economic circumstances. Neither was the full deregulation of finance, nor the enforcement of austerity, nor the use of trade rules to further undermine domestic managed capitalism, nor the indulgence of globalized and systematic tax evasion. These turned out to be economic failures, except in the one sense that they shifted incomes to the top. But the crisis of the 1970s did alter power relations and did create openings for these policies, and a revived global financial elite soon took full advantage. The dynamics, and the damage to decent capitalism, were cumulative.

4

THE LIBERATION OF FINANCE

The free-market conservatives who regained power in the 1980s were beneficiaries of the reversion to global monetary turmoil and global financial deregulation. They used their incumbency, in turn, to move the global system and national policies further in the direction of laissez-faire. Between the late 1970s and 1990s, the remnants of global financial regulation were swept away. Domestic and global deregulation energized each other.

The IMF and the World Bank, dominated by the United States and its close allies, mutated into the opposite of the roles imagined at Bretton Woods. They became instruments for the enforcement of classical laissez-faire as a universal governing principle. The OECD, created in 1961 as the successor to the postwar Organization for European Economic Cooperation (which planned the allocation of Marshall Plan aid in Europe), had grown into a club of rich nations. For most of its existence, the OECD had no formal powers. By the Thatcher-Reagan era, however, OECD economists had become prime advocates of global deregulation and OECD membership came to be conditioned on member nations agreeing to eliminate capital controls.

Once, in its own 1961 code on capital movements, the OECD had made a key distinction between "hot," speculative money and long-term investments in the real economy. Its earlier rules had explicitly permitted policies to discourage or punish short-term cross-border speculation. Now, all capital movements had to be liberalized. In 1988 the European Council approved a formal directive to require all member states of the European Community to abolish all remaining controls on international capital movements.

The reversal in the norms and rules of international organizations had origins in the Reagan and Thatcher administrations, in the shifting ideology of the economics profession, and above all in the resurgent of power of private finance. Ideological preferences masqueraded as technical imperatives: there was a right way to manage an economy and a wrong way.

The so-called Washington Consensus became a one-size-fits-all recipe for developing nations. Its norms were exactly the inverse of the original Bretton Woods system. Poor countries needed private capital. To attract private capital, according to the Washington Consensus, they needed balanced budgets, modest taxes, privatization, limited welfare states, and above all, free capital movements.

In 1997, Michel Camdessus, director general of the IMF at the time, sought to make the dogma of free capital movement formal IMF policy. This policy was not adopted, but by then it was not necessary. The Washington Consensus was routinely incorporated into all IMF stabilization agreements with countries needing IMF aid, and it was part of OECD and European Economic Community rules. This policy was known as "conditionality." It was especially perverse for poor countries, since such nations are often vulnerable to investment fads that ignore economic fundamentals, and capital controls are one of the few defenses against speculators. (One of that era's leading exponents of capital market liberalization, economist and central banker Stanley Fischer, was appointed nearly two decades later as vice chair of the Federal Reserve—by Barack Obama, another indication of how Democrats had bought into the orthodoxy.)

In Latin America, which had been encouraged by the US government and by money-center banks to borrow vast sums in the mid-1970s to finance more costly oil imports, the shift to higher interest rates in the late 1970s created a debt crisis. The reliance of several Latin nations on IMF aid provided an opportunity to use conditionality to dictate austerity policies that turned a debt crisis into a general economic catastrophe, costing Latin America a decade of lost growth.

The East Asian financial crisis of the late 1990s was driven entirely by hot money pouring into nations with newly liberalized capital markets, creating bubbles, and then when the bubble burst, pouring out just as fast. IMF missions of supposed experts imposed similar terms of the Washington Consensus, requiring even more market liberalization as a condition of financial help. This intervention backfired, and the nations that recovered soonest were the ones that defied the IMF. Once in recovery, the affected countries responded by building up vast war chests of foreign hard currencies, so that they would never again have to rely on the IMF. (For more details, see my account in *Debtors' Prison*.)

By the early twenty-first century, even IMF economists agreed that the conditionality formula and its rigid imposition on Latin America and East Asia had been a bad idea. Yet something similar would be imposed on the debtor nations of Europe after 2009. All of this drastically limited the ability of nations to run full-employment, egalitarian economies, even when they had strong domestic majorities in favor of such policies.

The costs of these policies to economies were immense. The damage done by financial crises and the austerity that followed overwhelmed the putative efficiency gains of freer capital movements. The authoritative study on the subject, by two impeccably mainstream economists, Carmen Reinhart and Kenneth Rogoff, demonstrated an almost perfect correlation between global financial deregulation and the incidence of major financial catastrophes. Yet political support for these policies persisted, not because of the general benefit, but because they were so lucrative for financiers.

A TALE OF TWO SOCIALISTS

In the spring of 1981, François Mitterrand was elected president of France. Since French conservatives had been in power in the 1970s, the timing of ideological rhythms in France was the opposite of those in Britain and the United States.

Mitterrand was the first socialist president under the Gaullist constitution of 1958, which created a strong executive. His Socialist Party also won an absolute majority in the Chamber of Deputies. French voters had rejected the high-unemployment austerity policies of the 1970s. Mitterrand resolved to pursue a strongly socialist program. That meant Keynesian "reflation"—public spending to create jobs and increase demand, surtaxes on the wealthy so that the new outlays would be only partly financed by deficits, nationalization of major banks so that capital would be invested productively, and an expansion of social benefits.

But in the newly deregulated global financial environment of 1981, France could go only as far as private international money markets would permit. Almost immediately, both domestic and foreign capital fled France. Taking advantage of what was left of a nation's right to rely on capital controls in an emergency, Mitterrand's government imposed controls that became increasingly draconian, and then silly. At first, the controls were applied to investment capital. Then the government prohibited the ability of importers and exporters to use futures markets to hedge against a falling franc. Finally, controls were extended to French tourists, including limits on personal credit cards. The outcry was immense, and even with these severe controls, France was fast running through its gold and currency reserves. In the spring of 1983, the government simply gave up. The franc had already been devalued three times since 1981.

This sequence of events was precisely what the architects of Bretton Woods had feared. The changed international financial system now made it impossible for a single nation—even a large one such as France—to pursue a program of high growth and full employment when the rest of the system was worrying about inflation and demanding austerity.

The U-turn in French policy came only after a bitter debate inside the government. The losers of the debate, the nationalist/left faction of Mitterrand's Socialist Party, led by the minister of industry, Jean-Pierre Chevènement, was committed to French sovereignty. Chevènement wanted France to go its own way, even at the cost of letting the franc float downward and doubling down on controls. This move in the direction of a self-contained command economy was ridiculed as the "Albanian solution" (communist Albania being a tiny, closed nation). The winner of the debate and architect of the course that followed, putting even French socialists into the neoliberal camp, was Jacques Delors, the finance minister, who soon became the father of a surprisingly neoliberal European Union.

The new policy went by the name of *rigueur*—austerity—the very austerity that Mitterrand and the socialists had been elected to reverse. Under the Socialists, it was a gentler version of austerity, but *rigueur* nonetheless. Public spending was cut, deficits narrowed, interest rates raised, and controls gradually lifted. As outlays were slashed, the Socialists fought hard to protect some cherished programs, such as prekindergartens. Even so, the reversal was a plain humiliation.

The Mitterrand experience was a vivid demonstration of how changes in the global system of finance narrowed the policy space and policy options of any one nation. Mrs. Thatcher's strategy and famous doctrine—TINA, standing for "There Is No Alternative"—had been vindicated. Change the global system's rules and you limit the freedom of each of its constituent members to maneuver. A trading nation is, of course, subject to some constraints; its products need to be competitive. But those constraints are far more severe when speculative international capital is liberated. For the right, that altered reality had the additional benefit of hamstringing left parties—they could no longer deliver for constituents—and pushing them to become more centrist.*

The post-1983 strategy of center-left parties, in line with the changed power dynamics and new ideological fashion, became this: to liberate markets, accept market outcomes, and redistribute after the fact. But that turned out to be a much weaker and more difficult politics than the full-employment, universal welfare state that had been pursued a generation earlier. Politically, why should "winners" want to tax themselves to redistribute to "losers"? The losers in this bargain became the constituency for Le Pen, Brexit, and Trump.

For contrast, consider the experience of another socialist government, the British Labour government elected in July 1945. Like Mitterrand in 1981, the Labour prime minister, Clement Attlee, was presiding over the first majority socialist government in his country's history. Labour took office in a landslide, winning 393 seats in the House of Commons to 210 for the Tories. Despite the affection for Winston Churchill, who had saved Britain in its darkest hour, the voters were weary of wartime austerity—and of twenty years before that of unemployment that never fell below 10 percent.

---

*For a time, French governments did try to retain partial control over some industries, such as telecom, aviation, and energy, but EU policy increasingly eroded that option as well. See Chapter 7.

Under British law, Attlee had five years before he had to call a new election.

The economic circumstances that greeted Attlee's new government were, if anything, far less auspicious than the ones that confronted Mitterrand. Britain was facing appalling war debt equal to about 240 percent of one year's GDP, the loss of about one-quarter of all its wealth, and the task of rebuilding homes, public facilities, and factories that had suffered massive damage in the war. Labour had campaigned promising to build a cradle-to-grave full-employment welfare state including pensions and national health insurance, as well as expanded housing and education. The government also nationalized the "commanding heights" of the British economy—the railroads, steel mills, coal mines, banks—eventually about 20 percent of total GDP.

How was it remotely possible to build an expansionary full-employment welfare state in such circumstances? Had the usual international financial rules been in place, it would have been plainly impossible. The command economy of the war, and the psychology of wartime solidarity, had laid the groundwork for postwar national purpose. In addition, the war had created new technologies available to be exploited, and pent-up consumer demand awaited only opportunities to buy. Yet all of these auspicious circumstances could easily have been short-circuited. Private capital, sensing inflation, would have triggered a run on the British pound, causing a drain on what remained of Britain's reserves and requiring the Bank of England to drastically raise interest rates, which would choke off the recovery, much less the construction of a welfare state.

But fortunately, even though the actual Bretton Woods institutions bore little resemblance to those proposed by Keynes and White, the rules of the emergency situation created a rough functional substitute, for at least the critical first few years. The value of the pound was pegged, and speculation against it was effectively prohibited. Britain could and did tightly control dollar imports. Its brief experiment with currency convertibility in the summer of 1947, under pressure from the Americans (and soon reversed), created a run on the pound and showed just how unwise free-market policy in currency and capital movements was in such circumstances.

Freed from the tyranny of speculative money markets, Britain was able to combine postwar reconstruction with the creation of a generous welfare state. Capital could not flee, because capital was not permitted to. Speculation against the pound was not a factor, because it was precluded by the system's rules. Eventually, in 1949, Britain did have to devalue its currency, because the dollar-pound exchange rate had been pegged too high since the beginning of the postwar period. For a time, living conditions were Spartan. Rationing continued after the war, since there was simply not enough money available to finance rebuilding, modernization, the new welfare state, and expanded personal consumption. Yet, more than any other government of the postwar era, the British Labour government of 1945 delivered its major campaign promises, and in arduous economic circumstances.

It's also worth taking a closer look at the Labour government's "Keynesianism." In the watered-down version of Keynes foisted on generations of students and policy makers by orthodox economists (and in pop shorthand), Keynes is associated with government budget deficits, notably during periods of private-sector slumps. Yet for most of the late 1940s, the British budget was in surplus. So how did the Labour government pull off its version of a postwar miracle, much less finance a welfare state?

With its immense war debt, the British government needed to run a modest budget surplus to begin paying down debt and reducing interest costs on the debt, even with the exchange value of the pound protected by the pegged rate. But the Labour government was able to take advantage of the very high wartime tax rates, especially on the better-off, to finance postwar reconstruction. Thus the strategy was doubly redistributive—both on the tax side and via a full-employment economy—and massive deficit financing was not required. The British unemployment rate, stuck at over 10 percent throughout the interwar period, averaged 2 percent or less not just during the total mobilization of the war, but for a full decade after the end of World War II, thanks to public investments in reconstruction and expanded social income.

Many economic historians, as noted, contend that the European economic miracle was powered by postwar reconstruction. That's true, but in addition to missing the key role of capital controls, that conclusion misses this other key dynamic: the miracle was built on the continuation of other wartime controls, high rates of taxing and spending, and a strong state role in the economy, into peacetime. Basically, the British government took the wartime economy, which had spent over half of its GDP on the war, and converted most of that taxing and spending (and immense stimulus) to peacetime use. The fact that the public outlay was tax-financed rather than deficit-financed did not weaken its impact. Powerful unions ensured a generous distribution of the enhanced purchasing power.

The British welfare state, while highly redistributive on the spending side, was less so on the tax side, since it was financed mostly by relatively flat charges. Yet people who had never been to a doctor or dentist could now get comprehensive medical care. Doctor salaries were not exorbitant, but they were decent. New jobs were created in the expanded education and social service sectors as well. Education at all levels was now comprehensive and free. The entire wage and salary structure was compressed, with notable increases for the working classes, and Britain enjoyed the most equal distribution of income in its history. Though Britain did not have the kind of corporatist wage bargaining of much of the continent, the unions were supportive of the new Labour government and appreciative of full employment; despite some strikes, wage demands did not destabilize the government's larger strategy.

So, Britain grew at a somewhat slower rate than other European nations did (and with good reasons), but it still turned in a performance that has not been equaled before or since. The British, unlike the continent, had not been invaded. British industrial plants did not have to be rebuilt from scratch, and the country's relatively antiquated factories were somewhat less competitive than the newer ones in Germany. Despite Marshall Plan aid, there was not enough money to rebuild everything at once. British industrial relations were more fractious than others. And perhaps most important, Britain had an immense war debt, while Germany's war debt was all but wiped out.

The point is that immensely indebted Britain would never have been allowed to run its recovery program in the fashion that it did, much less to build an expansive welfare state, if speculative international capital had been in charge as usual. By the time Mitterrand took over in France, the new rules of international finance already precluded any kind of effective democratic-left program like Attlee's.

Though France in the 1980s was far wealthier and better capitalized than Britain in the 1940s, Mitterrand found himself entirely stymied by liberated global capital markets when he sought to pursue policies not unlike those of the postwar British Labour government. The disabling constraints were the result of drastic changes of the rules in the global financial system in the more than three decades between Attlee and Mitterrand.

The constraints on domestic freedom of action have only increased over time. In 1983, when Mitterrand's program was stymied, there was no euro, no global financial crisis, and no austerity imposed by the rules of the EU and the European Central Bank.

THE EUROPEAN LEFT LEARNS TO LOVE NEOLIBERALISM

After Mitterrand's humiliating policy reversal, the French socialists made an even more remarkable turnabout. They sought to make a virtue of necessity. Jacques Delors, the architect of *rigueur*, and other relative moderates close to Mitterrand became convinced that liberal capital movements and deregulation were now inevitable. There was no point in fighting them. The next best thing to policy sovereignty in France was policy sovereignty in Europe, through a more powerful European Community.

Delors saw the German model of monetary discipline, tight fiscal policy, and extensive investment in workers and industrial innovation as a viable alternative to the traditional French policy of *étatisme* (statism)—*if* neoliberal financial principles could be combined with generous social policies. So, Delors set about deepening the European project. On January 1, 1985, he became the president of the European Commission, a post he would hold for a crucial decade.

Delors's epic contributions to the new Europe included the Single European Act of 1986, at last completing the creation of a true, borderless common market by 1992; the Maastricht Treaty, which came into force in 1993, creating the European Union; and as part of Maastricht, the move to the euro, which became the currency throughout the EU in 2002.

The Maastricht Treaty buried the last vestiges of capital controls, explicitly guaranteeing free movement of goods, services, people, and capital throughout the EU as constitutional doctrine. What the treaty did not do was guarantee either a regulatory or a social policy floor, except on some issues, such as antitrust, food safety, and women's rights. These were very important, but peripheral to the core project of containing finance. The result was an intensified pattern of member nations trying to compete by lowering wages, taxes, labor safeguards, or regulations. Delors once told me that he regretted his failure to put social policy on an equal par with free-capital movement. Instead, the follow-up Treaty of Lisbon of 2009, intended partly as a social complement to Maastricht, merely set goals for a common social policy. This process was given the grandiose euphemism the "Open Method of Coordination," a pretentious way of saying that governments should compare notes and attempt policy convergence. The Maastricht and Lisbon treaties also failed to create a fiscal union, in which the EU as a whole would take responsibility for the public finances of member nations—except to impose strict, deflationary limits on deficits and debts. Such rules would have condemned Attlee's Britain to prolonged depression.

It was another accidental convergence that put fiscal austerity at the heart of the post-1999 European project. In the late 1980s, Helmut Kohl, the conservative chancellor of the German Federal Republic, was a somewhat ambivalent supporter of a common currency, since it would mean giving up the cherished deutschmark, Europe's strongest currency and the rock of German postwar prosperity. Then, in 1989, the Berlin Wall abruptly came down, and Kohl, seeing a brief historic window, moved to annex the former East Germany, without consulting his allies or even his own coalition partners.

This move appalled other key European leaders, but Mitterrand and Delors were persuaded that it opened the door to a deal. Suppose they acquiesced in Kohl's fait accompli—and in exchange Kohl agreed to accept the euro? After much negotiation, Kohl agreed, but with one stringent condition: the new, deeper EU and its common currency would have to follow German fiscal norms. The resulting Maastricht Treaty, at German insistence, included strict and enforceable limits on budget deficits and debts. Current deficits could not exceed 3 percent of GDP, and debts had to be held to 60 percent. Later, enforcement measures and penalties were stiffened.

The euro, in effect, would become a pan-European deutsch-mark. Thus, the deepening of Europe—whose prime architect was a reformed French socialist—ended up gutting two of the prime elements of the compromise of 1944: controls on speculative capital, and the ability of states to run their own fiscal policies in pursuit of full employment. For all of Europe, *rigueur* became *de rigueur*, in good times and bad. Europe had one monetary policy and twenty-eight fiscal policies, all of which were relatively contractionary.

These policies would come back to haunt Europe in the aftermath of the 2008 collapse. Instead of the vigorous, countercyclical fiscal, monetary, and debt relief policies called for in the wake of a 1929-scale crash, Europe's institutions promoted austerity reminiscent of the post–World War I era. The debt and deficit limits of Maastricht precluded strong fiscal stimulus, and the government of Angela Merkel resisted emergency waivers. Germany, an export champion, which in effect had an artificially cheap currency in the euro, profited from other nations' misery. Germany could prosper by running a large export surplus (equal to almost 10 percent of its GDP), but not all nations can have surpluses. The European Central Bank, which reported to nineteen different national masters that used the euro, had neither the tools nor the mandate available to the US Federal Reserve. The ECB did cut interest rates, but it did not engage in the scale of credit creation pursued by the Fed. The Germans successfully resisted any Europeanizing of the sovereign debt of the EU's weaker nations, pressing them instead to regain the confidence of capital markets by deflating. Sovereign debt financing by the ECB went mainly to repay private and state creditors, not to rekindle growth.

Thus did "fortress Europe," which advocates and detractors circa 1981 both saw as a kind of social democratic alternative to the liberal capitalism of the Anglo-Saxon nations, replicate the worst aspects of a global system captive to the demands of speculative private capital. The Maastricht constitution not only internalized those norms, but enforced them. The dream of managed capitalism on one continent became a laissez-faire nightmare—not laissez-faire in the sense of *no* rules, but rather rules structured to serve corporations and banks at the expense of workers and citizens. The fortress became a brig. There was plenty to criticize in the US response to the 2008 collapse—too small a stimulus, too much focus on deficit reduction, too little attention to labor policy, too feeble a financial restructuring—but by 2016, US unemployment had come back down to less than 5 percent. In Europe, it remained stuck at more than 10 percent, with all of the social dynamite produced by persistent joblessness.

Maastricht, combined with the post-1980 norms and requirements of the OECD and later the WTO, undercut the ability of states to run a managed form of capitalism in two other respects. The agreements sponsored by all three institutions reflected the view of the resurgent economic orthodoxy that Europe's economic strength was hobbled by "rigid labor markets" and by too much state involvement in the economy. A variety of European Commission directives (more about these in Chapter 7) pressured individual nations to loosen safeguards for workers, and to privatize state enterprises, which also had the effect of undermining wages and worker bargaining power. The postwar model, of high growth led by rising wages, public investment, and a strong democratic state, was simply precluded by the rules of several transnational or global institutions. An alternative view of Europe's stagnation—that it was the result of overly tight fiscal policy combined with reckless financial deregulation—might win the intellectual argument but had no chance of being implemented, because of the constraints of the new, neoliberal European fortress.

One other fact is worth keeping in mind. During the heyday of strict financial regulation, there were literally no cases of bank failure, except in the isolated instance of deliberate financial fraud, and there was no case of a general crash induced by chaos in the financial sector. Yet the real economy got all the capital it needed. This was the road once taken. There was no economic need for a different one.

WHAT HAPPENS IN NEW YORK
DOESN'T STAY IN NEW YORK

While the international financial environment was becoming a haven for speculators, domestic deregulation of capital continued apace. In the United States, between the late 1970s and the early 2000s, every single element of the New Deal schema of financial regulation had been repealed or weakened by non-enforcement, setting the stage for two successive speculative bubbles and the great collapse of 2008.

As Wall Street invented new products of byzantine complexity, most notably credit derivatives, the response of the regulators was studied disinterest. If the market created something new, it must be efficient, and market forces would discipline it. The use of derivatives, supposedly, would make markets more efficient, by pricing credit risk more accurately, and by creating more "liquidity," which turned out to be a euphemism for infinite leverage—bets made with borrowed money. This attitude, of course, displayed a willful ignorance of the capacity of unregulated financial institutions to profit by creating unlimited debt and passing along the risk to others, and then to crash the entire economy.

The inflation of the 1970s, produced in part by the collapse of the Bretton Woods system of fixed exchange rates, undermined the domestic regulatory regime of strict limits on interest rates. Banks found themselves making long-term loans at fixed rates, while the cost of their own money rose with inflation. Banks and savings and loan institutions, suffering losses, successfully lobbied for an end to interest rate regulation. Commercial banks, noticing that investment bankers were still making nice profits, pressed to be allowed into some of the investment bankers' lines of business. At first, the Federal Reserve permitted some limited incursions via regulatory waivers. It took a quarter century, but eventually Glass-Steagall was repealed entirely by Congress in 1999.

After one skeptical regulator, Brooksley Born, chair of the Commodity Futures Trading Commission, began expressing alarm about the proliferation of financial derivative securities and the need for regulation—this in a Democratic administration—she was dressed down, isolated, and driven from office by an economic team headed by Robert Rubin, former co-CEO of Goldman Sachs and later chair of Citigroup's executive committee. Just to be sure, Congress passed bipartisan legislation, signed by President Clinton in 2000, essentially prohibiting regulation of financial derivatives. When AIG collapsed in 2008, it came out that the giant insurance conglomerate had been selling credit derivatives as a kind of insurance policy for bondholders, but with no capital reserves in case the policy had to be paid. The 2000 legislation had prohibited regulation of such derivatives either as insurance or as securities—and just for good measure, it prohibited state authorities from regulating them as gambling!

Lobbying from the savings and loan industry also led Congress to permit S&Ls to make highly leveraged investments far removed from their original franchise to provide mortgage funding. Soon came the first of several waves of crashes and bailouts, in the S&L collapse of the early 1980s. In the same era, financial engineers were inventing new techniques and complex products, and regulators responded with the same studied disinterest.

Until the 1980s, the secondary mortgage market created by the original Federal National Mortgage Association (FNMA, which came to be known as "Fannie Mae") was a dull affair. Mortgage lenders simply sold loans to a secondary mortgage market sponsored by a government agency, FNMA, which had its own high standards for purchasing a mortgage. The system was deliberately "plain vanilla," and one side benefit was that it kept financial engineers from complicating something that was basically pretty simple. Fortunes were not made, but neither were they lost.

In 1969, FNMA was privatized. In the 1980s, Wall Street bankers came up with the idea of creating private mortgage-backed securities, later combined into collateralized debt obligations. The claim was that these inventions allowed investors to better manage risk. Mainly, they were pyramid schemes, in which several layers of opaque forms of debt were piled onto underlying packages of mortgages. Through the alchemy of finance, mortgages that were at high risk of nonpayment metamorphosed into triple-A securities. The private bond-rating firms, to which regulators had delegated the responsibility of assessing these securities, later admitted that they never looked at the underlying mortgage loans.

In 1968, in a harbinger of things to come, a twenty-nine-year-old upstart named Saul Steinberg got the idea of borrowing money and attempting a takeover of a much larger corporation using the company's own stock as collateral. When Steinberg succeeded in having his small computer-leasing firm take over the Reliance Insurance Company, and then almost succeeded in taking over the far larger Chemical Bank, and the regulatory authorities did not object, a whole industry of "leveraged buyout" operators, capitalized by high-risk, high-yield "junk bonds," proliferated. Michael Milken, who later went to prison for securities fraud, turned junk bonds into a major financial industry in the 1980s. These operators were originally known as hostile takeover artists. Supposedly, they represented a new, radically fundamentalist incarnation of the invisible hand. If they could succeed, the reason must be that incumbent management was not running the company in the true interest of the shareholders. In practice, many such deals either resulted in bankruptcy or failed to increase the long-term value of the company and enriched mainly the middlemen.

Hostile takeover artists were rebranded in the new century as the private-equity industry and its close cousin, hedge funds. The manager of a narrowly held private investment enterprise need not comply with the SEC's elaborate system of public disclosures. By the early 2000s, hedge funds and private-equity companies were offering shares to the well-to-do investing public, but as nominally private entities, they remained exempt from the disclosure requirements.

Despite the higher-toned name, "private equity," most such firms did not create equity capital. Mainly they did the opposite: they increased the debt on the operating companies. The same claims of maximizing shareholder value were made, but careful research showed that the business strategy of general partners was often to *extract* value by reducing investment in the long term, cutting wages and pension benefits, and resorting to bankruptcy when that proved expedient.

In an early warning, one such firm, Long-Term Capital Management, had borrowed so much money, unbeknownst to regulators, that when a massive bet went bad, LTCM nearly bankrupted all of New York's money-center banks. It took a heroic and extralegal rescue operation organized by the Federal Reserve to make the system whole. LTCM was treated as a one-off, and no reforms were forthcoming. Even in the 2010 Dodd-Frank Act, private-equity firms, hedge funds, and bond-rating agencies were basically left alone.

FROM MAGGIE'S BIG BANG
TO THE COLLAPSE OF 2008

In Britain, meanwhile, Margaret Thatcher, in an effort both to promote laissez-faire principles and to reestablish London as a preeminent global financial center, massively deregulated British finance in October 1986 in a single stroke, a policy package known as the "big bang." The shift began as an effort to settle a regulatory dispute dating back to the previous Labour government, but it turned into something far more revolutionary. Fixed commissions on stock brokerages were abolished, as were the regulations separating stockbrokers from stock promoters and investment bankers. Britain had no Glass-Steagall Act, but by long-standing custom, commercial banks and brokers/investment bankers stayed out of each other's lines of business. With the sweeping deregulation of the big bang, finance became far more lucrative and far more speculative. Thatcher's chancellor of the exchequer, Nigel Lawson, speaking in a 2010 interview, termed the financial collapse of 2008 an unintended consequence of the big bang.

Thatcher's deregulation of Britain's financial markets, intended to give the City of London advantage as a global financial player, increased competitive pressure on the US and other nations to do likewise. Banking itself became internationalized. In the 1950s, with capital controls and other national regulations in place, banks for the most part did not have retail operations in each other's countries. Banking itself was also plain vanilla, with no complex derivative instruments. Bankers took in deposits and made loans. Investment bankers underwrote securities and sold stocks and bonds. Both aspects of the system made banking more transparent and banking regulation much more straightforward. If you could understand banking and if it stayed put, you could regulate it.

As controls came off, American banks very gradually began expanding to Europe to service their US-based multinational customers. The assets in foreign branches of US banks grew from just $9 billion in 1965 to $219 billion by 1976. In a paper for the Federal Reserve Bank of Boston on the history of the expansion of overseas US banking operations, the noted international economist Robert Z. Aliber concluded, "The U.S. banks set up offshore offices to circumvent domestic regulation, especially the interest rate ceilings and reserve requirements."

With partial deregulation and globalized banking, it was only natural for banks to seek the locale with the weakest regulation, and to manipulate their product lines to evade reporting and capital requirements. This practice, known as regulatory arbitrage, was part of an accelerating pattern in which internationalization of free-capital movements and domestic deregulation fed on one another.

For example, as long as banks were tightly regulated and prohibited from making speculative investments, it made sense for governments to allow banks to have relatively low ratios of equity to debt. In the US during the regulated era, the ratio was typically about $5 of equity capital for every $100 of loans. This meant that banks could do a lot of lending without having to tie up large amounts of equity capital. It meant that 95 cents of every dollar could earn interest.

The problem came when foreign-based banks began invading each other's home markets. US and foreign regulatory systems have different rules and norms. Germany, France, and Japan have no Glass-Steagall, but by long-standing custom German banks had interlocks with large corporations, as well as close government supervision, and were averse to purely financial speculation. The same was true of Japanese banks. As a consequence, German banks had lower capital costs and were permitted higher debt ratios than their US counterparts. French and Japanese banks had the implicit or explicit backing of the state, which also permitted higher leverage ratios and lower capital costs. For instance, in 1981, Chase Manhattan had a capital ratio of 4.77, while BNP of France had just 1.28, Deutsche Bank had 3.10, and Sumitomo had 3.13.

In addition, the lack of a Glass-Steagall wall meant that a British or German bank might provide a US-based multinational corporation a full range of services—both commercial banking and underwriting securities—that an American competitor could not match. As banking became more internationalized, the American banking industry argued that these disparities were giving foreign banks a competitive advantage.

Thus did globalization increase domestic pressure for greater deregulation. Ostensibly, globalization necessitated the convergence of banking regulations, especially of capital standards. But these efforts, dominated by the banking industry and its political allies, further weakened rather than strengthened the structure of regulation, by creating incentives for innovative evasion that made the system even less transparent and harder to regulate.

In this era, the United States had a growing trade deficit. Its prime export was ideology. The Thatcher counterpart included an obsession with budget balance, shrinkage of the public sector, and the use of deregulation to restore deindustrialized Britain to its former role as supreme global financial center. The Reagan version was more indulgent of big fiscal deficits but embraced the same deregulation, privatization, and cuts in public spending. Under their successors, some support for public outlay was restored, but both Bill Clinton in the US and Tony Blair in the UK doubled down on financial deregulation. With the immense American influence over global institutions such as the IMF and the World Bank, along with the spread of foreign banking by US commercial banks, both the practice and theory of neoliberalism were rapidly globalized.

Because of the internationalization of finance, a new word entered the lexicon: "contagion." Securities that bore the names of prestigious blue-chip firms like Lehman Brothers, and that offered slightly-above-market returns, were attractive investments to pension funds and other conservative buyers worldwide. The terms of securitization were so opaque and the marketing so fraudulent that passive investors were kept ignorant of the true risk. When the whole scheme collapsed in 2008, large numbers of European institutions, from municipal pension funds in Norway to state *Landesbanken* in Germany, lost trillions. Europe suffered a second round of contagion as financial markets fled the sovereign debt of several EU member nations and neither the European Commission nor the European Central Bank came to their rescue. Europe's fledgling economic and political institutions had neither the institutional authority nor the ideological permission to pursue the necessary recovery policies.

It is a testament to the massive power shift to capital that even a global financial collapse, comparable in scale and damage to the crash of 1929—and with similar causes—did not shake the political hegemony of finance.

SWISS CHEESE

Domestic regulation can keep up with domestic finance when the political stars align. But international financial regulation has proved inadequate to police liberated international finance.

The first major international effort to pursue greater regulatory coordination took the form of a committee of experts based in Basel, Switzerland. Basel is headquarters of the Bank for International Settlements, a kind of central bankers' central bank, but with little real power. In 1974, after a rare banking failure (of the Herstatt Bank), the Group of Ten leading industrial nations (the so-called G-10) created the informal Basel Committee of Regulations and Supervisory Practices. It was, at first, purely consultative. The Basel Committee eventually sponsored three rounds of negotiations, resulting in Basel Accords I, II, and III, aimed at greater convergence of capital standards and supervisory principles.

All three were notable failures—and worse. Each accord virtually invited bankers to take advantage of loopholes and invent new ones. Each promoted new forms of regulatory arbitrage and engendered new complications, such as the use of "off-balance-sheet" assets.

A basic problem was that the Basel Accords categorized different kinds of bank assets into "risk buckets," each of which would require different ratios of capital to debt. For example, government bonds were considered safer than collateralized mortgage loans, which in turn were safer than complex derivative securities. Each, in theory, should require a different ratio of capital reserves, and different countries should use the same rules. But it was child's play for bankers to manipulate these categories, and to further complicate them.

Most students of the Basel Accords conclude that they accelerated the development of off-balance-sheet items such as credit derivatives, which made the system that much more opaque, speculative, and prone to abuse. Daniel K. Tarullo, who later served as a governor of the Federal Reserve, wrote in his authoritative 2008 history of the Basel Accords, titled *Banking on Basel*, "Opportunities for manifold forms of regulatory arbitrage are inherent in the Basel approach of a limited number of 'risk buckets.' . . . The exemplary case is securitization."

If a securitized asset is not on a bank's balance sheet—even if the bank has a complex contract that puts the bank at risk of loss—then the bank is not required to put up any reserves under the terms of Basel. Note the extreme double standard relative to ordinary borrowers and lenders. If I apply for a loan and fail to disclose that I'm on the hook for a large mortgage that I've cosigned for my son, or that I have a gambling debt I'm paying back to a loan shark, I'm guilty of fraud pure and simple. I'm very likely to be prosecuted. It doesn't work to tell the loan officer (or the DA), "Oh, *that* debt? That's off balance sheet." But if bankers come up with creative ways to hide their true exposure, that's considered financial engineering, and the issue of its legality gets lost in the morass of impenetrable accounting standards. Nobody is vulnerable to personal prosecution.

Thus does complexity serve fraud and, in this case, heightened systemic risk. Deregulation invites complexity that does not improve efficiency. Globalization adds another layer and also increases the risk of contagion, since regulators in one country often cannot keep up with the maneuvers of bankers in another one. The feeble efforts to internationalize regulation, under the Basel Accords, which accepted the basic premises of the new, Wild West banking, only exacerbated the problems.

A lot falls into place when one appreciates that the basic political driving force behind the Basel Accords was not improved regulation, but the demand, mainly by US banks, for a level competitive playing field. The industry's concern was that the different ground rules, norms, and capital structures in a multinational bank's home country might give it an artificial advantage when it operated in someone else's country—say, the United States. Concern about reducing risk was decidedly secondary.

At a congressional oversight hearing on Basel I in April 1988, not a single member of the House Banking Committee asked about the impact of the standards on the banking system's safety and soundness. Nearly every question, Tarullo recounts in his history, focused on whether US banks "would be competitively disadvantaged." The entire Basel process occurred during an era when regulators were inclined to trust markets. The Basel Committee, for the most part, was content to accept the financial industry's own risk models, which turned out to be badly flawed and in some cases rigged.

The essence of the game was to create risk, reap gains up front, and transfer the risk to someone else, so that if the bet went bad, the originator of a dubious security would be long gone. Somehow, the real economy had done just fine—better, in fact—in an era when the financial sector was extracting less of the economy's output. Globalized finance was the handmaiden of fraudulent financial engineering, since a lot of the marketing of these high-risk products occurred offshore, and the maze of inconsistent national regulatory standards (and perverse transnational ones such as Basel) created a playground for speculative finance.

In sum, globalization of banking had multiple consequences for the viability of managed capitalism. It weakened financial regulation. It promoted the development of far more complex financial instruments, which in turn enriched financiers, increased their political power, put the real economy at risk, and—again—made banking itself less transparent and thus harder to regulate. And it put governments and public policy back at the mercy of private speculators.

The cumulative liberalization of global capital markets destroyed what was left of the paramount goal of 1944—that individual nations should have the ability to pursue high growth, full-employment econ-omies, free from the deflationary pressure of private international creditors. The harsh, disciplinary effect of liberated global finance on national governments became starkly obvious whenever one gov-ernment, such as France, ventured an expansionary program in the spirit of the mixed economy of the postwar boom.

TAKING OUR MARBLES AND GOING TO LONDON

The power of regulatory arbitrage and of threats to move offshore was vividly demonstrated in the aftermath of the financial collapse, a moment when some reregulation of finance had renewed credibility. But would-be reregulators in the US who challenged ill-considered forms of deregulation, nonregulation, and non-enforcement were repeatedly told that transactions that could not be booked in New York would be booked in London or perhaps Frankfurt. It was a sly threat passing for an empirical description of a new reality. Not sur-prisingly, their British and German competitors were telling their own national regulators exactly the same story.

One of the conflicts of interest revealed by the collapse was the practice of bankers, freed from Glass-Steagall, of making big, risky bets trading for their own accounts (as opposed to making trades for customers). This practice put at risk depositor money and, ulti-mately, the government's guarantee of "too-big-to-fail" institutions.

When Congress attempted to partially reregulate finance in the Dodd-Frank Act of 2010, one of the most contentious provisions was the so-called Volcker Rule, drastically limiting the ability of banks to engage in speculative, proprietary trades.

Banks, not wanting to be deprived of this lucrative line of business, made multiple arguments against the Volcker Rule. To review a sample of the hundreds of comment letters from the big banks to the regulatory agencies is to appreciate the mischief in the sheer complexity wrought by financial engineering. There are today so many different kinds of securities and other financial products that it is all but impossible for regulators to draw a clear, bright line and say that this counts as proprietary trading and that does not. The simple solution, perhaps the only solution, would be to return to Glass-Steagall and divide banks into those that may not trade at all (commercial banks) and those that may underwrite and trade (investment banks), but with no government guarantee.

For our purposes, the comments are revealing in one other aspect. One of the most frequent objections to the Volcker Rule is the contention that it would make US-based banks less competitive internationally. This claim occurs in all of the major comment letters filed by big banks and other financial players. Here is one example from the International Swaps and Derivatives Association, the lobbying and self-regulatory organization of large banks active in derivatives trades:

> The proposed rule would isolate the US swap market from the global market and decrease US market capacity, competitiveness and liquidity, to the detriment of US customers and all banking entities (US or non-US based) that would try to continue to serve them.

Goldman Sachs, shedding crocodile tears for the perils of globalization, wrote:

> "The Proposed Rule may push trading activity offshore or to less well-regulated sectors, leaving regulators with a less comprehensive view of market risks and a reduced ability to anticipate and address periods of market stress."

In other words, if US regulators insist on limiting the ability of US-based banks to engage in trades that potentially put the system at risk yet again, the banks will just move that business overseas. Of course, Goldman itself, with operations worldwide, would be the first to take advantage.

A man named Dave Robertson, who runs a financial firm that consults to major banks, testified on behalf of the US Chamber of Commerce. Robertson warned:

> In order to avoid the territorial jurisdiction of the Volcker Rule, foreign financial firms may retreat from the U.S., further depriving American businesses of capital and degrading the ability of U.S. regulators to oversee and regulate financial activity. . . . U.S. business will increasingly turn to foreign banks in overseas markets. Perversely, this will simultaneously weaken U.S. banks while strengthening foreign banks.

So, according to Wall Street's biggest players, globalization makes it impossible, or at best unwise, to regulate a practice that was thoroughly discredited by the 2008 financial collapse. All of these comments are veiled threats to move overseas. In fact, similar threats have been used to argue against other aspects of Dodd-Frank that bankers don't like. Seven years after the Volcker Rule was enacted, Wall Street kept delaying it with endless requests for refinements, and kept it tied up both in court and then in awaiting its repeal by the Trump administration. Final rules were never issued. However, other provisions of Dodd-Frank that bankers warned against were, in fact, implemented. And far from losing business or taking its marbles and moving to Europe, Wall Street is making more money than ever.

5

THE GLOBAL ASSAULT
ON LABOR

The story of the lost social contract of the postwar era has two essential elements. One was the liberation of finance; the other was the undermining of the power of labor. Globalization was an instrument of both.

The idea that labor was a commodity like any other, whose price—people's livelihoods—should be set purely by market forces, had been discredited by terrible events in the 1930s and by new economic insights. It was a convenient story for financiers and corporate moguls. But their usual power had been usefully suppressed during the boom years—allowing a well-regulated, high-wage, full-employment economy.

In fact, labor markets are no more perfectly efficient than other markets. When the rules of the system let capital batter down wages, the result is not just extreme insecurity and gratuitous austerity, but also social disorder, because "labor" is *people*, and people rebel against needlessly worsened conditions.

Like much of the great reversal that commenced in the 1970s, the assault on labor began in the United States. Europe soon followed. The pattern was the exact inverse of what occurred in the 1940s, when a more progressive model of the economy and society spread from the US to Europe. The new rules of globalization—on finance, trade, and taxation—facilitated the undermining of labor. This chapter focuses mainly on the United States. The following chapter addresses labor in Europe.

TRANSNATIONAL CAPITAL VERSUS
DOMESTIC LABOR

A venerable union slogan declared, "Take wages out of competition!" Within broad limits, this demand was also shrewd economic policy. If employers of comparable workers could not compete by cutting wages, they would have to compete by devising better production processes and products. Expensive workers force employers to use capital more creatively. Automated gas pumps came to Scandinavia a decade before they reached the US because workers were too expensive to waste on pumping gas. Labor scarcity in the nineteenth century famously promoted American industrial innovation. In the twentieth century, trade unions, workplace safety laws, and collective-bargaining rights were all intended to make it more difficult for industry to compete by depressing wages and working conditions.

But globalization without labor standards put wages ruthlessly back in competition, at a time of high global unemployment. All by itself, liberalized trade would have put pressure on wages through outsourcing of work to lower-wage countries. But the neoliberal global regime went further. International institutions whose policies had been captured by corporate interests, such as the IMF, the World Bank, and later the European Commission, required the *deliberate* dismantling of many national labor protections. They made these demands first in the context of conditioning loans to third-world countries, and more recently as part of financial packages for southern Europe. This was done in the name of greater efficiency, but it reflected and reinforced the power shift from labor to capital.

National policies in the US and in Europe also systematically weakened trade unions. As we will see, new technologies did create opportunities to weaken labor—they always do—but the way those technologies were deployed, and for whose benefit, was a function of politics, policy, and ideology.

Just as there was a neoliberal story about the benefits of liberated capital, there was a companion story about the need to deregulate labor. Supposedly, the high unemployment rates of the 1970s resulted from labor market "rigidities." These alleged rigidities, such as minimum-wage laws, strong unions, and protections against arbitrary dismissals, gave labor too much bargaining power to price itself above its natural, "market-clearing" wage, leaving inefficient labor markets with some workers overpaid and others idle, while producing inflation. According to the theory, if we got rid of such protections and cut wages, market efficiency would produce full employment. In one report after another beginning in the early 1980s, the multinational institutions first urged, then required, policies to carry out this formula.

As a matter of macroeconomics, the fallacy in the call for labor market liberalization as the cure for a broader slump is that declining wages reduce demand and deepen the hole. If all countries pursue labor market "liberalization"—which is to say, wage cuts—that only cumulates to a collective loss of purchasing power and keeps the entire system in a downward economic spiral and a slow-growth trap. This occurred in the 1930s, again in the 1980s, and again after the financial collapse of 2007–8. History keeps disproving the idea that an economy can deflate its way to recovery, but the orthodoxy never looks back.

In reality, the slump of the 1970s was partly a casualty of a failed monetary system, partly macroeconomic, and partly the result of the OPEC price shocks. Somehow, the "rigid" labor protections of earlier postwar Europe coexisted beautifully with high growth and full employment when the fiscal and monetary context was more auspicious. There is, however, a kind of labor market flexibility that serves both workers and managers. This strategy, as we will see in Chapter 6, was devised and refined in Scandinavia, but then undermined by pressures of global deregulation and directives from the European Union.

WEAKENING UNIONS
AND REGULAR EMPLOYMENT

For centuries, workers and their unions fought to regularize the relationship between employer and worker. The postwar era, with its combination of strong unions and well-regulated economies, allowed for a system of labor markets in which workers could count on getting a regular paycheck, often complemented with fringe benefits.

Virtually all the worker protections added by legislation from the 1930s through the 1970s assumed standard payroll employment. Lately, however, management has found more and more ways to turn regular workers into casual ones—part-timers, temps, or contract workers. Street-corner "shape-ups" for day labor have again become common in once well-regulated occupations such as construction.

Some economists have contended that this shift must be the result of changes in technology. A closer look suggests that the move to contingent work reflects mainly increased management power over labor, tolerated or facilitated by government. Many jobs that could be regular have been restructured as contingent, not because this is more efficient but because it is more profitable and more conducive to total management control.

In the decade between 2005 and 2015, literally all of the net US job growth was in nonstandard, contingent work, according to economists Lawrence Katz and Alan Krueger. Total US employment during that decade increased by 9.1 million jobs. But in the same period, nonstandard employment grew by 9.4 million. In other words, during a decade that included a steep recession followed by what appeared to be a strong recovery, all of the net job growth—and more—was in jobs that most people would take only as a last resort.

Temporary, part-time, contract, or on-demand jobs typically have no benefits, no stability, and scant prospects of something better. Employers have largely ceased offering the standard package of a generation earlier: payroll employment with regular raises, plus health insurance and pensions. Treating employees as contingent allows employers to avoid minimum wage, overtime, and antidiscrimination laws. This strategy also exempts employers from contributing their share of Social Security, Medicare, workers' compensation, and unemployment insurance taxes, as well as from the employer obligations of the Affordable Care Act.

Since the 1990s, new management strategies and new uses of digital technology have interacted to reinforce these trends. Entrepreneurs began taking advantage of digital technology to create "platforms" to connect consumers with on-demand workers, to whom the employer owed nothing other than the matching service.

The company TaskRabbit is emblematic of hundreds of others. TaskRabbit offers clients a list of approved workers who are available, on demand, to perform a variety of miscellaneous tasks, such as cleaning out a garage or doing a grocery run or assembling furniture kits from IKEA. Uber and Lyft provide rides on demand with a pool of approved drivers using their own cars. Mechanical Turk, created by Amazon, allows people to perform microtasks for clients, such as scanning bar codes or transcribing interviews, using their personal computers during downtime or brief periods of distraction. Instacart, mostly for grocery deliveries, connects freelancers with clients and guarantees just $3 an hour (less than half the minimum wage) for their services.

To avoid any responsibility under labor laws, employers insist that such workers are not their employees in any legal sense. Enthusiasts tell a happy story of a gig economy that maximizes flexibility and freedom. But most of the benefit flows to a very small number of entrepreneurs who operate the platforms, such as the billionaire Travis Kalanick, formerly of Uber. While a small minority of these gigs, mainly in tech fields, provide decent opportunities, the vast majority are held by part-timers trying to earn a living while they look for something better. Some work at it full-time, and they work very long hours to bring in a minimal income.

From a labor market viewpoint, computer-mediated, on-demand work not only saves on employers' payroll taxes and blunts other forms of protective legislation. The model realizes a long-standing fantasy of both employers and free-market economists (and a nightmare for those concerned about decent wages and reliable jobs): it turns labor markets into spot markets.

In economics, a spot market is one where the price, in this case the wage, fluctuates continuously, with shifting supply and demand, like the price of a stock or the price at an auction. The best thing of all, from the employer's perspective, is that platforms like Task-Rabbit enable a process in which *workers compete with each other to see who will accept the lowest wage.* The customer puts in a request for a specific piece of work, and prospective "taskers" offer bids. The worker with a plausible track record who offers the lowest price tends to get the job. That process drives down the prevailing price, in this case the wage.

Worker competition to lower wages is exactly what unions, minimum wages, and other labor protections are designed to prevent. The new gig economy, combined with weakened labor safeguards, restores a Hobbesian labor market of each against all. Such labor markets are brutal—and not even efficient. Economic theory and history suggest that there are low roads and high roads to an efficient labor market.

Spot markets, in standard theory, improve efficiency by producing a frictionless match of supply and demand. But labor markets are partly social institutions. Economist George Akerlof won the Nobel Prize in 2001 for pointing out that the most "efficient" wage is not necessarily the one that clears the spot market, because worker effort, worker knowledge, and worker loyalty fluctuate, both from worker to worker and in the behaviors of individual workers, depending on how they are treated.

Akerlof and his wife, economist and future Federal Reserve Chair Janet Yellen, first noticed this reality in their own domestic life when they were looking for a reliable babysitter. It was intuitively clear to both of them that the cheapest available sitter was not the one to whom they wanted to entrust their child. A light bulb went off, and Akerlof and colleagues developed what came to be called efficiency wage theory: the worker who will do the job for the lowest pay is not necessarily the one you want to hire.

Management loyalty (or its absence) tends to be repaid (or not) with worker effort. It's also hard to measure productivity minute to minute, though employers keep trying. Historically, these are some of the reasons why employers hire most of their workers as employees with fixed salaries or wages, and not as temps.

However, worker power is another force for regularization of work. While technology gets the credit or blame for some of the newly insecure labor market, employer attempts to casualize work are a very old story. If you think about it, in the history of capitalism, regularized jobs for regularized pay are a relatively recent institution. Throughout the industrial revolution, most workers were casual.

Long before the digital economy, employers sought to lower labor costs by turning payroll employment into casual work. An instructive example is a 1902 strike of 30,000 Italian immigrant workers hired to build New York's first subway. The prime city contract was held by a bankers' syndicate, which in turn used *padroni*—bosses—to recruit and pay day laborers. The workers, savvy about the dynamics of pay and power, were striking to be paid *as employees* directly by the syndicate, and not as casual labor by middlemen.

Similarly, in the garment industry, for more than a century employers have undercut wages and worker power by contracting out work through middlemen known as "jobbers." The subcontracting forced workers to compete with one another over who could offer the lowest piece rates. Only during the peak influence of garment workers' unions was this system rejected in favor of direct payroll employment. In that era, bookkeepers used ledgers and pencils to calculate workers' wages. These struggles had nothing to do with technology and everything to do with power.

The new digital economy, combined with the weakening of labor protections and labor bargaining power, does create more opportunities for employers to treat workers as just another spot market. But the digital economy doesn't *require* casualization. The other part of the story is the weakening of trade unions, labor regulation, and labor power. Strong unions are able to take jobs that could easily be structured as on-demand work, and turn them into more standard forms of employment.

For example, hotel work is a classic case of an occupation where demand (for rooms) fluctuates daily. Management would love to have most of the scheduling risk fall on employees: if we need you, we'll call you to come in. That system, of course, wreaks havoc on the lives of workers, who often have families and need to juggle arrangements for the care of their children. Even worse, on-demand scheduling makes it impossible to supplement one bad job with another one. This is the practice in much of the hotel industry. In unionized hotels, however, the union contract provides that most employees work regular shifts, with advance notice of schedule changes. Only a minority, typically those with less seniority, are on call to come in if needed. Rather than all the risk of fluctuating demand being piled on workers, it is shared with managers and owners.

Another instructive case is flight attendants. As with hotel rooms, demand for airline tickets is hard to predict far in advance (though algorithms that discount advance purchases and exact heavy penalties for changes now produce greater predictability). From management's viewpoint, it would be convenient to dispatch flight attendants where they are needed, on short notice. But a strong union and creative collective bargaining have created a system that both serves management and protects workers.

Flight attendants bid for schedules and routes and are awarded their preferences on the basis of seniority. The system enables those who can handle more flexible schedules to trade that flexibility for routes they want. Others who need more predictability (for example, attendants with families) are able to obtain it. Workers are protected, and management is able to get the mix of regular shifts and on-call workers that it needs. The costs and benefits of flexibility are shared. This system dates to the 1960s, the era of regulated airlines and strong unions. It's a high-road solution. Here again, this kind of collaborative strategy that also protects workers exists only because of unions and their role in providing worker power and worker voice. For 95 percent of workers in the private sector, the high-road option is gone.

THE THEFT OF STANDARD EMPLOYMENT

On-demand drivers for Uber and odd-job freelance workers for digital platforms such as TaskRabbit are just a small part of the contingent economy. Millions of workers who perform the same job for the same employer day after day are nonetheless treated as contract workers or temps, because that strategy denies workers rights and allows employers to direct the work but take no responsibility for the workers.

FedEx, for instance, pretends that its drivers are independent contractors. They drive FedEx-branded trucks, wear FedEx uniforms, and are subject to rigorous FedEx supervision. But the pretense that they are something other than FedEx payroll employees saves the company billions and denies these workers basic rights. Lawsuits by federal and local government have contended that if it quacks like an employee, it must be an employee, but largely to no avail. Even the IRS has gone after FedEx for failing to pay its share of employer payroll taxes for workers who, in effect, are employees. Unionized UPS, which treats its drivers as standard employees, offers a far better compensation package, but UPS is becoming the exception in the contingent economy.

The use of intermediary companies as labor contractors often plays the same role. In warehouse districts, workers who effectively are employees of Walmart are nominally the temporary or contract hires of intermediary staffing firms, whose sole client may be Walmart. Increasingly, the employer of record is no longer the corporation, but a web of intermediaries. This distancing of true employer from worker makes a whole range of labor abuses that much easier. The outside contractor demands stringent worker performance, even as it drives down wages, job security, and benefits.

At many leading hotel chains, desk clerks and room cleaners work for management companies or staffing agencies, not for Marriott or Hilton. The technician sent by Comcast to fix your cable TV may well be a freelancer, not an employee. When you go into a government building, the receptionist/guard is likely not a civil servant, but the low-wage hire of a security firm. That firm, in turn, may well be owned by a private-equity company. Apple employs some 63,000 workers directly, and more than 750,000 in a variety of contract relationships. When horrific working conditions were revealed in a Chinese plant that made iPhones and iPads, Apple—one of the world's most exacting companies when it comes to technical quality—could blame the contractor. McDonald's demands precise conditions of food handling, preparation, worker training, and the precise look and feel of a retail store, but its structure as a franchise allows the parent company to claim that any issue involving wages or treatment of workers is the business of the franchisee, and not the parent corporation. When NYU was embarrassed by a front-page article in the *New York Times* depicting slave-like labor conditions in the construction of its new campus at Abu Dhabi, university officials could use the excuse that the exploitation was the fault of the contractor and not NYU's responsibility.

A half century ago, at the peak of the postwar boom, large employers took direct responsibility for their employees. Today, according to labor economist David Weil, about one worker in three is hired not by the corporation identified with the product, but by someone else, and the connection between employer and employee is fractured—"fissured," in Weil's metaphor. Large corporations "have it both ways," Weil writes. "While a major restaurant brand may set out standards and guidelines that dictate to a minute degree the way that food is prepared, presented, and served, and specify cleaning routines, schedules, and even the products to be used, it would recoil from being held responsible for franchisees' failure to provide overtime pay for workers, for curbing sexual harassment of workers by supervisors, or for reducing exposure to dangerous cleaning materials."

This new system frees corporations from the obligations of a tacit social compact in which employee loyalty is reciprocated, companies have an incentive to invest in workers, and people can look forward to predictable careers. By contrast, a casual worker has fewer rights, and even rights that exist on paper are harder to enforce. Such workers are more likely to experience wage theft, subminimum wages, overtime violations, and working conditions that violate health and safety laws—and have less practical recourse to legal remedies.

The disguising of regular employees as contract workers or temps is a violation of law. It goes under the innocent-sounding name "misclassification." Labor activists have begun using a more accurate term, *payroll fraud*. Generally, the penalties are so light that employers treat the occasional slap on the wrist as a cost of doing business.

A standard conceit of orthodox economics is the idea that if the free market invents something, it must be efficient. But the evidence shows that the distancing of legal responsibility by management for labor is less about efficiency in the sense of improved productivity than about battering down wages and shifting income from workers to corporations.

If all of this casualization of work were really more efficient, it would have shown up in improved statistics on labor productivity or GDP. But there has been no such improvement. In addition, the use of labor staffing agencies, contractors, and logistics companies to manage supply chains added more layers of middlemen, all of whom took a cut and thus added costs. Again, all this was less about improving efficiency than about depressing wages. Many of the workers performed exactly the same job as before, but for lower pay and benefits and with less job security.

Accumulating evidence suggests that, with different politics and policies, most on-demand and contract jobs could be regulated in ways that protect workers—without damaging the technical innovations that are genuine gains to efficiency. The value that Uber provides to consumers is mainly in the convenient digital technology and the shorter response times that it makes possible, not in the low driver pay. How profits are divided between drivers and owners is a separate question. In cities where Uber drivers have organized, or where local laws have held that minimum wages apply, drivers do better.

Several state, local, and federal officials have sought to better regulate the on-demand economy. Unions have attempted to organize it. As a number of labor law scholars have suggested, employers of contract workers could be required to provide the same rights and benefits that payroll workers enjoy. In addition, government could organize a portable safety net of benefits that would apply to bona fide freelancers. Under Obama, the general counsel of the National Labor Relations Board held that a parent corporation with a franchise business model, such as McDonald's, should be considered an employer jointly with the local franchisee, and be subject to regulation as such.

But too few of these measures and proposals have had sufficient political support to make much difference on the ground. The net effect of the escalating shift to more on-demand jobs continued to degrade work and wages. These trends contributed to the overall (and entirely accurate) political perception of voters that the conditions of work were getting worse.

Obama himself, under prodding from the unions, issued a few executive orders requiring federal contractors not to violate labor laws. Yet the Obama administration did not choose to make its creative, if modest, pushback against the degradation of work a high-profile initiative; Hillary Clinton barely mentioned it. What did get a lot of attention was the administration's full-court press, and exaggerated claims, for the Trans-Pacific Partnership (TPP), a deal created by and for business and not to help labor. And in 2017, the Trump administration overturned the initiatives of both the Obama Labor Department and the TPP.

ABUSES BELOW THE RADAR

The weakening of unions, the shift in power from labor to capital, and the new possibilities for management abuse degraded employment in a variety of other ways. An obscure but potent source of job degradation is the use of compulsory arbitration. Large employers increasingly require both contract workers and regular payroll employees to sign contracts that steer virtually all complaints of violations of worker rights to arbitration. An increasingly conservative Supreme Court has upheld these requirements. This use of rigged arbitration, which superficially sounds fair, should not be confused with voluntary recourse to impartial arbitrators in cases of union collective bargaining with management. In compulsory arbitration, an individual worker with a complaint must take it to an arbitrator selected by corporate management, and is denied recourse to the courts. Class action suits against broad patterns of abuse are prohibited by these binding, compulsory agreements that a worker must sign as a condition of employment.

According to Professor Katherine Stone of the UCLA School of Law, who has written extensively on these abuses, compulsory arbitration has been used to deny workers a broad range of rights and remedies legislated by Congress, including protection from race, sex, and age discrimination; from being cheated out of pay; and from abuses of workers' compensation claims. The arbitrator, who is retained and paid by management, invariably sides with management. Penalties, when levied, are usually so minimal as to deter the use of arbitration altogether.

Do most working people understand the dynamics of this covert form of undermining worker rights? Not likely. It was news to me, until I started researching it. But they do notice that the conditions of work are becoming steadily worse.

Another case in point is workers' compensation. For most of the history of capitalism, when a worker was injured on the job, it was deemed to be the worker's fault. In the Progressive Era, however, reform-minded judges in a few states occasionally ruled in favor of workers, in cases where management negligence was too flagrant to ignore. Large corporations became alarmed and persuaded legislatures to step in, with what was sold as a grand bargain. Employers would be required to take out what was then called "workmen's compensation" insurance policies. Accidents would be treated as no-fault. An injured worker could claim compensation without having to go to court to prove who was to blame. And premiums would be "experience rated." Employers with a high volume of claims would face higher premiums. Thus the genius of the market mechanism would induce managers to operate safer workplaces over time.

All this sounds great. But it wasn't. The deck was stacked in favor of management. Payouts were a fraction of what injured, maimed, or sickened workers had earned when working. Far from inducing employers to operate safer workplaces, the comp system was such a failure that Congress had to enact direct worker safety legislation under the Occupational Safety and Health Act (OSHA) of 1970. But the medical part of the system was the worst, and it has worsened over time to save companies money, as corporations have lobbied to game the rules.

When you seek treatment for an injury or illness, the first question asked when you present your insurance card is whether the injury occurred on the job. If it did, your health insurer and customary doctor must dispatch you to the tender mercies of the comp system— where the reimbursements are typically lower, the waits longer, and the denials of care more arbitrary. Not surprisingly, the physicians who put up with these conditions are often the last ones you'd want to patronize. And here's the worst part: even though the workers' comp system involves private insurers and private corporations that have gamed the rules, the payroll tax financing and Kafkaesque paper chase lead workers to think it has something to do with the government—the damn government, again. Like the Affordable Care Act, government takes the blame for dissatisfactions with a substantially private and deteriorating system.

PRIVATIZATION AND PRIVATE EQUITY

Large numbers of jobs that were once public have either been privatized or contracted out by government. Prisons, as government institutions, employed guards who were typically unionized and were paid a civil service salary, with the usual fringe benefits and labor protections. Since prisons have been privatized, their workers, with less training and professionalism, have pay structures more in line with those of private security guards. The private company wins, and government saves money, not because private prisons are more "efficient" in the sense of better managed—they are usually worse—but because labor costs (workers' paychecks) are so much lower. And treatment of inmates worsens, too.

The same epidemic of privatization, with the same effect on earnings, has afflicted a broad range of human service jobs, from EMTs to home health workers. The superior-efficiency claims of privatized ambulance companies are instructively bogus. When a local government contracts out ambulance service, it saves money by removing from the town budget what used to be a public service, and shifting the cost to the patient's health insurance. The actual quality of the EMT service is often degraded. It is inefficient to have multiple private ambulance companies cruising for business, and their medics typically have less training and income, and often inferior medical equipment and supplies, than their public-sector counterparts.

In one case investigated by the *New York Times*, TransCare EMS, an ambulance company owned by private-equity partners, squeezed costs to the point where paramedics were so short on critical supplies that they were reduced to stealing them from hospital emergency rooms when they deposited patients. The *Times* found that three such companies owned by private equity had recently filed for bankruptcy.

The standard business model of private equity is to look for an operating company to purchase, and then borrow money against its assets, extract immense amounts of cash, and savagely cut operating costs, often in the form of worker wages and benefits. Private-equity companies have even found legal ways of looting employee pension funds.

In the case of ambulance companies, the business model called for aggressively billing patients and their insurers, often at inflated rates. A problem, however, was that large numbers of patients picked up by ambulances are on Medicaid or Medicare, which won't pay exorbitant charges. But when a particular venture fails, the private-equity owners can simply use bankruptcy, often to "reorganize" the operating company—that is, not pay its debts—and then just start over at no cost to themselves.

The private-equity industry now owns about 4.3 trillion dollars' worth of operating companies that employ about 12 million workers. Invariably, a private-equity takeover means an even deeper squeeze on worker wages, benefits, and job security. The truly nefarious aspect of the private-equity business model is that windfall profits are typically extracted *in advance*, so that when the actual operating company falters, the equity partners experience very little loss, if any. This model turns on its head the usual incentives to operate a business prudently and to view workers as long-term assets. Private-equity partners accomplish this trick by borrowing heavily against a newly acquired company, paying themselves an exorbitant "special dividend," as well as management fees, that together typically far exceed the actual equity they have invested in the company. They then move to aggressively cut costs. If they succeed, they often sell the stripped-down company to someone else. If they cut too deeply, they've already made their fortune up front, and they can use bankruptcy either to shut down the operation or to shed its debts and restructure it.

As an example, when Bain Capital took over KB Toys in 2000, it put up just 6 percent and borrowed the rest—using KB Toys' own assets as collateral. Before KB went bankrupt, at a cost of 10,000 jobs, Bain realized a gain of 360 percent on its original investment. In their authoritative book on how private equity affects workers, *Private Equity at Work*, economists Eileen Appelbaum and Rosemary Batt recount how Sun Capital, a private-equity company, acquired the ice cream chain Friendly's. Sun loaded the company with debt, extracted dividends, laid off workers, and took Friendly's into bankruptcy. But then a second affiliate of the same Sun Capital took steps to reacquire the restaurant chain. A third Sun Capital unit provided a loan to finance operations while the chain was technically in bankruptcy. Such maneuvers enabled Sun to strip assets from the operating company and shed debts, including pension obligations—yet retain control. This is one of thousands of comparable cases.

The losers in these maneuvers are invariably the workers. They lose wages, benefits, pensions, or their jobs. Private equity is just one more strand in a complex tapestry of degraded work. Ordinary workers may not grasp the complex strategies, but they surely understand the results. Why is this legal? How can private-equity companies get away with these moves? They invest heavily in political influence. The result, as someone said, is that "the rules are rigged" against working people.

Hold on; who said that? Actually, Elizabeth Warren said it first, in 2012, followed by Bernie Sanders—both left populists. They were talking specifically about how the financial industry had used its influence to alter the rules of managed capitalism to the disadvantage of workers, homeowners, consumers, and students. But then Donald Trump picked up the phrase, sometimes to suggest that elections were rigged, sometimes to criticize Wall Street and the rules of trade. Trump's twisting of the meaning suggests how badly scrambled the debate and the politics became.

Exhibit A is Trump's commerce secretary, Wilbur Ross, one of several private-equity billionaires appointed by Trump to top-level posts. For the most part, private equity is toxic to the interests of workers—the very sort of downwardly mobile workers attracted to Trump. Many of Ross's deals over the years followed the same playbook: borrow money, extract dividends, savagely cut costs. However, Ross was the rare private-equity operator who occasionally worked with unions to restructure failing companies. In a typical Ross deal, workers would take pay cuts and provide some equity via their pension funds, and if the company survived, workers would get some of the upside.

In 2002, Ross worked with the United Steelworkers to buy several shuttered steel mills out of bankruptcy. Ross persuaded the unions to cut wages and benefits, and he restored the mills to profitability. Ross himself contributed only $90 million in cash; the rest of the multibillion-dollar purchase and upgrading was financed by debt and investment capital contributed by Ross's limited partners and by union concessions or contributions. Thousands of jobs were saved at reduced wages. When Ross cashed out in 2005, his personal profit was fourteen times the money he had invested. Appelbaum and Batt calculated that "his three year investment netted him $4.5 billion—just equal to what retirees lost in their health and pension plans."

And here's the political kicker. Most Democrats and progressives were appalled at the Ross nomination. But the steelworkers' union, whose members had deserted Hillary Clinton in droves, endorsed Ross, and for good reason. When there are no good choices on the menu, you take the best available. Beggars can't be choosers.

Most working people did not have a sophisticated sense of the dynamics of these diverse policy changes. They mainly knew that daily economic life had grown more precarious. They knew that available jobs were mostly lousy, that factories were shutting down and jobs moving overseas, hollowing out entire communities where the available employment now meant working at Walmart, at Burger King, or maybe as a security guard or a temp. These jobs paid a fraction of the blue-collar jobs they replaced. You could not aspire to a middle-class way of life in jobs like these. When Donald Trump blasted trade deals like NAFTA or TPP for exporting jobs, Democrats either had sponsored such deals or hemmed and hawed about reforming them. And working-class voters got the message.

THE UNION DIFFERENCE

The workers with a more sophisticated, class-based understanding of what was occurring were members of unions. The experience of being part of collective bargaining gives ordinary workers a front-row seat at how capitalism actually operates. Unions have democratic elections for local and national officers, and the process of participating in them is a form of worker civic education. Polls typically show that members of unions and their families vote for Democrats and for progressives at about twice the rate of demographically identical voters who are not union members, and who tend to vote more on the basis of their social conservatism. But as the assault on organized labor has caused unionization among private-sector workers to collapse, the union offset makes less and less difference. In 2016, with unions increasingly unable to protect their members against job losses and wage and benefit cuts, Trump's faux populism made deep inroads even among union workers, about 35 percent of whom voted for Trump.

The decline of unionization also created a "tipping point" psychology that harmed public-sector unions. As other wages declined, collectively bargained civil service workers, whose pay and benefit packages once had seemed merely normal, now seemed privileged. In Wisconsin, conservative governor Scott Walker was able to turn worker resentment against unionized teachers, social workers, and other public employees. In her ethnographic study of populist backlash in Wisconsin, Professor Catherine Kramer conducted a focus group with blue-collar and mostly rural Wisconsinites, around the time of Governor Walker's successful efforts to weaken the collective-bargaining rights of teachers and other public employees. She recounted this conversation between two white, working-class Wisconsin conservatives:

HAROLD, A FORMER MEMBER AND SHOP STEWARD OF THE UAW: The teachers' union . . . they were in there like the cat at the bowl of milk. Then they turned it to cream. Then they turned it to *ice-cream.*

STU: Oh, no, it's not only the teachers' union, it's all the unions—state employees.

HAROLD: You name me one thing they've given up over the past forty-five years. It's nothing, nothing, nothing.

It takes a remarkable warping of politics for worker rage to be directed against a $50,000 schoolteacher rather than against a $5 billion hedge fund operator. But as other worker wages and job security have declined, ordinary public-sector workers look privileged, especially when Democrats do not seem to be looking out for blue-collar workers generally. The time span that Harold, a former UAW shop steward no less, picked in his rant against schoolteachers—the past forty-five years—takes us to 1973, exactly when the terms of engagement began turning against production workers like himself.

SKILLS, TECHNOLOGY, AND TRADE

There is a debate between those who believe that technology is primarily responsible for widening inequality and deepening insecurity, and those who pin responsibility on shifts in the postwar institutional rules. Most of the evidence suggests the latter. With a different politics, we could have preserved the egalitarian income structure of the postwar era.

After all, the income distribution bounced around for 150 years, from highly unequal in the Gilded Age of the late nineteenth century, to moderately more equal during the Progressive Era, to highly unequal again in the 1920s, to dramatically more equal in the 1940s through the 1960s, and then increasingly unequal since then. It is awfully hard to give an account of these trends that reflects mainly technology. Rather, the two prime culprits were the deregulation of finance and the use of a particular form of globalization to restore laissez-faire and undermine labor.

Allowing imports of duty-free products from nations without decent labor, social, or environmental standards was a political choice, not an economic imperative. Permitting multinational corporations to outsource at will, and permitting China to game the rules of the trading system, were also political decisions that advantaged capital and harmed labor.

During the postwar boom, factory workers with barely a high school diploma (or not even that) were paid a middle-class wage. What changed was less the demand for advanced workers than the alteration of a social contract that once had protected the unskilled along with the skilled.

In the heyday of trade unionism, strong unions had fought to narrow the gap between skilled and unskilled, as a mark of worker solidarity. Forty years ago, unskilled baggage handlers in the machinists' union received wages not far below those of skilled airline mechanics. As unions were weakened, airlines were able to shift many baggage handlers to casual contract labor. Those who could get away with it outsourced even the highly skilled machinist labor of rebuilding engines to cheaper workers offshore, in the Caribbean. The protected class—highly skilled mechanics—was narrowed.

Many centrist Democrats and their economic advisers persuaded themselves that the entire story of declining wages and widening income inequality was one of machines replacing workers who had inadequate skills for the advanced economy. In this story, the new economy required levels of education and technical skill that routine workers did not possess. In a free market, skills were rewarded accordingly. At the same time, semiskilled or unskilled jobs were pre-cisely the ones easily moved abroad, and the ones that tended to be replaced by machines.

It was a convenient, pat story—one that gave political leaders an alibi that blamed workers themselves, rather than blaming the eroding social compact, for the worsening terms of employment. The story was known in the economics literature as the "skills mismatch hypothesis." The only problem was that it was mostly wrong.

More recent research shows that the economy's demand for new skills in the recent era of widening inequality has proceeded at no faster a pace than in previous eras. Moreover, other advanced coun-tries use roughly the same new technologies and require the same new skills as the United States does, but most do not display the same extreme wage and salary disparities. So, labor regulation and social arrangements seem to matter a lot more than skills.

As the economist Ha-Joon Chang has pointed out, a taxi driver in Delhi makes about one-fiftieth the pay of a driver in New York, even though both jobs require comparable skills (in fact, the driver in Delhi must be more skilled because his car is probably less reliable and he is also dodging cows and small children). Why the disparity in pay? Because the Indian driver is paid in relation to the overall living standard in India and norms of where a taxi driver fits into that hier-archy. And so is the American driver. The point is that within a very broad range of possible pay structures, norms can vary, and likewise the power to influence those norms.

David Autor of MIT, one of the leading economists to have embraced and articulated the skills explanation for widening inequality, made waves among economists when new data persuaded him to acknowl-edge the importance of other factors. In a widely cited 2014 arti-cle, he wrote:

> The decades-long decline in the real value of the U.S. mini-mum wage, the sharp drops in non-college employment oppor-tunities in production, clerical, and administrative support positions stemming from automation, the steep rise in inter-national competition from the developing world, the secularly declining membership and bargaining power of U.S. labor unions, and the successive enactment of multiple reductions

in top federal marginal tax rates, have all served to magnify
inequality and erode real wages among less educated workers.

In the same article, Autor noted that the disparity in earnings
between well-educated workers and less educated workers was far
higher in the US than in other countries, because of the decline in
other pro-equality mechanisms in the US.

Education does broadly correlate with higher earnings. Yet even
the well-educated have suffered from stagnant or declining earnings
in recent years. For nearly two decades, a college degree has been no
defense against income losses, especially for the young. Earnings for
young college graduates peaked in 2001, at just over $19 an hour, and
fell steadily to under $17 by 2014.

THE FAMILY WELFARE STATE AND
INTERGENERATIONAL INEQUALITY

Economic success for the children of nonrich families has become an
ever-steeper climb. The accurate perception that your children are
likely to be worse off than you are is one more source of political
disaffection rooted in a shifting economy. It wasn't like that when
America was Great.

A rich student in the bottom one-fourth of high school students
is more likely to graduate from an elite college or university than is
a low-income student in the top one-fourth. A 2016 study by Stanford University economist Raj Chetty and colleagues found that
several prestigious colleges and universities, including Tufts, Mid-
dlebury, Kenyon, Colgate, and others, had more students from the
top 1 percent of the income distribution (parents' annual income at
least $630,000) than in the bottom 60 percent (under $65,000). At
Washington University in St. Louis, more than three times as many
kids came from the top 1 percent as from the bottom 60. Children
whose parents are in the top 1 percent of the income distribution are
seventy-seven times more likely to attend an Ivy League college than
those whose parents are in the bottom income quintile.

Chetty and his colleagues, applying a broader lens to intergenerational inequality, found that the percentage of grown children

who enjoyed a higher living standard as adults than their parents did, declined from 92 percent for those born in 1940 (today's retirees) to less than 50 percent for those born in 1984 (earners in their prime working years). The older generation benefited from rising GDP growth and increasing equality. The younger generation suffered more from rising inequality than from slower growth, with the hardening of class lines, and advantage passed along from parents to children. The researchers found that reverting to the income distribution of the 1940s would wipe out most of the recent decline in mobility and that higher growth rates are not sufficient to restore the ability of lower-income people to climb the economic ladder. Contrary to conventional economic wisdom, the rules of the game matter more than raw growth rates.

The phenomenon of most gains being captured by the top while earnings decline for the nonrich, coupled with decreasing social supports and rising college tuitions, means that the life chances of a young person are far more a function of the economic circumstances of their parents than was the case when public college was effectively free and jobs with decent earnings were plentiful. A young person benefiting from what I've termed the "family welfare state" gains numerous positional advantages throughout the life course, beginning before birth, when prenatal care is likely to be better.

A child born to affluent parents has a mother and father who are likely to engage the infant in conversation far more their working-class counterparts do—a practice that is good for both social and cognitive development. The child is likely to be sent to a high-quality preschool, and then a good public or private elementary and secondary school, all of which contribute to educational success. Expensive enrichment activities are part of the package, while public schools are dropping programs in art, music, and foreign language. And when the child attends college, affluent parents pay the tuition, sparing the new graduate crippling debt. In an age when unpaid summer internships are key to networking, the wealthy child can afford to partake of them, while the poorer student must take paid summer jobs, as well as part-time jobs during the school year, at the expense of academic performance. Then the young graduate of means benefits from parental contacts, as well as the subsidy of an apartment or a starter home. And so it goes on into the next generation, when grandparents often subsidize the costs of grandchildren. No such family welfare state benefits the nonrich student, who is sometimes working part-time to subsidize parents and younger siblings.

An astonishing statistic from a 2017 study indicated that almost half of young adults reported that their parents helped them with the rent, with monthly subsidies averaging $250. Not surprisingly, the proportion receiving help was greater the higher up the income ladder you went. Older parents who themselves were struggling economically were in no position to help their offspring get launched. It was one more confirmation of the intergenerational transmission of class lines.

A number of economists have documented that the income correlation between a grown child and the child's father has hardened over time and is more extreme in the US than in other nations that still have more equalizing mechanisms intact. Nations that are relatively more equal have more social mechanisms, such as inexpensive or free college, universal health care, preschool and good day care, and good public primary and secondary education. All of these social supports give kids from poorer families a better shot at thriving as adults.

With the substitution of a family welfare state for a genuine, public welfare state, more and more Americans found themselves exposed to risks that they could not insure against. In his great blueprint for the postwar welfare state, Britain's William Beveridge in 1942 wrote of the need for social insurance to protect citizens against the risks of ill health, injury, unemployment, or inadequate incomes in retirement. FDR captured much of the same spirit, both in the Social Security Act of 1935 and in his Four Freedoms speech of 1944.

In the US, some benefits of the welfare state were literally provided by the government, via programs like Social Security and Medicare, but many of them were provided by good employers, through health insurance and pension plans. As both the public and private aspects of the welfare state frayed, more and more risks were shifted to individuals and families. Political scientist Jacob Hacker documented these several trends in his 2006 book *The Great Risk Shift*. Like vanishing good jobs and stagnant or falling incomes, these risk shifts had political consequences.

Increasing risk went hand in hand with dwindling income and unreliable employment. A family can cushion itself against the risk of unforeseen setbacks if the household has enough income to save. But socialized risk and private capacity to handle risk were declining in tandem. Elizabeth Warren first came to prominence with her 2002 study of the true causes of rising rates of personal bankruptcy. It wasn't credit card spending binges, but economic reversals such as loss of employment, catastrophic medical expenses, or the death of a breadwinner.

What is true of income disparities is also true of wealth building. In the heyday of the American postwar social contract, there was a set of wealth-building institutions—some explicit, some tacit. A pension provided secure retirement in old age. By the 1960s, about half of all employers provided good pension plans. Today the proportion is about one in eight. Rising real wages made supplemental savings possible. Debt-free college for the vast majority allowed some portion of discretionary income to flow to savings rather than paying off debt accumulated before full-time employment even began. For the nonrich, home ownership became the single most important source of wealth accumulation over the life cycle.

Every one of these wealth accumulation mechanisms has been thrown into reverse. Falling real incomes have reduced the capacity to save. Real pensions have given way to 401(k) plans. College now requires debt. The need to pay off college loans not only depresses the capacity to save, but also delays or prevents the purchase of a house, diminishing another form of lifetime wealth accumulation. The mortgage collapse of 2008 devastated the home equity for millions, and the home ownership share plummeted, especially for young families. None of these shifts had anything to do with technology or the new digital economy. Each was the result of policy changes, which in turn reflected shifts in political power.

These trends occurred earlier, and with more intensity, in the United States. But by the turn of the twenty-first century, every single element was evident in Europe. Surprisingly, the European Union had evolved into a prime instrument of weakened labor protections and widening income inequality.

6

EUROPE'S BROKEN SOCIAL CONTRACT

As recently as the 1990s, Europe was widely hailed as having a mixed economy more egalitarian than America's—one that managed to reconcile dynamism with security. Though there were significant national differences among EU nations, Europe had a more comprehensive welfare state, a more equal income distribution, and stronger unions and worker rights than the United States had. Overall growth rates roughly tracked those of the US, but life was far better for the bottom 80 percent.

Over the past two decades, the European dream has been substantially squandered. The leaders of the EU and its most influential member nations have come to blame Europe's protracted depression on its social protections, rather than recognizing the continent's deep slump as the consequence of perverse austerity policies. The same social protections and more, after all, existed during the heyday of growth and prosperity. The fiscal trap of slow growth, high unemployment, and increased debt has become both an excuse and an opportunity for the EU's leaders to impose more fundamentalist neoliberal policies on member nations.

GLOBAL RULES, WEAKENED STATES

With stronger EU rules under the Maastricht Treaty beginning in 1993 and the adoption of the euro in 2002, it has become conventional to view Europe as an emerging state. Yet Europe, for our purposes, is far from a polity. It is a lot more like an instrument of global governance on one continent. Viewed through that lens, Europe illustrates all too vividly how transnational institutions promoting laissez-faire can produce far-right backlash by undermining the capacity of national democracies to broker decent social contracts.

Why is the EU not a state? The EU's budget spends only about 1 percent of the continent's collective GDP. The EU doesn't have a common fiscal policy, and its efforts to have a common monetary policy via the euro have been calamitous. In the EU, unlike the US, there is very little fiscal redistribution or collective responsibility for public debt, except with quid pro quo demands for deeper austerity. The European Central Bank, a unique case of a central bank reporting to nineteen countries, lacks the emergency powers of the American Federal Reserve. There is also what is politely termed a "democratic deficit." The European Parliament is directly elected by citizens but is mostly consultative. The real power is exercised by the unelected European Commission and its bureaucracy, and by the Council of Europe, made up of the leaders of Europe's member states.

Yet this relatively weak confederation has been strong enough to impose mandatory rules on its member nations, limiting their sovereign rights to define their own labor and social policies. An unregulated market with budget austerity has become the EU's default setting and ideal. This odyssey should be a warning to those who imagine that some form of global government could be a counterweight to the market. More likely, deepening of global governance would help corporate and private financial forces dismantle what remains of the managed capitalism of an earlier era—precisely what such transnational institutions as the IMF, World Bank, WTO, and, increasingly, the EU already do.

During the early postwar period, the European project had been a balance between bringing a freer common market for goods and services to an ever-larger region, and sheltering domestic mixed economies with strong social standards and labor protections. Europe's nation-states were the sources of the social protections, while the European Community represented the market part of the bargain. The founding generation of pan-Europeans appreciated the need for reliable jobs and good wages. They did not contend that labor rights violated market rights and needed to be countermanded by supranational authority.

With the Maastricht Treaty, Europe's political leadership became committed to a broadening and deepening of the European Union. This meant more member nations and more Community-wide rules to facilitate market liberalization. There is no logical reason why a federal state would need to depress social standards. The United States in the New Deal/Great Society era demonstrated quite the opposite. It was the national government that guaranteed workers the right to organize, legislated wage and hours laws, and enacted Social Security, as well as national rules for private pensions and worker safety. Individual states could go beyond these federal minimums, but in no case did the federal government undercut efforts by state governments to protect workers. The US, however, is a genuine polity.

The EU, well short of a true polity, ended up doing the reverse. The new rules of the confederation, enacted in the name of efficient markets, forced states to reduce social standards. The new EU also required extensive privatization of public goods and services, which further reduced wages and labor standards. This, too, was not part of the original bargain. The Treaty of Rome, creating the predecessor EEC in 1957, had explicitly provided, in Article 222, "This Treaty shall in no way prejudice the rules in Member States governing the system of property ownership."

Even in that era, when the emergent European Community left plenty of room for strong nation-states with national social contracts, some on both the left and the right foresaw where this project might be headed. Friedrich Hayek, a key libertarian theorist of the era, pronounced himself a European federalist. With a federation, he wrote in 1939, "certain economic powers which are now wielded by the national state could be exercised neither by the federation nor by the individual states." This is precisely what has occurred. On the other side of the political spectrum, a young Denis Healey, as the Labour Party's international secretary, issued a prophetic warning in 1950: "No Socialist Party with the prospect of forming a government could accept a system by which important fields of national policy were surrendered to a supranational European representative authority, since such an authority would have a permanent anti-Socialist majority."

It's true that the post-1993 EU has been a force for raising social floors in some areas, such as rights of women and environmental and consumer protections. EU enthusiasts also believe it has reinforced basic democracy in the former Soviet satellites of eastern Europe, though it has tolerated an alarming drift to neofascism in Hungary and Poland with mild slaps on the wrist. But when it comes to labor, the EU has actively worked to undermine wages and unions.

In some countries, such as France, Italy, Spain, and Greece, there is a case for more adaptive labor markets, in which workers would trade employment protections for employability assurances. A grand bargain of this kind is the goal of France's president Emmanuel Macron. The nations with Europe's most dynamic and egalitarian labor markets, notably Denmark and Sweden, had devised just such policies by the 1980s. They were at the heart of Scandinavian social democracy. But these arrangements require substantial public outlays for jobs, retraining, and transitional assistance for displaced workers. However, the combination of austerity and declining social investment characteristic of the present era makes such bargains all but impossible and leaves vulnerable workers defending the protections they still have. The combination creates a political and economic climate almost as poisonous as the American counterpart—of declining job opportunities, layoffs, wage cuts and diminished labor protections, and an understandably anxious working class.

THE NEW EU: LIBERATING CAPITAL, SUPPRESSING LABOR

The structure of the post-Maastricht EU gives its executive branch, the European Commission, the power to issue directives, which are binding on member nations. A European Court of Justice issues rulings that also have the force of domestic law. A key constitutional provision of the Maastricht Treaty guarantees free movement of goods, services, capital, and people within all of the EU's member states. This means that a citizen of the European Union is free to seek work in any EU country. In principle, workers who move, say, from Poland to France enjoy the same protections as French workers. But in practice, they are far less protected and they undercut the bargaining position of their French counterparts.

The problem intensified with the admission of ten new member states in 2004 and two more in 2007,* most of them eastern European nations with lower prevailing wages, lower levels of social protection or regulation, and center-right governments committed to free markets. These free-market governments were partly a popular reaction against the years of Soviet occupation; the disgust with communists often left voters skeptical of social democrats as well. But center-right policies were also a deliberate strategy of low-road economic development. Nations such as Slovakia, Romania, and Bulgaria frankly advertised themselves as venues with low taxes, weak regulation, and cheap workers. And those cheap workers could now migrate freely to the West as well. On the eve of the 2007–8 financial collapse, youth unemployment was already upwards of 20 percent in some of the new EU member states, such as Poland. With the crash and the general austerity policies that followed, unemployment rose markedly, pushing more to seek work in the West.

Note that this pressure on local labor markets involves fellow Europeans. This westward flow of workers from eastern Europe began well before the more recent surge of migrants and refugees from the Middle East and Africa, legal or illegal—people who are even more vulnerable to dismissal and typically willing to work for even lower wages. In 2016 the English backlash against the EU and the Brexit vote were not aimed mainly at Muslims, but at eastern Europeans.

In 1996, carrying out the Maastricht mandate, the European Commission issued a directive on "posted" workers. In EU jargon, these are workers hired by a multinational corporation or private labor agency in one country and sent (posted) to another. The primary appeal of these workers is that they will work for lower pay and can be sent home on very short notice. Local workers, by contrast, are likely to be protected by an array of rights, including union representation and protection against arbitrary dismissal.

A twenty-year review of the impact of the Posted Workers Directive (PWD), published by the EU in 2016, was quite explicit about its purpose. "Posting is framed as an expression of employers' freedom

---

*New members admitted in 2004 were Cyprus, the Czech Republic, Estonia, Hungary, Latvia, Lithuania, Malta, Poland, Slovakia, and Slovenia. Romania and Bulgaria were the two added in 2007.

to provide services in a market environment of fair competition rules and *does not entail the right of workers to equal treatment* [emphasis added]." The review continued, "Therefore, posted workers have no claim to equal treatment or equal pay in comparison with workers in the host state. Instead, the PWD requires the Member State only to apply a certain 'hard core' of labor rights, consisting of a catalogue of working conditions and terms of employment."

The 1996 directive was not a logical consequence of intensified economic integration. The Commission, if it had so chosen, could have required that individual migrant workers, or those sent by multinational corporations or temp agencies, would have exactly the same rights as local citizens. But given the shifting ideological fashion and balance of political power, the Commission chose not to.

How does this work out in practice? Jobs for large corporations are often farmed out via a chain of subcontractors, sometimes through temp agencies. Just as in the American case of the "fissured" workplace, labor rights are harder to enforce the further down the chain you go. The foreign worker often ends up at the bottom of the local labor market, unprotected by either unions or regulators.

Under the rules, a contractor need pay only the (typically lower) social security contributions of the worker's country of origin—giving an additional cost advantage to the contract worker over local workers, a gap estimated at about 25–30 percent in France or Germany or the Netherlands, relative to workers from eastern Europe. Such workers, whether posted by an employer or recruited by an agency, are also far more vulnerable to being cheated out of wages owed them—the counterpart of wage theft in the contingent labor market in the United States. One common technique is to overbill posted workers for lodging and transportation costs, or underpay them for hours actually worked. These workers, as EU citizens, are, in principle, free to quit and look for other employment, but in the context of European unemployment, typically in excess of 10 percent, most have few other options.

Further, a lot of the power of collective bargaining in western and northern Europe is informal. It depends on worker solidarity and concerted action to make it costly for employers to attempt to profit by saving money at the expense of worker incomes and rights. But posted foreign workers, desperate for employment, speaking a different language, and at the mercy of the corporation or contractor that sent them, are not part of the local worker subculture and are far more vulnerable to retaliation than their local counterparts. So, the posting directive serves not only to undercut wages directly; it undercuts them indirectly by fragmenting the workforce and weakening labor power relative to corporate power, accelerating what was already a decline in collective-bargaining coverage in Europe.

Combined with company freedoms to pursue commerce anywhere in the EU, the migrant labor system invites multiple abuses. On one UK construction project, the prime contractor, the Paris-based firm Bouygues, subcontracted work to Polish and Portuguese contractors, who paid employees working in the UK less than the British minimum wage. In Ireland, an Irish subsidiary of the Turkish construction company Gama imported Turkish workers to do construction jobs on a variety of public projects, including power plants, highways, and public housing, but paid them well below Irish minimum wage. Turkey is not a member of the EU, but the European Commission's posting directive is supposed to protect both imported workers from exploitation and local workers from unfair competition. Ultimately, after multiple complaints, Gama paid these workers €8,000 per year of service to cover unpaid overtime. In another UK case, a subcontractor paid posted Hungarian workers at rates below the British minimum wage, and then added insult to injury by deducting a management fee from their monthly net pay.

A German-Latvian agency called Dinotrans recruited workers from the Philippines, using the argument of "a shortage of skilled labour for international trucking" in Latvia. But as soon as they entered Latvia, the drivers were hired out all over Europe. The contractor was paying these drivers approximately €2.36 per hour, about one-quarter of the going rate in the West.

In the US, the closest counterpart is the H-1B visa program, which allows corporations to import foreign workers to fill positions that are allegedly in short supply in the domestic labor market. This program has been subject to similar abuses. Often the employer simply wants cheaper workers. There may be no real shortage if the employer pays decent wages. But at least in the US there is a single national government, and counterpressure from Democrats and from organized labor has held down the total number of such visas to just 65,000 per year, and cumulatively about a million such workers all told. The EU, by contrast, has twenty-eight member countries, each with different enforcement standards, making abuses far easier. And there are no limits on numbers or criteria for entry. The number of European posted or legal migrant workers is well into the millions.

In another landmark directive, the European Commission hastened the race to the bottom by providing that services of all kinds, including financial services and labor contract services, should be governed by the regulatory schema of the country where a service firm was based and not by the rules of the country where it was doing business. This rule, the so-called Bolkestein directive, after Frits Bolkestein, the Dutch EU commissioner who drafted it, produced a political uproar. The draft directive was put forth in early 2004, just as ten new member states with weak regulations and labor standards were about to be admitted to the EU. It went well beyond the Posted Workers Directive (PWD), which at least required posted workers to be accorded basic rights of the country to which they were sent.

After extensive public outcry, the final services (Bolkestein) directive was revised to leave some room for national regulation, but the combination of the PWD, the services directive, and Maastricht itself was sufficient to give the European Court of Justice ample grounds to issuing rulings that severely undercut both collective bargaining and national labor regulation.

UNDERMINING COLLECTIVE BARGAINING

Interpreting the European Commission's directives on posted workers and services, the European Court of Justice has gone well beyond the broad provisions of the Maastricht Treaty, further liberating corporations and undercutting the ability of member states to balance the rights of capital and labor. The *Viking* decision (2007) involved a Finnish company that provides ferry service between Finland and Estonia. Viking Line decided to "reflag" its ferries in Estonia, a newly admitted EU member nation, and then hire cheaper Estonian labor. The Finnish unions threatened collective action, but the ECJ held that union pressure was a violation both of the company's freedom of establishment and the right of free movement of labor. The union was liable for financial damages if it persisted.

In the second such case, a Latvian construction firm, Laval, contracted to send Latvian workers to refurbish a public school in the Swedish town of Vaxholm. Laval refused to negotiate a labor agreement with the Swedish building-workers' union. The union voted to take action against Laval, which sued first in the Swedish courts and then before the ECJ. Collective bargaining is especially well entrenched in Sweden, and broadly accepted by Swedish industry. Swedish law had clearly established the rights of unions to act in such circumstances. A 1989 ruling known as *Lex Britannia* reaffirmed the right of Swedish unions to take action against foreign companies if their policies undermined existing collective agreements. But the ECJ, in the *Laval* decision, found that any actions by the Swedish unions violated the company's freedom to operate and also held Swedish law to be inconsistent with EU law. A related source of damage in the Laval episode was a breach of long-standing norms of management behavior, which set a precedent for other corporations. Adding insult to injury, the Swedish Employers' Confederation provided Laval with financial support to bring the suit. Even in Sweden, norms of industry-union comity have drastically eroded, spurred by EU rules.

Germany, a high-wage country, has long permitted its state governments to enact regulations requiring contractors bidding on public construction projects to pay local wage rates negotiated with unions. This is the German counterpart of the American Davis-Bacon Act, which requires federal construction contractors to pay "prevailing wages." Davis-Bacon is a central pillar in upholding collective bargaining on public works.

However, the European Court of Justice held, in the landmark 2008 *Rüffert* ruling against the German state of Lower Saxony, that this prevailing-wage requirement violates the fundamental Maastricht doctrines of freedom of commerce and labor. The case involved a German contractor, Objekt und Bauregie, which had hired a Polish subcontractor to build a local prison. The subcontractor, in turn, brought in fifty-three Polish workers and promised to comply with the wage scale provided by the collective-bargaining agreement, but it actually paid them less than half the required wage. The state authority then canceled the contract and demanded payment of contractual penalties. The company sued. After the case worked its way through the German courts, the ECJ found in favor of the company, setting a broad precedent.

Occasionally, worker power and labor solidarity have been sufficiently strong to defeat corporate attempts to take the low road. Ryanair is one of several no-frills European airlines that have entered Europe's deregulated market in the past decade. For the most part, these airlines pay lower wages than established national flag carriers pay, but still meet national minimum standards. But Ryanair, based in Ireland with a swashbuckling CEO, is more of a bottom-feeder. It adjusts wages according to fluctuating demand, and cabin attendants report wages as low as €500 a month, about half that of other discount airlines.

Among its other routes, the upstart airline serves Denmark, a nation that still has very strong unions. When Ryanair attempted to expand its Danish operations by creating a base at Copenhagen airport in 2014, the company refused to bargain with Danish unions. Ryanair, which pays its employees a fraction of the going rate in Denmark, claimed that all of its employees were governed only by Irish labor law. The unions mounted an all-out campaign to shut down the proposed base, and were successful. Among other tactics, they blocked service to Ryanair planes. The city government of Copenhagen collaborated with the union boycott, refusing to permit city employees to use Ryanair. In a landmark ruling in 2015, the national Danish Labor Court held that the unions were within their rights under Danish law.

Ryanair threatened to take the case to the European Court of Justice. It is not clear whether the company would have prevailed, since its behavior in Denmark, violating several provisions of Danish labor law, fell below even the lenient standards of the *Laval* and *Viking* decisions. But Ryanair decided to cut its losses. The carrier still flies in and out of Copenhagen, but it abandoned its plans for a full-service Danish base. After decades of serial assaults, however, few nations have unions as strong as Denmark's.

The overall thrust of these directives and court rulings has been to substantially weaken Europe's collective bargaining. The one-size-

fits-all set of requirements has undermined Europe's long tradition
of having labor laws and norms grow out of national traditions and
social compromises. The Swedish and Danish systems, for example,
rely heavily on consensual agreements; the French and Italian systems depend more on government rules. But in both contexts, rigid
directives imposed by Brussels have undermined the power of unions
to bargain on behalf of workers. Conservative national governments,
bent on pursuing a strategy of low wages, weaker unions, and diminished worker protections, have worked hand in glove with neoliberal
directives of the Commission and companion rulings of the European
high court.

Both union membership and coverage of workers under collective
union agreements have declined across Europe since the 1990s. Sweden, Denmark, and Finland still have unionization rates of about 70
percent—a modest loss from two decades ago, when rates were about
90 percent. In Germany, the unionization rate has fallen to 18 percent, a decline of almost half. French unionization is just 8 percent.

In contrast to the United States, however, in much of Europe collective agreements negotiated by unions cover all comparable workers.
So the rate of coverage exceeds that of union membership. But in the
face of a sustained assault on collective bargaining, this kind of protection also tends to erode over time. A reduced membership means
less union income, fewer activist members, less overall solidarity,
and less leverage to negotiate agreements. The multiple restrictions
emanating from the EU, combined with national policies in some
countries, have depressed both union membership and collective-
bargaining coverage. About 90 percent of all workers are still covered by collective agreements in Austria, Belgium, France, Sweden,
and Finland, compared to less than 50 percent in Norway, Germany,
Spain, and the UK. But the coverage rate is declining everywhere,
and the agreements offer less protection than they once did.

In Europe, the decline in collective-bargaining coverage since 2008
was most dramatic in the southern European countries that received
emergency loans from the European Central Bank and the International Monetary Fund. These institutions used the leverage of loans
to demand drastic weakening of labor protection. In Greece, Spain,
and Portugal, the rate of collective-bargaining coverage between
2007 and 2015 was cut approximately in half.

Weaker unions mean loss of wages and widening income inequality. Between 1980 and 2012, the labor share of total world income
fell from 62 percent to 53, and the inequality of labor income also
widened. Income inequality has risen in every OECD country with
the exception of Turkey, where it narrowed very slightly, but those
statistics are less reliable than others. The increases were most dramatic in the US and in Mexico, where inequality was higher to begin
with, but they were also high in Sweden and Finland, where effective equalizing mechanisms came under assault from globalization.
Inequality also rose modestly in Norway and Denmark, but from a
low level. The standard Gini coefficient indicates that inequality in
Norway and Denmark has risen from about 0.22 to 0.25, compared to
0.40 in the US and almost 0.50 in Mexico.

Low-wage work, defined as work paying less than two-thirds of the
median wage, has increased almost everywhere in Europe, though the
percentage has stayed below 10 percent in Scandinavia and France.
There is a close correlation between the percentage of workers earning decent wages and the percentage covered by collective-bargaining
agreements. In Denmark and France, where over 80 percent of workers are covered by collective agreements, those who are paid sub-
standard wages amount to 8 percent and 11 percent, respectively. In
Germany, about 60 percent of workers are covered by labor agreements, and the low-wage work share rises to 22 percent. In the US,
where collective bargaining covers only about 12 percent of workers,
more than 25 percent are in low-wage work. The dynamics are both
direct and indirect. Where unions are weak, not only do fewer workers get direct protections, but unions have less impact on politics and
policy generally.

ENFORCING PRIVATIZATION

With the effort to create a seamless European internal market came
pressures for EU member states to privatize well-established public services, such as national post offices, rail service, gas, electricity, telecommunications, waste management, subways, and buses.
The logic was that government should be responsible for maintaining the network, but that private-sector suppliers or operators should

be free to compete on it. Preexisting national privatization policies, such as the extensive sale of public assets by the Thatcher government in Britain, had produced a very checkered record. Often, the private purchaser was out for quick profits and underinvested in the infrastructure it had purchased from the state, leaving the taxpayer and the ratepayer to make up the losses. The London Underground, after several rounds of privatization, has Europe's most expensive subway fares.

However, the generation of EU leaders who were in power after the creation of Europe's Single Market in 1992 concluded that substantial privatization would promote competition, and that private enterprises had a right under the Maastricht Treaty to compete with public ones. A 1991 directive, for example, requires national governments to allow substantial private competition on national rail networks. In 2010, the European Commission initiated legal action before the ECJ against thirteen member nations that had not fully complied with the directive. Conservative national governments that wanted to privatize could cite EU rules.

Other directives mandated substantial privatization of electricity and gas (1996) and of postal and telecom services (1997, 2002, and 2008), and required all EU members to devise deregulation timetables to open these public networks to private operators. What's notable here, once again, is that creation of a single market did not require privatization of public services. The United States is a single market, and arguments over what to privatize have been waged on ideological grounds, not based on the claim that private postal services are an inherent requirement of a continental market. European nations could easily have been allowed to keep postal services, rail services, and other goods public. But free marketeers of the center right and the center left, who were in power after 1993, convinced themselves that a single market necessitated extensive privatization.

The record is, at best, mixed on whether commercialization of public goods produces net efficiency gains or merely windfall profits and wage cuts at the expense of consumers and workers. Studies have found that the gains from competition and private-sector management expertise are often offset by corruption and network fragmentation and inefficiency.

British Rail was privatized by the Conservative government of

John Major in 1994, and the result has generally combined less efficient service, higher prices, and reduced wages. When a private rail franchise, Connex, was restored to public ownership from 2003 to 2006, performance and passenger satisfaction improved. After the East Coast rail network was renationalized in 2009, it became the most efficient rail system in Britain, returning hundreds of millions of pounds to the government. When the system was again privatized in 2015 by the Conservative government, ticket prices on some journeys doubled, and public satisfaction declined.

But even giving privatization the benefit of the doubt, one finding is beyond challenge: privatization has been devastating for labor. Consider postal service. Under a wave of national policies, postal services were gradually opened to private competition, beginning with postal banking, then courier and package services and business-to-consumer mail. The services reserved for traditional post offices were gradually reduced and then eliminated by a European Commission directive in 2011. Some nations, such as Germany and France, with strong traditions of public postal service, fought back and managed to retain traditional post offices, though with incursions by private contractors. Other nations, such as the Netherlands, enthusiastically embraced the privatization. Traditional service deteriorated, as new competitors focused on business clients and densely populated areas, sacrificing the tradition of universal postal service.

For workers, this shift has meant the loss of full-time jobs with decent civil service pay and benefits. In the Netherlands, where 34,000 jobs were lost, pay in the postal sector has fallen by an average of 40 percent. Full-time positions have been replaced with part-time jobs, many of which go to freelance couriers who are paid by the piece and sometimes earn less than minimum wage. The promise of better service at lower cost has not materialized. Professional postal carriers who know the terrain are being replaced with freelancers who often duplicate each other's routes. Thus, network efficiencies and professionalism have been sacrificed to a low-wage model that not only fails to improve cost-effectiveness, but also harms both workers and consumers.

The experience in other countries has been similar. German postal wages fell by an estimated 30 percent following the introduction of postal competition in 2001. In Austria, the decline was 25 percent.

Whereas traditional post offices typically had collective-bargaining agreements with unions representing workers, the new, fragmented structure of postal service generally precludes collective agreements. Where traditional post offices invested heavily in technology, the low-cost rivals tend to use a low-tech model and a chain of subcontractors, often ending with self-employed part-time drivers.

As Europe's nations have privatized a range of public institutions, the buyers have often been offshore hedge funds and private-equity companies, financial players out for quick returns with little sympathy for the postwar European model of stakeholder capitalism that valued collaboration between labor and management, technical excellence, and creation and preservation of high-wage jobs. A classic case is the privatization of the Danish national telephone company, TDC. This action was taken in 1994, by a Social Democratic government after extensive cabinet debate, under pressure from the European Commission. According to the then prime minister, Poul Nyrup Rasmussen, it was one of the worst mistakes of his nine-year tenure and may have cost him reelection.

In December 2005, TDC was resold to a consortium of five private-equity groups, including the Blackstone Group and Kohlberg Kravis Roberts. A private-equity purchaser typically looks for companies with strong positive cash flow and valuable assets, both of which can be diverted to the new owner; a well-run telephone company, accordingly, is a sitting duck. As Rasmussen explained, "It is hard to imagine a worse match than private equity and a telephone company. The company needs substantial capital to keep investing in technical improvements. Private equity is interested in extracting that capital." The private-equity consortium purchasing TDC borrowed about 80 percent of the money for its purchase, creating new liabilities that weakened TDC's balance sheet. The company's financial condition was further raided when the new owners voted themselves a cash dividend of €5.6 billion.

Before it was acquired by private equity, TDC had a healthy balance sheet of about 80 percent equity and 20 percent debt, and thus had plenty of money for new technology. Following its acquisition, the debt-to-total-assets ratio of the company rose to over 80 percent, increasing its debt-servicing costs and causing its credit rating to be downgraded. Hundreds of workers lost their jobs.

This precedent represents an existential threat to core principles of Danish labor-management relations. Layoffs necessitated by business conditions have traditionally been tolerated by unions as long as owners operate in good faith. But in the case of TDC, layoffs were mostly the result of private-equity owners stripping assets for windfall gains. If offshore private equity brings this model to broad sectors of Danish industry, the entire social model is at risk.

In one emblematic episode, the Danish Social Democratic government actually fell because of a sweetheart private-equity deal brokered in 2014 between the finance minister and Goldman Sachs. (For both symbolism and reality of how the new global economy works, it doesn't get any more vivid than this.) At the time, the government was a three-party coalition with a Social Democratic prime minister, Helle Thorning-Schmidt, reliant on the support of a centrist party and the left-wing Socialist People's Party. The deal involved selling 18 percent of the state-owned energy company, DONG, to Goldman, at a price that critics considered well below market. The left party was outraged and withdrew its support for the coalition. The government fell, new elections were held, and the right came back to power. Then, in 2016, when Goldman sponsored a stock sale (an IPO to take the company public), it valued the company about three times higher than it had when it purchased its 18 percent from the government, in 2014. So, in less than three years, Goldman roughly tripled its money, thanks to an insider deal with a Social Democratic government.

THE FLEXIBILITY DEBATE

Much of the rationale for the imposition of measures to weaken labor is based on the claim that labor markets in Europe are too rigid, which is a polite way of saying that workers enjoy too much security. The need for labor market flexibility has been a relentless theme of the IMF, the World Bank, the OECD, and more recently the European Commission, in a long series of reports. Flexibility, in this case, means treating workers more like another factor of production, whose price should be set by the market and whose skills should adapt to shifting demands. In orthodox economics, if the "price" of labor (the wage) more closely follows a market-clearing price, then the economy operates with more efficiency. Measures such as long-term labor contracts or protections from arbitrary dismissals can make labor markets less flexible and thus less efficient. As noted, in the context of a deep slump, making it easier to fire workers or cut their pay will only deepen the macroeconomic hole. The gains to pricing efficiency do not make up for the loss to collective demand. Conversely, in the postwar era, when the economy was enjoying a virtuous circle of high employment, ample worker purchasing power, and full production, well-protected workers did no harm and likely helped the macroeconomy.

Flexible labor markets are definitely beneficial as long as they don't add up to relentless cuts in worker pay. The irony, however, is that Europe's most productive and egalitarian societies have long had just such a system—one that is now under assault from the directives of the European Commission, the rulings of Europe's high court, and the neoliberal policies of some member governments. The system goes under the name "active labor market policy."

This approach, with Swedish and Danish variations, grew out of these nations' traditions of consensual social bargaining and their need to reconcile highly competitive, open export economies with economic security for workers. Sweden's ingenious system was substantially the work of trade union economists. They wrestled with a three-part challenge: First, how to keep Sweden at or near full employment through the ups and downs of the business cycle, given that the demand for Swedish exports was substantially dependent on economic conditions beyond Sweden's control. Second, how to keep the skills of the Swedish workforce and Sweden's technological advances at the frontier of the possible, without having the burden of adjustment fall on workers. Third, how to retain and deepen an egalitarian economy, when market forces tended to pay skilled workers in short supply at much higher rates than less skilled workers.

Two brilliant Swedish economists working with the Swedish Trade Union Confederation (the LO), Gösta Rehn and Rudolf Meidner, came up with a strategy that solved this conundrum and literally defined Swedish economics during the long half-century period when the Social Democratic Party dominated Swedish politics. First, when unemployment was low, the unions, as good stewards of the larger social bargain, would resist the temptation to take advantage of the labor scarcity and would restrain their wage demands. Wage increases would be limited and would go disproportionately to the lower-paid, thus compressing the Swedish pay structure. This approach was known as a solidarity wage policy. With this commitment of wage restraint from the unions, the government could run a fairly hot macroeconomic policy, confident that tight labor markets would not produce inflation.

Second, when unemployment rose, the government, through a system of labor market boards known as the AMS, subsidized extensive retraining, temporary public employment, and wages. Workers could take sabbaticals and learn the latest technologies, rather than wasting public funds on the dole. Active labor market policy was also used as a tool of regional development policy. When a particular sector or regional economy was soft, rather than allowing a skilled pool of workers to dissipate, the labor market board could approve training funds and even wage subsidies to attract new industry and keep workers productively employed.

New concepts and terminology entered the labor market lexicon. In addition to novel ideas such as "wage restraint" and "solidarity wage policy," Swedes spoke of the "open unemployment" rate, defined as the rate that would have prevailed in the absence of active labor market policy. At a given time the open rate might be 8 percent, while the effective rate was less than 4 percent. "Wage drift" referred to local collective-bargaining settlements that set wage hikes exceeding targets agreed to by national unions and employers. "Peak associations" referred to these national representatives of corporatist social bargaining.

With this model, Sweden stayed at or near full employment while its workers continually became more competitive and affluent over time. The whole economy became more equal, as well as more productive. The Swedish Employers' Confederation bought into the strategy and helped refine it. For decades, this economic model went by the initials EFO, which stood for Gösta Edgren, Karl Olof Faxén, and Clas-Eric Odhner, the economists then representing the union of clerical workers, the employers' confederation, and the blue-collar workers' union. The three even jointly wrote a book on how the model functioned.

The Danish counterpart includes an unusual and counterintuitive provision allowing employers to lay off workers at will. So confident were the Danish unions in the capacity of the system of active labor market policy that they strongly supported this right. In return, the employers supported substantial outlay on retraining, which in effect was a subsidy for their employees. At its peak in the 1990s, the Danish system spent about 4.5 percent of its entire GDP on active labor market policies. The equivalent in the US would be $700 billion a year. Workers were entitled to as much as four years of education or retraining, with stipends of up to 95 percent of their previous pay. They were expected to use this time to become skilled for a new job, not to sit idle. This premise has been strongly supported by Scandinavian unions.

The Danish system, like Sweden's, is based on the core principle of delinking employment security from the security of a particular job. What makes the model both attractive to workers and dynamic for society are five key features that are logically interconnected: a national commitment to full employment; strong unions recognized as social partners; fairly equal wages among different sectors, so that a shift from manufacturing to service sector work does not entail a pay cut; a comprehensive income floor; and the set of active labor market programs. These programs allow the Danish workforce to invest heavily in upgrading their lifetime skills, and to be very relaxed about changing jobs.

To the extent that the labor market rigidity hypothesis has validity, it refers to laws or union contracts that make it prohibitively expensive to fire workers. These are a genuine problem in some countries, such as France and Italy, and arguably dissuade employers from creating long-term jobs (though the same temp patterns are increasingly evident in countries with no such protections). But Denmark, which has socialized *employability* rather than protecting attachment to a current job, has Europe's highest rate of labor turnover. One in three Danes changes jobs every year. And with employers free to deploy workers as they wish, and all Danes eligible for generous social benefits, there is no inferior temp industry because there is no need for it. As precarious short-term contract employment has grown in most other countries, the number of Danes in temporary contracts has decreased since the mid-1980s. Where most other OECD nations have a knot of middle-aged people stuck in long-term unemployment, in Denmark the vast majority of the unemployed return to work within six months, and the number of long-term unemployed is vanishingly small.

So, while the European Commission, the OECD, and the IMF were obsessively demanding greater labor market flexibility, the Nordic nations *had already invented it*—but in a fashion that benefited workers as well as national competitiveness. In the 1990s, this approach was rebranded "flexicurity," a term invented by a Dutch sociologist to describe the rather different system of the Netherlands, which is more about extending labor standards to part-time workers.

In principle, the international organizations embraced the concept of a social bargain that blended security and flexibility, but the fine print of their demands was all about flexibility at the expense of security. The stabilization programs of the EC and the IMF are silent on the security part. Their directives and court rulings have impinged on the ability of Scandinavian nations to broker their own national social contracts. So the actions of the EC, the IMF, and the European Court of Justice, perversely, have undermined the world's most ingenious system for combining labor market flexibility with continuous skill upgrading of workers.

Not long ago, students of Scandinavia's social democracy could marvel at the fact that these small countries could be open to global trade yet still maintain their own domestic social policies shielded from imported neoliberalism. Some contended that the social buffers were precisely what allowed popular consent for the openness. But it's much harder to make that argument today, because the global pressures to weaken labor rights have become ferocious and ubiquitous. Even Scandinavia today finds it far harder to exist as an island of social democracy in a neoliberal sea (see pages 173–78). Power has been transferred both to the global marketplace and to transnational institutions that do its bidding rather than enabling national governments to lean against the corporate market. Left governments have moved to the center, to accommodate new economic and political pressures.

AUSTERITY AND WAGE SUPPRESSION

The financial collapse of 2007–8 gave the European Union and the IMF even more leverage to impose the neoliberal formula and suppression of wages on the EU's more vulnerable members. The panic that began in the financial markets of New York and London quickly spread to continental Europe. However, the Europeans experienced a deeper and more prolonged depression and higher unemployment because of structural weaknesses in the EU, compounded by perverse policies.

In the US, despite partisan acrimony and blockage, the Obama administration in early 2009 was able to convince Congress to approve a stimulus package of nearly a trillion dollars. The legislation was accompanied by a Federal Reserve/Treasury bailout of insolvent banks and a government rescue of the auto industry, followed by a Fed policy of buying Treasury bonds in record quantities in order to keep interest rates at zero. This suite of policies did not restore broadly shared prosperity, but it did spare the US a deeper depression, and recovery (with persistent inequality) eventually ensued.

Nothing comparable was accomplished in Europe. For one thing, governance of the EU is fragmented among twenty-eight member countries, and there was no appetite for a Union-wide stimulus program. "We are not a transfer union," became a rallying cry among Europe's conservative leaders. In addition, the European Central Bank did not have the Fed's power to engage in what were effectively unlimited bond purchases. Germany, as the EU's most powerful member state, adamantly opposed expanded ECB rescues and viewed the crisis as an opportunity to impose German-style budget austerity on other member nations that had been more indulgent of deficits.

The other structural flaw was the weakness of the euro. The single currency, intended as the ultimate solution to the continent's chronic monetary instability, was introduced into general circulation only in 2002. With the advent of the euro, investors made a colossal error of judgment. Since all member nations' bonds were now denominated in euros, there was no longer a risk of currency devaluation, so investors assumed that one nation's bonds were as good as another. They overlooked the more dire risk of default.

Before 2002, governments of nations with weaker currencies, such as Italy, Spain, and Greece, had to offer higher interest rates to sell their sovereign bonds, because they had a history of devaluations. But with the euro, the spread on rates between ultrasafe German bonds and those of the riskier bonds of southern Europe shrank to a percentage point or less. Capital poured into these nations from investors wanting to take advantage of the slight premium. The suddenly cheap capital fueled an investment boom, which was later recognized as a bubble. Overbuilding was endemic, especially in Spain, Ireland, and Greece. When a bubble pops, policy makers have a choice. They can work to save banks and restore purchasing power of the economy, or they can shoot the wounded. After 2007, the US opted for the former course. The Europeans went with the latter— and it didn't go well.

Unlike its American counterpart, Europe's economic crisis came in two phases. The first phase, beginning in 2007, paralleled that of the US. Both crises were triggered by the collapse in the value of toxic securities such as credit default swaps and other opaque and overleveraged financial vehicles. The loss of trillions of dollars in asset values caused insolvencies of banks and threatened the entire financial system. But the second European phase had no US parallel; it was a crisis of sovereign debt.

In the fall of 2009, as the United States was beginning its climb to economic recovery, Greece's socialist party, Pasok, won a resounding election victory after five years of opposition. The new prime minister, George Papandreou, had campaigned as a pragmatist and a structural reformer. Shortly after taking office, Papandreou's financial advisers reported that the outgoing conservative government had been using phony budget statistics. With the help of Goldman Sachs, no less, the government had created obscure bond issues that allowed it to disguise borrowed money as current income. The current budget deficit, reported as 3.5 percent, was actually about 12 percent, or four times the limit allowed under Maastricht.

As a reformer, Papandreou dutifully reported the discrepancy. While the new prime minister appealed to the European Commission, the European Central Bank, and the German government for help, speculators began betting against Greek government bonds. Such bets were made possible by a deregulated financial system. These bets, of course, were pro-cyclical; they intensified market panic and deepened Greece's plight. This was an epic case of the inefficiency of private-market behavior—the very sort of damage that the original Bretton Woods system was designed to contain.

Ordinarily, sensible government action responds with counter-cyclical policy to contain the damage. Greece's entire debt was about €300 billion. Refinancing half of it would have contained the crisis. A modest amount of aid from the EC or ECB to a country that represented only 2 percent of Europe's GDP would have given Greece some stability to get its finances in order and pursue a recovery. But the ECB's charter, unlike that of the US Federal Reserve, prohibited it from lending directly to governments. Even so, the ECB might have intervened to purchase Greek bonds on the secondary market, signaling speculators to quit their game. But German chancellor Angela Merkel was adamantly opposed to either course. Instead, Brussels and Berlin decided to treat the Greeks as an object lesson in the costs of fiscal profligacy, never mind that the new government was an innocent bystander seeking to rectify the damage.

Greece's cooked books were treated as a morality play and as evidence of the need for much closer surveillance and intervention in that country's national institutions and practices. In December 2009, credit-rating agencies downgraded Greek government bonds. By January, Greece was paying 7 percent to roll over its debt. By April, the rates were 15 percent and Greece was on the edge of default. With great reluctance, the EC and the ECB agreed to a rescue package. But the new loans would go mainly to keep current with interest payments to bondholders, not to dig Greece out of its hole. And the price would be crushing austerity, much of it directed at Greek labor.

In exchange for a wholly inadequate aid package, Greece had to agree to cut its deficit by 5.5 percent of GDP in a single year—a perversely deflationary policy that made no economic sense. In the American context, 5.5 percent of GDP is just under a trillion dollars. Greek civil servants took an immediate pay cut of 16.7 percent, followed by two additional reductions. All pensions in excess of €1,200 per month were cut. Extensive privatizations of public assets were ordered, forcing hundreds of thousands of workers into lower-paying jobs. The Greek government, under pressure from Brussels, cut the minimum wage by 22 percent.

Preposterously, these austerity measures were advertised as restoring confidence in financial markets. The official EC report on Greece forecast that Greece would return to positive GDP growth of 1.1 percent in 2012. The actual economy that year shrank by 7 percent. The austerity, not surprisingly, created a self-fulfilling prophecy. The more the real economy tanked, the more financial markets doubted Greece's capacity to service its debt and the more speculators kept betting against Greek bonds. After each round of inadequate and heavily conditioned bailouts, Greece's crushing debt service costs spiked again.

As early as 1706, English law created bankruptcy as a legal device to enable debtors to wipe the slate clean by setting debts at so many pence in the pound and begin anew. The 1706 Statute of Anne was the predecessor of the modern Chapter 11 of the US bankruptcy code.

But when it comes to nations, there is no bankruptcy code, and no provision for writing off or reducing old debts. In other circumstances involving heavily indebted third-world countries with no prospect of paying back debts, creditor nations have worked out relief packages that allow debtors a fresh start—but not in the case of the EU and southern Europe. Ten years into the crisis, EC officials have not learned from the perversity of their policies—recalling the definition of insanity, attributed to Einstein, of repeating the same mistakes and expecting different results.

At the start of the crisis, Greece's ratio of debt to GDP was about 107 percent. In mid-2017, after several rounds of austerity intended to reduce Greece's debt, the ratio was 185 percent. Following each round of punitive austerity and meager financial help, Greece's masters predicted that the country would return to growth. This conceit was known, preposterously, as "expansionary contraction."

Recall that Britain, after World War II, had a debt ratio of 240 percent. Nobody pushed Britain into an austerity program as a cure. And Hitler's war debt, an all-time record 675 percent of German GDP, was simply written off by the Allies. Whatever the sins of the Greek budget finaglers, they were tame compared to those of Hitler. But this remarkable act of macroeconomic mercy, which jump-started Germany's postwar recovery, somehow vanished from Germany's collective memory. What stuck was the less relevant lesson of Weimar—namely, that extreme recourse to the printing press can kindle hyperinflation. Ironically, Germany's disastrous inflation of the reichsmark in 1923 was itself a response to punitive debt, inflicted on Germany at Versailles.

In the Greek case, the IMF was doing exactly the opposite of what it was created to do in 1944. Greece's new minders, representing the ECB, the EC, and the IMF, known as the "Troika," sent regular delegations to monitor Greece's progress in tightening its belt, required as a condition of the next bailout. They were especially eager to see wage cuts, ostensibly to make the Greek economy more competitive in global markets. This course became known, euphemistically, as "internal devaluation." As a nation that used the euro, Greece could not devalue its currency—a common remedy for countries that have problems servicing debts. Devaluation is a far gentler medicine than general austerity, since it raises prices only for imports, while prices and wages in the domestic economy can go on pretty much as before. But an internal devaluation of deep wage cuts hits the entire economy, without necessarily having the offsetting benefits in improved exports.

As Joseph Stiglitz observed in his 2016 book on the euro, the crisis programs imposed on the nations of southern Europe invariably made things worse, because "the Troika's grasp of the underlying economics was abysmal." He added, "These outcomes were always a surprise to the Troika, which would forecast a quick recovery after an initial drop." When deeper depression ensued, they would blame the country for not following the orders to the letter. But "Greece's depression wasn't because Greece didn't do what it was supposed to do; it was because it did."

Greek citizens became so disgusted with austerity demands imposed by the Troika that in January 2015, they elected a radical coalition of far-left parties known as Syriza, headed by the charismatic Alexis Tsipras, who vowed to reject austerity. But after flirting with both a default and an exit from the euro, Tsipras sized up his realistic alternatives and was soon meekly acceding to the demands of the EC, the ECB, and the IMF. Wages and living standards continued to fall.

In response to the requirements of the Troika, Greek collective-bargaining law was weakened, first under a socialist leader (Papandreou) and then under a radical left government (Tsipras). Greek sovereignty has been lost, and its new minders are far worse stewards than the Greeks. Overall, in the years between 2008 and 2016, Greek GDP fell by close to half, and wages declined between 30 and 40 percent. The decline of Greek GDP from $354 billion in 2008 to $194 billion in 2015 was the worst national economic decline outside of a war in the past century, and it exceeded any country's economic rate of decline during the Great Depression.

The *diktat* on labor rights, demanded by the Troika and signed by the Tsipras government, committed Greece to "undertake rigorous reviews and modernization of collective bargaining and industrial action," as well as acceptance of "collective dismissals." In plain language, this meant no strikes and no protections against arbitrary layoffs. A massive cut in wages was not sufficient. The Troika needed to weaken unions as well.

The Greek crisis that began in 2009 soon spread to other countries that had experienced investment bubbles in the euphoric years between the introduction of the euro in 2002 and the financial collapse of 2007–8. The fiscal condition of Spain was far superior to that of Greece. In 2007, Spain had a debt ratio of just 35 percent of its GDP, well below the Maastricht ceiling of 60 percent and below Germany's. But financial speculators soon began betting against Spanish bonds as well. And they also bet against the bonds of Ireland, Portugal, and Italy. These five nations became coyly known in financial circles by their initials—the PIIGS, as if they, rather than the bond traders, were the greedy parties. Similar austerity medicine was dished out, in exchange for loans that were just sufficient to keep the payments to bondholders flowing but not adequate to dig out of depression.

By 2016, the spreads on interest rates between German bonds and those of southern Europe had narrowed, but Europe as a whole was still in deep recession. The austerity medicine had "worked" to stabilize the bond market, but the patient—the real economy—was sicker than ever.

What is truly remarkable about the pan-European austerity program imposed by the EC and the IMF is that it goes well beyond the policies that the IMF and the World Bank once demanded for developing countries. Indeed, in their own internal reports, the fund and the bank have backed off austerity and wage cuts as a cure-all. The EU and IMF country specialists monitoring Greece were operating from a rigid playbook that the IMF itself had substantially discarded for developing nations after the fiasco of the late-1990s Asian crisis.

The IMF's own chief economist, Olivier Blanchard, warned in a May 2010 memo to Poul Thomsen, the IMF official in charge of the Greek austerity program, that "a 16 percent cumulative fiscal adjustment [deficit reduction] in such a short period has never been achieved." He added, "The program could go fast off-track, even with full policy compliance."

Blanchard was rebuffed. Even the then-head of the IMF, Dominique Strauss-Kahn, called for a full debt restructuring for Greece rather than a series of short-term bailouts whose main beneficiaries were banks and bondholders, but Strauss-Kahn was turned down by the head of the ECB, Jean-Claude Trichet. In the end, only about 10 percent of the funds advanced by the ECB, the EC, and the IMF actually went to benefit the Greek economy. Most of the money cycled through to pay creditors.

Though the austerity demands hit southern Europe with greatest force, the broader austerity program sandbagged the economies of the entire continent. Mainly because of the German commitment to budget balance, the rigid limits of permissible deficits and debt ratios were not waived, despite what was clearly an economic emergency. Instead, delegations of technocrats from the EC and the IMF paid regular calls on offending nations and required them to sign memoranda agreeing to additional belt tightening.

These country agreements contained an astonishing degree of micromanagement of what was once national sovereignty, even for major member states. The most recent EU Council report on France chided the French for that country's deficits exceeding the limits of the Stability and Growth Pact, and it called for national budget cuts, as well as wage cuts, reductions in unemployment benefits (at a time of unemployment exceeding 10.5 percent), and labor market deregulation "to provide more employers to hire on open-ended contracts" that enable firing at will.

Today, while austerity, excessive globalization, and micromeddling by the EC and the IMF are monumentally unpopular throughout Europe, it is mainly the far right that has reaped the benefit. No progressive opposition politics or program has been able to gain traction. Even when a nominally leftist government does come to power, as in

Greece or France, it finds itself straitjacketed by the larger neoliberal policy demands reinforced by the discipline of private speculative finance, and compounded by parliamentary fragmentation.

In the past decade, the popular reaction against immigrants and refugees and fear of terrorism has added to the partisan splintering. In Sweden, Denmark, Norway, Finland, the Netherlands, Britain, and Austria, much of the core voting constituency that once reliably backed social democratic and labor parties now votes for the ultra-nationalist right.

The consequences for the European democratic left are dire. Even when center-left parties form the government, they are reliant on centrist or center-right coalition partners that blunt their ability to offer any alternative to the hated neoliberal global austerity regime. Yet the marginalization of the social democratic left goes deeper. When these parties were in power in the 1990s, often with decent working majorities, they signed on to much of the neoliberal policy regime—whose effects they and hundreds of millions of citizens are still suffering.

7

THE DISGRACE
OF THE CENTER LEFT

As the rise of Donald Trump, Brexit, and far-right parties on the European continent all attest, global neoliberalism is a practical failure for the majority of the citizenry. Yet a progressive opposition program and politics are largely invisible.

What happened to the democratic left? Was there really no alternative, in the famous phrase of Margaret Thatcher? Was there something about technology, or the stage of capitalism that arrived in the 1970s and 1980s, that made the postwar brand of mixed economy no longer technically possible? Or did the postwar progressive left shrink into a feeble center left through a power shift, combined with bad luck, circumstance, and personal opportunism? And did the new rules of globalism subsequently make a progressive program all but impossible?

As we've seen in prior chapters, once global neoliberalism took hold, it became increasingly difficult for individual nations to resist. The process was cumulative. Political shifts created new power dynamics and structural changes, which in turn reinforced the political shifts. The rules of the EU, similarly, became a confinement. Yet the EU is the creature of its member nations, and its rules were not random. In the 1990s, when moderate leftists governed much of Europe, a cohort of leaders of the West's progressive parties, notably in the US, Britain, and Germany, decided that they had a more promising future as centrists. The policy straitjacket that ensued was as much their creation as it was the work of Thatcher and Reagan.

These leaders were all the products of distinct national circumstances that were unhappy, each in its own way. But contrary to Tolstoy's famous line about unhappy families, certain patterns were convergent. Common political shifts and ideological fashions pushed each of these leaders to embrace a deregulated global market with a reduction in social and labor protections at home.

The French Socialists, having been stymied in their effort to carry out more of a left program, had already executed this repositioning in the 1980s (see Chapter 4). The other key leaders—of the US, Britain, and Germany—had in common the fact that they, like François Mitterrand, each took office after a prolonged period of conservative rule, during which the political and economic foundations of the mixed economy had already been weakened.

THE NEW DEMOCRATS

The first and most influential of these was William Jefferson Clinton. By 1992, when Clinton was elected in a three-way race with just 43 percent of the popular vote, Ronald Reagan and the first President Bush had substantially deregulated the economy, deepened globalization, cut taxes on the wealthy, reduced social spending, and weakened labor relative to capital. Though Reagan enjoyed substantial personal popularity, the public had not exactly been agitating for these right-wing policies. But they reset the location of the perceived political center. Clinton also calculated that Democrats had lost ground because they were seen as too supportive of big government, too soft on crime, too culturally left-wing, and too indulgent of people who took advantage of the welfare state.

Clinton was part of a movement of Southern governors, corporate moderates, and centrist intellectuals who believed that Democrats needed to reposition themselves as friendlier to business and tougher on crime and defense. A closer alliance with business was also convenient for fund-raising. These players organized the Democratic Leadership Council after Walter Mondale lost forty-nine states to Ronald Reagan in 1984. They launched an affiliated think tank, the Progressive Policy Institute, and cultivated friendly policy experts and theorists. In the 1980s, the idea that Democrats needed to become more market-friendly was very much in the air. It was reflected in the views of prominent neoliberal journals such as the *New Republic* and the *Washington Monthly*. Clinton and the DLC rebranded their party as New Democrats.

Clinton used some lines that out-Reaganed Reagan. "The era of big government is over," he declared in his 1996 State of the Union address. He launched an initiative called the National Partnership for Reinventing Government, which was one small part making government work more efficiently and one big part simply shrinking it— adding a Democratic amen chorus to the Republican demonization of government.

Clinton promised to "end welfare as we know it," a sly formulation that appealed both to working-class whites who resented alleged welfare chiselers made infamous by Reagan and to liberals who had long been pressing for reform of a badly flawed system that punished work and broke up families. When Clinton, in the same vein, promised that people who work hard and play by the rules shouldn't be poor, he was also sending a coded double message. Conservatives heard the support for the work ethic. Liberals heard the commitment to end poverty.

Ultimately, Clinton did win big increases in both the earned income tax credit and the minimum wage, but he also signed a draconian cutback in welfare benefits that cost him the resignations of the three subcabinet officials who had been the architects of welfare reform. When unemployment subsequently rose sharply in the great recession, the new, block-granted welfare substitute helped only about 10 percent of needy people. Its predecessor, Aid to Families with Dependent Children (AFDC), had helped more than half.

To be modern, apparently, was to embrace the market. Clinton's health care plan followed this logic. It was a complex system of "managed competition," relying on a regulated marketplace to increase coverage and hold down costs. The approach did not win enactment under the Clintons, but it had a close echo in Barack Obama's Affordable Care Act. The model overestimated the capacity of competition to restrain costs and optimize choice in an insurance market dominated by a few oligopoly suppliers with substantial pricing power.

The backlash against "Obamacare" would not have been so potent, were it not partly rooted in reality. There was no comparable backlash against Medicare.

In 1989, two New Democrat intellectuals, William Galston and Elaine Kamarck, later leading Clinton advisers, wrote an influential manifesto for the DLC called "The Politics of Evasion." They argued that identity politics and the "liberal fundamentalism" of "litmus tests" were killing the Democratic Party. Clinton vowed to reject the politics of multiculturalism fashionable on the left. During the 1992 campaign, as Arkansas governor, he made a special trip back to Little Rock to order the well-publicized execution of a mentally impaired black prison inmate, Ricky Ray Rector, to signal distance from the soft-hearted left. He made a point of repudiating a black radical, Sister Souljah.

Yet, in office, Clinton was pressed by the Democratic base to embrace exactly the cultural policies that he had disdained. One of Clinton's first executive actions was a politically ambiguous change in the rules so that gays could serve in the military, as long as they stayed closeted (Don't Ask, Don't Tell). Clinton appointed large numbers of black officials, a cabinet, he said, "that looks like America." With his high personal comfort level around black people, it was a standing joke in the African American community that Clinton was the first black president. Almost in spite of himself, he ended up moving left on cultural and diversity issues, while he moved right on economic ones, *because this was the course of lesser resistance*—exactly the Democratic formula that would prove so lethal to the campaign of Clinton's wife, Hillary, twenty-four years later.

One could make a case that Clinton's repositioning of the Democrats on issues such as crime, defense, and welfare was necessary politics in the 1990s, though his welfare reform and mass incarceration policies were far more brutal than necessary. But on three key issues, which came back to haunt the Democrats as the less and less credible party of working people, the most important Clinton decisions were optional. They were gratuitous—motivated more by a desire to get closer to business—rather than necessary politics.

The first of these issues was intensified deregulation of finance, which boomeranged in the financial collapse of 2007–8. The second was the embrace of trade deals like NAFTA, designed by the Bush

I administration, totally oversold in terms of its benefits, and badly divisive for the Democratic Party. The third optional policy was the embrace of budget balance as an end in itself. None of these were necessary as economics or as politics. There was no clamor for such policies, except among the business elite.

When Clinton took office, one of his first actions was to negoti- ate an understanding with then-chairman of the Federal Reserve Alan Greenspan to trade a cut in the budget deficit for a reduction in interest rates. Clinton used every ounce of his political skill to get Congress to agree to a deal that was part higher taxes and part spending cuts. The deal reduced the deficit by $500 billion over five years by cutting $255 billion of spending and raising taxes on the wealthiest 1.2 percent of Americans. It passed the House by two votes, and it took Vice President Al Gore to break a tie in the Senate.

Greenspan's premise that a cut in rates required tighter fiscal policy was itself dubious economics. At the time of the budget deal, unemployment was 7.3 percent. Quite independent of budget cuts, there was plenty of room for a low-interest-rate monetary policy with- out triggering inflation. But the conventional wisdom was that the rate cut and the deficit cut needed to be a package. With that deal done, fiscal conservatism became an article of faith and a token of virtue within the Clinton administration. By the late 1990s, Clinton was promising to put the budget into surplus. The two parties had switched roles. Republicans had become the party of "deficits don't matter," and Democrats, the party of the green eyeshade.

The budget was duly balanced by 1999, and money that might have gone toward long-deferred investment in public needs went instead toward paying down national debt. Economists began predicting sur- pluses as far as the eye could see, to the point where serious people fretted about how the Federal Reserve would conduct monetary pol- icy when the national debt was paid off and Treasury bonds were no longer in circulation. They needn't have worried. By 2001, George W. Bush had sponsored the first of three massive tax cuts and the budget was back in deficit.

But Clinton's worship of budget balance reinforced perverse views about the economy. It left Barack Obama with an unfortunate legacy. Fiscal probity became more important than a robust recovery. After initially supporting what turned out to be a modest fiscal stimulus, senior officials around Obama talked him into embracing austerity economics. Nearly all were Clinton administration veterans.*

Whatever problems Democrats of the Clinton era might have been having with both base and swing voters, there was no mass constituency pressing either for deregulation of Wall Street or for NAFTA, or for budget balance as an end in itself. The only such demands were coming from mostly Republican financial moguls, and they delivered nothing for base Democratic or swing voters. Clinton also very nearly succeeded in delivering another long-standing Wall Street goal: partially privatizing Social Security, the signature Democratic public program and a very important ideological message about the value of public provision and of Democrats as stewards. Clinton was restrained only by congressional Democrats, who held their noses and stood by him throughout the Lewinsky-impeachment mess. The House leadership sent word to forget about privatizing Social Security.

THE PIED PIPER OF THE THIRD WAY

Clinton proved to be a potent role model for several key European leaders of the late 1990s. As a triumphant Clinton was preparing to take office in January 1993, social democratic and labor parties were out of power in Britain, Germany, Sweden, and the Netherlands. British Labour was in a particularly sorry state, having just lost the fourth election in a row to the Tories. Even though Thatcher's successor, John Major, was a lackluster leader, Labour's hopes for victory were dashed in the election of April 2, 1992, when the Conservatives defeated Labour, 42 percent to 34. Much of the anti-Conservative vote went to the Liberal Democrats, who won a record 18 percent of the vote but, under the British system, got only twenty seats in Parliament.

Compared to other mainstream left parties stuck in the political wilderness, Labour had problems peculiar to Britain. As the UK became more of a middle-class society—aspirationally, if not in the

*The exceptions were Jared Bernstein, Vice President Joe Biden's chief economist; and Christy Romer, chair of the Council of Economic Advisers. Neither was a former Clinton official.

income statistics—efforts to move the Labour Party beyond its self-conscious working-class base had been repeatedly frustrated.

Unlike other social democratic parties, the British Labour Party was organized as a creature of the trade unions, which kept an iron grip on the party machinery. The annual party conference, where policy was made, was governed on the principle of bloc voting, and dominated by the unions. British labor is the antithesis of Scandinavian labor, in that the Nordic unions take responsibility for the economy as a whole, while British unions have a militant tradition of looking first to their members.

In 1969, the government of Labour prime minister Harold Wilson sought to move the trade union movement in a more Scandinavian direction, with employment minister Barbara Castle's white paper titled "In Place of Strife," suggesting a British version of corporatist social bargaining. The unions wanted no part of it. The rank and file were committed to raw class struggle, and preferred strife. The paper so divided the Cabinet that it led to several resignations, later including Wilson himself. Instead of demonstrating to a broader public the party's new flexibility, the fiasco showed that the party was still captive to inward-looking unions.

The half century between the successful postwar government of Clement Attlee and the ascent of New Labour under Tony Blair was a period marked by repeated battles between the Labour Party left and right. As early as the 1950s, following the return of the Tories to power in 1951, modernizers like Hugh Gaitskell, the party leader between 1955 and 1963, tried to turn Labour into more of a middle-class party, and largely failed.

Wilson, who succeeded Gaitskell as party leader, served as prime minister between 1964 and 1970 and again between 1974 and 1976. Wilson was the one postwar Labour leader after Attlee who, for a time, managed to bridge the party left-right divide. Wilson was known both as a protégé of the fiery champion of the Labour left, Aneurin Bevan, and as a onetime research assistant to the ultimate pragmatic leftist, William Beveridge, architect of the postwar welfare state and a proud member of the Liberal Party.

Once in a position of leadership, Wilson jockeyed between the party's left and its moderates, not fully trusted by either but recognized for his strategic brilliance. For a time, circumstances also helped

Wilson. Compared to what followed, it was easy to succeed in the booming 1960s.

Wilson's successor, James Callaghan, had no such luck. With Britain's heavy dependence on trade, a British government—especially a Labour government—is invariably whipsawed by competing needs: to hold down the rate of inflation, to defend the pound and the balance of payments, to promote a decent growth rate, and to address the demands of the unions for wages and benefits. This balancing act is hard enough in normal times. It became untenable in the stagflationary 1970s, when real wages lagged behind inflation, leading to broad unrest among both the unions and the battered middle class. After a series of fumbles, the coup de grâce for Callaghan was the so-called winter of discontent, 1978–79.

In an attempt to break the spiral of wage hikes and price hikes, Callaghan had been trying to get the unions to agree on caps on pay settlements. Several such efforts had collapsed in the face of pressure from the rank and file. In the coldest winter in two decades, a rash of wildcat strikes, mostly among public workers, broke out. Rubbish piled up on the frozen streets, corpses could not be buried because of a gravediggers' strike, ambulances refused some calls, and drivers of oil tankers struck for higher pay, causing petrol stations to close. The Labour government, meanwhile, had lost its tiny majority of three in a series of by-election reverses, and was forced to rely on the tacit support of Liberal members of Parliament to keep governing.

The British middle class had had enough. In the election of 1979, Thatcher and the Tories won by a modest 7 points, 44 percent to 37. But like Trump, Thatcher treated her election as a landslide and a mandate, ushering in eighteen years of Tory rule.

After the defeat of 1979 and the rise of Thatcherism, the Labour left gained influence, electing as party leader Michael Foot, a supporter of unilateral disarmament and withdrawal from Europe. His economic program called for increases in taxation, an interventionist industrial policy, and nationalization of the banks. Whatever the merits of such policies, Foot was far from a credible spokesperson, and his views on Europe and disarmament split his party. At sixty-seven and looking frail, Foot seemed a throwback to a bygone era. He was famous for stumbles and was known by his detractors as "Labour's Left Foot." The party's leading moderates, including several former cabinet members—Roy Jenkins, David Owen, Bill Rodgers, and Shirley Williams—quit Labour in 1981 to form Britain's first new political party in nearly a century, the Social Democrats.

For a time in 1982, an alliance between the Social Democrats and the Liberals was outpolling both the Conservatives and Labour. In the general election of June 1983, Thatcher trounced Foot, gaining the landslide that had eluded her in 1979 and increasing the Tory majority in the House of Commons from 43 to 144. The less extreme Neil Kinnock succeed Foot as party leader, but in the 1987 election, Labour remained stuck at just 31 percent of the vote.

Figures such as Tony Blair were determined to defeat this legacy once and for all, to finally turn Labour into a modern party that could be trusted by the middle class, as well as serving as a general instrument of social uplift. Even before Bill Clinton's victory, several of the Labour Party's self-proclaimed modernizers were very taken with the Arkansas governor. Clinton knew something of Britain, having been a Rhodes Scholar. Philip Gould, one of Tony Blair's top strategists, made a pilgrimage to Little Rock after Labour's defeat in April 1992. Several senior figures from Labour's centrist wing even worked in Clinton's presidential campaign. Memos were written describing Clinton's formula as something for Labour to emulate. Gould later wrote, "The Clinton experience was seminal for the Labour Party."

After Clinton was elected, Tony Blair and Gordon Brown, the two senior architects of Labour's repositioning as a party of the center, conferred with Clinton and his aides. Brown got to know some of Clinton's inner circle, such as Robert Reich and Sidney Blumenthal, and the Clinton people, in turn, helped the Blair-Brown faction work on kindred policies and ideological appeals such as welfare reform and the idea of a "supply side of the left," emphasizing improved worker skills, assuming that market outcomes would deal with inequality. As soon as Blair became party leader in October 1994, he rebranded the party as New Labour, borrowing directly from Clinton's New Democrats.

When Blair did succeed in leading Labour to a landslide win in 1997, his policy package was a blend of Thatcherism when it came to maintaining the deregulation of finance, the weakening of trade unionism, privatization, and fiscal conservatism—plus some reinvestment in a modernized welfare state. Internally, Blair, Brown, and their strategists were determined to jettison what remained of the Labour Party's socialist tradition and to break the influence of trade unions and left factions on the internal party machinery. One of Blair's first successes was to get the party to eliminate the famous Clause Four of its charter, which had committed Labour to nationalizing basic industry and finance.

Blair's governing strategy was also to make a close alliance with the City, the British counterpart of Wall Street, and with right-wing press barons such as Rupert Murdoch. The alliance with the City was good for the financing of the Labour Party. It meant deregulation of capital—the euphemism was "light-touch regulation"—as well as greater reliance on London's dominance as a world financial center to somehow replace Britain's collapse as a manufacturing center. In the EU governing institutions, the Labour Party was part of the caucus of social democratic parties. But in the wake of the financial collapse of 2007–8, it enraged other governments of the democratic left that British representatives invariably vetoed tougher financial reforms.

While the Labour governments in power between 1997 and 2010 did make some gains in rebuilding the National Health Service, broadening public education, and reducing child poverty, the deregulation, privatization, and anti-union policies of the Thatcher era continued. Even with the social investment, after three terms of Blair and his ally and successor Gordon Brown, Britain was even more deeply divided between a successful financial and professional elite and nearly everyone else.

Despite thirteen years of New Labour, Britain today has a more unequal income than all other European nations except Spain, Greece, and Estonia. Its Gini coefficient of 0.33 is only slightly better than that of the US, at 0.37. Income transfers do reduce inequality somewhat. On the earned income front, however, the Blair-Brown version of a Third Way did not do much for wages and job opportunities for the non-elite. The earnings ratio of the top 10 percent to the bottom 10 percent was essentially unchanged between 1997 and 2010. One of New Labour's widely acknowledged successes was its creation of a national minimum wage, about 50 percent of the median wage. The minimum wage helps only about 7 percent of British workers, who would otherwise fall below it.

New Labour made the same political mistake as the New Democrats, targeting help to the very poor but largely ignoring the plight of the broader working class. Unemployment rates in the industrial Northeast remained about double those of the more prosperous South and Greater London.

New Labour, with minor adjustments, also continued the Thatcher policy of using the welfare state mainly to coerce work, any work. In British director Ken Loach's brilliant 2016 film, *I, Daniel Blake*, a fifty-nine-year-old carpenter in a depressed northern town suffers a serious heart attack and is advised by his doctor that he needs three months of rest. When he applies for temporary disability aid, he is told that he must undertake a job search as a condition of assistance. He dutifully searches for a job that he mustn't take. There is a wide range of administrative penalties for failure to comply with a Kafkaesque set of routines. Sitting in a mandatory résumé-writing class, Blake blurts out, "It's a monumental farce, isn't it . . . there aren't enough jobs," and gets himself sanctioned with denial of benefits. The movie is a brilliant parody, just a bit removed from reality, of how the British welfare state became a dispiriting and humiliating affair whose primary purpose is to cut costs rather than to help people. Beveridge would have been appalled. The Tories were more extreme, but Labour colluded.

Meanwhile, the percentage of workers covered by collective-bargaining agreements continued to fall during the Blair-Brown period. Under Thatcher, union representation had dropped from 56 percent of the workforce to 31 percent. Under Blair and Brown the decline continued, to 27 percent in 2009. Its even steeper decline in the private sector accelerated—from 20 percent in 1997 to 15 percent in 2009.

John Monks, the leader of the Trades Union Congress in 1997, was also something of a modernizer. Monks was eager to achieve a more Scandinavian style of social bargaining with British industry and government. He was mostly rebuffed. Blair was not prepared to give the unions, even more docile unions, any legitimacy as social partners. Visiting Monks in his TUC office, Blair pointed to photos of the two most recent Labour prime ministers, Wilson and Callaghan, both of whom had been done in partly by union strife. "Is that your trophy gallery?" Blair demanded. "Well, you're not going to have my head on that wall."

One modest union-friendly reform under Blair provided for union recognition, either if a majority of employees were already union members, or if 50 percent of eligible employees voted in favor. But little new organizing was possible in the climate of deindustrialization and privatization, which had been devastating to unions. Blair also retained Thatcher's legal restraints on strikes, including on picketing, secondary boycotts, and the need for supermajorities to declare strikes.

Like Clinton's conversion to fiscal conservatism, some Blair internal party reforms turned out to be inadvertent time bombs that detonated two decades later. The New Labour wing of the party, now in firm control, did its best to ensure that Labour candidates for Parliament were Blair loyalists and not people further to the left. By the time of the general elections of 2010 and 2015, both won by the Tories, the Blair-Brown purge of the left had been so thorough that a whole generation of "sensible left" Labour figures was missing—leaving mainly Blairites and a remnant of older, hard-left members of Parliament who had been in office since before the Blair takeover of 1994. In the New Labour era, Blair and Brown also succeeded in wresting control of the party machinery from the unions, and then in 2014 the party leadership pushed through a reform that required the party leader to be chosen via a one member/one vote system that gave the voting power to individual dues-paying members.

But the result of these two reforms was the opposite of what the moderates intended. After the defeat of Labour leader Ed Miliband in the 2015 election (following a Shakespearean struggle for the party leadership against Miliband's own brother, David), the new party-voting system chose, of all people, Jeremy Corbyn, one of the unreconstructed leftists, who had been serving in Parliament since 1983.

The relatively low cost of Labour Party voting membership led leftist organizers to promote a mass enlistment drive among radicals in order to elect Corbyn leader. Corbyn is also a radical on such issues such as Israel-Palestine and disarmament. He was opposed by more than three-quarters of Labour members in the House of Commons. Under the traditional system, where the parliamentary caucus has a substantial say, Corbyn never would have prevailed.

Margaret Thatcher once remarked with malicious irony that her greatest achievement was Tony Blair. One might add that Blair's unintended legacy for New Labour was Jeremy Corbyn.

The Conservative prime minister David Cameron took his disastrous gamble in 2013 of calling for a referendum on leaving the EU in the hope of appeasing and then silencing the Tory party's noisy anti-European wing. But the ploy only energized the nationalist far right. Cameron and the nation were stunned when Brexit was narrowly approved in the 2016 referendum, and a disgraced Cameron lost his job.

In April 2017, Cameron's successor, Prime Minister Theresa May, taking advantage of Corbyn's low standing in the polls, called a snap election for June. Having been an opponent of British withdrawal from the EU, May now repositioned herself as the leader who could make Brexit work. She increasingly allied herself with the hard-line critics of the EU, stealing the clothes of the right-wing UK Independence Party. May sought a big victory on the premise that an increased majority in the House of Commons would strengthen her hand in the upcoming negotiations with Brussels. This claim was less than believable, since the EU held all the cards, whether the British leader had a majority of 2 or of 200.

In the general election of June 8, 2017, Labour—to the surprise of all—very nearly pulled off an upset win, picking up seats and losing by just 2 points in the popular vote. May, who was against Brexit and then for it, against a snap election and then called one, came across as an opportunist. Corbin downplayed his foreign policy radicalism and campaigned mainly as an economic progressive. Labour, which gained over 40 percent of the popular vote for the first time in decades, was able to win back at least some voters who had supported British exit from the EU. Corbyn, rather like Bernie Sanders, did exceptionally well among the young.

Yet the result was an ideological muddle and a political stalemate. The Tories were deprived of their majority in the House of Commons but remained the party with the most parliamentary members, and had to govern in a weak coalition with the tiny, far-right Democratic Unionist Party, representing Protestant Northern Ireland. The arithmetic did not allow for a coalition government led by Labour. The splintered politics of exit from the European Union, with both major parties having pro- and anti-European wings, only added to the muddle.

The narrow referendum vote, 52 percent to 48, in favor of quitting the EU is best understood as a spasm of popular protest against the declining living standards of ordinary Britons. It was far from nuanced analysis of the EU's complex role in promoting free trade and the rights of finance while undermining jobs and social protections. The protest vote was mostly about in-your-face migration. Working-class voters who backed Brexit, especially in devastated industrial regions like the areas around Manchester, Liverpool, and Newcastle, were rebelling on a visceral level. They didn't like Bulgarians and Poles taking local jobs, dark-skinned people invading their pubs, radical Islamists producing homegrown terrorists, and bureaucrats from Brussels adding insult to injury with silly rules. But mainly, they were rebelling against lost livelihoods. Yet a shaken ruling elite interpreted the narrow vote as the solemn will of the people.

The remedy of quitting the European Union may keep out some foreigners, but it would worsen the deeper economic grievances. The United Kingdom sends half of its exports to the nations of the EU, while continental Europe sends only 10 percent of its exports to Britain. As Britain has deindustrialized, its remaining auto plants are Japanese and Korean export platforms, whose main markets are the countries of Europe. With the loss of tariff-free trade, they will likely relocate to EU member nations. Britain is heavily reliant on finance, and the big banking houses are already making contingency plans to relocate to Dublin, Amsterdam, or Frankfurt. Leaving the EU, especially under the auspices of the Conservative Party, which has no interest in rebuilding a mixed economy in one country, will do nothing for those who supported Brexit.

Labour, meanwhile, remains bitterly divided between Blair-style "modernizers," who want to put a human face on neoliberalism, and the more progressive camp led by Corbyn. In 2017, a much diminished Tony Blair, dropping any pretense of being a man of the left, was unrepentant. In a *New York Times* article titled "How to Stop Populism's Carnage," Blair called for a new center that embraces technology and globalism: "The center needs to develop a new policy agenda that shows people they will get the support to help them through the change happening around them." But this man was prime minister of

Britain with a working majority in Parliament for ten years, and that is precisely what Blair failed to do.

For further insight into the embrace by social democrats of full-on neoliberalism and a brand of globalism that excluded ordinary citizens, it's worth bringing in one other major leader who repositioned his party in a strikingly similar fashion: Gerhard Schröder of the German Social Democrats, the SPD.

SCHRÖDER'S THIRD WAY

Like Blair and Clinton, Schröder came to power following the long incumbency of a successful conservative, Helmut Kohl of the Christian Democratic Union (CDU), who served as German chancellor from 1982 to 1998. Schröder became the first SPD chancellor since Helmut Schmidt nearly a generation earlier, serving in coalition with the new Green Party and its popular leader, Joschka Fischer.

The SPD had already completed the business of renouncing its earlier socialism. The party's Bad Godesberg program of 1959 repealed the German counterpart of the British Labour Party's Clause Four, by dropping the commitment to nationalize the means of production and the attendant Marxian rhetoric. Instead, the SPD promoted a more egalitarian version of a labor-business-government partnership. Beginning in 1966, the SPD served in several governments, either leading them (starting with Willy Brandt in 1969) or as junior coalition partners with the CDU.

The SPD's relationship with its unions and the unions' place in German society were drastically different from counterparts in Britain and the United States. German unions were both powerful and docile. Much of the German corporatist postwar social compact was based on a negotiated partnership between capital and labor. Under the German system of co-determination, German unions get seats on boards of all large German corporations. Works councils, on which union representatives serve, are important institutions of both corporate governance and worker voice. The unions are also full partners in Germany's widely acclaimed system of apprenticeship training, which combines classroom and practical experience. The result is unions committed to maintaining Germany's industrial excellence and a well-trained labor force to go with it. German unions, like those of Scandinavia, are also mindful of the need not to push for wages that outstrip productivity growth and undermine German competitiveness.

The other key element of what was known as stakeholder or block-holder capitalism was the German system of patient capital. German banks traditionally had large holdings of stock in large German corporations, and shares were seldom traded. This was the antithesis of the financialization that infected the US and Britain in the 1980s, in which the goal was to "maximize shareholder value." The two approaches reflected different theories of competitiveness and accountability, and each had pluses and minuses.

In the Anglo-Saxon system, activist shareholders would supposedly keep anxious managers on their toes. Managers who did not maximize the value of shares would be replaced. Those who succeeded in pumping up share prices would be rewarded with stock options. The downside of this system was that it often rewarded financiers and senior executives at the sacrifice of the actual enterprise. And the shareholder-as-king model treated workers as cost centers to be dispensed with when convenient, rather than as long-term assets.

In the German system, managers did not need to focus on the quarterly balance sheet and could plan for the long term. Debt capital in the form of bank financing was cheaper than equity capital, as well as more patient. Accountability was more social. Corporate executives were accountable to unions via co-determination, and to bankers, who were also their most important shareholders and board members.

Germany had long been indulgent of cartels. In the view of Joseph Schumpeter, the prophet of creative destruction, large oligopolistic corporations with deep pockets for innovation can sometimes achieve the creativity without the destruction. They do this by enabling continuous innovation to take place within the corporation, rather than having a high rate of business failures and social dislocation as the price of invention. The system of bank-company interlocks, affectionately termed *Deutschland, A.G.* ("Germany, Inc."), was quintessentially Schumpeterian. The hands-on involvement of secure and skilled workers helped drive precision and innovation too.

Germany also had other elements of a kind of soft industrial policy, via state banks and the government's development bank, the KfW, as well as industry research collaboratives that financed or subsidized new technologies. Germany, a nation without much natural sunlight, has nonetheless become a world leader in solar energy production, thanks to these government-industry partnerships.

But the system was also criticized as too clubby. Critics looked longingly at Silicon Valley and complained that Germany was falling behind the United States in its rate of innovation (though there was little if any connection between the rise of the US tech industry and the shift to financialized capitalism). The German cartels and the absence of "risk-bearing" equity capital were held partly responsible for the relative weakness of German small and medium enterprise, the *Mittelstand*, which was a prime source of German manufacturing excellence. In addition, bankers, private-equity moguls, and hostile takeover artists were becoming billionaires under the new Anglo-Saxon system. Some German bankers, who took relatively modest compensation in their role of suppliers of patient capital to German industry, wondered whether they were being suckers. Such was the state of debate about the German industrial system in the 1990s.

At the time Gerhard Schröder became chancellor, Germany was suffering its worst slump of the postwar era, but for reasons that had nothing to do with its industrial, financial, or co-determination system. In 1989, when the Berlin wall came down and the Cold War ended, the government of Helmut Kohl had seized the moment to annex the former DDR. To win East German consent for reunification and keep residents of the East from flooding the West, Kohl's government in early 1990 offered to exchange deutschmarks for the far lower valued East German mark at the giveaway rate of 1 to 1, which compared with an official rate of 4.8 to 1 and a black-market rate well above that.

Even so, massive investment in the poorer East was necessary to prevent a massive migration to the thriving West. The government of the Federal Republic of Germany ended up investing about €1.3 trillion in the former DDR between 1989 and 2003, a massive sum equal to about half of one year's German GDP. This burden functioned as a dead weight on healthy West Germany. The always inflation-phobic Bundesbank responded to the higher deficits and the giveaway of deutschmarks by raising interest rates, slowing German growth still further.

As a result, ordinarily prosperous Germany as a whole found itself in the rare position of having slower growth and higher unemployment than many of its neighbors. Economists began calling Germany "the sick man of Europe," a phrase once applied to Turkey. With reunification and the exposure of the command economy of East Germany to the more productive West, some 4 million of the 9.8 million jobs in the former DDR were lost. These were not replaced by economic growth. In 1998, when Schröder took office, the overall German unemployment rate was 11 percent, and in the East it was close to 20 percent. GDP growth was close to zero. The result of the high rate of joblessness was to put downward pressure on wages. In the late 1990s the US economy was booming, and Schröder looked to the more neoliberal American model for lessons. Yet the factors special to Germany were almost entirely the consequence of the costs of reunification and the economic policies pursued by Kohl and the Bundesbank to accommodate it.

This was the economic climate that allowed the SPD to finally oust the aging Kohl, and the policy puzzle that awaited Gerhard Schröder. The new chancellor was a veteran of SPD politics, having been minister-president of the important state of Lower Saxony, also in a coalition government with the Greens. In that post, he had become close to a number of bankers and corporate leaders. They belonged to the same clubs, and Schröder was often photographed puffing an enormous cigar with one corporate leader or another. Since the state of Lower Saxony was a major shareholder in VW, Schröder had a seat on the VW board and also became chummy with the carmaker's president and other executives, one of whom was VW's chief of labor relations, Peter Hartz. The SPD's left and the press mocked the nominally socialist Schröder as the "comrade of the bosses," a sobriquet that rhymes in German: *Genosse der Bosse*.

Schröder's theme was social and economic modernization. Upon taking office in 1998, Schröder sponsored some social policies dear to his partners in the Green Party, including phasing out nuclear power, promoting renewable energy, legalizing same-sex civil unions, and liberalizing immigration policy. He soon moved on to a core shift in Germany's economic model. In this, he basically accepted the neoliberal story of what was ailing Germany. Like Blair, he also found a friend and role model in Bill Clinton. Blair and Schröder would publish a joint manifesto titled the "Third Way," of which more shortly. The German version, the *Neue Mitte*, became Schröder's own brand.

Two aspects of Schröder's policy shift are noteworthy. In December 1999, Schröder announced changes in the tax law that made it possible for banks to sell appreciated stock in corporations without paying a prohibitively costly capital gains tax. The tax, which was cut from 54 percent to zero, had been one of the pillars of the "blockholder" system. With this change, the system of German corporate finance became rather more Anglo-Saxon. *Der Spiegel* termed this shift "a type of financial deregulation that Helmut Kohl would never have dared." Like Blair and Clinton, Schröder seemed to find a shift to a more market-oriented system both modern and personally rewarding, as well as conducive to better economic performance.

After narrowly winning reelection in 2002, Schröder unveiled a manifesto titled "Agenda 2010." It proposed a drastic liberalization of Germany's social welfare, tax, and labor system—as if these were somehow responsible for the sluggishness that had afflicted Germany since the Federal Republic's costly absorption of the East. Many of Schröder's allies in the SPD argued that the right policy response to a macroeconomic slump was macroeconomic stimulus, but this required taking on the powerful Bundesbank to lower interest rates and indulge larger deficits, and Schröder was already wedded to a more neoliberal course.

Agenda 2010 included cutting taxes, reducing unemployment benefits, raising the pension age, and reining in other welfare spending. Some of this was legitimate—especially the pension reform; Germany, with one of Europe's most generous pension systems and lowest birth rates, had a genuine fiscal challenge in its retirement policies. But the program's most controversial aspect was its shift in labor policy. As architect of that program, Schröder turned to his friend Peter Hartz, of VW. Four sets of reforms recommended by the Hartz Committee were enacted. The most controversial of these, known as Hartz IV, created a two-tier system of labor protections.

The Hartz reforms were intended to force unemployed workers

to take low-wage jobs. One instrument was drastic cuts in unemployment benefits. Before Hartz, long-term unemployed people could collect indefinite benefits of about 55 percent of their prior net income, with higher benefits for older unemployed people. The benefits were reduced and the duration capped at eighteen months for most workers. If people refused to take even dismal jobs, they would be cut off.

Hartz defined a new category, known as mini-jobs, that paid well below prevailing wages and received less than full social protections. The result of these reforms was to drastically increase the size of the low-paid workforce, widen income inequality in Germany, and weaken the bargaining power of labor generally. A research study by two German labor market scholars, published by the Russell Sage Foundation, found that even though wages are supposed to correlate with skills, the Hartz reforms pushed many skilled as well as unskilled workers into low-wage work. Though the policy changes were explicitly aimed at workers not protected by collective-bargaining agreements, the unions saw the move as the threat to labor solidarity that it was. Union membership and collective bargaining proceeded on a relentlessly downward path.

In policy terms, this was a low-wage response to what was basically a macroeconomic problem—proposed by a center-left government and with the enthusiastic support of the conservative parties. Germany's unit labor costs fell, boosting its exports, but its inequality of earnings increased dramatically. Neither policy shift—the liberation of financial capital or the weakening of labor—was necessary economics. In political terms, this was a gift for the right. When Schröder's popularity eroded and he was defeated by Angela Merkel in 2005, Merkel's victory speech slyly complimented Schröder, whose SPD was now her junior coalition partner, for his courage in pushing through the Hartz reforms.

Both changes enraged the unions and more progressive leaders of the SPD. Schröder, a Social Democrat, made policy shifts that a German conservative would not have dared attempt. With the liberalization of German capital markets, British and American hedge funds began mounting takeovers of some German industrial firms—something that had been all but impossible under the blockholder system. Private-equity firms had no respect for the delicate corporatist social bargaining, and no solicitude either for workers or for German production.

In April 2005, the SPD chairman, Franz Müntefering, gave a speech bitterly criticizing excessive marketization under Schröder and famously denouncing foreign private-equity companies as "locusts" that were buying up German companies with no appreciation of the German industrial system. *Der Spiegel* featured a caricature of a giant locust on its cover and warned, "Be it television stations, large machine builders or auto-parts suppliers, international investors are buying up large swaths of the German business landscape. The new lords of business want one thing: profits, profits, profits."

A month later, one of the leading SPD figures, former party chair and finance minister Oskar Lafontaine, who had been the SPD candidate for chancellor in 1990, quit the party. He soon spearheaded the creation of a new German party, *Die Linke* (the Left). The Left party was a combination of disaffected Social Democrats and leaders of the former, ostensibly reformed, communist party of East Germany. Such was the bitterness on both sides of the split that leaders of both the Left party and the SPD declared that it would take a generation before these wounds would heal sufficiently for *Die Linke* to form a coalition with the SPD. In the federal elections of 2005, the SPD, the Greens, and the Left together won more seats in the Bundestag than the parties of the center and the right, but Schröder chose to disdain an all-left coalition and have the SPD become Merkel's junior partner.

The prediction of a lost generation was too pessimistic. A decade after Lafontaine's walkout, the first SPD-Left-Green coalition took power at the state level in Thuringia in the former East Germany in 2014, led by a Left minister-president. And a similar coalition formed the government in the city-state of Berlin, led by a Social Democrat, in 2016. Under the SPD's new leader, Martin Schultz, there was talk of an SPD-Left-Green coalition at the federal level in the national elections of September 2017. But Merkel's party was re-elected, the SPD garnered a modern low of just 20.5 percent of the vote, while the far-right AfD got 12.6 percent and entered Parliament for the first time.

LEFT OUT

What conclusions should be drawn from these experiences? At the time, each repositioning seemed sensible politics and necessary economics. But a good case could be made that superior alternatives were possible on both counts. Bill Clinton's extreme financial deregulation and embrace of austerity seeded the ground for a financial collapse and narrowed his party's perceived and actual commitment to the downwardly mobile working class. Only for a couple of years, in the period of true full employment in the late 1990s, did US real wages rise at the bottom and the income gaps narrow.

Blair's mix of neoliberal financial and labor policies, coupled with some modest redistribution, ultimately failed both as economics and as politics. His legacy was a divided Labour Party, an angry working-class base of onetime Labour voters that looked to ultranationalists, and a period of Conservative rule.

Schröder's policies split the left, and put Germany on a road to much wider income inequality. Unemployment did eventually abate, but strong evidence suggests that this was more the result of Germany enjoying a severely undervalued currency, the euro, leading to the world's largest export surplus;* it was not the fruit of the cut in social benefits and wages. German unit labor costs, a measure of competitiveness, did fall—but not very much. Many German critics contend that German wages have been held down more than necessary, and that a better cure both for Germany and for the larger EU economy would be increased domestic demand within Germany—namely, more public investment and higher wages, especially at the bottom. Germany has been remarkably generous when it comes to investing in the recovery of its own eastern region—and equally niggardly when it comes to the rest of Europe.

These policies were also good for the personal finances of their sponsors. Clinton went on to become a rich man, using his corporate contacts to underwrite the mix of personal and philanthropic business known as the Clinton Foundation. His net worth is about $80

---

*If Germany had kept the deutschmark, its chronic surpluses would have led to periodic revaluations and a currency worth at least 40 percent more than the euro.

million. Blair became even richer, with an annual income of between $5 million and $10 million from corporate clients and wealth estimated at $80 million and rising. Schröder became the richest of all, worth upwards of $200 million, from deals that many Germans consider corrupt. Shortly before leaving office, in September 2005, Schröder approved a $4.7 billion pipeline deal with the Russian gas giant Gazprom. In December of that year, he was rewarded with the chairmanship of the venture. Comrade of the bosses, indeed.

The senior economic officials who advised Clinton and Obama to embrace deregulation and austerity—Robert Rubin, Lawrence Summers, Timothy Geithner, Jack Lew, Gene Sperling, Peter Orszag, Michael Froman—went back and forth between government and seven- or eight-figure jobs on Wall Street. Even if this revolving door broke no laws, it was corrupt in a deeper sense. It ensured that center-left governments would share the outlook of the financial elite at the expense of ordinary people. The exceptions were a few, lower-ranking officials, such as Jared Bernstein, who returned to academia or think tanks—and three leading women progressives: the chair of the Congressional Oversight Panel and acting head of the Consumer Financial Protection Bureau, Elizabeth Warren, who went on to the Senate; FDIC chair Sheila Bair, who became a college president; and former chief commodities regulator Brooksley Born, who had warned against the toxic potential of derivatives. Born continued to practice law.

To the extent that the repositioning of center-left parties was not based on opportunism or cupidity, it was based on mistaken economics. Neoliberal theorists made the error of blaming a macroeconomic drag on "rigidities" in labor market institutions. The remedy was to expose workers to the crude force of the market at a time of high unemployment, and to compound the damage with budget austerity.

An alternative, ruled out of bounds by the new pressures of globalism, would have used public investment, decent wages, and the proven recipe of active labor market policies. (The United States, where unions and wages had been on the defensive for decades, had no labor market "rigidities" to oppose.)

The joint Blair-Schröder manifesto of 1998, The Third Way/*Neue Mitte,* is a telling artifact of the hopes and miscalculations of that era. It began by caricaturing policies that Third Way social democrats were rejecting:

In the past,

> The promotion of social justice was sometimes confused with the imposition of equality of outcome. The result was a neglect of the importance of rewarding effort and responsibility, and the association of social democracy with conformity and mediocrity rather than the celebration of creativity, diversity and excellence. Work was burdened with ever higher costs.

> The means of achieving social justice became identified with ever higher levels of public spending regardless of what they achieved or the impact of the taxes required to fund it on competitiveness, employment and living standards. . . .

> The belief that the state should address damaging market failures all too often led to a disproportionate expansion of the government's reach and the bureaucracy that went with it. The balance between the individual and the collective was distorted. . . .

> Too often rights were elevated above responsibilities, but the responsibility of the individual to his or her family, neighborhood and society cannot be offloaded onto the state. If the concept of mutual obligation is forgotten, this results in a decline in community spirit, lack of responsibility towards neighbors, rising crime and vandalism, and a legal system that cannot cope.

These claims were all exaggerated or just plain wrong. Blair liked to define the Third Way as working with the grain of the market rather than against it. Clinton was fond of talking about the need for a government that "rows less and steers more." For many Third Wayers, it was about values—encouraging people to take personal responsibility and then rewarding that behavior, specifically moving people from welfare to work. The Third Way also embraced globalization, as both inevitable and conducive to innovation. A popular refrain was a supply side of the left, meaning greater investment in people that would enable them to become more productive citizens.

Most of this turned out to be empty slogan. The actual policies liberated market forces from social constraints but delivered few of the promised offsetting benefits. Earned incomes continued to slide. The "supply-side socialism" adopted by Blair as the source of a more equal and productive society was a palpable failure. After a decade of Third Way governments, citizens were more exposed to the full force of a resurgent, even more brutal market than before, but without the better jobs and with far fewer social buffers.

Unlike the America of Bill Clinton, Germany and Britain both had parliamentary systems. Clinton, with a Republican majority during six of his eight years in office, had to move his policies somewhat to the right to gain Republican support and get legislation through Congress. Blair and Schröder had no such excuse. They had the votes to deliver on the promised gains of the Third Way for diligent working people, had they so chosen. But they did not.

The irony is that the original use of the phrase "the Third Way" or its variant, the "Middle Way," was a description of Swedish social democracy—a robust commitment to full employment, comprehensive social benefits, genuine partnership with the unions, and continuous refinement. The reference, of course, was to a third way between capitalism and communism—namely, modern social democracy anchored in strong political democracy. The Third Way of Clinton, Blair, and Schröder, by contrast, split the difference yet again—this time between social democracy and the full-throated neoliberalism of Reagan and Thatcher. Meanwhile, the original Scandinavian third way found itself under pressure from similar forces—and made similar missteps.

EVEN SCANDINAVIA

The success of the Nordic social democratic model, of an efficient economy combined with social justice and solidarity, was all the more remarkable because Norway, Sweden, Denmark, and Finland all depend heavily on trade. As other chapters have demonstrated, the rules of globalization before the 1980s left ample room for countries to pursue their own economic and social arrangements.

In the postwar Scandinavian model, with relatively minor national variations, labor market policy is central, and complemented by a comprehensive welfare state—but one that rewards work, not idleness. Public services are of high quality, used and supported by the broad middle class, not targeted to the poor. Education is universal and free, at all levels. Health care is first-rate, and financed socially. The key point is that all of this is of a piece. Each element of the model works in tandem with the other elements and earns majority public support because the welfare state is for all, not just for the dependent poor.

Many observers have contended that it was easy for the Nordic nations to pursue this sort of social bargain because of their homogeneity. This claim may be true as a matter of ethnicity, but it is overstated. At the turn of the twentieth century, when the roots of the modern Scandinavian social model began, these nations were cauldrons of class conflict.

It took substantial struggles and gains by the labor movement and the new social democratic parties for business elites to agree on a détente and then on a model of collaborative social bargaining. These roots go back to the Danish class settlement of 1899, following a decade of bitter strikes. This was the world's first agreement to institutionalize collective bargaining. In Sweden the counterpart was the Saltsjöbaden Agreement of 1938, which committed capital and labor to an alliance. These references may sound arcane, but in Denmark and Sweden they are universally understood landmarks in national histories.

The Social Democrats astutely nested their welfare state in a benign form of nationalism. In the 1920s and 1930s, a right-wing version of nationalism was sweeping Europe. Sweden's Social Democratic leaders realized that they could define a progressive form of nationalism by building on their country's traditions. In that era, they often governed in coalition with the agrarian party, whose views reflected Sweden's unique tradition of a strong, landholding free peasantry, even in feudal times. As the Swedish scholar Lars Trägårdh observes, Sweden's Social Democrats "gradually abandoned the divisive language of class and class struggle in favor of the language of 'folk' that served to create political bridges to both the rural peasantry and the urban middle classes." In 1928 the Social Democrats embraced the originally conservative notion of the *folkhem* ("people's home"). This idea proved so resonant that by 1932, the Social Democrats had become the predominant governing party.

A decent society, in this view, was something that the Swedish people deserved, as Swedes. In addition, Swedish corporatism was consistent with Swedish values. A fortuitous blend of social conformism, modesty, and respect for community, partly rooted in the Lutheran religion common to Scandinavia, happens to interact nicely with social democracy. This is the aspect of the homogeneity story that rings true—and helps explain Swedish ambivalence about immigration. Sweden has the world's largest per capita share of refugees. On the one hand, the generous policy toward refugees reflects longstanding traditions of social compassion. On the other hand, with social democracy defined as a "people's home"—for Swedes—large numbers of immigrants from outside the local culture undermine tacit social norms and breed resentment.

The most important ingredient in the secret sauce of Sweden and Denmark during the half century after World War II was the fact that the Social Democrats were the party of government most of the time. Long-term stewardship of the social model allowed the government to continuously fine-tune the details, consistent with an overall social democratic approach. The economic and social parts of the model were mutually reinforcing, and a coherent whole.

The Swedish Social Democratic Party (SAP) governed Sweden almost continuously from 1932 to 1991, with the exception of a six-year interlude of two center-right governments between 1976 and 1982. Not surprisingly, it was the turbulent 1970s that broke the Social Democratic monopoly. Sweden, of course, was far from a one-party state. Swedish political democracy was robust, voter turnout high, and the fact that the nonsocialist parties invariably got at least 40 percent of the vote kept the government on its toes.

Denmark was not quite as consistently social democratic, but from 1929 through 2001, the prime minister was a social democrat for fifty-five of those seventy-two years. Even during the Nazi occupation, which failed to reduce Demark to a puppet state, social democrats were in charge of the Danish government.

In Norway, the Labor Party (social democrats) governed continuously between 1945 and 1981, and about two-thirds of the time between 1986 and 2013. Thanks to the windfall benefits of North Sea oil and very creative policies for the social investment of its proceeds, Norway was buffered against some global trends. Yet today, conservatives govern in coalition with the far right.

In the heyday of Scandinavian social democracy, there was no coun-terpart anywhere else in the West. In other countries, left regularly alternated with right, leaving a far less coherent social and economic strategy. In nations with proportional representation and coalition governments, the model was further watered down. But since the 1980s, Scandinavia has become more like the rest of Europe, in its fragmented party system, in its alternation between left and right, in its exposure to globalization, and in its neoliberal policies.

In Sweden, the two center-right Swedish governments in power between 1976 and 1982 reduced taxes, cut social benefits, and intro-duced elements of privatization. The Social Democrats took the center-right's political success as a sign that their model had gone too far and was losing public support. They also attributed some of the sluggish economy to elements of rigidity. So they decided to take a page from the neoliberal playbook when they returned to power in 1982. The repositioning was not as drastic or as extreme as the shifts pursued by Blair or Schröder, but it turned out to be a slippery slope.

The Social Democrats kept some of the privatization, on the prem-ise that this would introduce more consumer choice. They expanded school choice options, imagining that creative groups of parents and teachers would found alternative schools. Instead, offshore corpora-tions sponsored voucher schools, which creamed off high-performing students, leaving the state schools with fewer resources to deal with often harder-to-educate pupils.

The center-right government that had led Sweden between 1976 and 1982 was relatively moderate and did not seek to undermine core aspects of the Swedish model. The more staunchly conservative coali-tion government that took power in 2006 explicitly sought to drive a wedge between people who relied on the welfare state and those who had steady jobs. The new prime minister, Fredrik Reinfeldt, pro-claimed that his was the party that "valued work." The message of his campaign was that if you rely on public benefits, you should vote for the Social Democrats, but if you are self-reliant, you should vote for us. "Two thirds take part in the productivity-driven society," he said after his election. "But one third or so are standing aside and living on subsidies—bystanders who have excluded them-selves from the labor force. Basically, what the Swedish electorate said is there are too many bystanders."

The conservative coalition government demolished Sweden's active labor market policy. Instead of a long-term strategy for retraining, the program was converted to an Anglo-Saxon-style "work first" system, where jobless people sit in offices to work on their CVs and job search plans, and must take available low-wage jobs. Both the value and the duration of benefits were cut, as was the training.

The government also went after a core source of union strength: union sponsorship of the system of unemployment insurance and coverage. In 2006, the new government created a new system, delinked from the unions, in a kind of declaration of war on the unions. Encouraged by the Swedish Employers' Confederation, the government stopped promoting centralized wage bargaining, in favor of market determination of wages. This action both weakened labor solidarity and contributed to widened income inequality. The government also changed hiring rules so that corporations could try out new workers at reduced wages for as long as twenty-four months, without giving them regular employment. These young workers, marginally attached to the labor force, are harder for unions to reach. As one senior trade unionist, Ola Pettersson of the Swedish Trade Union Confederation (the LO), told me, "These cumulative policy shifts undermine both the high-wage, high-equality, high-productivity Swedish economic model and the Social Democrats' political support."

By the time a Social Democratic government returned to power in 2014, Swedish politics had fragmented further, and an anti-immigrant people's party received 13 percent of the vote. The prime minister, Stefan Löfven, hoped to restore some of the traditional Social Democratic policies, but his party won only 31 percent of the vote and he headed a weak coalition government reliant on centrists. Major policy innovations were not possible; this was more like a caretaker government.

Löfven was also a fervent supporter of the rights of immigrants and refugees. When I was in Sweden on a research and reporting visit in 2015, I attended a pro-immigrant rally in a Stockholm suburb. The featured speaker was none other than the prime minister. This stance is noble, but risky. With weak governments unable to improve the dynamics of economic growth, job creation and wages in an ever-more-deeply-global economy, high unemployment and large numbers of immigrants are a toxic brew. As of August 2017, Sweden's right-wing populist party, the Sweden Democrats, was polling in the midtwenties, almost double its 2013 showing, just below the governing Social Democrats. So, even in the nations where the social democratic model of managed capitalism is most powerfully anchored, global pressures and domestic compromises by the center left are undermining the system's political and economic logic.

FEAR AND FRAGMENTATION

In March 2017, many commentators expressed great relief when Geert Wilders, head of the Dutch far-right anti-immigrant party, polled 13.5 percent, only slightly better than he had done in the previous 2012 election, leaving the center-right government of Prime Minister Mark Rutte largely intact. Hardly remarked on was the wipeout of the Dutch democratic left. The Dutch Labor Party, the mainstream social democratic party affiliated with the Dutch labor movement, was reduced to just 5.7 percent and nine seats in parliament, down from twenty-nine seats in the previous parliament.

In the heyday of Clinton, Blair, and Schröder, the Dutch prime minister was Wim Kok of the Labor Party, sponsor of much the same Third Way ideology. Kok's version of labor market reforms delivered some protections for part-time workers but accelerated the growth of a low-wage workforce in the Netherlands. By 2002, the incidence of low-wage work among the young had risen to a staggering 61 percent. Since then, the Dutch Labor Party has been part of several coalition governments that sponsor austerity and has lost a great deal of credibility. All told, the three Dutch left parties, Labor plus the Left Greens and the Socialists, won only 37 seats out of 150 in the 2017 election, the left's worst showing ever.

One of the consequences of the right-wing populist upsurge is the growth of new parties that further fragment the parliaments of European countries, most of which elect their members via some variant of proportional representation. A related consequence is that much of the populist right's support comes at the expense of social democratic parties, which traditionally draw on the same working-class demographic. The Danish People's Party takes the position that it supports the Danish welfare state even more fervently than the Social

Democrats do; it just wants the benefits strictly limited to Danes. The People's Party now gets about half of the votes of trade unionists, who used to be reliable voters for the Social Democrats. Elsewhere in Europe, far-right nationalist parties are all over the map when it comes to social and economic policies.

All over Europe, the support for social democratic parties has been cut from its traditional range of more than 40 percent to less than 30 percent in Denmark, Sweden, Norway, and Austria—and in some cases, like the Netherlands, below 10 percent. This fragmentation has narrowed the political center and required coalitions, usually led by the center right, that embrace deeper austerity. The left's sometime involvement in these coalitions further depresses its credibility with voters.

The echo from the pre-Hitler period is chilling. Following the German elections of March 1930, as votes for the Communists and Nazis were narrowing the political center in Germany, the new chancellor was Heinrich Brüning of the Center Party. Brüning presided over a five-party grand coalition that succeeded a cabinet led by Hermann Müller of the SPD. Though Müller had tried to restore growth, his government had been done in by the deepening depression. The five parties in Brüning's cabinet, which excluded the SPD, were a fractious brew, but they agreed on one thing—the need for austerity. Budget tightening and spending cuts were duly carried out, deepening the depression and increasing German unemployment. The Nazi vote surged from 18 percent in 1930 to 37 percent in 1932, making the Nazis the largest party in the Reichstag and paving the way for Hitler.

While Hitler was taking office as German chancellor in January 1933, Franklin Roosevelt was building his new administration in Washington. The stunning contrast between the two leaders underscores the fact that deep economic grievances can energize the far right and destroy democracy, or animate a democratic left that both harnesses capitalism and strengthens democracy.

8

TRADING AWAY
A DECENT ECONOMY

The structuring of the world trading system in the era after World War II is at the heart of our story of how the rules of globalization were used, first to promote a democratically controlled form of decent capitalism in the 1940s and then, beginning in the 1970s, to destroy it. In trade policy as in the global monetary system, the resurgent power of finance is central to this reversal.

The United States was the prime architect of the trading system, both in the immediate postwar era and in the later reversal of its original terms. At first, there was little contradiction between America's diplomatic goals for the system and its pursuit of self-interest as a nation. US presidents could promote an open trading system, secure in the knowledge that American companies were the world's most productive, and would thrive. As Europe and Japan recovered and increased their capacity to export, access to the immense US consumer market would reward Cold War allies and cement the alliance. The US could look the other way as loyal allies honored the principles and rhetoric of free trade but not the practice. Japan, for example, was the model Cold War client state—and also the prime protectionist.

President Eisenhower, brushing off criticisms of the plain double standard in US-Japan economic relations, declared in 1955, after enactment of a US-Japan deal that tolerated multiple forms of Japanese protectionism, "All problems of local [US] industry pale into insignificance in relation to the world crisis. Japan cannot live, and Japan cannot remain in the free world, unless something is done to allow her to make a living."

Japan soon demonstrated how a system of cartels with close ties to banks and government planning objectives could be nominally open while frustrating the ability of US firms either to export or to defend against imports whose production was subsidized and sheltered. Japan, which grew prodigiously, became the model for South Korea, Taiwan, and later China. This set of policies came to be known as neomercantilism—and it worked.* American manufacturing and wages suffered. The American trade deficit widened, to half a trillion dollars by 2016. A trade deficit of that scale adds up to massive losses of jobs and industries. Yet the US government's strategy of giving priority to system-maintaining goals, even at the sacrifice of both American industry and the mixed economy, persisted as a diplomatic habit, to the point of magical thinking.

To some extent, it made sense at the height of the Cold War in the 1950s and 1960s for the US to bend the rules to accommodate Japan, South Korea, and Taiwan, which were still relatively poor, as well as close geopolitical allies. Yet the same habits of denial and acquiescence persisted long after they became rich nations—and were even extended to China, which was far from an ally.

All this seems a mystery, until one grasps that the accommodation of China's mercantilism served US-based corporations that no longer produced much domestically but enjoyed extensive offshore manufacturing partnerships with China. Tolerating China's system of state-led capitalism also provided profitable opportunities for US finance. Banks and investment firms got to underwrite deals with China and to play in China's own, previously closed market, as long as they played by Beijing's rules. So the winners of this entente were American multinational companies and bankers that made a separate peace with Beijing. The losers were a broadly egalitarian, competitive domestic economy and American workers. The strategy also backfired geopolitically, with China emerging as a global power, not just via its production machine but as leader of a rival economic system with deep penetration in Africa, Asia, and Latin America.

*The original mercantilism of Europe in the seventeenth and eighteenth centuries emphasized positive trade balances, accumulation of gold and silver, and state promotion of industry. It was opposed by Adam Smith and David Ricardo as contrary to economic efficiency. Modern neomercantilism is a much more supple blend of state and market.

REVERSALS OF FORTUNE

We can divide the evolution of US post–World War II trade policy and the global trade regime into roughly four phases. The first can be dated from about 1947 through the late 1960s. In that era, several rounds of multilateral negotiation reduced tariffs, but nations retained plenty of room to fashion their own national brands of managed capitalism. Nations remained free to use quotas, subsidies, cartels, public ownership, or preferential procurement arrangements as part of their national industrial policies. American industry, heavily unionized and with a huge head start from the war, continued to dominate world production.

Under the original 1947 agreement creating the General Agreement on Tariffs and Trade (GATT), member countries were also permitted to limit imports to maintain national security, to promote product standards, to ensure consumer safety and environmental goals, and to protect domestic agriculture. States could also restrict imports for balance-of-payments purposes, and impose countervailing tariffs when it appeared that a rival nation was subsidizing production. These exceptions to the laissez-faire norm of free trade were part of the early postwar system's commitment to managed egalitarian capitalism. The stillborn International Trade Organization, whose charter the US government helped draft but the Senate refused to ratify, went even further, allowing nations to restrict trade to protect labor and social standards.

In the second phase, beginning in the 1970s, leaders of Japan, then Korea, and eventually most of East Asia, including China, refined and expanded their system of state-led capitalism. These incursions began seriously damaging US manufacturing and American unions—not because American industry was uncompetitive or because US workers were overpaid, but because Asian markets were largely closed to US exports in sectors targeted for development, while Asian exports were subsidized. Over time, these industries came to include both basic and advanced products—inputs such as machine tools, steel, and semiconductors, plus the entire range of consumer goods. Asian exports, by contrast, could enter the US essentially barrier-free.

Europe's leaders, meanwhile, promoted a protected internal market via a steadily expanding tariff-free European Community. Successive American presidents continued to give priority to the Cold War alliance rather than a balanced trading system.

As domestic industry suffered and deindustrialization and the rust belt became all-too-familiar concepts, the US Congress, first in 1974 and again in 1979, gave the president broad new powers to retaliate against foreign mercantilism. But for the most part, American presidents declined to use the new powers, lest they offend key allies. Instead, diplomats negotiated ad hoc palliatives for injured domestic industries, such as "voluntary export restraints" by trading partners, which gave US industry a bit of breathing room and preserved the convenient fiction that all parties were practicing free trade. Puny outlays under a program called Trade Adjustment Assistance, begun in 1962 as part of President Kennedy's Trade Expansion Act, were supposed to assist displaced domestic workers. The unions called it "burial insurance."

In the third phase, beginning in the 1980s and intensifying with the creation of the World Trade Organization in 1995, financial and corporate interests waged a successful campaign to transform the trade agenda into one of general deregulation. Trade policy became an all-purpose tool to dismantle managed capitalism, especially for finance. Business interests succeeded in portraying these measures as nothing more than the deepening of free trade. Therefore, anyone who raised qualms was to be disparaged as a self-interested or ignorant protectionist. Most economists piled on, and the nation's editorial pages obliged.

Congressman Richard Gephardt of Missouri, who campaigned for the Democratic presidential nomination in 1988, calling for a more reciprocal set of trade rules, was pilloried as a vulgar protectionist. Noting the failure of American cars to sell in Korea, Gephardt calculated that Korean protectionist measures raised the sticker price of a $10,000 Chrysler K-car to $48,000 in Seoul. "Take off those taxes and tariffs," he warned in a TV commercial. "If you don't, you're going to leave the negotiating table wondering how you are going to sell $48,000 Hyundais in America." Gephardt's arithmetic was spot-on. But the nation's opinion leaders had accepted the premise that it was protectionist to challenge someone else's protectionism, and Gephardt was dismissed as an opportunist who was ignorant of basic economics. Four decades later, a Jeep Wrangler with a sticker price of $40,530 in the US retails for about $70,000 in Beijing because of China's tariffs, which make US auto exports uncompetitive in China's domestic market.

"Protectionist" became an all-purpose epithet to condemn both narrow-interest groups and more complex critics of the resurrection of laissez-faire. This branding of the dismantling of the mixed economy, by corporate moguls and their allies in government, as nothing more than "free trade" was one of the most effective propaganda campaigns ever. It continues to this day.

In the fourth phase of US trade policy, beginning in the 1990s with NAFTA and extending into the new century, trade agreements defined a broad range of domestic financial, health, consumer, environmental, and labor regulations as infringements on free commerce. A radical reinterpretation of private property rights adopted the far-right claim that regulation was an uncompensated "taking" of property. Business elites had failed to persuade US courts that this was a reasonable reading of the Takings Clause of the Constitution, which requires compensation for property seized via eminent domain, but the doctrine became part of the common structure of international law, via the back door of trade.

None of the newer trade agreements even attempted to restore a trading system with policy space to rebuild a decent form of capitalism, as the architects of the Bretton Woods system had done. Instead, newly invented rights of corporations to challenge regulations as illegal restraints crowded out the ability of national democracies to manage capitalism. Agendas for these trade deals were set mainly by corporations, facilitated by allies in government; the official advisers to trade deals were mainly corporate.

Center-left governments did attempt to better the lot of workaday voters with modest programs of job training, public investment, labor regulation, and education. Yet the commitment to laissez-faire trade undermined those small good deeds, and the net impact on most citizens was a worsening of economic security. The 2008 financial collapse and the austerity policies that followed, reflecting the enhanced global influence of financial elites, compounded the damage. Thus did the capture of the trading system and its rules by financial elites set the stage for Trumpism.

In the 2016 election, Donald Trump made opposition to trade deals like NAFTA and the proposed Trans-Pacific Partnership the centerpiece of his nationalistic appeals to American workers. The details of these agreements were numbingly complex to most people. But ordinary citizens, watching factories close and wages collapse, grasped that the deals were serving the interests of someone else.

Trump got a lot of the specifics wrong; he got the politics right. His opponent, Hillary Clinton, was left to waltz around the fact that she, her husband, and the outgoing Democratic president, whom she had served as secretary of state, had all relentlessly promoted such deals, with little concern for the impact on working people. These trade agreements not only harmed ordinary workers and communities. On balance, they did not even promote net economic growth. There were benefits, but they went mainly to the top. The fact that American political leaders, Democrat as well as Republican, had made these deals the core of their foreign economic policy reflects a blend of bad economic theory, muddled diplomatic goals, and the deepening corporate capture of both parties. In March 2018, Trump ordered tariffs on steel and aluminum, and was widely denounced as a protectionist risking a trade war. But his trade negotiators then narrowed the target to the state-led, predatory capitalism of China. He also negotiated a market-opening deal with South Korea. Trump thus managed to pursue a strategy that had long eluded the free-trade mainstream.

THE ROAD TO HELL

To understand how US trade policy and the postwar trading system became engines for the return of laissez-faire, it's worth a brief review of how governments have promoted economic development. Despite the claims of free-trade theory, literally no nation has industrialized by relying on free markets. State involvement in economic development has been pervasive—not only for newly emergent manufacturing titans like Japan, Korea, and China, but also in earlier times for Germany, France, and Italy, as well as Latin American industrial powers such as Brazil, Mexico, and Argentina. State-led development even describes early England, which later invented the gospel of free trade. And it emphatically describes the United States.

Under England's Queen Elizabeth I in the late sixteenth century, there were tariffs, embargoes, export taxes, and royal grants of monopoly, all intended to build up Britain's domestic manufacturing capacity, initially in woolen textiles, and to protect that industry from imports. These protections were later extended to other industries. Britain imported only those raw materials that it could not produce at home, but not those that competed with British agriculture and industry. Its extensive network of colonies was part of this system, and Britain also banned exports from its colonies of products that competed with British goods. In addition, the Navigation Act of 1651 prohibited foreign ships from transporting goods to Britain. Trade between Britain and her colonies operated under a discriminatory system known as Imperial Preference. Only in the mid-nineteenth century did Britain convert to free trade—as other nations practiced variations on the brand of state-led development that had produced Britain's temporary commanding lead.

The United States had been a protectionist nation since its founding—to escape from British domination. The Tariff Act of 1789 was the second bill signed into law by George Washington. US economic nationalism began with Alexander Hamilton's "Report on Manufactures" of 1791, pointing to the key role of manufacturing in economic development and devising the nation's first industrial policy. A stronger manufacturing base was seen as necessary for national defense, as well as for the producer and consumer sides of the economy. Like other catchup economies, the US used both public investments and tariffs as tools of development.

Thomas Jefferson, a free trader, became a convert to the use of tariffs. With the War of 1812, tariffs were raised to 30 percent on iron imports and 25 percent on cotton and woolens, and they were further increased in 1828. US tariffs never fell below 40 percent until the mid-1930s. The so-called American system also relied on substantial public investment in canals, railroads, highways, agricultural extension, and government investment in manufacturing and technology. The land grant college system and agricultural extension, beginning in 1863, subsidized research into new technology and incubated many inventions that provided American industrial leadership, just as the National Science Foundation, the National Institutes of Health, and DARPA did after World War II.

Meanwhile, Britain in the 1840s shifted to unilateral free trade, making the same self-annihilating assumptions that the US would make more than a century later. Presumably, Britain had such an overwhelming lead in manufacturing that it could afford to set a good example. If other nations could be persuaded to practice free trade and buy cheaper and better British goods, the British manufacturing lead would persist indefinitely. This stance has been termed the "imperialism of free trade." Embracing free trade would also help British capital, which stood to benefit by being the prime financier of global commerce, and would help British consumers, who would get cheaper foreign products.

Other nations, however, also grasped the logic, and wouldn't play. They wanted to manufacture too. If other nations protected, that tactic was said to be irrational—because they were denying themselves cheaper imported goods. And if they subsidized exports, free-trade theory said that consumers should accept the gift.

The result of Britain's unilateral free trade? Germany and the US—both with national development strategies and protected internal markets—rapidly surpassed Britain. A virtuous circle of tariffs, government assistance, American inventions, and demand for American inputs such as steel drove the US manufacturing economy. Germany, which never accepted free-trade theories, had its own counterpart to the American system, as the Prussian state helped Germany to industrialize behind high tariff walls.

Clyde Prestowitz, formerly Ronald Reagan's senior counselor on trade and a close student of comparative industrial policy, tallied the numbers on American growth and British decline: "In 1870, Britain accounted for about 32 percent of total global manufacturing, with the US second at 23 percent, and Germany third at 13 percent. . . . By 1913, the United States accounted for 36 percent, Germany for 16 percent, and Britain for 14 percent."

Economic growth of the more protected US exceeded 4 percent per annum during this period, while that of laissez-faire Britain lagged at about 2 percent. By 1914, American GDP per capita had surpassed Britain's. Whatever static loss American consumers might have suffered from the tariffs on imports they more than gained over time in the dramatic growth of GDP.

Note that all of this reversal of fortune occurred *before* Britain went deeply into debt during World War I while the US wartime economy soared. A big part of the story was the hyper-reliance of the British political economy on finance, at the expense of British manufacturing. Other nations exported goods; England exported capital.

None of the British fade was the result of natural economic forces allowing the US to catch up. Rather, it was a textbook case of how one-way laissez-faire weakens a dominant economy, while a more deliberate industrial policy and selective protection allows a challenger to surpass it. Nor was this a case of a "mature" economy (Britain) naturally suffering a reduction in the rate of economic growth as it reached the so-called frontier of technological possibility—a favorite contention of economic orthodoxy. The US in 1945 was a far more mature economy than Britain was in 1870, but thanks to a managed form of capitalism, the United States once again enjoyed three decades of nearly 4 percent growth, until American industry was battered by one-way free trade and the dominance of finance.

At the level of economic theory, the great fallacy in the logic of David Ricardo, the father of free-trade theory, was to view the gains and losses of trade in a static fashion, as a snapshot at a single point in time. In Ricardo's theory, whose variants are espoused by free-market economists to this day, if nineteenth-century Britain offered better and cheaper manufactured goods, the US should buy them and export something where it could compete—say, raw cotton and lumber—even if that meant the US never developed an industrial economy. By the same token, if twentieth-century America made the best cars, machine tools, and steel, Japan and Korea should import those, and continue to export cheap toys and rice. And if other nations subsidized US industries, Americans, rather than being fearful of displacement, should accept the "gift."

What Ricardo missed—and what leaders from Alexander Hamilton and Abraham Lincoln to Teddy Roosevelt grasped (likewise statesmen in nations from Japan to Brazil), as well as dissenting economists like the German Friedrich List and the Americans Paul Krugman and Dani Rodrik—was that the dynamic gains of economic development over time far surpass the static gains at a single point in time. Economic advantage is not something bestowed by nature. Advantage can be deliberately created—an insight for which Krugman won a Nobel Prize. Policies of economic development often required an active role for the state, in violation of laissez-faire.

EMBRACING LIBERAL TRADE,
LOSING ECONOMIC LEADERSHIP

America's shift to free-market exemplar in the 1950s and 1960s repeated Britain's mistakes of the late nineteenth century, with the same negative effects on manufacturing and the same bloating of the financial sector. The shift required turning a blind eye not only to America's own economic history, but to its extensive use of the military as a de facto form of industrial policy.

During and after World War II, US defense spending both incubated new technologies with commercial spillovers and guaranteed a huge domestic market for them. In everything from aircraft to metallurgy and machine tools, and later semiconductors and the Internet, the US had a disguised planning system that helped it to be an export powerhouse. The military role was both a convenient dodge for the dominant free-market ideology and an embarrassment in trade negotiations. The diplomatic reaction of America's free traders was to insist that defense was its own realm—that if commercial spillovers did operate, they were an unfortunate accident.

Even in the 1920s, a decade famous for its embrace of free-market economics, the US had several de facto industrial policies, many of them spin-offs of government involvement in World War I. The Radio Corporation of America was sponsored and subsidized by the US Navy so that patents and technologies vital to transatlantic military communication would be kept in the United States. With that head start, RCA retained leadership in the development of consumer technology for half a century. In 1915, as Germany threatened to become the world's leader in aircraft technologies, Congress created the National Advisory Committee for Aeronautics (NACA), the forerunner of NASA. During World War I, NACA promoted cross-licensing agreements of key technologies among rival aircraft producers, and it used the wartime power of procurement to develop more advanced production. After the war, the Kelly Air Mail Act created a subsidized market that, in turn, stimulated aircraft production and paved the way for commercial aviation.

Until the 1930s, high tariffs were simply one part of the American system of economic development. For free traders, the Smoot-Hawley Tariff Act of 1930 is proof positive of the evil of tariffs. It is widely held responsible for deepening the Great Depression. As more detailed scholarship has revealed, however, about two-thirds of goods in that era entered the United States duty-free and were not affected by Smoot-Hawley. Trade was depressed mainly by the Depression itself, not by the tariff. Between 1929 and 1933, trade in dutiable and nondutiable products fell by almost the identical amount, according to the dean of trade historians, Alfred E. Eckes.

America's goals for its own policy and the trading system as a whole changed during the Roosevelt administration—in two stages. The first was via a law passed in 1934, the Reciprocal Trade Agreements Act, giving the president broad authority to negotiate tariff cuts. The second was American sponsorship of a postwar trading system that would aim for the freest possible trade among nations. Both were substantially the work of Roosevelt's secretary of state, Cordell Hull.

Hull was the exception in an administration that believed in regulating and managing capitalism. In contrast to FDR's other senior officials, Hull, a senator from Tennessee, was a free-market man. Roosevelt appointed him mainly to accommodate the Southern wing of the Democratic Party. Hull hailed from a region that depended on exports, of tobacco and cotton. He internalized the free-trade gospel, and as the US was emerging into world leadership, the policy seemed logical. As long as the hegemonic nation has highly competitive industries and other nations actually let in its exports, the systemic goals and the national-interest goals converge. But just like the US and Germany facing a dominant Britain in the nineteenth century, other nations looked to their own national advantage.

As the states of Europe and Asia planned their own recoveries after World War II, they resorted to a wide variety of measures that violated norms and practices of free trade. By the time these disparities became a flagrant source of imbalance starting in the 1970s, ideology and national interest had diverged, but free-trade ideology had hardened into a core article of faith: America would continue practicing free trade both to set a good example and to reward Cold War allies, even if it destroyed US manufacturing in the process. Later, as finance regained the political influence lost in the New Deal era, American presidents did vigorously insist on foreign market access—*for banks*—even as they largely ignored the fate of US manufacturing.

Between the 1960s and the current era, US employment in manufacturing declined from over 25 percent of total jobs in 1965 to just under 8 percent by 2016. This decline occurred across the board, in basic industries and advanced ones. Entire sectors, such as textiles, were wiped out. The United States did regain leadership in some advanced consumer electronics via tech leaders such as Apple, but virtually all of the production occurred offshore. Only because of the military applications and an industrial policy initiated by the Reagan administration did the US hold on to part of the semiconductor industry. Manufacturing lost 5 million jobs between January 2000 and December 2014 alone.

During this entire period, worker productivity more than doubled, but manufacturing wages stagnated. In January 1979, the average manufacturing wage was $20.83 in inflation-adjusted dollars. In July 2017, it was $20.94. You might think that as machines replaced workers and worker productivity soared, each remaining worker logically should have commanded a higher wage. That had long been the case in unionized sectors. But after the 1970s, the opposite happened, as corporate power increased and worker bargaining power was reduced.

Economically and politically, the consequence was to hollow out entire sectors and regions. Thriving industrial regions of the upper Midwest were all but wiped out.

Efforts by local leaders to have the government either intervene more aggressively against foreign mercantilism, or launch domestic industrial policies for replacement of jobs and industries, fell on deaf ears. Both demands violated the faith in free markets. From Carter to Obama, small token programs made little difference to these devastated cities and regions. And these were precisely the locales that supported Trump and breached the supposed blue firewall of the Democrats.

It has become conventional to blame the decline in US manufacturing either on robots or on a natural shift of production to nations that can provide cheaper workers. While some loss in human employment reflects increased productivity and more efficient machines, other nations with high wages have not suffered the same decline. Germany, with some of the world's highest-paid workers, still has 20 percent of its workforce in manufacturing. The difference reflects not just Germany's famed engineering prowess, but the fact that German national policy works hard to keep Germany as one of the world's leading industrial powers, while the US has no such policy.

Even more significant is the manufacturing share of GDP. The American share is about 12 percent. In other nations that have made a commitment to manufacturing, the share is 29 percent for South Korea, 27 percent for China, and 23 percent for Germany. Note that these are, respectively, medium-wage (Korea), low-wage (China), and high-wage (Germany) countries.

By 2016, the US was importing about three dollars of manufactured goods for every dollar it exported. Even the manufacturing facilities that remained in America tended to be low-value final-assembly plants, while the advanced production was done overseas. The remaining leaders, such as aircraft, semiconductors, and medical devices, were fruits of earlier or continuing unacknowledged industrial policies. Potential new leaders, such as solar cells and wind turbines, were quickly displaced by the more aggressive industrial policies of other nations.

Manufacturing went from having a rough trade balance with the rest of the world in the early 1980s, to having a deficit of over $700 billion in 2006. The trade deficit in goods in 2016 was $347 billion with China alone, a ratio that had tripled since 2001. And that had serious consequences for domestic employment. If the trade accounts in manufacturing were roughly balanced, the US today would have had at least 5 million more jobs. The growth of US imports from China alone in the decade between 2001 and 2011 displaced nearly 3.3 million US jobs, according to Robert Scott of the Economic Policy Institute. On average, jobs in these import-competing industries paid $1,022 per week, or well above the median US income.

Despite a tendency to blame the loss of manufacturing jobs on automation, even orthodox economists who took a closer look concluded that China was a big part of the story. David Autor of MIT and two colleagues, writing in the flagship *American Economic*

Review, calculated that about a million jobs lost between 2000 and 2007 were the direct result of displacement by imports from China. "The 'aha' moment," Autor explained, "was when we traced through the industries in which China had surging exports to the local addresses of their U.S. competitors and saw the powerful correspondence between where China had surged and where U.S. manufacturing employment had collapsed." And those addresses tended to be in the upper Midwest.

All of this displacement occurred because US trade policy, under Republicans and Democrats alike, paid little attention either to the neomercantilism of other nations, or to the value of keeping a strong manufacturing sector. Donald Trump's slogan "Make America Great Again" resonated because workaday voters viscerally understood what had been lost.

SPRINGTIME FOR BANKERS

Over the four decades since 1980, two profound changes occurred in corporate goals for the trading system. First, even relatively patriotic domestic manufacturers finally realized that the US government was never going to effectively defend their interests against foreign mercantilism. So they decided to make a separate peace with foreign governments and substantially abandon domestic manufacturing.

China used both carrots and sticks to enlist large US corporations as allies. It kept out exports that competed with fledgling Chinese domestic industries, much as Britain had done under the Tudors. But it also created incentives for manufacturers to move production to China—for export back to the West, not for sale within China. A US-based multinational could get subsidies in the billions for constructing its latest, state-of-the-art factory in China, and transferring technology to a Chinese partner (which would soon become a rival). In addition, there was the appeal of a very cheap and regimented workforce. One by one, large companies such as Intel, which had once been leading advocates of tougher trade negotiations to defend US-based production, took the deal. In February 2017, a California-based manufacturer of semiconductors, GlobalFoundries, announced the largest such deal yet—a $10 billion chip plant, heavily subsidized by the Chinese. All told, the Chinese government is currently spending $100 billion to attract state-of-the-art chip fabrication.

By the turn of the new century, a once-potent lobby of manufacturers proudly representing made-in-America products had all but vanished, as giants like Intel and GE realized that if the US government wasn't committed to making it in America, they would be damned fools to blow against the wind.

Further, as organized business and finance regained political power generally, financial elites realized that even if the rules of the trading system could not defend American industrial interests, they could accomplish something else: they could open the world to US banking. And with a shift in emphasis, trade rules could be used as a battering ram to destroy a regulated form of capitalism at home, in Europe, and in much of the Global South.

Thus, the new form of globalization did not compel Asian nations to give up mercantilism. But it was superb at dismantling the social and regulatory elements of the mixed economy in North America and Europe—the home base of financialized capitalism.

In the 1970s, as critics on both the left and the right pointed to the double standards of foreign mercantilism, the term "nontariff barrier" was used to refer mainly to foreign practices, such as cartels, subsidies, and regulatory blockages, that harmed American exports. By 1995, after a fifteen-year lobbying, rebranding, and publicity campaign by the banking industry, a nontariff barrier was understood to mean mainly foreign and domestic *financial regulation*. The objective of trade diplomacy shifted—from token efforts to pry open foreign consumer markets for American-made goods, to a full-court press to deregulate global banking.

A core element of the negotiating goals at the series of trade talks begun in 1986, the so-called Uruguay Round, was a set of provisions known as TRIMs, which stood for Trade-Related Investment Measures. This was the brainchild of the big investment banks and American Express, which were eager to gain greater footholds in nations that still had well-regulated national banking systems. The idea was that even if the US could no longer compete in manufacturing—a debatable premise and one that reflected the abject failure of US presidents to defend manufacturing—it was still superbly competitive in services, especially "financial services," the new term for banking invented and disseminated by American Express.

In 1978, Harry Freeman, then-president of American Express, launched a campaign to popularize the phrase "financial services" as part of a strategy to globalize US banking. In 1982, Freeman's successor, James Robinson, joined with John Reed of Citibank and others to create the Coalition of Services Industries (CSI), to lobby for a set of trade negotiations that would dismantle restrictions on global banking.

American Express in that era was far more than a charge card or travel company. Under Freeman and then Robinson, Amex had sought to become a financial conglomerate. Under Robinson, Amex bought the brokerage Shearson Loeb Rhoades. Shearson then acquired the investment-banking firm Lehman Brothers in 1984, as well as one of the leading retail brokerages, EF Hutton, in 1987. The company, then known as Shearson Lehman/American Express, also bought the mass-market investment company Investors Diversified Services. Later, the whole conglomerate blew up, and Amex reverted to plain old American Express, while Lehman Brothers suffered one of the most spectacular collapses of 2008. But in the 1980s, Amex's invasion of other areas of finance reflected the early breaches of the Glass-Steagall Act.

Amex of that era also wanted to get into commercial banking. It was barred in the US by what remained of the Glass-Steagall wall, but thanks to one of the early bilateral trade deals, the Canada–United States Free Trade Agreement of 1993, Amex was able to operate as a bank in Canada, much to the consternation of Canadian regulatory authorities.

The CSI pushed for a formal advisory panel to the US Trade Representative on services. The panel was duly created in 1984, with Robinson as chair. Robinson also was named head of the business advisory committee on trade to the US president, who at the time was Ronald Reagan. President Reagan's chief of the USTR, former Republican senator Bill Brock of Tennessee, was a key ally of the banking industry.

In the early 1980s, Robinson, Reed, and their associate Joan Spero went on an extensive publicity blitz, giving literally hundreds of speeches and interviews to sell the proposition that with US manufacturing in decline, America could recoup its trade balance by prying open other markets for "financial services." Insisting on more symmetrical trade rules for trade in goods was not part of their pitch. Goods were passé; services were the next new thing.

Clyde Farnsworth, in a November 1982 *New York Times* piece, bought the Robinson story—hook, line, and sinker. Quoting both Robinson and Bill Brock, President Reagan's chief trade negotiator, on the growing importance of services in world trade, Farnsworth concluded, "The United States, with the most advanced service sector, has the most to gain from liberalization."

The services provisions of the Uruguay Round were being incubated during the same period when finance was being deregulated at home, the Basel Accords were attempting to create (weak) ground rules for international banking completion, and the IMF and OECD, prodded by the US Treasury, were pressuring nations to get rid of the last vestiges of capital controls. The 1990s were also a period when the US was pressing Mexico to open its financial system to speculative US dollar investment—a move that had proved disastrous to Mexico in the peso crisis of the mid-1980s.

The final Uruguay Round deal, conceived under Ronald Reagan and George H. W. Bush, but approved by Bill Clinton's administration in 1995, committed the signatories to open up their banking systems. The entire process of trade negotiations had undergone an epochal shift. Whereas trade negotiations had once been about reciprocal tariff reductions and (half-hearted) pressures against the mercantilism of other nations, the key measures in the Uruguay Round were written by and for financial interests. They were all about opening up a deregulated world for banks.

The fact that successive US presidents went to bat to pursue the interests of American finance in the same trade deals that threw American manufacturing industry and its substantially unionized workers under the proverbial bus is another powerful reflection of the restored political power of finance. The Clinton administration picked up this set of priorities where Reagan and Bush I had left off.

During this period, Robert Rubin, who had been co-CEO of Goldman Sachs and would later be chair of the executive committee of Citigroup, served Clinton first as a fund-raiser, then as chair of the new administration's National Economic Council, and in Clinton's second term he was the Treasury secretary. Rubin became a key player in the negotiations over China's accession to the WTO. In that era, China was barred from the WTO and its predecessor, the GATT, as a state-led, antimarket, communist dictatorship. But Rubin took the position that China could be welcomed into the new WTO if it opened up its financial system to American players such as Goldman and Citi. At one key negotiating session with China's reform leader, Zhu Rongji, in April 1999 that was supposed to finalize China's WTO membership, Rubin sent Zhu packing with no agreement because the Chinese premier had refused to make enough concessions on financial access. When Zhu later sweetened the terms, the Clinton administration did its part and delivered WTO membership. There were no comparable commitments on manufacturing.

DELEGATING SOVEREIGNTY TO PRIVATE CORPORATE POWER

Unlike the GATT, which relied on ad hoc retaliatory bluffs and compromises to resolve disputes and create rough justice in the balance of costs and benefits for member nations, the WTO has real power and mandatory rules. These represent lost sovereignty—nominally to a transnational institution, but effectively to "the market"—as personified by the invisible hands of large banks and multinational corporations. In this respect, the WTO regime is not only deliberately destructive of the mixed economy but also antidemocratic, since entire realms of social and economic policy have been removed from national democratic deliberation, while WTO procedures are far less transparent or observant of due process than are the procedures of national democracy.

One can almost identify a rule of thumb: The US fiercely resists subordinating its sovereignty to international bodies or treaties when the purpose is the exposure of US practices in human rights, labor rights, or environmental practices to international scrutiny and law, much less prosecutions through the International Criminal Court. But the US welcomes compromising sovereignty when the effect is to liberate finance and commerce from binding national rules. This double standard speaks volumes about how power is exercised. Indeed, the US has been more willing to constrain its own behavior on sensitive issues of national security via arms control treaties than to bind its labor, environmental, and human-rights practices to international law.

Alongside the GATT process, the US began sponsoring bilateral trade agreements in the 1980s, starting with Israel and Canada. These deals contradicted the GATT principle of general nondiscrimination and equal treatment of all members, since the essence of a bilateral or multilateral trade deal is special treatment.* This contradiction was present at the founding of the postwar trade system, which included colonies with preferential arrangements and, later, the European Common Market as a preferential trading area. In recent years, American presidents have rationalized this double standard by arguing that even if "progress" toward freer trade was blocked at the level of the unwieldy, 177-member WTO, at least it might be achieved among smaller coalitions of the willing. With the failure of the latest proposed WTO trade round to launch after the Seattle protests of 1999, Washington intensified its efforts to negotiate bilateral or multilateral deals. By 2016, the US had bilateral "free-trade agreements" with twenty countries, and investment agreements with several others.

But there was a deeper rationale to the shift in strategy: export of the conservative Washington Consensus. In the several bilateral deals with poorer countries starting in the 1990s, the United States wielded disproportionate power against smaller nations, which were eager both for investment and for access to the US consumer market.

In agreements with developing countries that often had corrupt governments and weak systems of rule of law, US financial interests persuaded the US government to demand parallel systems of private law enforcement, ostensibly to protect their investments from expropriation or extortion. Poor countries that sought more US private investment or better market access had to agree to private adjudication panels to resolve any disputes (usually in favor of the investor because the United States stacked both the membership and the rules).

---

*The same contradiction applies in the case of the WTO, successor to the GATT.

In pressuring smaller nations to go along with this system, the US had powerful allies in the IMF and the World Bank, which urged developing nations to open their economies to private investment, often demanding greater openness as a condition of approving loans. Both institutions applauded a parallel system of private law to safeguard the rights of investors.

The financial industry realized it had a device for circumventing national governments and courts—one that was too good to limit to deals with the third world. Why not use it generally? The concept became known as investor-state dispute settlement (ISDS). The idea was that any disputes under trade deals should be referred to special panels that would supersede national courts and laws. The first major agreement among advanced economies to use this device was the North American Free Trade Agreement, approved in 1993.

Under NAFTA, a Canadian company could sue a US state to challenge a regulatory policy as trade-distorting, in a special NAFTA court from which there was no appeal. American companies, or their affiliates in Mexico, could bring similar cases against Canada. Unlike the public legal systems of advanced democracies, which had well-established norms of transparency, due process, and strictures against conflicts of interest, ISDS panels were private, and riddled with conflicts. A panel member could literally serve as a "judge" one day and a lobbyist the next. Ex parte contacts—secret undisclosed lobbying to work the referee—were permitted, and flagrant.

Under NAFTA, Ethyl, a US chemical corporation, challenged a Canadian ban on imports of its gasoline that contained the additive MMT, a suspected neurotoxin. The Canadian government repealed the ban and paid the company $13 million for its loss of revenue. At this writing, Canada is defending corporate suits running into the billions, including a $775 million suit by T. Boone Pickens's Mesa Power Group that is challenging the Ontario Green Energy Act, which promotes local wind farms. Another $500 million suit, by the pharmaceutical giant Eli Lilly, requests that the NAFTA panel override rulings by three tiers of Canadian courts that turned down Lilly's request for a patent extension of one of its drugs. ISDS clauses were part of dozens of other bilateral trade deals negotiated in recent years.

In the proposed TPP with Asia and the parallel Transatlantic

Trade and Investment Partnership (TTIP) with the European Union, such private resolution panels were central to the deals. As innumerable critics have pointed out, it's one thing to insist on private arbitration panels in nations with weakly developed systems of law and transparency or out-and-out corruption. Such extraterritorial panels can move closer to a rule of law. It's quite another matter to use these panels in advanced democracies that have well-developed systems of due process. In those cases, private dispute resolution moves away from the rule of law. In the case of the US and the EU, there is no need for extralegal private dispute panels, except as instruments of corporate end runs.

The TTIP with Europe, launched by the US and the EU in 2013, was billed as a complement to the TPP and a kind of transatlantic counterweight to China. Absurd claims were made for the supposed increases to GDP in the US and Europe if only the deal would be approved. But in the four detailed economic studies on which sponsors relied, only trivial economic gains were projected. And these calculations were based on unrealistic assumptions such as full employment. The TTIP was also billed as promoting "regulatory harmonization," though the fine print made clear that the harmonization was mainly downward.

This was a case of fixing something that wasn't broken—unless "broken" was defined as what remained of the mixed economy. European and US multinationals have no difficulty selling in each other's markets, buying each other's companies, and using extensive supply chains to source production. Tariffs are almost nonexistent, except in farm trade, where both parties desire some protection to stabilize the notorious cyclical nature of agriculture. US-EU trade has roughly doubled, from about $600 billion in 1997 to over $1.1 trillion in 2016. Foreign direct investment has grown at an even faster pace. The main obstacle to a robust recovery in the Atlantic area is not the lack of yet another trade deal, but the drag of austerity policies demanded by the same financial interests that promote the TTIP. China, by contrast, does present real trade challenges, which US trade diplomacy does not begin to address.

However, Europe is more tacitly nationalist than the US in its trade policy. German manufacturers, without being directed by government, know that a national goal is to keep high-value production in Germany, even as lower-cost components may be outsourced. The German apprenticeship system is devoted to keeping high-end industry at home. So is Germany's national development bank, the KfW. The Europeans have insisted on a Common Agricultural Policy, which protects agriculture and violates the norms of free trade, because no European nation wants to lose its farming sector (as a matter of social policy), even if imports from Canada or America are cheaper. Europe also takes justifiable pride in locally produced food. It's very hard to demonstrate that this is a bad bargain, when all factors are considered.

European leaders are also less doctrinaire when it comes to promoting domestic manufacturing. The state-created and state-subsidized Airbus consortium is now competitive with Boeing. In a textbook world, Europe would simply have bought American planes. European trade negotiators also tend to take a tougher line with China, since they don't sacrifice their economy to geopolitical goals the way the US does. Europe has plenty of trade disputes within the EU. But as a consequence of Europe's more heterodox approach to extra-European trade and industrial policy, the EU's trade accounts with the rest of the world are roughly in balance, while America's are chronically in deficit.

A DEEPER LOOK AT THE CHINA PARADOX

In the period after the 1989 massacre at Tiananmen Square, the West had immense leverage over Beijing—leverage that was largely squandered. China in that era was far from a free-market economy. It was also a Leninist, one-party dictatorship. After Tiananmen, Japan suspended a $5.2 billion package of loans. Chinese economic growth dropped to near-recession levels. As James Mann, former Beijing correspondent for the *Los Angeles Times*, wrote, "If ever there was a time when the U.S. held considerable economic leverage over China, this was it."

China desperately needed WTO membership to attain some international legitimacy, to reduce tariffs on its exports to the West, and to facilitate deals with Western multinationals. In those years, the US kept the terms of trade with China on a short leash. They had to be approved by Congress annually. The House of Representatives, then controlled by Democrats, was more sensitive both to complaints from constituents of the harm done by China's state-led exports, and to China's human-rights violations. American presidents tended to be more attuned to the interests of large multinational corporations eager to do business with China.

The first President Bush twice vetoed trade bills that tied annual approval of China's ability to freely access US markets to demonstrable progress on human rights. Candidate Bill Clinton supported those bills. As president, however, Clinton reversed course and persuaded Congress not to enshrine those requirements in law, but to accept instead an executive order to deny benefits to China, absent clear progress on human rights and market opening. When the first deadline approached in May 1994, Clinton acknowledged that little had changed. But instead of imposing penalties, he revoked his own order.

Much of this shift reflects the influence on Clinton of Robert Rubin and others close to Wall Street. Subsequently, in 2000, after extensive lobbying by the Clinton administration, Congress granted China "permanent normal trade relations," sparing presidents the need to do this annual dance. The law still required the Treasury to judge annually whether China was manipulating its currency, the renminbi, to keep it artificially low in order to promote Chinese exports. Though the evidence on this was unambiguous, successive Treasury secretaries kept giving Beijing a pass on that question as well.

Why the coddling of Beijing? American finance was eager for deals with China and had close allies in both the Bush I and Clinton administrations. This relationship continued through the Bush II and Obama presidencies. And thanks to the immense and growing US trade deficit, the US needed foreign banks and governments to buy its Treasury debt. China was now America's largest creditor. American manufacturing industry, meanwhile, was accepting Beijing's terms and producing goods for export in factories located in China.

In both geopolitical and economic terms, it would have made sense to create a timetable for China to reform politically and to temper the state role in the economy. A kind of WTO candidate status could have been created. At the consummation of reforms, China would be rewarded with full WTO membership. Instead, once China promised to cut American financial firms in on the action, it was rewarded with full WTO membership, in 2000. During Clinton's presidency, America's trade deficit with China grew from $20 billion to about $70 billion. One of the benefits of Chinese WTO membership, the administration forecast, was greater trade balance. By 2004, the deficit had grown to $200 billion. At this writing it is about $400 billion.

US presidents, from Bush through Obama, tried to convince themselves and world public opinion that China's mere participation in the WTO would nest Beijing within a global rule-of-law system and promote both political and economic liberalization. Such thinking proved naïvely wishful. "Almost 15 years after China joined the World Trade Organization (WTO) in 2001, the vision of China embracing a rules-governed, market-based global trade system has yet to materialize," wrote Stephen J. Ezell and Robert D. Atkinson, of the Information Technology and Innovation Foundation, in 2015. "If anything, the country's aggressive innovation mercantilism has grown stronger in recent years, as China seeks absolute advantage across a wide range of advanced technology industries."

Surely American diplomats are not that incompetent. The China exception was indulged not because they believed their own fantasies, but because an expanded role for China was so lucrative both for US financial players and for manufacturers no longer committed to domestic production—who welcomed the Chinese low-wage labor market as an export platform.

One set of players was left out of this grand bargain: American workers, who continued to lose decently paid domestic jobs. The idea that labor standards could be exported to China along with US-style democracy and free markets has proved entirely illusory. The communist government of China represses independent trade unions. China today represents a hybrid of capitalism and communism that promotes Chinese nationalism, rewards billionaires, and suppresses wages, worker rights, and dissent. There is an old-fashioned word for that sort of regime: "fascism." Meanwhile China's influence as a world power has only grown.

These chickens came home to roost in 2017, when the Trump administration, which had taken a rhetorical hard line against China, needed Beijing's help on containing North Korea as a nuclear threat. Trump repeatedly had to back down, in exchange for only modest diplomatic help. Despite Chinese president Xi Jiping's posture as a friendly mediator, the North Korean nuclear threats nicely served Beijing's efforts to undercut any hardening of the US policy on trade. In containing China, as both an economic and a geopolitical rival, the US had simply waited too long.

President George H. W. Bush, a former ambassador to Beijing and proponent of closer ties, explained the China fantasy this way: "Economic freedom creates habits of liberty. And habits of liberty create expectations of democracy. . . . Trade freely with China, and time is on our side."

The same belief was echoed by advocates of naïve globalization in the media. "China's going to have a free press. Globalization will drive it," Tom Friedman wrote in *The Lexus and the Olive Tree.*

Eighteen years later, China is no closer to having a free press. Beijing's aggression toward its neighbors in East Asia continues. China has escalated territorial disputes with Taiwan and the Philippines. It has not increased cooperation with the US in the containment of North Korea. China is no closer to having a free press.

Despite claims that WTO membership would accelerate China's progress toward rule of law domestically, China's one-party rule continues, and so does its state-led, intermittently corrupt semi-capitalism. America's trade deficits with Beijing keep setting new records, and China is a far more potent regional and global power in 2018 than it was in 2000, when it was welcomed unconditionally into the WTO. China holds more US public debt than ever—and whenever the Chinese want to pull Washington's chain, they sell some Treasuries.

US diplomacy toward Beijing might be seen as totally incompetent and baffling—were it not for the explanation of how neatly it serves the interests of American global finance and corporate offshore production. Remember: the United States is a nation that for four decades was willing to take the world to the brink of nuclear war in order to contain communist Russia. But with the emergence of China as a military and economic superpower, the US government response has been feeble, even though China becomes more of a force over time.

What explains the difference? American capitalists got nothing from the USSR, so geopolitics and commercial economics aligned.

The China connection, by contrast, confers immense economic benefits for US economic elites.

"Engagement" with China was the all-purpose fudge word. In his 2007 book, *The China Fantasy*, James Mann wrote prophetically that rather than the illusion that integration with China would make China more like the West, the risk was that the West would become more like China.

> The fundamental problem with this strategy of integration is that it raises the obvious question, "Who is integrating whom?" Is the United States integrating China into a new international economic order based on free market principles? Or, on the other hand, is China integrating the United States into an order where democracy is no longer favored and where a government's continuing eradication of all political opposition is accepted or ignored?

China, Mann added, was on the verge of serving as a role model for dictators throughout the world, just as its economic system of state-led semi-capitalism, rather than America's professed economic liberalism, was seen as the preferred approach to development. Ten years later, there is no progress whatever in China moving toward Western-style political liberalism. The United States is becoming its own version of a corporate authoritarian state.

After the 2016 election, MIT economist David Autor, relying on a research study with two colleagues, calculated that if Chinese imports had grown half as slowly after 2000, the manufacturing economy of the American Midwest would have been so much healthier that Hillary Clinton would likely have won Michigan, Wisconsin, Pennsylvania—and the presidency.

The proposed, now defunct Trans-Pacific Partnership is a window on America's self-defeating China policy. Pathetically, the TPP was marketed in contradictory fashion as both a strategy for containing China and a potential outreach to China. Mainly, the deal had a number of special-interest provisions sought by industry. It would have countermanded national patent regimes and given pharmaceutical companies longer terms of patent protection. Special-interest provisions written by the tobacco industry would have undermined national antismoking regulations. These and other measures were sold as nothing more than promotion of freer global commerce. The TPP also included the now standard provision on investor-state dispute settlement, giving private, industry-dominated pseudocourts the power to overrule national laws.

The TPP supposedly would have increased market access for US companies into Asian nations whose national economic development strategies were built around restricting such access or conditioning it on the sharing of trade secrets. The trouble with this premise is that most of the twelve member nations of the proposed TPP already had bilateral deals with the US that had promised the same market opening. But most, notably South Korea, had simply resorted to new subterfuges. There was no reason to believe that the TPP would succeed in market opening where the bilateral deals had failed.

When the effort was launched in 2009, it was marketed as a "pivot to Asia." This claim was preposterous on its face, since the US had never left Asia. The United States maintained about a hundred thousand troops in the region, and the US Seventh Fleet was in its seventh decade of patrolling the western Pacific. The TPP was also promoted as a kind of US-led co-prosperity sphere, in whose absence China would "write the rules" for Asian trade. But this was also ludicrous, since that horse was already out of the barn. Every major nation that had agreed to participate in the TPP already had its own bilateral deals with China. Many did, indeed, fear China's outsized influence in Asia and did want the US to serve as a regional counterweight to Beijing. But nothing in the TPP—mainly a series of special-interest provisions for US industry and finance, combined with token market-opening gestures—would serve that end.

In the propaganda pitch for the TPP, US officials left open the possibility that it would be so attractive that Beijing might someday join. "They've already started putting out feelers about the possibilities of them participating at some point," President Obama said in 2015. This remark created great amusement in China, which had just launched its own rival to the World Bank, the $100 billion Asian Infrastructure Investment Bank. The AIIB enlisted several close US allies as charter members—and pointedly excluded the US. For much of the world, the AIIB instantly became a more attractive alternative to the US-led World Bank. The Beijing Consensus came with its own strings—including preferential trade deals—but in many respects it was preferable to the Washington Consensus, since the strings left national domestic policies alone.

Flush with cash from its immense trade surplus, China has emerged as a global economic superpower—and the sponsor of a rival co-prosperity sphere. By the time the TPP was pronounced dead, China had not only displaced the US as the leading manufacturing nation. The Chinese state was the prime engine of economic development in Africa and Latin America, filling a role once played by the British and later by the Americans. Chinese state capital was financing railroads and port facilities in Africa, in exchange for preferential access to minerals. American companies such as Bechtel, seeking business in Africa, found themselves regularly underbid by the Chinese.

In 2013, the Export-Import Bank of China stated that the central government, including state-owned banks, would provide $1 trillion of financing to Africa in the years to 2025, with the bank accounting for 70–80 percent of direct investments, soft loans, and commercial loans. In December 2015, China pledged $60 billion in new grants, loans, and export credits to help Africa. This scale of investment dwarfed anything committed by the United States or the West. China was already providing the capital and the technology for several ambitious rail projects, including a 466-mile transnational line linking the port city of Djibouti with Addis Ababa, capital of Ethiopia. Chinese state banks provided all of the $4 billion of financing. China has also spent some $50 billion on ports, highways, and airports across the African continent. With these investments come commercial ties and diplomatic influence that the US or its multinational institutions can't match.

Meanwhile, in the Western Hemisphere, where the Monroe Doctrine once warned foreign economic powers to stay out of America's backyard, China had become the dominant source of development capital. In 2000, Latin America sent just 1 percent of its exports to China. By 2010, that number had risen to 10 percent, or $110 billion.

China became a leading customer for Latin American oil, soybeans, iron ore, copper, and wool. Chinese companies poured about $50 billion into the region between 2005 and 2013. In 2015, Beijing committed $250 billion in investment capital to Latin America over a decade. And unlike US capital investments, these came with no requirements about Latin American domestic policies.

These incursions were a serious challenge both to American geo-economic leadership, and to the system of market capitalism that the US was ostensibly promoting. Several Latin American nations that gamely signed onto the TPP at Washington's prodding were among the leading participants in these Chinese deals. But the TPP, a cover for corporate narrow-interest deals, did not address the challenges of China's expansionist mercantilism. The height of irony is that while Marxists are described as ideological proselytizers and American businessmen as pragmatists, China was not in Africa or Latin America to sell communism. China was there to do business and, not incidentally, to extend its geopolitical reach as a great power.

US trade diplomacy began in the 1940s by recognizing the necessary balance between free commercial markets and a regulated form of capitalism. After seven decades of shifting goals, its two notable achievements were these: the destruction of the economics and politics of a mixed economy in the US and Europe, and the enabling of a communist dictatorship that practiced the opposite of free markets, as America's main global rival.

President Obama's top trade official, the man who had engineered the failed TPP, was Michael Froman, formerly chief of staff to Robert Rubin in the Clinton administration. In the ten years between these two government gigs, Froman was a managing director at Citigroup, again working closely with Rubin. The TPP was already in deep trouble legislatively when the election of Donald Trump administered the coup de grâce. Most Democrats in Congress had voted against the TPP. Progressives were in a race with right-wing populists to devise a better trade policy, but Trump got there first. Maybe, if Presidents Obama and Clinton before him had not put the interests of finance first in their trade deals, Trump would not have gotten there at all.

THE TRADING SYSTEM
AND THE THIRD WORLD

This book addresses mainly the negative impact of a pro-corporate brand of globalization on citizens of advanced democracies, and on democracy itself. A defense of this version of globalization holds that a freer flow of capital, goods, and people helps poor countries to develop. Defenders of globalism often blame working people in the Global North for wanting to hold back their even poorer brothers and sisters in the Global South. Don't these protectionists care about the poorest of the poor?

In fact, there is no evidence that laissez-faire trade is the best route to the economic development of poor nations—or of rich ones. As this review of the trading system has suggested, countries such as Japan, South Korea, and China that violated free-market norms with strategies of neomercantilism have gained from the greater openness of the West. But this opportunism does not exactly make the case for free trade. It merely shows that one-sided trading nations that push exports but resist imports and coerce "partnerships" can gain by gaming the system. And while the planned capitalism of Japan and Korea has improved the equality of wages and salaries in those countries compared to much of the West, Chinese inequality has risen dramatically. The same is true of most of Africa, where abject poverty continues to coexist with the staggering wealth of a few corrupt potentates and their capitalist allies.

The most authoritative recent work on global income distribution finds that the world has grown significantly more unequal in recent decades, both within countries and between countries. Rich people in the rich countries have grown even richer, while at least half of their citizens have lost ground in absolute terms, despite increases in average GDP per capita. In the case of China, *average* income has grown relative to the West but internal inequality has increased dramatically.

In one of the most comprehensive studies of global inequality, the former World Bank economist Branko Milanović found, looking at the world as a whole, that between 1988 and 2008, 44 percent of all the income gain went to the top 5 percent of earners. The question of whether the West should destroy its own social contract in order to aid the Global South is precisely the wrong question. The right question is whether a different form of globalization is possible. And of course it is.

Let's not forget that the era after World War II was good not just for Europe and North America. It was a period of much higher growth for

Latin America too, as well as for Japan and Korea. Limits on finan-cialization were salutary for the entire system. A more limited form of globalization would allow more policy space for nations to have a social compact, using traditional tools of public investment, planning, and regulations to protect labor and limit predatory finance.

There are limits to the capacity (or the right) of nations to impose social standards on other nations. However, democratic nations could and should use policies such as tariffs to limit the damage to their own systems and to encourage trading nations to have at least minimally decent labor and human rights protections. If some nations choose not to, that's their right, but they shouldn't get the same trade privi-leges as others do. Such restriction was exactly the road not taken when American leaders were considering whether to grant China full privileges of WTO membership. Beijing actually got more than full privileges: China was granted the right to barrier-free exports as an advanced nation while retaining its right to block imports as a devel-oping nation.

Wouldn't conditional trade retard the economic growth of the developing world? To believe that, you would have to believe that the best road to growth is exploitation of a country's own people. China has achieved growth rates of close to 10 percent by grossly underpay-ing its own workers relative to their productivity and undercutting the wages of workforces in the rest of the world. By contrast, Japan's version of state-led capitalism at a comparable stage of development, despite some tactical similarities, achieved prodigious growth and yet created a more equal Japan. China, as a number of development economists have urged, could shift to a strategy that pays its workers better and relies more on efforts to increase domestic demand and consumption rather than on predatory exports.

It's also possible to revise the rules of globalization to reduce the amount of damage done by speculative private finance and to expand the role of transparent social investment. We could provide a lot more debt relief, as well as imposing a Tobin tax (see Chapter 3) on short-term financial transactions. Though the West has less economic influ-ence than it once did, the markets of Europe and North America are still the world's largest, which gives the West immense power to influ-ence the rules for the global economy as a whole. Those rules were once used to promote balanced domestic social contracts. Lately, they have been used to enrich the already rich, often in concert with the repression of labor in the third world, and at the expense of decent labor standards in the West as well.

The point is not that Japan, South Korea, China, and other emergent economies are doing something fundamentally wrong or inefficient by having industrial policies, subsidies, and managed trade strategies to promote their own economic growth. This is precisely what the West did at earlier stages of its own development. The point, rather, is that the system needs more realistic rules and norms, so that there is a fairer balance of benefits. That means balance between developing and developed countries, balance between capital and labor, and balance between market norms and social standards. Today, both the global trading system and US trade policy are promoting imbalance.

If we care about global as well as national income distribution, the laissez-faire market is not the place to look. Free markets tend to produce extremes. A more egalitarian income distribution, combined with strong rates of economic growth, requires a democratic polity. The global trading system is no polity, but is a rampant market increasingly led by an alliance of corporate and government autocrats—one that steadily weakens democratic states and societies.

9

TAXES AND THE CORPORATE STATE

L ike much of the postwar social and economic system, a progressive tax structure was a legacy of World War II—yet another element of egalitarian capitalism that was gradually eroded as power shifted back to financial elites. In the US and the UK, wartime income tax rates for the rich were set as high as 94 percent in the US and 98 percent in Britain. This high rate of taxation was tolerated as an exigency of war. Yet when the war ended, taxes did not revert to prewar levels. Far from it.

In the US, the top bracket remained at 91 percent until 1964. In the UK, the Labour government that took office in July 1945 kept top marginal tax rates on capital income at 98 percent for the wealthy until 1951. The top rate on labor income was as high as 83 percent. Because of exemptions and deductions, effective rates were lower; however, the well-to-do still paid upwards of 60 percent of their incomes in tax. Taxes on corporations were also high—over 50 percent of corporate profits in most of Europe and North America. Governments were serious about tax enforcement, and the opportunities for evasion were scant.

This anomaly of steeply progressive taxation is worth some reflection. Normally, rates would have dropped substantially after the total mobilization of a war. That's what had happened after every other major war, in both the US and in Europe. But in the postwar era, the Cold War provided a rationale to maintain a costly military establishment, while an expanding welfare state also soaked up revenues. The political balance of power had not yet shifted back to business, especially to financial capital, and public spending was popular. So, inertia was on the side of keeping tax rates both high and progressive. The taxes, in turn, funded a substantial public sector.

On the continent, most of which had been occupied by the Nazis, the fiscal system had to be rebuilt. As in the US and Britain, this was an era of extensive public investments. As the welfare state expanded, tax-financed public spending rose to about half of GDP. By the 1970s, the top rate on wage and salary income in most of continental Europe was between 60 and 70 percent. Germany's was the lowest, at 56 percent, and Sweden's the highest, at 83 percent.

Progressive taxes were part of a valued social compact, yet they were not the most egalitarian part. One can only redistribute so much after the fact. The most important aspect was the egalitarian distribution of what economists call primary income—wages, salaries, income from capital—as well as the public investment that served a broad public.

In addition, the financing of welfare-state programs was relatively flat, mostly via payroll charges. This fiscal structure was part of the logic of social insurance. Payroll deductions were seen as comparable to insurance premiums. Politically, benefits were experienced as prepaid and earned. Roosevelt famously defended the flat financing structure of Social Security as political assurance that no future politician could kill the program, because voters believed they had paid for it in advance. (In fact, the system was mostly pay-as-you-go, with one generation's taxes paying for the previous generation's retirement.)

Another source of Europe's relatively flat financing of public services was the turn to value-added taxes (VATs) beginning in the 1950s and expanding further in the 1960s. VATs, now used throughout Europe with rates of typically 20–25 percent, are a kind of sales tax, where the tax is levied at each stage of value creation. A business is able to take a credit or deduction for a VAT paid on inputs. So the tax cycles through the system and is effectively paid on final consumption.

Despite the relatively flat financing, social insurance is inherently redistributive—from the well to the sick, from the employed to the unemployed, from the rich to the poor, and from working-age people to the old and the young. A public welfare state was a giant step toward a more equal society because it allowed for a broad diffusion of benefits such as pensions, health coverage, decent housing, free education, subsidized public transit, and unemployment insurance—what the British usefully call social income. These are in-kind services, free or partly subsidized, that one gets as a citizen, as distinct from one's market-derived income.

Taken as a whole, counting the flat payroll taxes and graduated income taxes, the postwar fiscal system was moderately progressive, on both sides of the Atlantic and on both sides of the revenue and outlay equation. More important, it was regarded as broadly legitimate. Taxes paid for benefits that people valued. Individuals of high income and wealth paid at a notably higher rate. In the US in the 1940s and 1950s, people of median income paid a very low rate of tax—under 10 percent of gross incomes. In 1952, the corporate income tax accounted for 33 percent of all federal tax revenue. By 2016, for comparison, that share was down to just 8 percent.

The overarching social contract, known in some quarters as tax-and-spend, enjoyed wide public support. The origin of that phrase, which Ronald Reagan turned into an epithet, was a saying attributed to Roosevelt's aide Harry Hopkins: "Tax and tax, spend and spend, *elect and elect*." For two generations, it worked—as economics and as politics.

UPENDING A FISCAL COMPACT

The loss of tax fairness and legitimacy came in three phases: first domestic, next global, and then, in a convenient feedback loop, global competition to cut taxes supercharged further domestic tax cutting. In the middle and late 1970s, as economic growth and corporate profits sagged, financial and corporate lobbies began pressing for what were soon branded "supply-side" tax cuts. This campaign slightly anticipated but prefigured the election of Thatcher in the UK in 1979 and of Reagan in the US in 1980.

At the level of economic theory, the supply-side vogue was part of the counterrevolution against John Maynard Keynes. The economics of Keynes had stressed demand: keep aggregate demand strong, via both wages and public outlays, and the economy will perform at or near its capacity. Wrong, countered the supply-siders: if taxes are too high, they will destroy incentives and kill the golden goose of invention and entrepreneurship. Indeed, if you cut taxes, especially on capital and on income from capital, the resulting jolt to economic growth will supposedly make up the revenue loss, despite lower tax rates.

As part of this rebranding, an obscure lobby called the American Council on Capital Gains and Estate Taxation changed its name in 1975 to the American Council for Capital Formation. Who could be opposed to that? Headed by Charls Walker, one of Washington's superlobbyists, the council soon signed up as clients GM, Ford, GE, Gulf Oil, Bethlehem Steel, Procter & Gamble, and Union Carbide, as well as several trade associations, including the new Business Roundtable, which Walker himself had helped to launch.

Six rounds of so-called supply-side tax cuts followed, beginning in 1978 under Democrat Jimmy Carter. The result was one of the most robust natural experiments ever conducted. In every instance, rosy projections fell short; revenues fell below what they would have been at higher rates. The ensuing economic stimulus resulted mainly from the enlarged deficits, not from increased investment. Nor was there any evidence that taxes had killed growth. The sources of the sluggish 1970s lay elsewhere—in the collapse of the Bretton Woods system and the OPEC price increases, compounded by the tight money policy of the Federal Reserve.

The driving force behind these tax cuts was not economic theory; it was politics. The supply-siders were fond of invoking the first of the major postwar tax cuts, proposed by President Kennedy in 1962 at a speech to the Economic Club of New York. Congress approved the cut in early 1964, three months after Kennedy's death, taking the top marginal rate on personal income down from 91 percent to 70.

Kennedy had campaigned on the theme that America was underperforming. His Council of Economic Advisers included the leading Keynesians of their generation, Walter Heller and James Tobin. In his kitchen cabinet was the most famous Keynesian of all, John Kenneth Galbraith. But Kennedy had only the barest legislative majority in Congress. A debate ensued about what sort of economic stimulus to apply. Galbraith, who in 1958 had written movingly about the shabbiness of America's public household in *The Affluent Society*, wanted a deficit-financed increase in public investment. The policy would do double duty. The deficit itself would be a tonic; likewise the public improvements.

The more centrist neo-Keynesians on Kennedy's Council of Economic Advisers argued that a deficit was a deficit. If the goal was stimulus, a dollar of tax cut was as good as a dollar of public spending. That premise has subsequently been disproved. A dollar of tax cut is less efficient as stimulus, especially when some of it goes to the rich, because the rich don't spend all of it. By contrast, when you increase public spending by a dollar, every penny is injected into the economy.

But far more important than the economics was the politics. With Congress narrowly divided, key committees such as House Ways and Means were in the hands of conservative Democrats, in this case Chairman Wilbur Mills of Arkansas, and business lobbying was already resurgent. So a tax cut was a far easier sell than an increase in public investment. The moderate neo-Keynesians won the debate. The cut was duly enacted in 1964, after Kennedy's death. A succession of deeper supply-side cuts followed, and sponsors invariably invoked the wisdom of John Kennedy.

Under Jimmy Carter, the economy in the late 1970s was in far worse shape than the one that Kennedy inherited in 1961. Carter, not much of a liberal, was in desperate need of some kind of economic tonic. Deficits incurred under Keynesian auspices were in bad repute. But suddenly, deficits resulting from tax cuts could be blessed by conservatives as supply-side medicine. Carter got on board, proposing cuts in both the personal income tax and the capital gains tax. Given this opening, the business lobbies went into high gear. The eventual 1978 law modestly reduced income tax rates but included a whopping cut in the effective rate on capital gains from 49 to 28 percent, and capital gains are, of course, heavily tilted to the wealthy.

In the United States, the late 1970s also witnessed a state-level revolt against property taxes, which had spun out of control as inflation pushed up housing prices. The property tax is based on assessed valuations, which were soaring. Citizens, facing earnings that lagged behind the cost of living, had no power to vote themselves a raise. They did have the power to approve ballot initiatives capping or cutting property taxes, and they used that power in state after state, beginning in California.

The tax revolt of the 1970s reflected the accident of inflation coupled with a political failure that created an ideological windfall for the right. As inflation increased assessments, California politicians could not agree on a formula to reduce tax rates so that homeowners would be held harmless. Taxes kept rising, mechanically. Voter anger gave legitimacy to a fringe figure, Howard Jarvis, who had long been regarded as a crackpot. The success of Jarvis's Proposition 13 in June 1978, cutting property taxes by over $6 billion, signaled that the tax-and-spend bargain was losing credibility with ordinary people. It energized the national drive to cut taxes. Proposition 13 prefigured Reagan—and in a sense prefigured Trump. When mainstream politics does not address core concerns about people's livelihoods, voters look to the extremes.

Once Reagan took over in 1981, more massive federal tax cuts followed, heavily tilted to the upper brackets. The impact on revenue losses was partly camouflaged by a large increase in Social Security payroll taxes, approved in 1983. That tax hike, enacted at the recommendation of a bipartisan commission, was intended to create a surplus to pay for the retirement of the baby boom generation three decades later.

The cause of the shortfall in Social Security reserves is widely misunderstood. Social Security's actuaries did not fail to notice that a huge wave of boomers would retire early in the twenty-first century. Social Security planned accordingly, basing payroll tax projections on long-term trends in wage growth. But that growth did not hold. So the real source of the larger-than-anticipated shortfall in projected Social Security balances was stagnant wages. When worker earnings fell below the postwar trend, starting in the 1970s, so did payroll tax receipts. Had wage increases continued to track productivity growth, as they had during the three decades after the war, Social Security would have been in surplus.

As a result of the payroll tax hikes enacted in 1983, a whole generation of workers was hit with a substantial tax increase, since payroll taxes are levied on the first dollar of income, with no deductions or exemptions. But thanks to consolidated government accounting, this massive revenue increase is scored as general government income; there is no separate Social Security "lockbox."

Thus, as Reagan's supply-side cuts were draining the government of revenue, higher Social Security taxes were making up part of the loss. The incidence of taxation was dramatically shifting to workers—higher payroll taxes, along with cuts in less progressive taxes on income, capital gains, and corporate profits. But with consolidated accounting, the supply-siders could attribute higher revenues to the magic of supply-side incentives. Reagan's tax cuts were tilted upward. For median-income taxpayers, the hikes in payroll taxes exceeded the income tax cuts. So, ordinary citizens experienced a net tax increase, at a time when public services were being cut. The tax-and-spend bargain was becoming steadily less attractive, just as the right intended.

Soon, however, even with the payroll tax increases, net deficits did go up. Though supply-side tax cuts were an economic failure, the formula was a stroke of political genius: cut taxes, express alarm when deficits increase, slash social spending to reduce the deficit, and then repeat. Such was the routine under Presidents Carter, Reagan, Bush I, Bush II (twice), and most recently was also the program of Trump. The strategy also converted the hapless Democrats from the party of possibility to the party of the green eyeshade. Somebody had to worry about fiscal responsibility, and Democrats stepped into the vacuum. In this shift, the Democrats were also prodded to embrace austerity by their Wall Street donors and policy advisers, who were often the same people.

PROGRESSIVES AS FISCAL SCOLDS

In 1984, the Democratic nominee, Walter Mondale, gave one of the most self-defeating acceptance speeches ever delivered by a Democrat. The centerpiece was a pledge to raise taxes. Mondale later confirmed that it was Robert Rubin, one of his largest donors, who had put him up to it. Mondale declared:

> Whoever is inaugurated in January, the American people will have to pay Mr. Reagan's bills. The budget will be squeezed. Taxes will go up. . . . By the end of my first term, I will reduce the Reagan budget deficit by two-thirds. Let's tell the truth. It must be done, it must be done. Mr. Reagan will raise taxes, and so will I. He won't tell you. I just did.

The crowd did not exactly go wild. Mondale expected acclaim for his honesty and probity. Not surprisingly, the voters were not moved by a Democrat's pledge to raise taxes to cut deficits. Mondale lost forty-nine states. For the next three decades, the pattern repeated. Republicans cut taxes, deficits followed, Democrats dutifully expended political capital to raise taxes. Republicans then excoriated Democrats for raising taxes, and gleefully cut them again. A core theme of Clinton's second term, and of the Obama presidency after 2009, was the urgent march to budget balance—hardly a theme to stir the imagination or allegiance of hard-pressed working- and middle-class families.

With higher taxes, and lower benefits to show for them, the social contract tilted further against ordinary working people. The Democrats lost their principal source of appeal. The Republican Party had two wings ostensibly opposed to each other: the supply-siders and the deficit hawks. But despite the plain contradiction, they worked in tandem to destroy the Democrats as a progressive party with a credible appeal to working people.

By the 1990s, a nominally bipartisan coalition of mostly Wall Street conservatives had mounted a public relations campaign, issuing dire warnings about the perils of deficits. The first incarnation was the Concord Coalition, and several others followed, many of them bankrolled by the private-equity billionaire Peter G. Peterson. They had close allies in top Clinton officials with Wall Street connections, such as Robert Rubin, and in the late 1990s Clinton made budget balance one of his paramount themes. The pattern was repeated under Obama, who shifted his emphasis from recovery spending to budget balance in late 2009, long before the recovery was robust.

In 2010, Obama created the Peterson-inspired Bowles-Simpson Commission, which recommended an automated formula to bring down the deficit. The commission's plan was not adopted, but it gave broad legitimacy to the bad idea that the economy's paramount problem was not a sluggish recovery and low wages, but public deficits. A slightly different version of the same policy was enacted in the budget deal of 2013, which included an automatic "sequester" mechanism to ratchet down spending.

This perverse shift in what Democrats stood for was another reflection of the resurgent influence of Wall Street. Obama did appoint some progressives to other offices, but the key economic and budgetary portfolios went to fiscal conservatives, most of whom were protégés of Rubin. These were people who had personally benefited from the Wall Street–Washington revolving door.

These officials accepted the mistaken logic of what Paul Krugman scathingly dubbed the "confidence fairy"—the magical idea that if you cut deficits, business confidence will return and investment will soar. It was another variant on the supply-side claims. But the deficits were cut and the fairy never came. What dragged down the recovery was not a lack of business confidence caused by deficits. The culprits were flat wages, mortgage foreclosures, financial losses, overly indebted households, and traumatized banks. More public investment could have broken this stalemate. Cutting public outlay to reduce deficits only worsened the slump.

The logic of the deficit hawks was both bad economics and impossible politics for a progressive party. For Democrats to embrace fiscal probity and deliver little else was to do the right's dirty work, and to squander their own appeal. A pledge to balance budgets was no more resonant with hard-pressed working- and middle-class voters under Obama than it had been under Mondale three decades earlier. Both had been listening to the same people—billionaire investors and political donors more concerned about price stability, corporate profits, and limited government than about balanced economic performance that served working families.

Meanwhile, in the UK, the Thatcher revolution drastically flattened the tax system. Disproportionate tax cuts at the top and modest cuts at the bottom were more than offset by a slashing of social benefits. As in the US, the terms of the social contract thus worsened. Upon taking office in 1979, the Thatcher government reduced the top tax rate on wage and salary income from 83 percent to 60. In 1988, it was further reduced to 40 percent. Rates on capital gains and other investment income were also cut. The Thatcher government was obsessed with cutting public deficits, which the Tories rebranded as the "public-sector borrowing requirement," as a reminder that deficits had to be financed by government debt—which was supposedly crowding out private investment. Both the tax cuts and the reduced public deficits meant less money to finance public services, and reductions in welfare-state outlays followed.

All this put Britain's postwar social contract in a three-way squeeze. Taxation was now both lower and less redistributive. There was less revenue to finance social income, and the primary distribution of wage and salary income was becoming more unequal. Greater economic precariousness, especially at the bottom, meant a need for more public services, not fewer. But the British working and middle classes were getting less back for the taxes they paid.

The center left also became more indulgent of plain tax evasion. On his last day in office, President Bill Clinton pardoned a notorious tax felon named Marc Rich. A commodities trader and hedge fund billionaire, Rich had fled to Switzerland in 1983 to escape what was then the largest criminal tax evasion prosecution in history. Rich and his partner were charged with sixty-five counts of tax evasion, racketeering, wire fraud, and violating the oil embargo with Iran. For a time he was on the FBI's Ten Most Wanted list. The tax evasion scheme involved a bewildering array of offshore trusts and money-laundering maneuvers.

While Rich was on the lam in Switzerland, his ex-wife Denise donated an estimated million dollars to the Clintons and the Democratic Party, including $450,000 to the Clinton Foundation and over $100,000 to Hillary Clinton's Senate campaign—and lobbied hard for the pardon. Clinton's inner circle managed to keep the pardon deliberations away from the federal prosecutors in New York who had brought the case. The pardon of Marc Rich nicely epitomized the marriage of offshore tax evasion with corrupt wealth blessed by Democrats.

A GLOBAL RACE TO THE BOTTOM

Globalization supercharged the ability of corporations and very wealthy investors to avoid paying taxes and to play governments off against each other. This process took several forms. The most straightforward was competition among nations to cut tax rates. The supply-side mantra had an international dimension. Supposedly, high taxes on investment income were not only depressing incentive and entrepreneurship; they were also creating international competitive disadvantage.

In the 1980s, nations governed by conservatives began reducing their tax rates to attract investment. Other nations soon followed, ratcheting rates generally downward in a game of follow the leader. Between 1981 and 2013, corporate tax rates in OECD countries were cut, on average, from 47.5 percent to 25.5. In Germany, Britain, and Canada, rates were cut approximately in half. The US retained a relatively high nominal rate of 35 percent,* but an effective rate (thanks to loopholes) of about half that. Yet, American conservatives regularly warned that the US was an international outlier and needed to cut corporate rates to avoid losing business.

In addition to slashing corporate tax rates, several nations reduced taxes on dividends, interest, and capital gains—all forms of income heavily concentrated among the wealthy. Individual income tax rates were also cut during this period, from an average top marginal rate of about 75 percent among all OECD nations in 1980, to a top rate of about 40 percent by 2007. On capital gains income, the OECD average is now approximately 20 percent, and twelve OECD member countries have no capital gains taxes all, including Switzerland, the Netherlands, Belgium, and Luxembourg.

The new eastern European members of the EU aggressively cut taxes to attract Western capital. Slovakia in 2004 cut its personal and corporate tax rates to a flat 19 percent. Bulgaria and Macedonia went Slovakia one better, with a rate of just 10 percent. These moves pushed Germany to cut its own taxes defensively. When Ireland cut taxes, the Netherlands followed. For conservative governments, this tax competition trend created a rationale for policies they wanted to pursue anyway. Even center-left governments, such as British Labour after 1997 and the German SPD-led government under Gerhard Schröder beginning in 1998, felt compelled to follow. In 2007, Sweden, Europe's most resolutely social democratic nation, abandoned its long-standing (and modest) tax on wealth.

These trends made the tax system flatter and less progressive. They reduced the state's revenue, leaving an unpalatable choice of increasing deficits, cutting valued services, or raising other taxes that hit citizens more directly. As the international tax scholar Reuven Avi-

---

*The total nominal rate averages 38.9 percent, counting state taxes.

Yonah has observed, tax competition undermines the revenue base of the modern welfare state—creating a Catch-22 dilemma: "Globalization and tax competition lead to a fiscal crisis for countries that wish to continue to provide social insurance to their citizens at the same time that demographic factors and the increased income inequality, job insecurity, and income volatility that result from globalization render such social insurance more necessary."

Antitax conservative leaders welcomed and promoted the trend, using it as a rationale to cut their own national taxes. Speaking at the 2014 Conservative Party convention, Chancellor of the Exchequer George Osborne said, "In a modern global economy where people can move their investment from one country to another at the touch of a button and companies can relocate jobs overnight—the economics of high taxation are a thing of the past."

Even as nominal rates were coming down, neither corporations nor individual investors paid anything like the stated rates. An increasingly globalized economy, with national governments largely in the pockets of big business, creates multiple opportunities both for semilegal tax avoidance and flatly illegal tax evasion. With the rise of the multinational corporation and friendly conservative governments came a variety of creative accounting maneuvers, which caused taxes to be booked in locales with very low or zero rates of taxation—or booked nowhere at all.

Friendly governments in Washington and London facilitated international tax evasion through measures such as the Reagan administration's abolition in 1984 of the withholding tax on interest income earned abroad. This was a unilateral invitation for tax cheating. Subsequent tax treaties also got rid of the withholding tax on cross-border investments between the US and Japan and the US and Canada, making tax enforcement more difficult and tax evasion easier. In recent years, seven major European countries, including Germany, France, the Netherlands, and Britain, have repealed the withholding of taxes on bank accounts held by foreigners.

The Reagan administration not only cut taxes, but cut funding for the IRS, which was overwhelmed trying to track the complexity of offshore tax evasion deals. Its small audit force could keep up with only a tiny fraction of likely offenders. Some conservatives viewed tax evasion as a legitimate way of reducing tax burdens. As one commentator wrote, "Starving the beast by avoiding or evading taxes produces a benefit because it reduces the size and scope of government."

MORE SWISS CHEESE

Beyond tax competition (which at least is transparent), globalization has enabled both corporations and individual investors to hide assets and profits in tax havens, nations that do not share financial information with the tax and regulatory authorities of the corporation's or investor's true domicile. This use of tax havens lowers taxes in two ways—one barely legal because of creative accounting, the other illegal.

The legal way—but only because major nations permit it—is the booking of profits actually earned in the US or Europe in havens that have low or nonexistent corporate taxes. Major US-based corporations, including Starbucks and Apple, use such maneuvers to cut their tax liability to almost nothing. More on that part of the story in a moment. The illegal way is to use a combination of trusts and other straw entities to hide assets and earnings from tax authorities.

Until the 1970s, Switzerland was the only tax haven of note. Ever since the 1920s, the Swiss banking system had promised its depositors secrecy through anonymous, numbered bank accounts. Much to the consternation of tax authorities in neighboring nations, notably Germany and France, Swiss banks were complicit both in hiding money gleaned from criminal activity and in facilitating simple tax evasion by wealthy individuals.

A French or German investor could stash assets in a Swiss bank account, hide them from domestic tax authorities, and pay no tax on the income. In the 1920s, foreign funds held in secret Swiss bank accounts grew at a rate of 14 percent a year, according to the economist Gabriel Zucman. The Swiss built up a mythology that they were performing a humanitarian service by allowing persecuted peoples, such as German Jews, to hide assets from their tormentors. A postwar commission chaired by Paul Volcker on financial restitution for Jewish victims of Nazism revealed these claims to be nonsense. Most users of Swiss bank accounts were ordinary tax evaders—plus no small number of more serious criminals.

After World War II, the Swiss, neutral during the war and suspected of hiding a lot of Nazi loot, came under pressure from the United States to reform bank secrecy and share information. They responded by falsifying records, certifying that assets whose beneficial owners were Europeans or Americans belonged to shell corporations or to Swiss citizens. The US government soon dropped the matter; the revenue loss to the IRS was modest and the Cold War dictated other priorities.

In the 1970s and 1980s, Switzerland became an unfortunate role model, and the global tax system became a lot more baroque. Several other nations, in both the Caribbean and the fringes of Europe, became tax havens. A tax haven helps owners of wealth and income from capital to illegally evade taxation by failing to report the income or by disguising the true owner. As pioneered by the Swiss, bankers located in tax havens hold portfolios of stocks and bonds for Americans or Europeans, but do not report the income to the tax authorities of the nations where owners actually reside. Bankers may also provide useless information attributing the income to sham trusts that do not list the true owners of the assets.

By contrast, the other major Western nations have tax treaties with each other that require the sharing of information. So, if your intent is to cheat the IRS, it doesn't help to stash your fortune in France or Germany. Hedge funds and private-equity companies, whose actual operations are in the US and Europe, typically incorporate in offshore tax havens. In the meantime, Panama and Luxembourg specialized in welcoming the creation of shell corporations whose sole purpose was to disguise true ownership.

After the financial collapse of 2008, one of the worst offenders was revealed to be one of Switzerland's leading banks, UBS. In the investigations that ensued, the Swiss came under increasing pressure to cooperate with the authorities of other nations. The Swiss did work with other financial regulators, but Switzerland managed to preserve much of its role as an enabler of international tax evasion. In this enterprise, it has a partner in neighboring Luxembourg. In a convenient division of labor, Switzerland provides the banks, while the Grand Duchy of Luxembourg hosts shell corporations.

The Grand Duchy allows mutual funds for wealthy people (such as hedge funds and private-equity operations) to disguise their true owners. Tiny Luxembourg has a population of just 543,000, but it is the legal home to half of all the world's mutual funds. A fund based in Luxembourg can use a Swiss bank for its financial operations, but when the Swiss share tax information with other national tax authorities, the identity of the actual taxpayer is a black hole of anonymity, thanks to the Luxembourg-based trust. The Swiss can shrug and insist that they are complying with their own tax treaty obligations.

The EU has done nothing to address these illegal evasions. To add insult to injury, the current president of the European Commission, Jean-Claude Juncker, is a former prime minister of Luxembourg. In that role, Juncker courted multinational corporations to make Luxembourg their legal domicile, so that they could evade the higher tax rates of their true headquarters nations and pay corporate tax at Luxembourg's token levels. For instance, Amazon, on European sales of €9.1 billion, generated taxable profits of only €20 million, all of it in Luxembourg.

Investigations by the International Consortium of Investigative Journalists revealed hundreds of sweetheart tax deals, many of them brokered personally by Juncker when he was finance minister and then prime minister. The technical maneuvers were worked out by accounting firms such as Ernst & Young and KPMG. The corporations included Skype, IKEA, FedEx, GlaxoSmithKline, Accenture, Reckitt Benckiser, Disney, Pearson, and Burberry. Juncker was selected to lead the EC, the executive branch of the EU, despite an ongoing investigation by the EC's outgoing vice chairman, Joaquín Almunia, into whether Luxembourg's tax concessions amounted to illegal subsidies under EU rules.

The finance ministers of France, Germany, and Italy, following Juncker's 2014 election to head the EC, indignantly wrote a joint letter requesting action under the EU's (mostly useless) common tax rules, calling for mandatory and automatic exchange of information on cross-border tax rulings, including transfer pricing; a register identifying beneficiaries of trusts, shell companies, and other nontransparent entities; and measures against tax havens. No such action was forthcoming. Under EU law, it takes only one member government to veto such proposals.

The same Jean-Claude Juncker, meanwhile, was a leading architect and proponent of the Transatlantic Trade and Investment Partnership (TTIP). Though this overarching trade and investment deal covers countless areas of supposed regulatory harmonization, one can search the draft agreement in vain for anything that cracks down on illegal tax evasion.

On the contrary, under other trade deals with investor-state dispute settlement (ISDS) clauses such as the one proposed for the TTIP and the TPP, twenty-four countries have been sued by corporations or investors for enforcing tax policies in ways that allegedly reduced net profits. Countries that had tax policies challenged by corporations via ISDS clauses include India, Romania, Mexico, Ecuador, and Uganda. Vodafone has been suing India since 2007 over whether capital gains taxes were owed in an offshore transaction. Critics of the TTIP have warned that it will reduce the ability of governments to crack down on corporate tax evasion. The double standard in the use of trade agreements to thwart regulation but not to address the hiding of financial assets, money laundering, or tax evasion says a lot about who is ultimately calling the shots.

ISLES OF DECEPTION

While Switzerland and Luxembourg cater substantially to individual investors, other offshore tax havens have promoted themselves as locations in which corporations could fictitiously book profits. More precisely, lawyers and accountants for large multinational companies helped locales like the Cayman Islands play that role. The Caymans basically have no local economy other than tourism and a very small amount of agriculture. Yet they are home to thousands of banks, trusts, hedge funds, and other offshore entities whose Cayman address is a law office or a postbox and whose real homes are in New York or London. One five-story office building on Grand Cayman, Ugland House, is the registered legal address of 18,557 companies, some of which are nominally based in law offices, others only in postboxes.

The use of tax havens is not limited to offshore venues such as the Bahamas or Panama. It includes parts of Europe, notably Ireland, the

Channel Islands, Luxembourg, and the Netherlands. Ireland, in the "Celtic Tiger" era, sought to attract foreign investment by offering a very low rate on corporate tax and negotiating additional concessions in particular deals. Intel, which builds an average of one immense chip factory every two years, has played Mexico, Costa Rica, Ireland, and Israel against each other, and manages to avoid paying US corporate tax entirely.

At the heart of corporate offshore tax evasion is an accounting maneuver known as transfer pricing. A corporation such as Apple or Starbucks or Caterpillar can create a subsidiary based in a low-tax jurisdiction, and arrange for that subsidiary to bill the parent company for various goods or services. The profits are thus booked in the low-tax nation, and the corporation as a whole pays little or no tax.

The Congressional Research Service found that US-based multinational corporations booked 43 percent of their foreign earnings in five tax haven countries: Bermuda, Ireland, Luxembourg, the Netherlands, and Switzerland. Yet only 4 percent of these companies' foreign workforces were actually based in those countries. An investigation by three think tanks revealed that 367 of the largest 500 US-based corporations had set up at least 10,336 tax haven subsidiaries. The study reported that profits that American multinationals collectively attributed to operations in Bermuda and the Cayman Islands totaled, respectively, 1,884 percent and 1,313 percent of each country's entire annual output.

Apple Computer is the champion tax evader, using transfer pricing, tax havens, and special tax deals. Apple arranged to book most of its research costs to its Irish subsidiary, even though the actual research is done mainly at home, in Cupertino. But if 80 percent of the research is booked in Ireland, then 80 percent of the profits may be credited to Ireland, whose general corporate income tax rate is a low 12.5 percent. Not satisfied with that arrangement, Apple negotiated additional tax concessions with the Irish government to further reduce taxes owed.

Apple's Irish branch is considered an Irish company for US tax purposes, since it is incorporated in Ireland. But when the Irish tax authorities come around, they are told that Apple's Ireland subsidiary is an American company because it is managed and controlled from California. So Apple in Ireland professes to be a tax resident . . .

nowhere. A European Commission ruling found that Apple used this tax structure in Ireland to pay a rate of just 0.005 percent on its European profits in 2014. At this writing, the EC is now in a conflict with the US over whether Apple owes some $14.5 billion in back taxes to Ireland, or possibly to the US. Washington would not have pursued the case had Brussels not forced its hand.

All told, Apple has booked $214.9 billion in offshore profits, mostly in tax havens, the largest such holdings of any US corporation. If taxes on those profits were paid in the US, Apple would owe $65.4 billion. Apple is only one of hundreds of large US-based multinational corporations that play these games. Pfizer, the world's largest drugmaker, ranks second in profits held offshore for tax avoidance purposes, with $193.6 billion. All told, Fortune 500 corporations hold about $2.5 trillion in profits booked outside the US purely for tax avoidance purposes.

A series of regulatory easings by administrations from Reagan to Obama facilitated these maneuvers. Under Bill Clinton, in 1997, a ruling sought by the drug industry, known as check-the-box, allowed multinational corporations to consolidate all foreign income paid to an affiliate in a low-tax jurisdiction such as Ireland. Check-the-box makes it even easier for corporations to invent technically legal tax dodges and harder for the IRS to audit them. Some 55 percent of foreign US corporate profits (and about 18 percent of all US corporate profits) are attributed to offshore paper affiliates in six tax havens.

Maneuvers that skirt legal and potentially illegal are endless. Caterpillar Tractor has a huge and profitable spare-parts business, run from a warehouse in Illinois. The company's accounting consultant, PricewaterhouseCoopers, for a fee of $55 million, invented a complex tax dodge, in which Caterpillar billed its Swiss affiliate for the parts, even as it continued to ship them from its warehouse in Illinois. Caterpillar then declared 85 percent of the profits in Switzerland, which has a far lower tax rate than the US has. However, a whistle-blower tipped off the IRS that these paper transactions were bogus, and at this writing Caterpillar is under criminal investigation for tax fraud. However, these cases are vanishingly rare. In the absence of a whistle-blower, the IRS is simply overwhelmed.

A 2014 report by Citizens for Tax Justice, relying on company data filed with the SEC, found that of the 500 largest Fortune 500 corporations, 26, including Boeing, GE, and Verizon, paid no federal corporate income tax at all between 2008 and 2012. Another 93 paid an effective rate of 10 percent or less—far below the nominal rate of 39 percent. And for at least one year during that period, 111 companies paid no tax at all. Offshore maneuvers made up the largest part of these corporations' tax avoidance strategy.

In principle, taxes on corporate profits booked abroad are still owed on paper, but they are deferred until the profits are brought back home. As noted, US corporations have stashed about $2.5 trillion in profits that have escaped taxation.

If these profits were "repatriated," the corporations would get a small credit for the token taxes paid offshore, at an average rate of about 6.2 percent, and would owe the rest to the IRS—an estimated $717 billion. Periodically, a kind of tax amnesty is proposed for companies that repatriate their profits. They would be allowed to pay US tax on a onetime basis, at far below the usual rate. The argument is that all of this money could be invested, energizing the economy. This is a bogus argument and a bad idea. "Repatriation" is a misnomer, since it implies that when Apple keeps over $200 billion offshore, the company somehow doesn't have the use of that money. Typically, however, these funds are held by banks with branches all over the world. If Apple needs funds to finance its extensive operations outside the US, the company can simply tap its offshore accounts. Bringing this money "home" would do nothing for the US economy; it would simply wipe out much of a deferred tax obligation.

The economist Gabriel Zucman, in the most comprehensive study of corporate global tax evasion to date, very conservatively estimated that $7.6 trillion of upper-income wealth is held in tax havens, where it escapes taxation almost entirely. James Henry, former chief economist of McKinsey & Company, puts the figure of hidden wealth much higher, at about $21 trillion, or about one-fourth of all of the world's wealth.

Offshore havens not only cost countries money needed to finance public services. They also undermine the rule of law and facilitate the evasion of regulatory requirements as well as tax obligations. In the financial collapse of 2007–8, the same offshore jurisdictions that hide assets from the tax collector were used to hide illegal schemes in now familiar scandals that crashed the global economy. Long-

Term Capital Management, whose collapse in 1997 foreshadowed the more serious general financial meltdown, hid its transactions in tax havens. The financial maneuvers of Enron, Bear Stearns, Bernie Madoff, Citigroup, and Northern Rock, the epicenter of the financial collapse in Great Britain, among many others, were similarly obscured. Wall Street has long parked the assets of its "special-purpose vehicles" in the Caymans. The entire game of booking assets off the balance sheet, a major factor in the financial collapse, would have been much more difficult in the absence of tax and regulatory havens. Here again, the interest of the financial industry in evading regulation converges with the interest of other wealthy individuals and corporations in hiding income and assets from taxation.

All of these maneuvers simply overwhelm the tax enforcement machinery, even under relatively liberal governments. In 2010, under Obama, a special Internal Revenue Service division was created to pursue wealthy tax evaders with multinational holdings. By the time Trump took office, the unit, known as the "wealth squad," had enough staff to pursue only about two hundred cases a year. The IRS puts far more effort into pursuing low-income users of the earned income tax credit, mainly for innocent mistakes—which are a lot easier to track using computer matches.

WHY GOVERNMENTS TOLERATE TAX EVASION

In principle, all of these maneuvers could be shut down. The obstacle is not technical, but political. In 2010, while President Obama still had a working majority in Congress, the US enacted a law called the Foreign Account Tax Compliance Act, known as FATCA (which sounds, instructively, like "fat cat"). FATCA seems like a real breakthrough. It requires foreign banks with US business relationships to identify to the IRS account holders who are US citizens and to forward data on assets held and income earned. This is supposed to be done automatically, just as US banks and corporations must automatically provide information on domestic interest and dividend income to the IRS.

Under FATCA, failure to provide the information on transnational income triggers an automatic withholding tax on the income of 30 percent, with criminal penalties for evasion. However, the efficacy of FATCA is severely limited by the pervasiveness of shell corporations. If assets are held in the name of an offshore dummy trust, there is no documentation of whether the beneficial owner is a US citizen—and no data needs to be filed by the bank. Any fat cat with a smart accountant can avoid much of FATCA. And as weak as it is, FATCA is on the hit list of the Trump administration.

To go further and put shell corporations out of business or require universal disclosure of beneficial owners would require general coordination among all major nations. But there are invariably holdouts. Globalization thus makes the politics of tax enforcement more difficult, because all major nations need to cooperate and it takes only one defector with an antitax government at any given time to frustrate such efforts. In the 1950s and 1960s, there was less multinational corporate activity, less support for laissez-faire generally, and national governments were much tougher about issuing rules to defeat attempts at regulatory and tax evasion.

One of the most revealing stories of the complicity of the major Western governments in global tax evasion involves the OECD. In general, the OECD has facilitated the neoliberal economic model. But in the late 1990s, with nominally left-of-center governments in power in the US, Britain, and Germany, the OECD sponsored a bold initiative to force tax havens to share data with major governments. This was the result of a request by the Group of Seven nations at their 1996 meetings.

The OECD's initial report, released in April 1998, declared that tax havens "erode the tax bases of other countries, distort trade and investment patterns and undermine the fairness and broad social acceptance of tax systems generally. Such harmful tax competition diminishes global welfare and undermines taxpayer confidence in the integrity of tax systems." Strong stuff—or so it seemed. A follow-up OECD report in 2000 identified forty-one offending countries, and explicitly linked money laundering, bank regulatory issues, and tax evasion. Yet two decades later, tax havens and corporate tax evasion are more pervasive than ever.

The OECD's strategy was to devise a checklist of measures that cooperating nations were expected to take, including supplying authorities in other nations with relevant tax and banking data. The

OECD even established a blacklist of noncompliant countries. For the most part, however, the major governments among the OECD's member countries refused to apply any sanctions. So, the twenty-year history of this effort is an elaborate choreography of apparent progress that, in practice, made little difference.

Under the governments of Clinton in the US and Blair in Britain, the OECD task force was beginning to make some limited headway. Tax haven governments were negotiating how to stay off blacklists. But in 2001, the new Bush administration shut down US cooperation. America ceased to be any kind of a prod. Bush officials were quoted as saying that if corporations found ways to avoid taxes, this was constructive, since they were overtaxed anyway.

Conservative think tanks such as the Cato Institute lobbied the new Bush government to cease cooperating. A front group was created by Daniel Mitchell of Cato called the Center for Freedom and Prosperity, explicitly to defend tax havens. One Cato presentation was titled "The Moral Case for Tax Havens." It argued, "Tax competition is greatly beneficial in the battle for human rights and personal freedom. Low-tax jurisdictions, or tax-havens, are a safe refuge for oppressed people seeking to protect their assets." (Oppressed billionaires were not mentioned.) Supposedly, these small island nations were being bullied by big Western powers. It was a violation of their sovereignty. These were poor, mostly black countries whose economies needed the income. The right-wing think tanks and their business allies, who donate a lot of money to the Congressional Black Caucus Foundation, even got the Congressional Black Caucus to oppose the OECD initiative as racist. Cracking down on tax havens was depicted as a disguised form of a tax hike, at a time when taxes were said to be too high.

In February 2001, Bush's new Treasury secretary, Paul O'Neill, flatly accused the OECD of trying to raise tax rates. In April, House Majority Leader Dick Armey and his Senate counterpart, Don Nickels, sent strongly worded letters to the Bush Treasury Department demanding noncooperation. In May, the Bush administration formally ceased supporting the OECD tax competition initiative, claiming that it could raise costs to US taxpayers. O'Neill declared, "I am troubled by the underlying premise that low tax rates are somehow suspect and by the notion that any country, or group of countries, should interfere in any other country's decision about how to structure its own tax system."

But four months later came the attacks of September 11, 2001. The Bush administration suddenly woke up to the national security implications of sleazy, lucrative practices by large, multinational US banks. Financial institutions such as Citibank made billions of dollars by serving as conduits for foreign money laundering, and asking few questions. Money laundering went hand in hand with tax evasion—and also, in some cases, with terrorism.

For example, a US bank can serve as a "correspondent bank" for a foreign bank that knowingly hides assets for organized crime, for other white-collar criminals, for dictators who loot the treasuries of their own countries, for tax evaders—or for ostensible charities that finance terrorists. In the 1990s, the Bank of New York was revealed to have been earning $240 million a month for cooperating with an elaborate money-laundering scheme created by the head of its eastern Europe operations for Russian clients. Upwards of $10 billion was deposited into sham corporations in Russia in tens of thousands of separate transactions, and then laundered through the Bank of New York. Though two key executives—Lucy Edwards and her husband, Peter Berlin—did plead guilty to multiple counts of wire fraud and bribery, the government lacked the tools to charge the Bank of New York itself. This case was noteworthy because it was the exception. Edwards and Berlin had been careless and failed to cover their tracks.

In another emblematic case, Raul Salinas, brother of Mexican president Carlos Salinas, used private Mexican banks to wire-transfer over $100 million to Citibank's Mexico City office, using an alias. The money was then moved to New York, where Citi recorded no connection to Salinas and displayed no curiosity about the identity of the true owner. From there, the money moved to several offshore trust accounts based in London or Zurich, nominally owned by Cayman Islands shell corporations, but advised and managed by Citibank. The details of the Salinas case came to light only because of a whistle-blower. In a scathing report on Citi, the government's General Accounting Office faulted management for failing to determine Salinas's identity.

During this period, the Treasury secretary was Robert Rubin, a close ally of Carlos Salinas, who had facilitated Mexico's financial liberalization. Rubin was not accused of any wrongdoing in the Carlos Salinas affair. Rubin, after leaving the Treasury, soon became chairman of the executive committee of Citi.

After September 11, investigations soon revealed the financing of the terrorists via the laundering of money that had passed through US banks. Legislation was rushed through Congress. Under the International Money Laundering Abatement and Anti-Terrorist Financing Act of 2001, part of the USA PATRIOT Act, the government issued tough new reporting rules requiring banks to share detailed information with regulatory authorities so that possible laundering could be detected.

In many respects, the PATRIOT Act violated norms of privacy and due process to help the government track potential terrorists. In the case of money laundering, the Treasury was given broad mandates to issue regulations. But in working out these rules with the financial industry, the Bush administration effectively carved out a loophole for one kind of criminal enterprise: tax evasion by US corporations and investors. That was business as usual, not terrorism.

Even with the increased concerns about terrorism, the US government hesitates to crack down on huge banks that are too big to jail. Hong Kong–based HSBC, one of the world's largest, was caught red-handed laundering money for Mexican drug cartels. In 2013, the bank paid a fine of $1.92 billion, which sounds draconian until you know that its 2013 profits were $22.6 billion. The fine was a cost of doing business.

The Bush administration likewise devised a loophole for offshore tax havens. These governments were asked to provide financial information about possible money laundering to US and European authorities, but only "on request," and on a case-by-case basis. As Nicholas Shaxson, one of the closest students of tax havens, has observed, "You can't prove criminality until you get the information, and you can't get the information until you can show the criminality. Catch-22's Captain Yossarian would have appreciated the double bind."

Meanwhile, the charade of international tax enforcement collaboration staggered onward. The OECD effort came back to life when the Obama administration took office. But the OECD's checklists and blacklists are themselves full of loopholes. As we've seen, the true beneficial owner of an asset may still be disguised. And nothing in the OECD effort addresses either tax competition to lower rates or the common practice of transfer pricing and fictitious booking of profits in low-tax or no-tax jurisdictions.

In 2007, the OECD created its latest checklist of twelve commitments that tax havens were supposed to make. The simple act of making them got you off the blacklist; there was no serious follow-up to check compliance. Not surprisingly, everyone complied. At a press conference timed to coincide with a 2009 meeting of the G-20, the OECD released its latest blacklist of tax havens. A longer list of thirty-eight nations had been reduced to just four: Costa Rica, Malaysia, the Philippines, and Uruguay. Within five days, the blacklist was empty. For notorious havens like the Cayman Islands, Switzerland, Luxembourg, and Panama—none of which were even on the OECD's latest blacklist—it was business as usual.

THE ROAD NOT TRAVELED: SHUTTING DOWN TAX HAVENS

Western governments could close down tax havens and international tax evasion almost overnight, if they wanted to. The fact that they don't want to illustrates the power shift to capital over the past three decades—and the distance that government has come from the postwar era when governments and national social contracts served ordinary people.

Governments could begin by ceasing the use of tax competition to reduce corporate tax rates. Trade deals, instead of providing ways for corporations to play nations off against each other, could agree on a common corporate tax rate and common tax reporting requirements. Major Western nations could make it a crime for a bank with a license to operate in the United States (or Germany or Britain) to engage in banking relationships with entities incorporated in tax or regulatory havens.

Gabriel Zucman has a simple idea for tracking true beneficial ownership. He proposes a universal registry that would cut through straw owners and trusts and show the true owners of all stocks, bonds, and bank accounts. The US currently has a very weak know-your-customer rule requiring banks to determine the true identity of their clients, but, as in the Citi-Salinas case noted above, the rule is often violated with impunity. A universal rule, enforced by the major nations, would disclose the true owners and end most money laundering and transnational tax evasion. The same digital techniques that banks, corporations, and investors use to evade detection could be used to track transactions. In an era when monitoring of calls, emails, and digital communication has become ubiquitous, this is one area of law enforcement where privacy concerns are not a legitimate excuse for inaction. If the law requires ordinary citizens to disclose incomes and tax liabilities to tax authorities, wealthy investors and corporations should do no less.

Further, governments could end the game of fictitious accounting via transfer pricing with a very simple rule known as "sales factor apportionment." A multinational company would pay corporate income tax according to where its final sales occurred. If 50 percent of Apple's final sales occurred in the United States, it would pay corporate income tax at US rates on those sales. If 10 percent of its sales were made in Germany, it would pay German rates on those sales. The complex games of booking costs and sales in tax havens would suddenly be useless, because almost no final sales occur in tax havens.

Tax cutting and tax evasion can also be practiced nationally, of course. But globalization promotes competition to lower rates and makes evasion easier to conceal and harder to track down. The fragmentation of national governments, the rise of multinational corporations, and the capture of many governments by financial elites create a general race to the bottom.

All of these maneuvers are highly technical and complex, and few citizens grasp the details. When the Bush administration stopped cooperating with the OECD, nobody cared except corporate lobbyists (who cared mightily) and a tiny handful of tax reform advocates. But at some primal, intuitive level, ordinary people—who have never heard of transfer pricing, or FATCA, or sales factor apportionment—somehow notice. They notice that someone else is getting a sweetheart deal, and it isn't them.

10

GOVERNING GLOBAL CAPITALISM

n January 2001, while the global political and economic elite gathered at the annual meeting of the World Economic Forum in Davos, a countermeeting convened in Porto Alegre, Brazil, called the World Social Forum. This gathering has become an annual event, usually in a third-world setting, bringing together thousands of activists and intellectuals who represent a diverse global opposition party. As markets and corporations have outrun the constraints of national governments, it is tempting to conclude that global civil society as counterweight is a major part of the solution.

True global government, once the ideal of postwar groups such as the World Federalist Movement, is utopian—or worse. Despite an increasingly global economy, the world is too diverse and complex, and any global government that somehow emerged would likely be even further removed from democratic checks, rather as the EU has become. At a conference discussing world federalism, I once heard the eminent diplomat and global idealist Harland Cleveland say that the trouble with global government is that I might not like it and it might not like me.

Yet it is undeniable that our most pressing challenges are global. Among these are climate change and nuclear nonproliferation—quite literally existential issues—as well as such causes as universal human rights and related norms of treatment for refugees, immigrants, and migrant workers. The challenge is to make necessary entities of global governance as transparent and accountable as possible, to imbue them with a social mission as well as a market mission, and to rekindle something of the spirit of 1944, when global institutions were designed to reinforce the national management of markets rather than to undermine it. But even more important is the need for national democracies to take back authority to govern capitalism.

GLOBAL GOVERNANCE AS ANTIDEMOCRACY

Numerous quasi-public bodies play a role in setting and enforcing international rules. The problem is that the ones with real power, such as the IMF, the World Bank, the WTO, and the EU, have been substantially captured by financial elites and have far less democratic accountability than their domestic counterparts. Conversely, in the areas where we really need global rules and bodies, such as international human rights, the agencies that exist have been kept too weak to do their jobs.

A deeper look at how the usual process of government actually functions shows that democratic governance of capitalism is difficult to achieve at a global level, for three core reasons. First, the enactment of most law at the national level requires merely a parliamentary majority. Even the United States, with its multiple legislative veto points and supermajority requirements, can enact such laws as the Clean Air Act or the Glass-Steagall Act and the standards are binding, including on foreign corporations that operate within the US. By contrast, the adoption of a binding global treaty requires *unanimity* of major nations, most notably the participation of the United States—or its legal force is dramatically weakened. This simple fact creates a bias in favor of inaction, or weak action, or action that accommodates or even enhances the power of corporate elites.

Second, nations have a well-established enforcement apparatus of the state that includes regulatory agencies, civil and criminal actions by government, and private litigation enforceable by courts. Government enforcement is a potent institutional ally of the political forces pursuing the regulation of markets. The enforcement counterpart at the global level, where there is no state, is far weaker. This industry-dominated patchwork requires civil society groups to devote immense monitoring resources in a grossly unequal contest.

Third, the process of domestic legislation has formal mechanisms of democratic participation that are relatively transparent. These include legislative hearings that are open to citizens, public legislative debates, and judicial review, as well as political accountability of elected officials after the fact. Citizens are often outgunned by the power of industry groups—yet the democratic process does allow breakthroughs in which the public can be mobilized and David sometimes beats Goliath. The global counterpart is far less transparent or participatory, and far more decisions are made by elites behind closed doors. Many standards for business conduct are set privately by corporate trade associations.

An emblematic example is the International Swaps and Derivatives Association, a membership association of large multinational banks that originate and trade derivative securities. The ISDA is simultaneously an industry lobby, a standard-setting body, and a quasi-judicial organ that decides when defaults trigger required payments under derivatives contracts. And there are hundreds of other cases where industry bodies have binding legal authority to set standards and adjudicate disputes.

National governments typically have well-established procedures for the enforcement of laws. In the United States, an agency creating rules to carry out the intent of legislation must issue advance notification, solicit comment, release draft rules, and then publish final rules that take into account public comments. In this rule-making process, genuine public-interest groups may be outgunned by industry advocates, but at least they may participate and the process is relatively transparent. There is the recourse of tipping off the press to forays by lobbyists and pending capitulations by the regulators. By the same token, the rules of courts are very well established, to prevent conflicts of interest, prohibit ex parte contacts or jury tampering, allow public trials, and so on. Domestically, additional transparency is provided by the Freedom of Information Act, rights of discovery in the context of trials, and other guidelines.

At the international level, literally no body of governance has a system of due process remotely as protective of the rights of citizens as the domestic counterpart. Dispute resolution tribunals range from pseudo-transparent, such as the WTO, to purely privatized and opaque. Agendas are often secret. Conflicts of interest, rather than being prohibited, are frequently the essence of private capture of a quasi-governmental entity. All of this tends to stack the deck in favor of financial elites.

The history of private law governing global commerce (with the necessary support of sovereigns) goes back to the Middle Ages. Alongside the legacy of Roman public law and church law, the trading culture of the late Middle Ages created a *Lex Mercatoria*—a system of common law for merchants that defined the sanctity of contracts and created generally recognized standards for property rights across national borders. In some places, such as England and some French and Italian states, merchant law could be enforced in the royal courts.

One of the most fundamental extraterritorial functions of merchant law was to guarantee and protect ownership of private property as it crossed national borders in commerce. Nowhere was this more vividly demonstrated than in the era of slavery, when a slave trader could buy slaves in Africa, underwritten by a British, Portuguese, or Dutch merchant, for sale in America, knowing that his ownership of the human cargo would be respected and guaranteed by several governments as it crossed the seas, should the issue ever be raised in any court of law. What was true of slaves was true of lesser commodities.

So, the global reach of private property law, enforced by states, is not a new phenomenon. Much of the de facto legal system that governs commerce across nation boundaries is, in fact, highly regulated, but via private systems of law that are largely opaque to the citizenry, and the business mainly of private-market actors. The great achievement of modern democracy was to make law public.

With increasing reprivatization and globalization of law in the twenty-first century comes the problem of double standards in extraterritoriality. Multinational corporations are content to live with extraterritoriality when it serves property interests. But application of labor, environmental, human-rights, and social standards is fiercely resisted as an interference with the sovereign right of developing countries (and their corporate partners) to exploit labor, despoil the environment, avoid taxation, and weaken social protections. The enforcement of austerity by the IMF, US Treasury, and European Union, in exchange for financial support of sovereign debts that were often incurred corruptly for private gain, is an emblematic case of the indulgence granted for the approved sort of extraterritoriality.

Occasionally, there is an instructive exception, as there was in the 1944 Bretton Woods rules constraining private financial speculation. I had firsthand experience with this dynamic in the 1970s, as a US Senate investigator under Senator William Proxmire, the chair of the Committee on Banking, when I conducted the hearings on bribery of foreign governments by US-based corporations and then drafted the legislation that became the Foreign Corrupt Practices Act of 1977.

We faced a united front of opposition from corporations on the grounds that this proposed law, prohibiting US corporations from bribing foreign governments, would prove a source of competitive disadvantage, as well as an unwise and unconstitutional extraterritorial overreach. But Congress did pass the law, and it was signed by President Carter and upheld by the Supreme Court. It has had modest success in reducing corruption—and was the rare case in which an extraterritorial law constrained rather than enabled corporate behavior. But this was the result of a brief window for domestic progressive legislation, in the wake of the Watergate downfall of Richard Nixon at a time when the political mood was anticorruption—an exceptional instance of the nation-state setting progressive rules for globalism. But this success shows that such rules are indeed feasible, when the politics align.

THE ILLUSION OF CORPORATE SOCIAL RESPONSIBILITY

The usual pro-corporate tilt in transnational governmental organizations has led some reformers to look to NGOs as counterweights. These range from disruptive groups willing to resort to civil disobedience, such as Greenpeace, to heroic service groups such as Doctors Without Borders, and tame, nominally independent organizations that are essentially fronts for multinational business—as well as lots of gradations in between.

For more than three decades, vast citizen effort has gone into the creation of "multi-stakeholder" coalitions to induce and then monitor voluntary reforms in the practices of multinational corporations concerned about their reputations. The first model for this approach was a set of codes of conduct called the Sullivan principles, created in 1977 by the Reverend Leon Sullivan as part of the pressure that the anti-apartheid movement put on multinational corporations doing business with or in South Africa, to press the Pretoria government for specific reforms.

The original Sullivan principles asked corporations to commit to a code of equal employment opportunity that, if actually implemented, would have reversed core tenets of the apartheid regime. Reverend Sullivan had some leverage because he was a prominent African American leader and a member of the board of General Motors, which had extensive operations in South Africa. Eventually, by the late 1980s, more than 125 corporations had committed to the Sullivan principles, and over a hundred others pulled out of South Africa. By then, the anti-apartheid movement had moved well beyond piecemeal reform demands.

Seemingly, the Sullivan principles demonstrate the value of such voluntary codes of conduct. Key differences, however, explain the weakness of most such monitoring initiatives. The Sullivan principles were not just about altering corporate behavior. Ultimately, they were part of a movement for revolutionary change, a movement that included pressure on Western governments and a divestment campaign, as well as radical agitation and civil disobedience on the ground. No small effort, of course, was contributed by South African insurgents themselves, and it is misleading to categorize a revolutionary movement as part of "civil society." This rare convergence of forces, coupled with the personal courage and moral witness of Nelson Mandela and thousands of others, produced transformative change that few believed possible. Ironically, however, the Sullivan principles inspired an elaborate ideology and practice of certification regimes whose goals are far more modest and incremental.

Since the 1990s, hundreds of monitoring and certification regimes have been created by NGOs or by corporations seeking to insulate their brands from reputational damage. These regimes, by definition, are voluntary. They require corporations to agree to cooperate. They depend on activating a global public in their role more as *consumers* than as citizens. This difference is key. A citizen can elect a government with the power to enact a law that is a mandatory constraint on corporate behavior. A consumer or group of consumers can pressure a corporation to follow norms, using reputational concerns as political leverage. The latter is far weaker than the former because it leaves enforcement to NGOs and corporate self-policing rather than to the direct legal and police power of states.

The certification approach seeks to raise standards within market norms, rather than by state regulation that explicitly alters market practices. This strategy inverts the schema made famous by Karl Polanyi, who observed that the goal of a managed form of capitalism is to re-embed economic transactions in social relations. But certification regimes, by contrast, turn Polanyi upside down. They proudly attempt to use market forces—consumer pressure, corporate enlightened self-interest—to achieve social goals. As Michael Conroy writes, in an enthusiastic book promoting certification regimes, these are "non-state, market-driven" strategies that rely entirely on market forces to achieve social goals. This is quite the opposite of Polanyi's sensibility, since it acknowledges and even reinforces the hegemony of markets as the mechanism for making decisions required by systematic market failures.

While there have been scattered successes of corporate social responsibility, some of the world's most powerful corporations, which have been responsible for large-scale catastrophes, such as the 2008 financial collapse, the ongoing degradation of the environment, and the war on labor standards, have eagerly signed on to voluntary certifications as part of their reputational efforts. Citigroup, a prime instigator of predatory deregulation, has collaborated with the World Bank on voluntary environmental standards for third-world lending. Walmart, the leading opponent of wage regulation, has branded itself as a pioneer in green retailing. As these corporate social responsibility efforts have burgeoned, so has financial corruption of basic democracy. Though there are occasional companies, such as the original Ben and Jerry's, whose owners put the public good ahead of profits, one could be forgiven for concluding that for large corporations, these multi-stakeholder partnerships are mainly public relations.

CERTIFIED COFFEE, SUSTAINABLE FORESTRY, CLEAN CLOTHES, ETC.

Fair-trade coffee, seemingly, is a good example of progress. Fairtrade International and Fair Trade USA have sought to brand fair-traded coffee, combining environmental and labor goals. Consumers in wealthy nations willing to pay $4 for a cup of premium coffee tend to be politically conscious. Because of the high retail price and the exquisite sensitivity of corporations such as Starbucks for their reputations as good corporate citizens, there was economic and political room to demand that "fair-trade" coffee justify its premium price with decent labor and agricultural standards. Growers could gain by being certified, and thus get a higher wholesale price for their coffee.

However, more than twenty years of experience with fair-traded coffee has led critics—many of them veterans of the fair-trade movement—to point to the several deficiencies that seem endemic to the approach. Only about 5 percent of world coffee is fair-traded. The cultivation practices are a gain for sustainable agriculture, but there is controversy about how much of the premium price results in improved net compensation for farmers, who incur added costs in gaining certification. The higher prices paid to growers, some critics contend, destabilized a reasonably effective price stabilization regime, the International Coffee Organization, which was aimed at preventing world coffee overproduction. Growers, attracted by the premium prices, increased the land under cultivation, adding to supply and depressing prices worldwide for the vast majority of coffee farmers who were not under the fair-trade regime.

There is now a proliferation of certification labels (four major international fair-trade networks), leading to consumer confusion. There is also controversy about the adequacy of compliance monitoring. FLO-CERT, the monitoring subsidiary of Fairtrade International, is a for-profit company. Some corporations, such as Starbucks, invite consumers with social consciences to pay extra for coffee that is branded as fair-traded, but offer the same customers other premium, non-fair-trade options. This is a far cry from a regulatory regime, such as OSHA or the Fair Labor Standards Act, that sets *universal mandatory minimums*.

Forest certification programs, one of the oldest such initiatives of international civil society, attempt to brand forest products that follow sustainable practices. The creation of the Forest Stewardship Council, in 1993, grew out of the Rio Earth Summit of 1992 and eighteen months of consultation between industry and environmental groups. What is noteworthy is that the FSC has brought together major industry players and the industry's fairly radical critics, such as Greenpeace. The FSC has enlisted not only major logging companies, but retailers such as Home Depot and IKEA. It has an elaborate system of governance, accreditation, and chain-of-custody certification. Its members range from environmental groups to major producers and end users such as Kimberly-Clark.

The FSC claims 440 million hectares of certified forest, about 10 percent of the world's total. However, that number should be placed in the context of 130 million hectares lost to deforestation in the past decade alone. While the FSC claims that about 15 percent of global timber sales now are covered by one certification regime or another, deforestation is still proceeding at the rate of 16 million hectares a year, according to the Food and Agriculture Organization of the UN, up from 13 million hectares a year in the 1990s.

On balance, the FSC process has raised consumer awareness and has slowed but not reversed the process of global deforestation, which has now destroyed more than half of the world's forests. Sustainable practices still cover only a minority of tree harvesting. What we do not have is an enforceable global treaty on forest standards. Though branding campaigns have helped, much of the credit goes to deliberate policy changes by two national governments, Brazil and Indonesia, which reversed earlier policies of promoting rapid deforestation.

THE ELUSIVE QUEST FOR LABOR STANDARDS

Consider the anti-sweatshop movement, which pressures companies to use a logo certifying that their products come from factories that provide minimally decent standards of pay and working conditions. One of two US-based organizations, the Fair Labor Association, partners with major corporations. The FLA was created in 1999. It grew out of a consultative process brokered by President Bill Clinton, and originally included unions as well as industry. But the industry couldn't agree on binding standards, and the unions soon left, later criticizing the FLA for settling for only token changes. When Apple selected the FLA to monitor its plants in China after revelations of gross abuses in the factories of its supplier Foxconn, critics noted that it had picked an entity partly funded by corporations and not noted for tough, independent scrutiny. Abuses continued, even after FLA monitoring.

In 1999, unions and United Students Against Sweatshops (USAS) created an independent group, the Worker Rights Consortium. The WRC has had some successes, but it also encounters great difficulty getting multinational corporations to reform labor practices—one of the most fundamental of which is the right to organize or to join a union. The WRC sometimes uses the leverage provided by the FLA process. For example, in 2008 a member company of the FLA, Russell Athletic/Fruit of the Loom, closed a factory in Honduras rather than recognizing the workers' decision to unionize. The FLA resisted taking any action against Russell. Eventually, some one hundred universities, mobilized by the WRC and USAS, denied Russell licenses to make products with its logos, and the company finally agreed not only to reopen the factory, but to allow others in Honduras to unionize. But successes such as these are rare.

A potential breakthrough occurred in May 2013, after a building collapse in Bangladesh killed more than eleven hundred workers in a garment factory producing for major fashion brands in Europe and the United States. The global labor movement and groups such as the WRC and the Europe-based Clean Clothes Campaign enlisted more than seventy mostly European major fashion brands, led by Sweden-based H&M and Spain's Inditex, the two largest European garment retailers.

An agreement signed on May 15, 2013, made front-page news. It creates a contractual obligation for the participating retailers to assume responsibility for safety conditions in the Bangladesh plants from which they source garments. In cases of dispute, there is a binding arbitration process. However, this Accord on Building and Fire Safety in Bangladesh did not address either wages or organizing rights. It did commit the companies to allow union representatives to train workers in health and safety, which the unions took as a foot in the door. The Bangladeshi government, whose economic development strategy has been to position Bangladesh as the world's low-cost garment producer, was far from enthusiastic. Reports by monitoring teams in 2016 and 2017 found modest progress in safety standards, but no meaningful access to union organizers and scant gains in wages.

Despite these limited successes, the ideal of consumer awareness has played almost no role in this process. Most consumers are too preoccupied with other concerns, including price, to pay much attention to whether a corporation's product boasts a union label. Rather, the unions' ability to convince corporations to accept unions has been almost entirely a function of the capacity of unions to influence national law enforcement of labor rights.

EXTRACTION, POLLUTION, AND CORRUPTION

Some fifty countries rely on payments from extractive industries such as oil, gas, iron ore, and minerals as their principal source of foreign exchange. Many are poor, and few are democracies. So the temptation to sacrifice both the environment and the labor force is immense. Widespread corruption in the flow of corporate payments to host governments only exacerbates the problem. This syndrome is often known as the "resource curse."

Resource-rich developing countries are typically clustered at the bottom of the UN Development Programme's Human Development Index and Transparency International's Corruption Perceptions Index. Oil money rarely flows to help the majority of the nation to develop, and it often underwrites wars. Heavy reliance on mineral wealth, especially in weak democracies or despotisms, promotes corrupt dealings between rulers and multinational extractive corporations, causing profits to flow out of the country rather than into balanced economic development. The result is that countries with few natural resources tend to grow at faster rates than resource-rich countries.

The link between corruption and wretched labor and environmental conditions in the extraction of raw materials has been the target of numerous NGOs. In December 1999, a London-based group called

Global Witness published a report titled "A Crude Awakening," an exposé of the multinational oil and banking industries' role in the plundering of public assets in Angola. The report showed that multinational oil companies were complicit in the embezzlement of oil revenues by corrupt local governments, including huge sums that went to finance Angola's three decades of civil war. The report called on the oil companies operating in Angola to "publish what you pay."

The London-based campaign soon enlisted such NGOs as Oxfam GB, Catholic Relief Services, and Human Rights Watch. Prime Minister Tony Blair embraced the cause as a way of combining corporate responsibility, poverty reduction, and energy security. In 2003, organizers created the Extractive Industries Transparency Initiative (EITI), and a campaign called Publish What You Pay, with a network of at least 350 affiliated NGOs worldwide.

This campaign was about as good as it gets. A broad coalition was possible because the cause was of interest to a wide range of groups that don't always collaborate—environmental and labor groups concerned that lax or corrupted regulatory standards allow environmentally destructive practices, as well as human exploitation of workers in extractive industries; social justice and antipoverty groups interested in ensuring that government funds in poor countries go more to human development and less to corrupted government officials; peace groups eager to reduce the flow of illicit funds that finance regional and tribal conflicts; and other NGOs pursuing transparency and honest government as both ends and means.

The presence and activism of the campaign set the stage for another fortuitous breakthrough. In the final round of jousting over the 2010 Dodd-Frank Act, one key Republican senator, Richard Lugar of Indiana, was not particularly friendly to the overall bill, but he had an interest in anticorruption measures in third-world countries. So, although a disclosure provision was not included in either the House or the Senate bill, it was added by sponsors to the final conference draft, in the hope of enlisting Senator Lugar's vote for the whole package. Multinational corporations were caught off guard, since there was no time for the usual corporate lobbying, and the final bill did include the publish-what-you-pay requirement.

Under Dodd-Frank, multinational companies in extractive industries must include in their public filings with the US Securities and

Exchange Commission their payments to governments. This requirement, in turn, makes outright corruption more difficult to hide, and it opens the way to greater substantive progress on labor and environmental conditions in mining and petroleum production.

This rare story of NGO success, however, does not have a happy ending. The election of Donald Trump reversed these gains. Industry pressure and litigation between 2010 and 2016 delayed the issuance of final regulations by the SEC. Those regulations were among the first to be killed by the incoming Trump administration. So, corporations need not publish their payments in their SEC filings after all.

In practice, social progress produced by certification and monitoring programs has been glacial. For all of the effort, there are huge areas of global commerce, such as financial practices, where it has not been possible to establish any such regimes. Corporate social responsibility, for the most part, is a branding and public relations maneuver. However ingenious global NGOs may be, if we want to restore democratic control of capitalism, the real action is at the level of the nation-state.

ADVOCACY WITHOUT ENFORCEMENT

While states have ceded real power to the IMF, World Bank, and WTO, the norm when it comes to human rights is institutions of global governance that are voluntary and hortatory. They have the power to name and shame, but too much of global commerce is simply beyond shaming. A case in point is the ILO.

Founded in 1919 as an affiliate of the League of Nations, the International Labour Organization and its secretariat, the International Labour Office (both somewhat confusingly abbreviated as ILO) are the most venerable of the UN-associated agencies. The ILO is organized as a tripartite body, bringing together business, labor, and government, though its outlook tends to be pro-labor. The ILO grew out of demands from nascent trade union organizations for a seat at the table at the Versailles Peace Conference, and reflected the tripartitism that was already in the air in the period after the First World War.

Within the limitations of its structure, the ILO is as close as it gets to a voice for labor within the international system. Over the years, in addition to conducting extensive research on labor conditions, the ILO has promulgated 188 "binding" conventions on labor rights and related human rights, most of which have not been ratified by the United States, as well as 199 nonbinding recommendations. However, these are not enforced. They have been ratified by dozens of nations that routinely repress labor rights with impunity. As globalization of production has spread, the conditions of labor in both the third world and more affluent countries have deteriorated, and the assault on trade unions have intensified.

The ILO machinery adds up to an elaborate jurisprudence, which is honored mainly in the breach. Every aspect of it depends heavily on action by member states, most of which accept the ILO norms as aspirations but not necessarily as policies. Unlike the WTO, the ILO has no independent standard-setting authority with the force of domestic or international law.

Nonetheless, these conventions have a certain moral authority, and the ILO has been useful as a quasi enforcement body in the rare cases when labor provisions have been added to trade agreements. The European Union, for example, offers "Community preference" (reduced tariffs) to trading partners that agree to abide by certain commercial norms, and one of the conditions is the adoption and enforcement of core labor rights as defined by the ILO. The EU has relied on the ILO to monitor whether nations seeking or obtaining Community preference are in compliance. In a world where trade unions are chronically understaffed, the ILO also provides backup resources, networking opportunities, and technical expertise from a perspective generally friendly to the expansion of worker rights. But enforcement remains the province of governments.

MIGRATION AND THE DILEMMA OF STATELESSNESS

Migration is a hallmark of the global economy, as well as a first-order challenge to the ideal of universal human rights. More than 244 million people find themselves living in someone else's country—most to seek work, some to pursue democratic liberties, many fleeing as refugees. A third to half of these migrants either are already citizens or are newcomers on a path to citizenship. But an increasing number don't really want to be citizens unless they can be dual citizens; they prefer to journey back and forth to their original homelands, perhaps to return permanently once they've accumulated a decent nest egg. Tens of millions of economic migrants send remittances. In some countries, such as Nepal and Haiti, remittances account for upwards of a quarter of domestic GDP.

Many migrants—the estimates exceed 40 million—are in destination countries illegally. They have no rights of citizenship, they are vulnerable to summary arrest, and their ability to normalize their status varies from country to country. The latest surge of refugees with no place to go has only exacerbated this challenge.

In countries that do not have democratic rights even for their own citizens, such as the Persian Gulf states, migrant laborers exist in a condition of indentured servitude akin to slavery. The governments of "sending" countries, such as Pakistan, the Philippines, and Nepal, seek to negotiate standards with the "receiving" countries to protect their citizens, but they have little leverage. Some governments attempt to regulate the labor brokers who handle this human commerce, but with little success. Nepalis regularly travel to India to connect with labor brokers who ignore the laws of Nepal.

In nations mired in poverty, people are so desperate for the work that they brave exploitation both by middlemen and by host governments. Their passports are often held either by their employer or by the labor broker, they incur debt to cover the cost of airfare, and they frequently experience theft of wages owed. There is nobody to whom they can complain. In addition to suffering exploitation, desperate workers with few rights, if any, drag down wages and social standards, and feed the kind of political backlash that brought us Brexit and Trump. Even if there is not a shred of racism in this reaction (and there often is), local workers who resent migrants are correct to observe that migrants tend to reduce prevailing wages.

In principle, this problem cries out for some kind of global governance regime to set minimal standards. On paper, the ILO is supposed to protect basic labor rights. The 1967 Protocol Relating to the Status of Refugees treaty, as one example, requires its 146 national signatories to admit persons seeking asylum who can demonstrate "a well-founded fear of being persecuted for reasons of race, religion, nationality, membership of a particular social group or political opinion . . . and being outside the country of former habitual residence as a result of such events, is unable or, owing to such fear, is unwilling to return to it."

Even that fairly clear criterion is subject to widely varying interpretation by different nations. The United States makes a stringent distinction between people seeking asylum for reasons of political persecution, and those who are merely fleeing economic destitution. Other nations, such as Japan, make a practice of discouraging the admission of refugees entirely.

There are no uniform standards or norms on such contentious issues as "birthright citizenship" (whether a child of immigrant parents is automatically a citizen of the country of birth) and whether dual citizenship is allowed. There are no global mechanisms for enforcing even the norms, such as admission of political refugees, to which nations have agreed in principle. Gara LaMarche, a long-time human-rights activist and leader, has proposed that even aliens should not be alien from the social contract—meaning that the basic norms of decent treatment should be extended to citizen, visitor, refugee, and migrant alike. But the global system is far from accepting that principle.

In the idealistic years after World War II, governments worked collaboratively to settle millions of victims of that war who were termed "displaced persons." That was the era when the United Nations committed its member governments to the Universal Declaration of Human Rights. But in subsequent years, migrants and refugees have been increasingly unwanted, except as temporary workers without rights. This legal limbo for migrants serves the narrow interests of corporations. It pits locals against others and undermines the long-standing struggle for decent capitalism.

THE GOLD STANDARD: BINDING TREATIES

In 1974, two scientists from UC Berkeley—Mario Molina and F. S. Rowland—found that chlorofluorocarbons (CFCs) used in refrigeration, air-conditioning, and aerosol spray cans could weaken the

Earth's ozone shield, increasing the risk of skin cancer and eye disease. Despite widespread industry opposition and the advice of conservative skeptics that people should just wear hats and apply more sunscreen, the major industrial nations acted to ban CFCs.

This one-off success for global governance by treaty took no small dose of luck. The chemical industry at first created the usual front group to oppose regulation, called the Alliance for Responsible CFC Policy. But faced with pressure from environmental groups and major governments, as well as clear scientific evidence, the industry soon split. In 1986, DuPont, a leading producer with reputational concerns, pledged to find a substitute for CFCs within five years. DuPont correctly calculated that this would be a shrewd business strategy. As CFCs were phased out, the company would become the leading producer of next-generation coolant products.

With the discovery of a dramatic hole in the ozone layer over Antarctica, leading nations agreed to the Vienna Convention for the Protection of the Ozone Layer, formalized by the 1987 Montreal Protocol, a legally enforceable treaty requiring all signatories to phase out CFCs. The United States, despite a conservative national administration under President Ronald Reagan, took the science seriously. Republicans had not yet become climate-change deniers, and CFCs were a niche product, not a major industry like oil or coal.

The US took the lead in enlisting major nations to reduce CFCs by 95 percent over ten to fourteen years. The initiative worked. CFCs now have better chemical substitutes. The ozone layer is expected to heal by about 2050, in a rare success for international environmental governance. Note, however, that the decision of a key national government, the US, to lead was critical.

A binding treaty enforced by member governments is far superior to campaigns by civic groups of publicity, education, pressure, or voluntary cooperation. It is superior to most global governing regimes, even those that allow limited participation by civil society, because a binding treaty *has the force of domestic law.*

Several other treaties have been negotiated and signed, but the United States has refused to ratify most—citing sovereignty. At the risk of repeating myself, I note that sacrificing sovereignty is something the US does willingly—eagerly—when the impact is to undermine regulatory constraints on capital and commerce. When the goal is to constrain business or advance human rights, the US usually balks.

Among the international conventions signed by most nations but either not signed or not ratified by the US are several core ILO conventions: the 1994 Law of the Sea Treaty, the 1998 Rome agreement recognizing the jurisdiction of the International Criminal Court, and the 1997 Kyoto Protocol on carbon emissions. The rather weak 2004 international "Seed Treaty" was not ratified by the US. Nor has the US ratified the 1992 Convention on Biological Diversity, the Basel Convention governing the trade of toxic wastes, or the Stockholm Convention on Persistent Organic Pollutants. Conservatives in the US Senate have a visceral tendency to reject almost everything that begins with the initials UN.

Of major human-rights treaties negotiated since 1980, only two have been signed by the US, though neither one has been ratified: the conventions on elimination of discrimination against women and on the rights of the child. Those not even signed by the US include treaties banning land mines and cluster bombs, the convention against torture, and the convention on rights of persons with disabilities.

Why the outlier behavior of the United States? It is explained by a combination of the influence of traditional isolationist conservatives, who either reject the substance of the measures or can't imagine the United States being subjected to any form of international law, especially measures that might hold the US accountable for breaches of human rights—plus the power of business elites who strenuously resist labor, financial, or environmental standards being imposed on their practices, by either domestic or international law.

What was different about the ozone agreement? For one thing, it was approved relatively early in the current era of environmental concern, before the massive corporate backlash set in. More important, it addressed a narrow and easily isolated problem, depletion of the ozone shield by CFCs, where both the science and remedy were straightforward and the economic dislocation was limited.

By contrast, serious global efforts to reduce carbon emissions, say, to 350 parts per million, raise complex questions of goals, means, and trade-offs. At face value, a universal goal would deny the world's largest and poorest developing nations—namely, India and China—the means of economic growth that the West used at earlier stages of its own development. In principle, China could leapfrog the West's entire stage of dirty development by using green technologies, and still raise living standards. In the meantime, China is bringing into service an average of one new coal-fired electric generator a week. China now consumes more than half the world's coal. And while China also leads the world in production of solar cells and wind turbines, it is adding capacity for dirty development far faster than it is adding renewables.

Achieving a carbon agreement perceived as fair to third-world countries would probably require substantial transfers of wealth and intellectual property. It would require the West to set binding goals that would be unpopular domestically, and to radically transform its own economies. All of this is necessary to save our environment. But it is a far more complex challenge and far heavier diplomatic and political lift than banning CFCs. So, treaties may be the gold standard of global governance, but once again, the trail leads back to national democracy and national politics.

Here again, the Bretton Woods agreement of 1944—a treaty that was binding upon signatory nations—is a model of both substance and process. A new Bretton Woods agreement would reduce speculation in exchange rates, restore authorization of capital controls, explicitly permit imposition of social standards in trade, and take back some economic sovereignty that has been captured by corporations

ONE CHEER FOR GLOBAL GOVERNANCE

This is not to say that global governance and the world of global civil society are useless—only that they are no solution to the challenge of governing capitalism.

NGO campaigns such as Publish What You Pay can shed light on abuses. Civil society bodies like the International Red Cross and Doctors Without Borders become players not only in direct humanitarian aid, but in efforts to get nation-states to reduce violence. The antiglobalization groups succeeded in shutting down a Seattle GATT meeting in 1999 that was expected to launch a new round of trade negotiations. Much of the spotlight on global climate change reflects the good work of NGOs.

Occasionally, a transnational governance body contributes directly to genuine progress. A good example is the Intergovernmental Panel on Climate Change. It was created under the auspices of the United Nations and serves as a trusted repository of the scientific consensus on the pace, sources, and consequences of climate change. Another case in point is the International Atomic Energy Agency, which has served as a widely respected body entrusted to monitor compliance with nuclear nonproliferation agreements. The IAEA's directors were willing to go public to challenge misrepresentations of the American administration during the Iraq War (Hans Blix, 1981–97, and Mohammed ElBaradei, 1997–2009) and to facilitate progress toward an Iran nuclear deal later (Yukiya Amano, 2009–present).

However, the efficacy of such agencies is only as strong as the willingness of the great powers to trust them with real authority. And the policies pursued by national governments are mostly functions of domestic politics, not of global civil society.

President John Kennedy, in his 1963 speech at American University, offered a pun on Woodrow Wilson's call to make the world safe for democracy. Kennedy declared that America was resolved to "make the world safe for diversity." This was both an acknowledgment of the Soviets' right to their own system and a pledge to resist the communist effort to impose a single totalitarian model—but also a subtle commitment to respect the rights of other countries to define their own course.

Today, it is not communists, but capitalists, who are seeking to impose a single economic model on the globe. On balance, the institutions of global governance tend to reflect and reinforce rather than challenge that dominance. Globalism has been great at advancing the interests of capital and feeble at defending or enlarging the domain of human rights. The home of democracy—or antidemocracy—continues to be the national polity.

11

LIBERALISM, POPULISM, FASCISM

Democratic theorists have long appreciated that the enemies of open societies can take advantage of their openness and seek to destroy democracy. As this book has suggested, there is a direct connection between the stress on liberal democracy and the vulnerability of citizens to economic reverses. In our own era, as in the 1920s, an excess of economic liberalism—supercharged by globalization—is destroying political liberalism. If democracy cannot harness capitalism, it runs the risk of subverting itself and giving way to neofascist regimes that will pretend to manage the market but more often ally themselves with corporations and substitute ultra-nationalist symbols and scapegoats for reforms. In the 1930s, this slide ended in both dictatorship and war.

For centuries, the spread of democracy has accompanied the rise of liberal values. Beginning with the Enlightenment, classical liberalism came to be associated with rights of the individual, constraints on rulers, and free inquiry, which in turn logically precluded censorship. Jeffersonian liberalism pursued religious tolerance but prized reason over faith. These core values gradually evolved into a conception of constitutional democracy.

Along the way, theorists such as John Locke, writing in the late seventeenth century, proposed an elegant theory of natural equality, the polity as a social contract, and checks on arbitrary rule. Locke, in turn, was a major influence on James Madison and the other American constitutional founders. The modern antecedents of these constraints on tyranny go back to the Magna Carta of 1215, the

English Habeas Corpus Act of 1679 and Bill of Rights of 1689, and the American Bill of Rights and French Declaration of the Rights of Man and of the Citizen, both in 1789. The assertion and definition of civic rights antedated the popular right to vote, which was expanded only gradually.

For centuries, there have been plenty of arguments within the broad liberal family about the nature and structure of government; about freedoms from government versus affirmative freedoms that require state action; about the relationship between free markets and free peoples; and about tolerable extremes of inequality. Two of the ideals of liberal democracy—liberty and equality—are in necessary tension, because liberty presumably includes the freedom to get rich, but at some point economic inequality undercuts political equality.

Beyond dispute, however, are a few core principles involving a large zone of individual privacy, limits on arbitrary power, and the contestability of public office. As the economist and political philosopher Joseph Schumpeter observed, for there to be genuine competition for leadership, the rest logically follows—free speech, free press, opposition accepted as loyal, and incumbent government not rigging elections.

Although it is comforting to believe in the myth of progress—in this case, the idea that the world is moving inexorably toward liberal democracy—the reality is long periods of dark ages, some of them all too recent. Democracy is more fragile than we would like it to be. It is particularly vulnerable when the economy deserts the common people.

There is a long history of illiberalism and antidemocracy in practice and in theory, both in traditional monarchies that continue to this day in the Middle East, as well as in newly assertive medieval theocracies such as Islamic State, and new autocrats claiming to speak for a mythic people. For a time, moderate religion and constitutional democracy managed a peaceful coexistence, epitomized by America's separation of church and state, but a new wave of fundamentalist absolutism challenges the assumptions of mutual tolerance, even in well-established democracies. It is hard to think of a major Abrahamic religion, whether Christianity, Judaism, or Islam, that is not more fundamentalist today than it was in the mid-twentieth century.

This trend, too, is an assault on liberalism, both in the new religious claims on the polity and in the liberal state's frequently awkward response to religious absolutism.

Liberal democracy has been attacked by the far left as a sham that serves the ruling class, and by the far right as naïve about human nature. Anti-liberal theorists from Joseph de Maistre writing in the era of the French Revolution, to fascists in the twentieth century, have insisted that the ideal of civic man is preposterous. Real people, they contend, are not the rational individuals of liberal theory, but creatures bound to ties of blood and soil. Carl Schmitt, a German philosopher influential during the Weimar and Nazi eras, contended that parliamentary democracy was just a front for special interests and that true democracy was organic.

Today's right-wing populism is a repudiation of liberalism in its multiple forms. Ultranationalist leaders are contemptuous of the norms of parliamentary democracy. Radically nationalist masses reject such liberal values as tolerance, compromise, universal rights, and informed deliberation. There are national variations, but the common elements include a feeling that the system has failed the citizenry; that the Nation must be taken back from the cosmopolitans; and a belief that a strong Leader who embodies the true popular will is preferable to squabbling and corrupt parliamentarians.

In this respect, twenty-first-century right-wing populism is disconcertingly reminiscent of important elements of twentieth-century fascism, though less vicious, at least so far. What is chilling is the rejection of many of the elements not just of liberal democracy—but of modernity itself, including rationalism and even objective truth. If the public cannot agree on what is true via recourse to evidence, democratic deliberation is impossible.

As Robert Paxton, a leading historian of fascism, observes, there is no single manifesto or program of fascism. "Its truth rested not upon the truth of its doctrine but upon the leader's mystical union with the historic destiny of his people." Indeed, fascism, unique among ideologies, took pride in having no program as such, beyond the intuitions of the leader. Asked by a critic from the paper *Il Mondo* what his program was, Mussolini replied, "The democrats of *Il Mondo* want to know what our program is? It is to break the bones of the democrats of *Il Mondo*."

In his synthesis of core principles of fascism, Paxton suggests these:

- A sense of overwhelming crisis
- The primacy of the group
- The belief that one's group is a victim
- Dread of the group's decline under the corrosive effects of individualistic liberalism, class conflict and alien influences
- The need for closer integration of a purer community
- A national chief who alone is capable of incarnating the group's destiny
- The superiority of the leader's instincts over abstract and universal reason
- The beauty of violence and the efficacy of will, when they are devoted to the group's success
- The right of the chosen people to dominate others without restraint from any divine or human law.

Leaving aside the purifying effect of violence (which seems to appeal mainly to a few despots outside of Europe, such as Rodrigo Duterte of the Philippines), every major populist leader in Europe today has invoked most of these themes. The sense of national victimhood, the perceived failure of democratic liberalism, the threat of alien influences, and the appeal of an authoritarian leader who embodies the true Nation are pervasive. And Trump is skilled at applauding violence of which he approves. Violence can be rhetorical and symbolic as well as literal.

Yet there is one big difference between the fascism of the 1930s and the far-right reaction today, that provides a sense of hope. Not long after seizing power, Mussolini, Hitler, and Franco destroyed parliamentary institutions and took total control. Opposition was not just risky. It was utterly crushed. None of today's far right parties in the West, even those in power, has gone that far. Describing the press as "enemies of the people," as Trump has, is not the same as shutting the press down. One could also make a case that Congress is stronger today than when Trump took office. This is no basis for complacency, but a reason to resist despair.

FROM NATIONALISM TO FASCISM

The history of twentieth-century fascism begins with the nationalist struggles of nineteenth-century Europe. That era was marked by rising consciousness on the part of nationalities without states. Poles, Czechs, Slovaks, Croats, Romanians, Hungarians, Bulgarians, Serbs, Albanians, Greeks, and more found themselves stuck in somebody else's empire. All wanted their own states that corresponded to their ethnicity, language, and culture. Jews were strewn across the continent, sometimes eager to be accepted as locals, sometimes wanting to be apart.

Germany and Italy, divided among several principalities, achieved a fraught unification—but far from a liberal one. For other nations, the project of neatly aligning state with nation proved all but impossible (short of ethnic cleansing). Nationalities were hopelessly intermingled, with Hungarians and Romanians, Serbs and Croats, Czechs and Slovaks, Albanians and Chechens, Greeks and Turks living cheek by jowl in surprisingly cosmopolitan towns like Sarajevo and thousands of others occupied by multiple ethnic groups.

The revolutions of 1848 pursued a liberal, republican form of nationalism. But the empires struck back, and all these revolutions were crushed. The eminent historian A. J. P. Taylor referred to 1848 as the year when history "reached a turning point, but failed to turn." Nationalist aspirations would have to await the carving of parts of the old Habsburg, Ottoman, and Russian Empires into nine new countries at the Versailles Peace Conference seventy-one years later.

The decaying empires of the era—the Austrian and the Ottoman— had one surprising virtue: they were far from totalitarian, and intermittently tolerant of ethnic diversity and a relatively free press. They became severely repressive only in the early twentieth century, partly in response to heightened nationalist uprisings.

This is a point to which we will return: liberalism and democracy do not necessarily go together. It is possible to be nondemocratic, but relatively liberal in accepting core values of the rule of law and respect for the individual. British Hong Kong did not allow even limited representative democracy until 1991, but it respected traditional English personal liberties. Conversely, fascism can be "democratic," in that tyrants are sometimes freely elected and even enjoy fervent mass support, but are profoundly illiberal.

With the widespread failure of liberal nationalism in the nineteenth century, the dominant form became tribal. Racial unity, as Hannah Arendt put it, became "a substitute for national emancipation." Common racial origin came to be defined as the essence of nationhood. This was the opposite of American nationhood, which was creedal rather than tribal.

The Great War not only destroyed the common European civilization of elites. It drastically weakened liberal constitutionalism. So, at the very moment that the Treaty of Versailles attempted a bold program of liberal nation building, parliamentary democracy was too weak to carry the project.

Woodrow Wilson's ideal of national self-determination was doomed in part by the problem of national minorities. There were ethnic Hungarians in Romania, Slovaks in Poland, Greeks in Turkey. Only about 60 percent of the new Polish state carved from Germany and czarist Russia were Poles. Italians found themselves in Yugoslavia, itself a cauldron of contending nationalities. With the shrinkage of Germany as punishment for the Great War, there were large numbers of Germans in Alsace and the Saar, now regions of France, as well as in the Czech Sudetenland and in Russia. Rather than melting pots of mutual tolerance, the result was heightened nationalism and irredentism. The project was further doomed by the prolonged economic distress of the interwar period.

RIGHT-WING POPULISM
AS AN ECHO OF FASCISM

Fascism thrived on the failure of parliamentary democracy to solve urgent problems. In the aftermath of World War I, these included national humiliation and economic catastrophe, never a good combination. The failures, in turn, discredited democracy itself, to the point where people were willing to turn to dictators. Even in the United States, at the pit of the Great Depression, there were calls to give Franklin Roosevelt dictatorial powers. In that era, "dictator" was close to a good word. Studebaker, for a decade beginning in 1928, manufactured a popular car called the Dictator. The model was prudently retired in 1937.

In 1932, on the eve of FDR's presidency, Benito Mussolini proclaimed, "The liberal state is destined to perish." He added, all too accurately, "All the political experiments of our day are anti-liberal." Unlike the dictatorships, which were willing to forcefully use a strong state, the democracies evidently could not fix their broken economies. Parliamentary systems were hamstrung politically by partisan blockage. The democracies were also war-weary, conflict-averse, and ill prepared to fight. The fascists, unlike the democracies, had solved the problem of who was part of the community. Fascism provided a state and society with organic unity.

Fascists, like today's right-wing populists, invoked a mystical "People"—a *Volk*. They proposed a direct alliance between Leader and People, unmediated by the pluralist institutions that are beloved by liberals like Tocqueville and modern parliamentarians. But these institutions had lost legitimacy with the masses; they were seen as corrupt, inept, and cosmopolitan, with no allegiance to the People. For Hitler, the enemies included international bankers, Bolsheviks, the decadent Weimar culture, and Jews. Fascism involved rituals of purification, and private armies. Fascist dictators soon swept away all institutions not controlled by the ruling party, though they made accommodations with both corporate elites and the Roman Catholic Church.

The idea of a maximum leader, uncorrupted by mediating institutions, predates both populism and fascism. When the Roman Republic gave way to Caesar, the appeal of a dictator was similar. Jean-Jacques Rousseau proposed a version of democracy—the leader in direct relation to the people—that was at odds with the carefully mediated civic republic of Locke and the Madisonian Constitution, whose checks and balances were directed as much against the passions of a temporary majority as they were against the abuses of a king.*

Fascism promised regeneration and purification of the long-suffering, long-humiliated true People. It was both antimodern, in its romantic, heroic conception of the Nation, and modernizing in

---

*Rousseau proposed a "law-giver" who would create a constitution that expressed the general will, and then somehow give way to democratic popular sovereignty.

its use of state-sponsored industry, technology, and public works. Its socialism was nationalist. Fascism represented a rejection of the liberal constitutionalism that was seen as corrupt, moribund, and ineffectual.

Italian fascism was the first to invoke—proudly—the word and concept of totalitarianism. All institutions not controlled by the ruling party were extirpated. "The Fascist conception of the State is all embracing," Mussolini wrote. "Outside of it no human or spiritual values can exist, much less have value. Thus understood, Fascism is totalitarian, and the Fascist State—a synthesis and a unit inclusive of all values—interprets, develops, and potentates the whole life of a people."

The party would embody the state, and the state would embody the people. The Leader (*Duce*) would represent the entire people as an organic community, in place of the failed, blocked, and squabbling form of parliamentary democracy that had discredited itself in the years right after World War I. Read today, many of the core precepts of fascism sound like mystical gobbledygook. But in the 1920s, an era of failed politics and failed economics, they spoke to a great many Europeans.

Against the collapsing parliamentary governments and chronic economic crises of the 1920s, Mussolini's Italy looked to be a rare island of competence and national purpose. The US ambassador to Italy, Richard Child, not only wrote a fawning introduction to the US edition of Mussolini's autobiography; he helped ghostwrite the book as a paid propagandist. Child wrote:

> In our time it may be shrewdly forecast that no man will exhibit dimensions of permanent greatness equal to those of Mussolini. . . . He has not only been able to secure and hold an almost universal following; he has built a new state upon a new concept of a state. He has not only been able to change the lives of human beings but he has changed their minds, their hearts, their spirits. . . . I knew him before the world at large, outside of Italy, had ever heard of him; I knew him before and after the moment he leaped into the saddle and in the days when he, almost single-handed, was clearing away chaos' own junk pile from Italy.

Mussolini and Hitler were broadly popular once they annihilated their enemies. They got their nations out of economic crisis faster than the democracies did.

As we have seen, the policy reversals that began in the 1970s and intensified in the 1980s restored classical *economic* liberalism via globalization, at great cost to *political* liberalism. As social democrats in Europe and left liberals in the US have failed to promote credible alternatives, the backlash against economic liberalism (laissez-faire) has increasingly been illiberal in the political sense.

Today, the packaging of laissez-faire with constitutional liberalism is coming unstuck, because broad publics don't like the result. If something is expendable, it is political democracy (with the all the trimmings of tolerance), which increasingly seems like a charade. It doesn't matter what mainstream party you vote for, your world is still going to hell. Elites imposed a form of economic liberalism but forgot about ordinary citizens. Thus the revolt against the cosmopolitan governing class and the retreat into nationalism. The Dutch political scientist Cas Mudde puts it very well: "In essence, the populist surge is an illiberal democratic response to decades of undemocratic liberal policies." And in some respects, this, too, is akin to the descent into fascism.

After World War II, sifting through the ashes of the failed experiment in fascism, a number of social scientists connected the appeal of the fascist ideology to personality traits of marginalized people who sought an "escape from freedom" by relying on hypnotic leaders. These followers were said to have authoritarian personalities. Yet, as the rise of Trump suggests, such people exist in every society if circumstances push them hard enough, and it is more important to pay attention to the circumstances. When global market society destroys livelihoods, tribal nationalism comes to the fore, even in well-established democracies.

RIGHT-WING POPULISM
AND ANTI-LIBERALISM

A review of the history of fascism and the deepening economic and political crisis of the 1920s, followed by the rise of Hitler, makes today's right-wing populism look almost tame—until one views that populism in power. In Russia, Turkey, Poland, and Hungary, the governments look much like classical fascism, though not quite as totalitarian.

Many critics have described the new far-right governments as "illiberal democracies," with the forms but not the substance of genuine constitutional liberalism. In 2014, after winning reelection, Hungary's dictator, Viktor Orbán, proudly embraced the concept, declaring, "We have to abandon liberal methods and principles of organizing a society, as well as the liberal way to look at the world." Sounding very much like a classical fascist invoking the organic unity of the nation, Orbán went on, "The Hungarian nation is not a simple sum of individuals, but a community that needs to be organized, strengthened and developed, and in this sense, the new state that we are building is an illiberal state, a non-liberal state."

The term "illiberal democracy" was popularized by Fareed Zakaria, who wrote an influential 1997 essay in *Foreign Affairs* titled "The Rise of Illiberal Democracy." His subject was mainly pseudo-democracies in the third world. This was before the upsurge of right-wing populism in the West, and it proved prescient. "Democratically elected regimes, often ones that have been reelected or reaffirmed through referenda, are routinely ignoring constitutional limits on their power and depriving their citizens of basic rights and freedoms," he wrote.

Many current critics have used the term "illiberal democracy" to describe the governments of Russia, Hungary, and Turkey. But one of the most careful scholars of right-wing populism, Jan-Werner Müller, objects that characterizing their regimes as any sort of democracy concedes too much to these autocrats. Basic personal rights, such as freedom of speech, assembly, and the press, and protection of minority views and groups, Müller warns, "are not just about liberalism (or the rule of law); they are constitutive of democracy as such." Even if ballot boxes are not stuffed, he adds, a seemingly free and fair vote can be undemocratic "if the opposition can never make its case and journalists are prevented from reporting the government's failures."

In Vladimir Putin's Russia, there are elections; opposition deputies even serve in the Duma; there is some semblance of a critical press. But it is a charade. The opposition never gets to govern. When critics make seriously threatening allegations, they are simply murdered.

Putin forms alliances with corporate magnates, but they are aware that their billions depend entirely on the favoritism of the regime. If they step out of line, they will be crushed. There is a secret police almost as pervasive as in the days of the KGB, from which Putin himself emerged. This is far from illiberal democracy. It is more like neofascism.

Russia under Putin is a milder version of the 1930s brand of fascism because dissenters are tolerated as long as they are basically harmless, and because Putin has not eliminated elections entirely; he has simply rendered the opposition meaningless. There is an opposition press of a kind, but it knows what lines not to cross. Like Hitler at the peak of his power, Putin enjoys broad popularity. Thus, populist neofascism is a form of democracy only in the sense that autocratic leaders command popular support and have the window dressing of parliamentary institutions, but at the expense of anything like liberalism. And Putin's version of capitalism is thoroughly corrupt, as far from Adam Smith as it is from Thomas Jefferson.

In Turkey, Recep Tayyip Erdoğan has pursued similar political strategies to render effective democracy close to meaningless. His Justice and Development Party reversed the long-standing Turkish support for secularism, using a closer alliance with Islam to rally rural and lower-income voters who feel scorned by the more cosmopolitan elements in Turkish society. He has increased spending on public works, while gradually converting Turkey to a more authoritarian state. Erdoğan was elected president in 2014 in a relatively free election, by the surprisingly narrow margin of 52 to 48 percent. Since then, he has offered a textbook case of how to use incumbency to turn democracy into dictatorship. A bungled coup attempt in 2016 gave Erdoğan the pretext for dismissing at least 130,000 civil servants accused of disloyalty, including teachers and judges; purging military personnel; and cracking down on the independent press. A referendum in April 2017 concentrated additional power in the presidency, making it all but impossible to dislodge him.

Neofascist populists like Erdoğan, in office, systematically move against independent power centers. In Turkey, and also in Hungary and Poland, ruling parties curtailed the authority of the courts to challenge extraconstitutional government actions. In all three countries, however, the semblance of parliamentary legitimacy is important to these leaders, and none has gone as far as Mussolini, Hitler, or Franco in eliminating parliament entirely.

Viktor Orbán is a classic case of a leader who preserves the semblance of democratic rule while rubbing out the ability of the opposition to challenge his policies, much less get elected. In opposition, Orbán's Fidesz party sponsored populist referenda, which among other things, abolished medical copayments and university tuitions.

After eight years of a left governing coalition that had lost credibility in a series of scandals, Orbán's party won an absolute majority and more than two-thirds of the parliamentary seats in the 2010 election, giving him the power to change the constitution. One of the changes reduced the number of deputies from 386 to 199, redrew the voting districts, and revised the voting bonus system to guarantee Fidesz a two-thirds majority and to make it even more difficult for the opposition ever to be elected. And there is an explicitly fascist party, Jobbik, to Orbán's *right*. The two far-right parties have the support of at least 60 percent of Hungarian voters, so this is nominally "democratic," in the sense of reflecting the will of the current majority, but profoundly illiberal and fundamentally antidemocratic in that the opposition cannot come to power.

Since being elected, Orbán has systematically destroyed the opposition press, the courts, and the universities as centers of dissent. In 2017 he moved to curtail the independence of the Central European University in Budapest, which had been founded and supported by George Soros to be a magnet for intellectual excellence and free inquiry. Orbán took the affiliation of Soros—a Hungarian-born Jew and the epitome of foreign money sponsoring "open society" institutions in central Europe—as a particular affront. Throughout Orbán's first six years, which corresponded with Barack Obama's presidency, he had been sternly warned by both American and EU officials that destroying the Central European University was a bright line that he must not cross. But with the election of Donald Trump, Orbán felt free to move.

In mid-2017, Orbán's Fidesz party plastered Budapest with posters of a grinning George Soros, with the words, "Don't let Soros have the last laugh." In case the message was not clear enough, friendly thugs then obliged by adding anti-Semitic graffiti, such as "Stinking Jew."

In another echo of the 1920s, the shrunken post–World War II boundaries of Hungary—a punishment for Hungary's wartime alliance with the Nazis—left several million ethnic Hungarians living in the surrounding states of Poland, Romania, and Czechoslovakia. So, another source of Orbán's populist appeal is lingering nationalist resentment, and his claim to speak for a "Greater Hungary." After Orbán won his supermajority in 2010, he acted to give the vote to ethnic Hungarians living outside Hungary. Over 98 percent of them voted for Fidesz. This result is suspicious, since polls in Romania showed about 20 percent of Hungarians supporting the even more extremist party Jobbik. The Orbán government also acted to make it far more difficult for liberal Hungarian citizens residing outside the country in places like London to cast votes.

In neighboring Poland, the government of Law and Justice Party leader Jarosław Kaczyński, which also has an absolute majority in parliament, has moved to restrict freedom of assembly by giving priority to demonstrations organized by the government, the ruling party, or the church, and narrowing the conditions for opposition meetings. The government has also undercut the financial footings of the opposition media, has made public media a tool of the ruling party, and has repeatedly tried to destroy the independence of the courts.

In Poland as in Hungary, the EU has sent delegations and issued warnings, but to no avail. In February 2017, the European Commission warned Poland to conform to the EU's basic democratic requirements or lose its voting rights. Kaczyński responded that the Commission's criticism "amuses" him. A more serious breach was averted in July 2017 when Poland's president, Andrzej Duda, following massive street protests, vetoed government legislation that would have ended Poland's independent judiciary. The Polish government's effort to fire the entire Supreme Court came just three weeks after Donald Trump delivered a fawning speech in Warsaw with no warnings against the Polish government's antidemocratic moves. And more such forays are expected.

The EU's tough punishment of nations that exceed deficit targets offers a painful contrast with its failure to act against member governments, such as Hungary and Poland, that sabotage democracy. This indulgence of autocrats is all too clear a reminder of the Union's deeper priorities; economic liberalism is far more important than political liberalism. The fact that the EU, which requires explicit constitutional liberties as a condition of membership, has been unable or unwilling to restrain Hungary and Poland is one more testament to the weakness of liberal democracy in the face of existential threats, just as the failure of Italian and German parliamentary democracy to constrain Mussolini and then Hitler reflected its terminal weakness. In a pithy summary of the totalitarian mind-set, historian Tony Judt wrote, "There were no disagreements in Stalin's universe, only heresies; no critics, only enemies; no errors, only crimes." One hears muted echoes of those sentiments in Erdoğan, Orbán, and Kaczyński.

Trump energized these and other dictators. In July 2017 he went out of his way to make Warsaw his first stop on a major European trip, lavishly praised the regime, and said not a word about its increasing assault on democracy. He passed up the usual presidential visit to the memorial to the uprising of the Warsaw Ghetto. Trump's "dog-whistle" anti-Semitism that played to the far-right base at home also reached Budapest, where American diplomatic pressure on Orbán not to go after the Central European University evaporated. During his May 2017 trip to Saudi Arabia, Trump signaled the Saudi regime that the United States would ignore human-rights abuses, saying, "We are not here to lecture." Given his mutual-admiration friendship with Vladimir Putin, any pressure on the Russian human-rights assault also disappeared. Oddly, Trump made an exception in his criticism of the Nicolás Maduro dictatorship in Venezuela, but then demolished his own credibility in Latin America by threatening an invasion.

FAR-RIGHT POPULISM IN WESTERN EUROPE

Comparing today's right-wing populism with twentieth-century fascism, one can find reasons for both reassurance and alarm. Far-right parties have made troubling gains in western Europe's democratic heartland, where they are now the second or third largest party in several national parliaments, but none of them is yet the lead party of government. But in Norway and Finland—the heartland of social democratic Scandinavia—a right-populist party is part of the governing coalition. The rise of far-right parties was abrupt, from about 5 percent of the national vote in the 1980s to about 20 percent in the current decade.

It's worth recalling that even in the 1930s, when unemployment rates averaged about 15 percent for much of Europe, fascism had little domestic political appeal beyond Germany, Italy, Spain, Portugal, Austria, and Hungary, all nations with very shallow democratic roots. In no nation other than Austria in 1932 and Weimar Germany in 1933 did parliamentary democracy bring a fascist regime to power. In western Europe, homegrown fascists gained little ground in the 1930s, despite the dire economic circumstances. All of the other fascist regimes in Europe came into existence through civil war, seizure, insurrection, military coup, or invasion by a fascist power. Ominously, neofascism has more popular appeal today in western Europe than in the decade of Hitler and the Great Depression. In a sense, Polanyi's description of too much free market producing social dislocation that would end in fascism was an even more prescient warning for our own era.

For now, liberal democracy in nations with strong constitutional traditions seems to be holding. Many observers credited Emmanuel Macron's strong defeat of Marine Le Pen to the negative role model of Donald Trump. Yet the parliamentary fragmentation and antisystem sentiments in the West are far from reassuring. As right-wing populist parties grow to upwards of 20 percent of the seats in national parliaments, they narrow the space for the political center (much less the political left) to redress popular grievances, and so the downward spiral of economic turmoil, government weakness, and loss of government credibility continues. The fragmentation and paralysis in national parliaments is compounded by the overlay of fragmentation in the EU.

The fact that far-right parties were marginalized in recent elections in Britain and the Netherlands conceals the fact they had significant influence on mainstream parties and politics. The UK Independence Party (UKIP) was wiped out in the British election of June 2017 mainly because Conservative prime minister Theresa May adopted most of UKIP's program. Likewise in the Netherlands, where the far-right party of Geert Wilders lost support, the center-right prime minister, Mark Rutte, adopted Wilders's anti-immigrant rhetoric. As

Jan-Werner Müller has observed, by pushing mainstream politicians toward the nationalist far right, right-wing populists win even when they lose.

Further, the relative marginalization of the populist far right is small comfort because democratic government continues to lose broad legitimacy as it fails to solve pressing problems. The two core problems, now as in the 1920s, are a persistent economic crisis and the question of nationality and membership. This was exactly the soil in which fascism developed in the interwar period. Barring a drastic and improbable change of course by centrist parties, the far right is likely to continue gaining ground in western Europe—deepening the cycle of escalating problems and lost legitimacy for the system, and growing support for antisystem parties.

In the newer and shakier democracies of eastern and central Europe, more neofascist parties may come to power. In several former Soviet satellites, the face of the new nationalist populism is a business leader with no direct ties to the political establishment. In Bulgaria, Veselin Mareshki, a wealthy independent who got rich on a near-monopoly network of pharmacy chains, garnered support by railing against the corruption of the political elite. In the Czech Republic, Andrej Babiš, the head of a large conglomerate, launched a personalist party that did so well that he joined the government as finance minister. In January 2018, Babiš's ally, the far-right nationalist Miloš Zeman, was reelected Czech president. Though the Czech economy has benefited from EU membership, 2017 Eurobarometer polls showed that only 25 percent of Czechs have a positive view of the EU. So economics is only part of the story. And in neighboring Slovakia, Boris Kollár, another wealthy businessman, launched his own political party in 2016 called Sme Rodina, or "We Are Family"— and won eleven seats in parliament, proposing a mix of libertarian economics, and opposition to the EU and to more immigration.

Similar figures have gained ground elsewhere in eastern Europe, and they are already the party of government in Poland and Hungary. In all of these former communist nations, democratic roots and party affiliations are shallow, creating openings for wild swings in elections, and the rise of antisystem figures.

The populist parties are all over the map in terms of their support for the traditional postwar welfare state. In Denmark, the far-right People's Party claims to be even more strongly in favor of welfare protections than the Social Democrats. It just wants to limit these benefits to Danes. The People's Party has succeeded in peeling away about half of the traditional voting base of the Social Democratic Party, notably among trade unionists, and has prompted an agonizing debate about whether Social Democrats might ever govern in coalition with populists. In the Netherlands, by contrast, the radically anti-Islamist Party of Freedom of Geert Wilders is more like a right-wing free-market party. It combines nativism with a call for a massive tax cut. The Norwegian Progress Party, which warns against the Muslim takeover of Europe, is similarly libertarian on economic issues.

This ideological indeterminacy, in traditional left-right terms, is another characteristic that right-wing populism shares with fascism. "NSDAP" (the Nazi Party) is an abbreviation for the party of national socialism. Hitler, once in office, won the affections of the German working class by sponsoring an improved welfare state and by promoting job-creating public works projects, even before the outlays on rearmament ended German unemployment. But Hitler also made close alliances with German industrial and banking cartels.

Today's populism represents an entirely understandable reaction to the dislocations of elite-led globalization. Yet the fragmentation and distrust produced by populism makes it that much harder to find our way back to a brand of mixed economy that will restore economic security and responsive government. Thus, populism is likely to feed on itself. Strange as it may sound at the beginning of the second year of the Trump presidency, the heartening exception is likely to be the United States of America.

THE TRUMP PARADOX

Of the several right-wing populist leaders on the world stage, the rise of Donald Trump presents the most intriguing paradox. On the one hand, he has displayed alarming elements that evoke aspects of 1920s and 1930s fascism. On the other hand, given the well-entrenched democratic institutions of the United States, constitutional democracy seems to be holding, at least for now.

On economic issues, Trump turned out to be about as far from populist as one can get. What remained of his alleged populism was an autocratic governing style and some jingoist effusions with scant meaningful parallels in actual policy. Rather, Trump has governed as a corporate conservative with an unstable personality.

Trump mixed business interests with national policies. In the spring of 2017, as he was revising his line on China to effect a rapprochement, ostensibly to combat North Korean nuclear ambitions, the Beijing government was granting Trump and his daughter Ivanka a slew of trademark protections on an unusually fast track, which will be of enormous help to the Trump family businesses. If a Trump-like president had been the incumbent in 2016, this would have been exactly the kind of corrupt swamp that candidate Trump would have excoriated. Yet his scapegoating of immigrants, foreigners, the media, and liberal elitists continued to shore up support with his hard-core base even as it alienated the rest of the country.

The classic fascist leader is a kind of crackpot genius, with an intuitive, almost feral gift for connecting to the grievances of the marginalized. This facility allows the leader to get away with breaking the normal rules of politics, and to be celebrated by his supporters all the more for every breach. It didn't hurt Trump that he resorted to shabby personal insults, grotesque comments about women, and ill-disguised appeals to racist sentiments. On the contrary, the breach of norms made him seem the champion of the outsiders whom the establishment had disparaged or ignored: a thug, but our thug.

An extreme form of cognitive dissonance kicked in. Trump, after all, was a billionaire from New York. At various points in his career, he had been a supporter of abortion rights. He never went to church. He ran as a champion of the forgotten working class, but he had cheated workers and subcontractors on his construction projects, and had swindled students at Trump University. His wife's convention address was plagiarized from the speech of *Michelle Obama*, of all people. But once Trump was seen as the emblem of the outsider, none of it mattered. Hitler, a swarthy Austrian, celebrated the blond purity of the ideal German, and somehow his fanatic supporters didn't notice the contradiction.

Fascists are not just charismatic, but entertaining. The Argentine populist Juan Domingo Perón and his wife, Eva, put on a terrific show. Likewise Mussolini, and of course Hitler. They were so compelling to their followers that the contradictions were effectively invisible. Trump was not only the first businessman-president; perhaps more important, he was the first reality TV entertainer.

Like the fascists of the 1920s and 1930s, Trump campaigned as the embodiment of a mystical true People that had been displaced from the respect it deserved. His phrase at the Republican National Convention, "I am your voice, I alone can fix it," could have been Mussolini speaking. Trump validated views and people who had previously been consigned to the far fringe.

He played to the belief that conventional politics was corrupt and "fake." Interestingly, fake was also a major concept for Mussolini, who regularly dismissed parliamentary democracy as "a sham and a fraud." Trump's populism sometimes tacked left and sometimes tacked right and was impossible to define ideologically.

Fascists use mobs or the threat of mobs to intimidate or physically assault opponents and silence critics. Hitler had his Brownshirt private militia of storm troopers, the SA, before he became chancellor. Then the SA became part of the state. The Internet adds a new wrinkle. During his campaign, Trump used tweets to incite cyber-mobs. Like the fascists, Trump exhorted his militant supporters to violence when protestors came to his rallies. He went so far as to say that maybe some gun nut—"the Second Amendment people"—could get rid of Hillary Clinton once and for all.

As president, speaking at a Long Island rally for crime victims, he urged police to be rougher on people they arrest, as a form of summary justice (ignoring that suspects are presumed innocent under our system). When neo-Nazis rampaged in Charlottesville, Virginia, in August 2017, Trump condoned their violence by proposing an equivalence with antiracist protestors. He thus energized the white nationalist far right, which was delighted with his comments.

Trump had a penchant for making things up, claiming that the system was rigged against him, and then turning the tables on his critics who dwelt in reality and accusing *them* of fakery. Obama's being born in Kenya, global warming's being a myth, Trump's actually winning the popular vote, vast numbers of immigrants' voting illegally—all this recalled Hitler's use of the Big Lie. Trump's intuitive strategy was to flood the zone. The press would be just catching up with one flagrant lie when Trump was on to three others. It was a brilliant tactic for undermining the free press—not by shutting it down, but by overwhelming it.

Trump also resorted to dog-whistle anti-Semitism, violating a long-standing gentlemen's agreement that Jew baiting had no place in American politics. And he did it in a way that allowed him to deny what he was doing, while still sending unmistakable signals to the white-nationalist base—by going out of his way not to commemorate Jewish events, and even using a poster from a white-nationalist website that pinned a Star of David on Hillary Clinton, and then claiming that it was a sheriff's star.

When Trump won his surprise victory, many commentators treated it as almost a coup d'état. As he prepared to take office, there was widespread alarm about whether the US Constitution would hold.

Previously, the United States had been extremely lucky in the self-restraint of presidents who governed in true national emergencies. The three greatest wartime presidents were paragons of restraint. George Washington could have been king, but he chose to cast his lot with a republic, to put a broad spectrum of Federalists and anti-Federalists into his cabinet, and to step down after two terms. Abraham Lincoln, as Doris Kearns Goodwin wrote, deliberately named rivals to his cabinet, who served as checks on his own predispositions. He implemented emergency wartime measures, such as suspension of habeas corpus, sparingly and with reluctance. There were calls for Franklin Roosevelt to assume dictatorial authority, but for the most part he did not ask for or use emergency powers. His appalling decision to round up loyal Japanese Americans into concentration camps was the exception. Trump, by contrast, contemplated the use of executive powers to excess and with relish.

The founders of our republic devised a complex system of checks and balances as a bulwark against tyranny. But much of our liberty depends on the internal constitutions of our leaders—their respect for democratic norms, and sense of restraint. When presidential restraint falters, the latent power of the two other branches of government kicks in—but sometimes it doesn't. Congressional Republicans, most of whom loathed Trump and resented him as an interloper, cynically decided that he could be used. If there was a deeper cost to democratic institutions, the Republican right and its corporate allies had already displayed little regard for democracy.

Critics began tallying all of the ways that Trump could bring a kind of soft fascism to America without even breaking the law. He could use the power of US attorneys and the IRS, Nixon style, to selectively target political enemies. He could sic regulatory agencies on hostile newspaper publishers and TV network executives who had other business interests to protect, such as *Washington Post* publisher Jeff Bezos, owner of Amazon (a corporation that surely deserves to have antitrust problems). He could exercise the awesome power of the commander in chief to govern as more of an autocrat, or use the next terrorism event to seek or seize emergency powers. Impeachment, let's recall, is ultimately a political remedy. Nixon could be impeached and driven from office only because the Democrats controlled Congress.

And then something unexpected and even heartening happened. Reality intruded.

REALITY BITES

Trump's personal habit of dwelling in an alternative reality where up was down and truth was lie could work to get him elected. But once in office, he bumped into the real world.

Trump discovered that he could not govern by decree. The FBI was not about to become his personal secret police. When Trump fired FBI director James Comey and failed to keep his story straight, the deputy attorney general, Rod Rosenstein, who had been used and then undercut, was quick to name a special counsel, former FBI director Robert Mueller. Republican legislators, who had been defending Trump, cheered Mueller's appointment and signaled that removing him would not be a good idea. Republicans in Congress joined Democrats and used legislation to block Trump's ability to waive sanctions against Russia.

Trump's alliance with a badly split Republican Party not accustomed to the discipline of governing resulted in a prolonged humiliation in the failure to repeal the Affordable Care Act. When he ordered Republican legislators to keep at it, Trump learned that they did not have to follow his orders, and they moved on. His sole legislative win, a tax cut, was the work of the Republican Congress. The cooling of Republican congressional support for Trump narrowed his room to govern as an autocrat. After tacking in opposite directions on the question of whether to deport "Dreamers" brought America as children, Trump ultimately punted the issue to Congress rather than attempting to seize more executive power.

Classical fascists had formed new political parties. As an incipient authoritarian, Trump was hobbled by the fact that he had come to power via a hostile takeover of one of America's two major parties, many of whose independently elected leaders were quite antagonistic toward him. As Trump's behavior became increasingly bizarre, that animosity only deepened. In short, separation of powers held, even though one party nominally controlled all three branches of government. A less impaired and more competent autocrat might have done far more damage.

In addition to the reality of America's separation of powers, the reality of the wider world intruded on the entire range of foreign policy challenges, from NAFTA and Mexico, to China's currency manipulation, to Syria, to North Korea's missile threats and the issue of Israeli settlements. In every case, Trump backed down from the oversimplified, aggressive stance of the campaign (though he continued buffoonishly insulting or flattering foreign leaders). Like health insurance, foreign policy turned out to be complicated.

Though Trump professed the characteristic far-right support for the military and proposed significant increases in weapons spending, the generals emerged as one of the most significant checks on his impulses. The military tends to be conservative in the best sense of the word. When zealous civilians (like Dick Cheney, Donald Rumsfeld, George W. Bush, Lyndon Johnson, Richard Nixon, and company) send American forces on fools' errands based on grandiose lies, it is the military that pays the price. And the generals know that.

It was a little strange for critics of Trump with no love of militarism to admit that the security of American democracy was substantially in the hands of three retired Marine Corps generals: the defense secretary, James Mattis; the national security adviser, H. R. McMaster; and the secretary of homeland security, John Kelly, who was elevated in July 2017 to White House chief of staff.

Though Kelly has often done Trump's bidding, these are serious men, with the patriotism and self-respect to tell the president when he is blowing smoke. As Trump discovered, he may love firing people, but he can't fire them all.

Trump's ultranationalist strategist Steve Bannon in a sense was right. The deep administrative state, otherwise known as the US Constitution, had a lot of staying power. Yet the deep state also includes Goldman Sachs, whose hold on politics has been redoubled under Trump.

Even if Trump does not manage to govern as a dictator, there is a huge amount of damage he can do as an ordinary, if somewhat personally deranged, far-right conservative. In 2017, key executive branch positions went unfilled. Public spending that serves ordinary Americans was gutted. Regulatory safeguards that protect consumers, workers, and investors were repealed. The assault on the right to vote at the state level was intensified by Trump's Justice Department and Orwellian commission on election integrity, chaired by Vice President Pence and Kansas secretary of state Kris Kobach. The immense far-right money machine continues to have strategic influence, beyond Trump's personal fate. Though Trump did not defy the courts or try to summarily remove judges in the manner of Erdoğan, or Kaczyński, the judiciary is becoming steadily more far-right thanks to ordinary Republican tactics of blockage. Whereas other right-wing nationalists bought off the populace with expanded public works investment and welfare-state spending, Trump's intermittent promises to improve health benefits and public jobs were mere campaign rhetoric.

All of this, of course, only deepens the economic frustrations that brought Trump to office. It's not quite a silver lining, but these policies are far from popular. Nor, after the novelty wears off, is a clownish, clueless president of the United States. In his first several months in office, Trump was the most unpopular new president since modern public-opinion polling began. Mark Twain observed that it is easier to fool a person than to persuade him that he has been fooled. But even cognitive dissonance has its limits.

Looking forward, America faces three broad possibilities. Trump could well be forced from office before his term ends. At the other extreme, he could continue turning America into an autocracy, relying on a national security crisis, real or contrived. Or opposition could continue gaining ground.

I do not have a crystal ball, but there is reason for guarded optimism. Despite all of the assaults against serious public discourse, voter suppression, and the abuses of the normal legislative process, we are a long way from dictatorship. The elections of November 2017 in Virginia, New Jersey, and New York as well as the Maine ballot initiative to expand Medicaid under the Affordable Care Act, displayed not just a popular revulsion against Trump approaching a "blue wave," but real grassroots energy on the progressive side. Brand-new activist groups with names like Indivisible, Flippable, and Run for Something looked to the future, trained candidates, and energized thousands of voters to win legislative seats that Democrats in prior years had not even bothered to contest.

Yet a blue wave, to succeed, will need to be large enough to overcome both voter suppression and gerrymandering. As we saw in Chapter 1, democracy has been under assault for decades, and with it, respect for government and politics as a source of remediation. The authoritarianism of Trump, despite the fact that mainstream Republicans don't like him, has operated in symbiosis with the Republican strategy of undermining of the right to vote, the growth of far-right media as propaganda, courts undermining public-interest regulation, and the gross corporate use of money to overwhelm speech. In addition, the Russian effort to sow confusion and mistrust through hacks, leaks, and misinformation damaged the credibility of the American political process, and these tactics will continue.

Even if a progressive gets elected in 2020, the undertow of antidemocracy will persist, and it will take time for government and politics as a counterforce to regain constructive impact and broad legitimacy. This effort must be deliberate and strategic, or it will fail.

It will be a long road back to a socially decent economy and a government that enjoys broad legitimacy. But assuming the Constitution continues to hold, the Democratic nominee in 2020 is likely to be more of a progressive populist than any of the party's recent standard-bearers—a candidate from the Elizabeth Warren wing of the party more in the spirit of Franklin Roosevelt. That shift, in turn, would allow a progressive form of populism to contest the white-nationalist brand of populism, and to rebuild a mixed economy of broadly based prosperity.

The Obama presidency, seen in this light, was something of a false start. Obama came to power as an outsider, at a moment when the financial collapse disgraced both the Republican laissez-faire ideology and the bipartisan deregulation of the financial industry. The new American leader, as I wrote in my 2008 book *Obama's Challenge*, was poised to be either a transformative president in the mold of Roosevelt, or another centrist Democrat captured by Wall Street. When Obama, a conciliator by temperament, proved to be more the latter than the former, a political moment was missed. But it will come round again.

Despite all of its sources of legislative blockage, the United States is ultimately a single country with a state capable of governing. In the EU, the blockage of an economic recovery program and the perverse regime of austerity are likely to continue—producing more support for neofascism.

Thus, if there is a road back to a strengthened democracy and a restoration of a balanced economy in the West, it will likely begin in the United States—a reprise of the benign role that the US played to promote a mixed economy in the era of postwar reconstruction. That will be far from easy; the fortuitous circumstances of 1944 have no obvious counterpart on the near horizon. But it is not impossible.

12

THE ROAD FROM HERE

Democratic capitalism today is a contradiction in terms. Globalization under the auspices of private finance has steadily undermined the democratic constraints on capitalism. In a downward spiral, the popular revulsion against predatory capitalism has strengthened populist ultranationalism and further weakened liberal democracy.

If democracy is to survive, the cycle will need to be reversed. This will require much stronger democratic institutions and a radical transformation of capitalism into a far more social economy. It will require different global rules, to allow more space for national policy. Conversely, if the current brand of capitalism survives, it is likely to become even more corrupt, concentrated, and undemocratic. So the emerging system will be either more autocratic and more controlled by capital—or more democratic and less capitalist.

In the 1990s, a formulation popularized by George Soros distinguished open societies from closed ones. An open society was pluralist, with a web of civic institutions not controlled by government, and respect for the whole range of personal and political liberties. After the fall of communism, the West was working to bring the liberal values of an open society to newly democratic eastern Europe, and to other autocracies worldwide.

Today, that distinction of open versus closed societies tells only part of the story. A more pointed distinction, as Soros himself has recognized, is democratic societies versus crony-capitalist societies. Corrupt capitalism seems to be gaining, while the number of democracies is shrinking. Some twenty-five democracies have failed just since 2000.

DEMOCRACY VERSUS CAPITALISM

The Russian or Turkish or Chinese versions of crony capitalism don't pretend to be democratic. The fact that democratic Germany does a lot of business with despotic Russia, and American corporations and their Chinese counterparts have no difficulty negotiating partnerships, suggests that there is more convergence than we might like to admit. As James Mann prophetically warned more than a decade ago, dampening the euphoria around China's admission to the WTO, China is not becoming more like us; we are becoming more like them.

Fascism, it's worth recalling, had two aspects. One was dictatorship, with worshipful or intimidated masses angry at the usual elites and seeking salvation in a strongman. The other face of fascism was corporate. Despite the apparent contradiction, dictators and corporations got along nicely. They both understood power. Donald Trump personifies a corporate alliance, in which the leader's political and business interests simply blend. Half the members of his cabinet have similar conflicts.

To its enthusiasts, capitalism is democratic in two key respects. Capitalist norms and democratic norms are said to converge via transparency and rule of law. But there is a fundamental divergence between the core democratic principle of one person/one vote and the basic market norm of one dollar/one vote. Democracy thrives to the extent that the raw power of money is contained.

Capitalism is also said to be democratic because everyone has the opportunity to become a shareholder or an entrepreneur. The American dream of upward mobility for all epitomizes those claims. The relative openness of capitalism in its idealized form is what gives the system its claim to both efficiency and legitimacy. American capitalism might still be considered "open" in the sense that a Jeff Bezos of Amazon or a Travis Kalanick, late of Uber, can dream up an idea, win venture-capital backing, introduce a new, must-have consumer product or platform, and become a billionaire many times over. But the rules of the game are increasingly rigged against ordinary workers, consumers, and even potential rivals. Public systems of regulation and transparency that are supposed to keep the game honest are increasingly corrupted. Donald Trump's mingling of his business and political interests is a caricature version of the corruption, but in much of American industry and finance, such conflicts of interest are the new normal.

Despite the myth of American mobility, for decades the more socialized economies of northern Europe have done a far better job of allowing people to rise above the station of their parents, while class lines in the US have hardened. The American dream has been alive in social democratic Scandinavia—alive, but not well. As we've seen, the pressures of the global market have breached even well-defended social compromises in Sweden and Denmark.

The preface of this book introduced a notional argument between Karl Marx and Karl Polanyi. Critics of capitalism writing in the spirit of Marx have long insisted that capitalism is doomed by its own contradictions. Polanyi, with Keynes, believed that given the right democratic mobilization and the right policy interventions, a mixed economy could adapt and thrive. That hope was realized in the three decades after World War II. Conversely, Polanyi argued that if markets were not harnessed in a broad public interest, their excesses would destroy both market society and democracy. This is what happened in the 1920s and 1930s, and it has echoes now.

Another, lesser-known figure from that era is also worth invoking. The Polish-born British economist Michał Kalecki, a student of Keynes, located himself somewhere between Keynes and Marx. He wrote a seminal essay in 1943 titled "Political Aspects of Full Employment," whose argument rings even truer today.

As a technical economist, Kalecki agreed with Keynes that capitalism, with the right policy interventions, could indeed be stabilized in the service of broad prosperity and legitimacy. But wearing his Marxian hat, Kalecki argued that the capitalists would strenuously resist such a program, because it would require them to give up too much power and wealth. So, if managed capitalism was possible in theory, it was unlikely in practice.

For the golden generation after World War II, Kalecki's view seemed too pessimistic. Popular mobilizations were keeping the power of elites at bay, and democratically elected governments were pursuing policies that stabilized a market economy and broadly distributed prosperity—and as a side effect, reduced the political power of private finance. But Kalecki's insight about the residual power of capital in a capitalist economy has surely been vindicated in the years since 1973.

Given that the stars aligned so perfectly for an interlude of a democratic mixed economy in the years after 1944, and given how out of alignment they are now, what might offer cause for optimism? Institutionally, as Kalecki predicted, the captains of industry and finance have succeeded in taking back so much power, and the backlash is so antidemocratic, that the politics of balanced capitalism seems even more improbable today than it was on the verge of World War II.

Indeed, in the 1930s we at least had a full-blown depression to undermine the legitimacy of raw capitalism and capitalists. We had the Soviet Union posing both a geopolitical threat and an ideological alternative. We also had the most effective progressive populist president in American history, using the powers of an expanded democratic state to constrain capital and help the common people—a virtuous circle that steadily built more legitimacy for government and the mixed economy.

Today, corporate and financial elites have substantially captured the machinery of the state and neutralized the nominally center-left party as a source of systemic reform. Galbraith's idea of democratic government, trade unions, and citizens' organizations as "countervailing" forces against private corporate power (a theory propounded in 1952 during the flush of the postwar boom) doesn't work when corporate power dominates the state too.

Government and politics as instruments of broad public improvement have lost credibility. Right-wing nationalist populism and neofascism have substantially filled this vacuum. Globalist institutions have further stymied democratic-left alternatives. How might we turn this vicious circle back into a virtuous one?

THE CASE FOR PROGRESSIVE POPULISM

In times like these, the entrenched power of financial elites is so potent that only a popular mobilization can begin to contest it. This is what Roosevelt was able to accomplish in the 1930s and early 1940s. It took inspired leadership backed by the power of mass movements. Many of Roosevelt's policies were radical. But once enacted, they became normal, economically successful, and beloved by the populace. Social Security is our most socialistic program, but citizens do not experience it as radical.

During the past century, radical democrats have often run for office, but the undertow of money in a market economy is so potent that they seldom get elected. In the West, the main exceptions were Roosevelt in the US, Attlee in Britain, and the long reign of social democrats in Scandinavia from the 1930s to the 1990s.

When radical democrats do manage to get elected and reelected, however, something remarkable happens. Their programs often turn out to be both practical and popular. They demonstrate that it is indeed possible to have a dynamic mixed economy that is also socially just. But their success requires a popular mobilization that is hard to sustain over time.

In past decades, the labor movement played the role of that sort of ongoing mobilization of the common people as an institutional counterweight to the ever-present power of capital in a market economy. When labor evolved from a radical shop-floor movement into a bureaucratic manager of contract settlements, that power was compromised. The further weakening of organized labor by resurgent business and deliberate antilabor policies has been a major part of the tilt back to raw capitalism.

One of the analytical mistakes made by many commentators is to conflate progressive populism and neofascist populism. When you read articles in the popular press that refer to populism and populists, you can almost see the writer raising an eyebrow of disapproval. Populism, whether of the progressive or reactionary variety, is usually seen as akin to demagoguery and to an embrace of fantastical, irrational assumptions about how economies work. Michael Kazin, a historian of populism, writes archly, "The 'populist' whose politics you abhor is always a demagogue disguised as a hero of the masses." Even Paul Krugman, nobody's idea of a conservative, accused Bernie Sanders of "demagoguing" the trade issue.

Sanders, though he doesn't share Krugman's view of recent trade deals, is as committed a small-d democrat as anyone in public life.

Yet Sanders was repeatedly condemned as a populist (in the sense of rabble-rouser) because he rallied the common people against economic abuses. Unlike right-wing populists who traffic in myths, Sanders dwelt in reality; he appreciated and helped interpret the arduous reality experienced by working people. Sanders invariably scored highest in the fact-check features published during the 2016 campaign.

Massachusetts senator Elizabeth Warren is another fine example of a progressive populist. When Warren declared that "the rules are rigged" (long before Trump did), she was not making false claims about illegal immigrants voting. She was describing—in accurate, well-informed detail—how bankruptcy laws are stacked to favor corporations over families; how the fine print in student loan contracts can leave even elderly parents liable for student debts imposed by fraudulent private universities; how misleading mortgage contracts can lead to astronomical interest rate increases; how health insurance plans are written to deny medical care when it is most needed; how arbitration clauses imposed as a condition of employment can deny workers their day in court even when employers break the law. And on and on. In these abuses and the inchoate mass sense that something is very wrong, there is a latent majority politics.

Altering rules that are rigged against ordinary people, often in obscure and insidious ways, requires populist leadership. The current abuses and Warren's efforts to narrate, explain, and remedy them are reminiscent of the politics of the populist grievances of the late nineteenth century, a time when monopoly railroads charged farmers extortionate rates to ship their crops, monopoly financiers denied farmers necessary credit, and local merchants kept farmers perpetually in debt to provide seasonal financing and materials for planting and harvests.

Though "populism" gets a condescending press, progressive populism is precisely what's required. As we saw in the 2016 election and in the political history of the US and Europe going back to the nineteenth century, popular frustrations about perceived economic injustice can go left or right. Trump and Sanders appealed to some of the same voters, but with very different narratives about what ailed the economy and the polity.

The tendency of commentators to blur neofascist populism with progressive critiques of the current rules of the economy is testament to just how thoroughly orthodox economists and the media opinion leaders have internalized the conventional wisdom about finance, trade, and market economics. Nowhere is this truer than in the defense of globalization. Critics of the particulars of proposed "trade" deals (which mainly promote deregulation) are grandly dismissed with irrelevant generalizations about the broad efficiency of trade.

Ideally, we should jettison the word "populism" and refer instead to neofascist nationalism versus progressivism. The trouble is that the word has broad currency (writers sometimes get to invent words, but not to banish them). But let us at least be clear in distinguishing between reactionary populism and progressive populism. Democracy will never keep financial elites at bay unless leaders rally ordinary people to understand the stakes, to participate in politics, and to use the instruments of political liberalism to keep elites from destroying a decent economy. That brand of populism is not abhorrent. It is indispensable.

WHY THE UNITED STATES NEEDS TO LEAD

Today, other nations are contending for global leadership. The Russian version combines nationalism, dictatorship, and corruption. Even nations on the periphery of Russia, such as Turkey, Poland, and Hungary, long wary of Russia's military reach, are attracted to the political formula. The Chinese model is a blend of one-party rule, state capitalism, and neomercantilism. Japan and South Korea are the exceptional cases that blend government-led capitalism, political democracy, and a good income distribution, but both are consumed with regional security challenges. India is becoming an economic superpower in its modern sectors, but it is mired in profound poverty, and its democracy is very shaky.

Not long ago, the EU offered a more social democratic–flavored mixed economy (but no longer), while the US was a beacon to the world because of its political and cultural openness, even if it left many people behind and its foreign policy was sometimes at odds with professed democratic ideals. Though America in the Trump era is increasingly self-isolating and not much of a beacon for anything, it is hard to imagine any other nation claiming the global mantle of political liberalism and economic equity. The United States was instrumental in disseminating a perverse version of globalism, and the US will have to take the lead in restoring a benign globalism. The post-Trump era will be a moment for American leadership, as urgent as in the era of World War II and the postwar.

A progressive EU, either as a diplomatic giant or as an economic leader pursuing continent-wide policies of economic expansion rather than austerity, seems tragically improbable. The EU also remains on the defensive against a wave of rising neofascism, and splintered because of its constitutional rules and political divisions. Maybe the European project will once again realize its promise, but not anytime soon.

In France, the centrist technocrat and modernizer Emmanuel Macron won an impressive victory in 2017. President Macron proposed a kind of grand bargain in which France would jettison rigid job protections, and in return, government would increase social investments. That way, more new job opportunities would arise and workers would not need to cling to existing jobs—a kind of Scandinavian solution.

Macron's approach, however, would require more public outlay, some of it deficit-financed, but France's budget was already over the Maastricht Treaty limits on deficits and debts. In his first months in office, Macron took steps to reduce spending. Despite his bold rhetoric as a *party* outsider, Macron is a consummate insider as a French centrist and member of the technical elite. In office he has turned out to be a fairly conventional center-right politician on economics, with liberal social views. France and the rest of the continent, led by Angela Merkel, have continued their austerity regime, breeding more nationalist neofascism. It would be nice to imagine a drastic change in Europe's suicidal course, but nobody has presented a plausible scenario. If the new center is represented by Macron, voters may feel a little better about the grandeur of France, but pocketbook grievances will continue to fester.

The rise of illiberal right-wing populist parties throughout Europe is particularly tragic because it was needless. In the postwar era, nations that had experienced fascism firsthand became citadels of successful democracy and broadening prosperity. With democratic regimes delivering good living standards and a broad sense of fairness, the nationalist far right had almost no appeal, and the emergent European project had broad support. History rarely provides opportunities for do-overs. But the postwar era was a kind of do-over for the failed efforts to build decent, capitalist democracies in the period after Versailles. A second do-over for Europe will be even harder.

America in recent years has been hamstrung by Republican legislative obstruction. In the US, by constitutional design, enacting activist policies requires substantial congressional majorities. Such progressive majorities have been put in place only twice in the last century—under FDR and under Lyndon Johnson's Great Society, when Democrats had majorities of almost 2 to 1 in the Eighty-Ninth Congress, of 1965–66. But with the repudiation of Trump and the election of a progressive Democrat to the White House, it could happen again.

America is not only more capable of shifting policy. It is also far better positioned than Europe to turn cultural diversity into a source of strength rather than mutual division and hostility. The United States has always done a better job than Europe of integrating migrant populations. Most immigrants to the US aspire to be Americans, and after two or three generations their grandchildren feel like Americans. In much of Europe, a great many migrants merely see a place to make a living free from the terror of their homelands. Typically, they are far less integrated than their American counterparts. The strongest bases of resurgent American progressivism today are in highly diverse cities such as Los Angeles and New York, where popular left governing alliances have been formed by broad multiethnic coalitions.

Therefore, if a decent balance of market, society, and democracy does regain ground, the shift will almost have to begin in the United States, as in the 1930s and 1940s, and then once again spread outward.

A RECOVERY OF PROGRESSIVE POLITICS

I noted at the outset of this book that history is a combination of deep structural forces and contingent events. Sheer luck can be good or bad, and here we are again. Unlike the EU, the United States, despite all its flaws, is structurally capable of governing the market, *if* the politics is aligned. For America to reverse political course and begin once again to harness a mixed economy in a broad public interest, a few things have to break the right way politically.

First, the progressive wing of the Democratic Party needs to emerge dominant from the infighting of the next few years, and the upsurge of activism needs to continue. That actually seems likely. The 2016 election pretty well discredited the Wall Street influence on the Clinton-Obama-Clinton wing of the Party. The momentum and energy were increasingly with the economic-progressive wing, and that tilt has only intensified since the election of Donald Trump. The resurgent grassroots activism on the Democratic side has been defined and led by progressives. Democrats elected to the House and Senate in coming elections, as well as the presidential nominee in 2020, are likely to stand for more of a pocketbook-populist program. The increased energy and turnout on the Democratic progressive side is likely to change the electoral calculus. Roosevelt won a landslide victory in 1936 less because formerly Republican voters switched sides than because of increased turnout that was overwhelmingly Democratic.

Second, for this scenario to unfold, the Republican Party needs to fragment along several axes—into Tea Party/Trump versus establishment factions on domestic policy; Putin-apologist and traditional national security factions on foreign policy; and white-nationalist/America First versus Wall Street globalist factions on economics. This fragmentation has already begun, and could well deepen.

Apart from the factors unique to Trump, it is normal in the first midterm election under a new president for the opposition party to have momentum and energy and for the president's party to lose seats. In every midterm election except 1934, the party of the newly elected president has lost House or Senate seats, and usually both. The average loss in the House has been about thirty seats. Trump's approval rating is far below that of other presidents, and his party is more divided. Even the sort of gerrymandering that has created a structural tilt against Democrats cannot be intensified between now and the 2018 election, since redistricting takes place only after each decennial census. Trump and Republican-led state governments will intensify voter suppression maneuvers, but even relatively conservative courts have acted to limit those tactics. Democrats may begin with a handicap of a few percentage points of the electorate in some swing states. Such a deficit is not insurmountable.

Bernie Sanders and Elizabeth Warren are from deep blue New England. But they are not unicorns. Democrats get elected in unlikely places running as economic populists. In the 2016 election, Donald Trump carried Montana by 23 points, but that state also elected a progressive Democratic governor, Steve Bullock, by 4 points. More than a quarter of the electorate voted for Trump but split their tickets for a populist Democrat. Bullock's two-term predecessor, Brian Schweitzer, who was barred from running again by term limits, was another Montana Democrat who had been elected and reelected as a progressive populist.

In neighboring North Dakota, which often elects right-wingers, one of the state's best-loved officials was its longtime populist Democratic senator Byron Dorgan, who retired in 2011. Dorgan first came to prominence at the age of twenty-six, when he became the state's tax commissioner. North Dakota is the only state with a popularly elected tax commissioner, a legacy of the prairie populism of the Progressive Era. At the time, federal contractors working at antiballistic missile (ABM) sites in North Dakota were claiming exemption from state taxes because of their association with a federal project, since states cannot tax the federal government. Dorgan taxed them and was upheld by the courts. He became wildly popular as the man who fought to tax the ABM. A number of other Democratic progressives, such as Ohio's Sherrod Brown, manage to be elected and reelected in swing ("purple") states, running as economic populists.

It's true that Democrats can also win in such states by running as economic and social moderates or as allies of Wall Street, appealing to crossover Republicans rather than rallying the populist economic base. Such was the case with the longtime, now retired, Democratic chair of the Senate Finance Committee, Max Baucus, a fervent advocate of laissez-faire trade and budget balance, a favorite of austerity activists, and one of Montana's wealthiest landowners. Another such Democrat is Virginia's recent governor, Terry McAuliffe, a wealthy centrist.

Pro-corporate Democrats can and do get elected with such views—but why bother? The policies they espouse will do nothing to change the economic fundamentals that breed the Tea Party reaction. After the era of Carter, Clinton, Obama, and finally Hillary Clinton, a two-party system that makes a constructive difference has to include a Democratic Party that is progressive populist. The hopeful news is that the party seems headed in that direction.

If a progressive Democrat is elected president in 2020, the House and Senate could also flip, reversing the situation of 2016. The new president could face a Republican Party somewhat divided and dispirited from the Trump interlude, as well as an electorate looking for a very different leader and set of policies. Even so, such a president would face an immense undertow of big money, as well as the entire apparatus of the Koch brothers, more reactionary courts, and right-wing think tanks and media—all of which bridge the "mainstream" Republican right with the neofascist right. The only possible antidote is a popularly mobilized progressive electorate.

If we can indulge the not-so-unlikely fantasy that a progressive Democratic president and Congress could be elected in 2020, what might that president actually accomplish—to restore faith in affirmative government, to counter and contain the power of finance, to damp down the appeal of neofascism domestically and globally, and to reclaim domestic policy space from the current golden straitjacket of globalism?

WHAT OTHER COUNTRIES CALL SOCIALISM

In his classic 1972 book *Inequality*, the sociologist Christopher Jencks and a team of collaborators examined all of the ways that schools were supposed to be instruments for achieving greater economic equality. They came away unimpressed with the capacity of schooling, by itself, to transform the deeper patterns of inequality, which were less extreme then than now. Jencks observed, "As long as egalitarians assume that public policy cannot contribute to economic equality directly, but must proceed by ingenious manipulations of marginal institutions like the schools, progress will remain glacial. If we want to move beyond this tradition, we will have to establish political control over the economic institutions that shape our society. This is what other countries call socialism."

This delicate wording was only prudent. In the United States, socialism has been the alternative that dare not speak its name. Since so much of the socialist tradition was discredited by totalitarian communism, democratic socialism got lumped in with, and presumably buried with, Stalinism. The lesson of the post-1973 era, however, is not that social democracy attempted too much, but that it left too much of capitalism intact. A successor brand of mixed economy will have to be a more robust hybrid—what other countries call democratic socialism. This imperative, as we've seen, is less economic than political. In a mixed economy, there is still a valuable role for entrepreneurs, but capitalists as a political class need to be constrained or they will destroy the foundations of a social contract.

Interestingly, nearly three decades after communism collapsed, Americans seem to have a far more benign view of socialism. In the 2016 campaign, Bernie Sanders made no secret of the fact that he had long considered himself not a liberal, but a democratic socialist. Yet the disaffection from what American capitalism had become was so profound by 2016—nominally a year of economic recovery and rising employment—that many voters no longer considered "socialism" a dirty word. Journalists rubbed their eyes in disbelief when they read public-opinion polls showing that 56 percent of Democrats, including a majority of Hillary Clinton supporters, reported that they held a favorable view of socialism. Indeed, long before the Sanders campaign, a Pew Research Center poll in 2011 showed that 49 percent of all Americans under age thirty had a positive view of socialism, compared to 47 percent who had a positive view of capitalism.

If we do find our way back to some form of equitable, mixed economy, it will not be a copy of the one that prevailed in the postwar era. A lesson of that era is that in a system that is basically capitalist, even when the destructive aspects of a market system appear to be contained and constrained, capitalism and capitalists have immense residual power. To keep power elites at bay, there need to be extramarket forms of ownership that are understood and valued by the citizenry, as well as a public that is in a high state of democratic mobilization.

Marxists spoke of nationalizing the means of production. The social democratic planners of postwar Europe, by contrast, understood that an entrepreneurial sector was essential for the dynamism of the economy. They hoped that by nationalizing the "commanding heights" of the economy, and combining that control with a measure of democratic planning, they could have the best of both worlds. Roosevelt's "yardstick competition" included some public ownership of utilities such as electric power to determine true costs and keep private providers honest. In Europe, the postwar economic system included substantial public ownership. In Sweden, municipal ownership of land has been central to Sweden's strategy of building and retaining affordable housing and connecting new housing development to expanded public transit and environmental advances—all objectives missed by myopic private markets.

At the zenith of the era of social democracy, progressive economists such as Rudolf Meidner of Sweden came to appreciate that the social control of financial capital was essential if the bargain was to hold. In 1976, Meidner proposed an ingenious plan that would require Swedish corporations to issue shares every year to be given to "wage-earner funds," so that within twenty years, workers collectively would become majority owners of Swedish capitalism. This plan proved too radical even for Swedes, including the Social Democratic finance minister, who was fiercely opposed. The Meidner plan never became law.

By the new century, just as Meidner feared, private control of finance had gradually eroded much of the economic and political base of social democracy. Once the postwar ideological entente had given way to fierce neoliberalism, public control over other major assets was steadily weakened as well.

EMBLEMATIC POLICIES
AND TEACHABLE MOMENTS

Starting in the United States, what might a twenty-first-century version of a mixed economy look like? In this climate, policy ideas need to pass several tests. They need to be sensible in their own right, produce real benefits for broad constituencies, contain the power of elites (especially financial ones), revive the power of the common people, rebuild democracy, expand the realm of "decommodified" forms of social income that are not dependent on market wages, and teach durable lessons about the failures of laissez-faire. They need to rebuild an ideology of solidarity and common purpose using national democracy, and reclaim space from the global market. And they need to restore confidence in public solutions and public institutions. In the US, the great progressive legacy of the Roosevelt and postwar periods did just that. A new version of a social economy needs to be even better defended institutionally and politically than the last one was.

Finance as a Public Good. A prime project of the next progressive administration should be the drastic simplification and containment of private finance. The financial system of the well-regulated postwar era efficiently provided capital to the rest of the economy, and it was all but scandal-free. Banks and thrift institutions of mortgage provision were effectively public utilities, and they need to become so again. With no opportunities for windfall profits and no exotic, opaque securities, banks were far easier to supervise and far less inclined to seek ways to corrupt public officials. Banks need to be turned back into something like public utilities, under either explicit public ownership or drastic regulation.

Politically, banks today are not exactly popular, except in the corridors of power. Wells Fargo was exposed to indignation and ridicule when investigations revealed that pressure to generate sales had caused thousands of low-level employees to break the law and create phony accounts that generated exorbitant charges in order to produce profits and commissions. These employees lost their jobs. The executives whose orders abused customers and employees alike were eventually made to disgorge some of their fortunes, but they kept tens of millions. Wells was only a more extreme case of abusive practices common throughout the financial industry.

The "tricks and traps" regularly criticized by Elizabeth Warren, such as subprime loans and exorbitant terms on student debt, have resurged with the weakening of the Dodd-Frank rules and the Republican administration. If banks were effectively public utilities, either publicly owned or drastically simplified in their permissible powers, the threat of moving offshore and the pursuit of regulatory arbitrage would be idle. With no more derivatives, there would be no risk of bankers moving derivative transactions to London. Some might think it demagogic to run against the regime of finance, but this is just what's required, both economically and politically. The core challenge always comes back to constraining finance, and any progressive populist worthy of the name should be leading the charge.

In American history, we actually have a lot of experience with public capital. As noted in Chapter 2, New Deal public and non-profit institutions such as the Reconstruction Finance Corporation and the Federal Home Loan Bank System literally recapitalized entire sectors of the economy that had been paralyzed by private financial collapse. Government electrified rural America with public power. North Dakota has had a state-owned development bank for a century. DARPA has functioned as an investment bank for new technologies needed for the national defense, many with commercial and public-good spillovers, such as the Internet. We need to reclaim this tradition.

Green Infrastructure on a Serious Scale. As even Donald Trump recognizes, America's infrastructure is rotting. The American Society of Civil Engineers puts the bill for deferred maintenance in basic infrastructure such as roads, bridges, water and sewer systems, public buildings, and the like at $4.6 trillion, and the gap in available funding at over $2 trillion. That doesn't even count the need to move to "smart grid" electric power systems, to devise new strategies of resilience to defend against coastal flooding, and transition to a post–fossil fuel economy. Trump's version of this is privatized infrastructure investment, subsidized by tax credits, which would further shrink the public, nonmarket realm. His administration has even sought to privatize the crown jewel of the Roosevelt legacy: the great hydropower dams of the West, which provide cheaper and cleaner power than anything offered by private electric utilities.

A program on the scale of a trillion dollars a year over ten years could accomplish four things: it could modernize the economy's infrastructure, provide millions of good domestic jobs, accelerate the transition to an economy based on renewable energy, and generate new technologies. These innovations, in turn, would make the United States more competitive, much as the World War II burst of public technology investment did, as well as restore confidence in government. In macroeconomic terms, such a program would be like the

World War II boom, but without the war. In contrast to Donald Trump's funny-money approach of using tax credits to enrich private entrepreneurs for investing in quasi-public infrastructure, this would be a true public program—financed largely by bonds via a federal capital budget, and partly by progressive taxes.

There is a related need for large-scale public interventions to address the trend of robots replacing human workers. Unlike some, I don't see evidence that this problem is insurmountable. New technologies have always displaced established ones, and there is always more work to be done. But market forces will not resolve this challenge. Without government intervention to keep a high level of employment macroeconomically, social investment to create decently paid service work, and the use of measures such as reduced working time and increased social income, we could end up with a small number of very well paid workers and millions of people underemployed, badly compensated, or idle.

Positive Nationalism and Different Global Rules. A massive commitment to rebuilding infrastructure and transitioning to a post-carbon economy would require complementary changes in trade rules. If American taxpayers and bondholders are creating $10 trillion worth of demand to modernize public systems and to shift to green energy sources, it is reasonable to insist that these resources promote US-based industries and US-based jobs.

Other nations have much tougher rules on domestic content—requirements that US-based multinationals such as Boeing or Intel must create local jobs as part of agreements to buy their products. If we want to maintain social, labor, health, and safety standards that don't relentlessly drop to the levels of the most wretched and undemocratic countries, it's also legitimate to impose social tariffs against the products of exploitive production.

The economist Dani Rodrik put it well: "Democracies have the right to protect their social arrangements. And when this right clashes with the requirements of the global economy, it is the latter that should give way." Government needs to explicitly assert its right to prevent global laissez-faire forces from undermining its capacity to devise and broker a decent social compact at home.

Other sovereign nations, often governed by despots, may accept appallingly low wages for their workers, break unions and tolerate unsafe working conditions, or subsidize domestic production. But they do not have a right to expect the fruits of those policies to enter the American domestic market duty-free and thus to undermine American social standards. When we have "free trade" with such nations, we import the low standards along with the products. Resisting this race to the bottom is an entirely defensible form of protection, and one that might even win back the affections of American workers for progressive populism.

American progressives spent more than a century struggling for domestic legislation to protect workers, consumers, and investors from the predations of laissez-faire. It is magical thinking to believe that those same predations evaporate merely because commerce is global.

Restore Regulation of Market Abuses. Deregulation generally has turned out to be a blessing for corporate titans, not for an efficient or equitable economy. It has also been an emblem of bipartisan collusion. Deregulation began in 1978 under the Democratic administration of Jimmy Carter, cheered on by Senator Ted Kennedy, who was influenced by his then chief counsel and later Supreme Court justice Stephen Breyer. Pro-corporate conservatives were so fond of Breyer that in 1994, his appointment to the Supreme Court was easily confirmed with only nine Republican senators opposed.

Beginning under Reagan, antitrust regulation was all but eliminated. Combined with the demise of antitrust, in industry after industry deregulation has led not to the efficient competition based on price and quality promised by free-market theory, but to concentration, price gouging, anticompetitive predation, deteriorated consumer service, and downward pressure on wages. As I write these words, United Airlines is trying to recover from a blunder in which a sixty-nine-year-old physician, Dr. David Dao, who came to the United States as a refugee from Vietnam, was seriously injured by police who were called in by the cabin crew of his flight after he refused to give up a confirmed seat. The arrogance of the airlines and the worsening conditions for passengers are the logical consequence of increased concentration and lack of meaningful competition wrought by deregulation. It's hard to believe that it would be good politics to defend the status quo. But it takes a leader to connect the dots between public disgust with corporate abuse and the case for regulation.

Companies such as Google, Amazon, Microsoft, and Apple have used their market dominance, combined with predatory mergers and acquisitions, to fend off competitors. Their profits relative to invested capital have been astronomical. They have employed techniques that would have been illegal under earlier antitrust enforcement, such as abusing intellectual property protections, buying out potential rivals, and demanding that vendors in their supply chains sell only to them and not to competitors.

The impact of the new economic concentration is deceptive because this is a general period of low inflation and falling prices for some products. Presumably, if there were monopoly power, prices would be rising. But because wages are stagnant or falling, it's possible to have monopoly pricing power and windfall profits, with the result averaging out to low inflation.

In many respects, the US has become a middleman economy. Private firms make a fortune in excess charges on student loans. Financial engineers extract needless charges on consumer credit and mortgages. Parasitic middlemen attached to the health-industrial complex extract fees for designing systems that handle billing, utilization review, pharmacy benefit management, electronic records, and a great deal more—raising costs to patients and making professional practice less fulfilling for doctors. Direct public provision would be more efficient and more equitable, and less of a hassle. It will take inspired leadership to explain how these abuses work before they can be remedied.

The Conundrum of Income, Work, and Wealth. As robots replace human workers, a program of public investment and transition to sustainable energy can replace a lot of the lost jobs. There is also plenty of work to be done caring for the young, the old, and the sick, at decent wages. Even so, as more physical production is done by machines, it makes sense both to reduce working time and to supplement labor income with other income. The very rich have always been aware of this. More of their income comes from capital than from labor.

As part of a new economy, supplements to labor income need to be broadened to the entire population. One way to achieve this end is via what the British call social income—good public services that include everything from health to free education to high-quality care for children. A complementary strategy is to give every citizen a share of wealth that is produced from the commons. The British Labour government briefly introduced a version of this approach with what were called "baby bonds." Every newborn was given a financial account that would grow over time. This initiative was promptly repealed by the Tories.

A more promising version has been proposed by the entrepreneur and social critic Peter Barnes, who uses the example of the Alaska Permanent Fund. Thanks to a renegade Republican governor back in the 1970s named Jay Hammond, when oil was discovered on Alaska's North Slope, the state didn't just give it to the oil companies, but treated it as a resource owned by all Alaskans. So, under the deal that Hammond and the legislature cut with the oil giants, each year every Alaskan man, woman, and child gets a share of the oil revenue.

The genius of the Alaska Permanent Fund is that the revenues don't go to the government. Every Alaskan gets a check, rather like a Social Security check. Try taking that away. Rugged individualists love it. In 2015 the check was $1,884 for every resident of the state. In some native Alaskan communities, it was the largest source of cash income. Even Sarah Palin supports the dividends; she can see the checks from her window. Efforts by the oil companies to roll it back keep being defeated.

Barnes suggests a similar citizen dividend not just for all extracted minerals, but for any private, for-profit appropriation of something taken from the commons. Examples could include various forms of subsidized knowledge creation, such as innovations that depend on the publicly created Internet, as well as profits that piggyback on federally funded biotech research, and windfalls that rely on publicly granted patents. As wealth becomes more concentrated, this is one good way of democratizing it.

Reclaim the Public Realm. Good public services that are superior to private ones provide another teachable moment—if leaders are clear about their own first principles and will teach. Medicare, for example, extended health coverage to tens of millions of older Americans that private insurance could not provide. There is some popular backlash that Republicans can exploit against the Rube Goldberg market contraption that is Obamacare, but not against public Medicare. Beyond its pragmatic success, Medicare taught the lesson that government could efficiently provide a basic need that private corporations could not. So, too, did the public power projects that brought affordable electricity to millions of Americans. The same is true of Social Security, which is superior to any comparable financial product offered by Wall Street. Efforts to privatize public services have often been shown to be less cost-effective, less reliable, and more prone to corruption than their public alternatives.

One policy that would be highly popular in its own right, and that would teach the lesson that direct government services work more efficiently, reliably, and fairly than private ones do, is Medicare for All. Such a measure is difficult to achieve in one fell swoop. It might be accomplished state by state. Alternatively, my colleague Paul Starr has suggested beginning with a subsidized buy-in option for people over fifty, called Midlife Medicare. Late-midlife voters are disproportionately Trump voters, whose insurance is becoming unaffordable. We could next give Medicare cards to all children under twenty-one, who are cheap to insure, and finally bridge over to include young adults and extend Medicare to the entire population. The savings in the wild inefficiencies and middleman costs of the current health system would more than cover the incremental costs of this transition.

The assault against an entire generation in the form of escalating college debt is another teachable issue that cries out for remedy. Higher education, at least at public universities and community colleges, should be tuition-free. Living expenses should be partly subsidized for moderate-income students, and debt should be eliminated as a form of student "financial aid." The load of the $1.3 trillion of existing debt should be dramatically lightened. During the financial crisis, the Federal Reserve found ways to purchase the securities of the big banks, to recapitalize banks that were effectively insolvent, to the tune of several trillion dollars. It should do no less for a whole generation of young adults, who begin their active life in debt—something unprecedented in American history since the pre-independence days of indentured servants. The Sanders campaign calculated that it would cost about $75 billion a year to end the system of student debt, and that the program could be underwritten by a tax on speculative financial transactions.

In addition, we should shore up the system of community colleges, the quintessential second-chance institution in American life. Community colleges provide two-year degrees that are tickets to middle-class technical jobs for which qualified workers are often difficult to find. The seven-year completion rate for two-year degrees is only about 30 percent. This poor record does not reflect a lack of student motivation or diligence. The problem is that most of these students have families and jobs, and can't find the time to squeeze in study. A stipend for community college students, to cover living expenses, would be an immensely efficient social (and political) investment. One of the reasons the original post–World War II GI Bill of Rights worked so well was that it covered living expenses as well as tuitions. In Middle America, working families who could benefit from associate degrees were part of the demographic that went heavily for Donald Trump.

RESTORING THE CREDIBILITY OF PUBLIC INSTITUTIONS

The overarching strategic and ideological purpose of policies that reclaim the public realm is to demonstrate that social institutions can often serve the needs of people more equitably and more efficiently than commercial ones can—to enlarge the space for social institutions and narrow the domain and political sway of purely commercial ones. Successes breed more successes. Republican efforts to block programs such as these smoke out whose side Republicans are really on.

However, recent Democratic presidents, for the most part, have been too intimidated or too compromised to maximize such moments. The 2008 financial collapse was a potential teachable moment that was largely squandered. The Democratic flirtation with everything from austerity economics to partial privatization of Social Security blurred differences and left voters unimpressed. The next Democratic president needs to be clearer in his or her own mind about first principles and grand strategy, and needs to be a better teacher and mobilizer.

The American labor organizer David Rolf has brilliantly remarked that *policy is frozen politics.* The epic policies that display still-functioning elements of universal social income, such as Social Security and Medicare, are legacy institutions of earlier political struggles against elites. But when the politics cease to be vigilant, even solidly frozen policies are at risk of erosion. The remark of a seventy-seven-year-old Florida man named Rolando Bocos quoted in a *New York Times* article on the eve of the 2016 election captures the challenge perfectly: "It doesn't matter, Republican, Democrat, to me anymore," he said. "I'm only interested in Medicare and Social Security."

This voter missed the fact that Social Security and Medicare are not random benefits or gifts of nature. They were enacted by Democrats, after years of political struggle, over the fierce opposition of the private financial, health insurance, and medical industries—and, of course, of the Republican Party. Bocos knew nothing of that, and his ignorance wasn't his fault; *the politics had grown cold.* Frozen policy, divorced from hot politics, is vulnerable policy. Effective politics requires—and nourishes—strong democracy. Weak politics undermines not just social justice, but democracy.

One of the reasons for the rise of the Tea Parties and Donald Trump is the effectiveness of the corporate and libertarian right at disparaging social institutions and at capturing government agencies— and the failure of Democratic administrations to adequately defend things public. Working-class voters were left to conclude that nobody was looking out for their interests, and they were right. In the wake of Trump's election, political scientist and public-opinion analyst Guy Molyneux polled white, non-college-educated voters (the usual definition of white working class) who had voted for Trump over Clinton by a spread of 67 percent to 28, and found attitudes overwhelmingly antigovernment. In response to the questions he asked, Molyneux reported:

32 percent chose: "When government tries to solve a problem, it usually does more good than harm."

68 percent chose: "When government tries to solve a problem, it usually does more harm than good."

27 percent chose: "Government has helped me achieve my goals."

73 percent chose: "Government has made it harder for me to achieve my goals."

These are precisely the people who rely on government to offset the insecurities of the market economy. If government fails to deliver and government is perceived as being in the pockets of elites, then democracy will never harness the mixed economy in a broad public interest, and such voters will keep being attracted to antisystem politicians—who don't serve their interests but who make them feel better.

The point of these ideas is not just to list policy proposals that could restore greater security and equality, but to demonstrate that policies also need to teach meta-lessons and rebuild political coalitions. Note also that all of these proposed policies are national, and substantially insulated from the undertow of global laissez-faire. The next generation of Democratic progressives needs to be far more strategic. What's required is a strategic coherence about how the policies add up to a reclamation of the public realm and an impeachment of the predatory market.

As I've suggested throughout this book, race remains the great fault line of progressive politics. In the months since Trump's election, racial grievance and hurt has sometimes overwhelmed the need for a common politics to resist the slide to neofascism. It's no good pretending that a strategy of class uplift, by itself, will restore a progressive majority. Nor, conversely, will a focus on the "rising electorate" of minorities, professionals, and the young do the job. The project of engaging lingering racism, injuries of class, and the unfinished business of gender equity needs to be undertaken with active listening, inspired leadership at all levels, open minds, and open hearts for trust to be restored.

BEYOND THE MUDDLE

As this book has suggested, one factor that has scrambled politics is gross confusion over which parties and which leaders are defending ordinary people against the predations of liberated, raw capitalism. In the absence of a robust democratic left, these frustrations have been embraced and articulated by ultranationalists, many of whom are in bed with the very same corporate elites that are the source of the dislocations. Donald Trump in the US and Theresa May in the UK are exhibits A and B, and some of their predecessors (Clinton, Blair, Schröder) representing nominally center-left parties only added to the muddle.

A prime aspect of the confusion is globalization itself. Even after all of the dislocations of free-market neoliberalism, commentators still tend to disparage challenges to the global regime as simpleminded protectionism. The fact that there is more than one kind of globalism tends to get lost in the muddle. But as this book has shown, we began the postwar era with a globalism that promoted managed forms of capitalism, national democracy by national democracy, and we now have a globalism that, by design, destroys nationally managed capitalism.

Despite the sense of a simplistic polarity of nationalists versus globalists, history shows that there are liberal forms of nationalism and reactionary forms. The New Deal era in America, the Swedish Social Democratic idea of a socially secure national homeland, and the postwar social settlement all are variants. Indeed, when liberal nationalism falters and working people feel vulnerable, right-wing nationalism fills the void. That is the tragic story of our own era.

As an example of the ideological and policy confusion, right-wing populists, for the most part, have not made a serious critique of the economics of the new globalism. Mainly, they have scapegoated immigrants. Dani Rodrik observed, "Brexit advocates in Britain presented free trade as an explicit objective. One of the advantages of leaving the EU, they argued, was that it would enable Britain to pursue policies closer to free trade!"

A restored democratic left could invoke Bretton Woods and call for a very different brand of twenty-first-century globalism that respects the exchange of ideas, of culture, and of people, as Keynes famously argued, but that leaves space for national democracies to manage capitalism in a broad public interest. If progressives were clear about this, it would restore focus to politics and to political choices. It would define a left that subordinated globalism to full-employment economies of decent earnings and opportunities, and a right that served corporations, bankers, and the one percent. The corporate right, despite the immigrant bashing of its far-right allies, would be revealed as no friend of working people, and the new progressive left would define a form of globalism that would be hard to disparage as simple protection and that would command broad political appeal. A lot of misinformation about raw capitalism as the quintessence of individualism would go back into well-deserved eclipse. The details of trade policy may be arcane and deliberately obscure, but the fundamentals of managed markets versus predatory capitalism are clear enough, if leaders will lead.

CAN DEMOCRACY SURVIVE GLOBAL CAPITALISM?

Some commentators, such as the brilliant student of comparative government and economics Wolfgang Streeck, see today's crisis as portending the long-deferred, terminal collapse of capitalism. The pathologies of capitalism, Streeck reminds us, have been vividly on display for decades and are now reaching a critical phase. These include a chronic fiscal crisis, in which the state goes broke trying to make up for the deficiencies of the market system; the falling rate of profit, in which capitalists squeeze workers to compensate for the impact of ruinous competition on their own diminishing returns and sacrifice the system's legitimacy in the process; the failure of capitalism to address the intensified replacement of workers by machines, further depressing worker incomes and increasing unrest; and a deepening propensity for structural crises, as the financial system keeps encroaching on the real economy and periodically collapsing.

All of these trends are, in some sense, real. But Streeck, a social democrat well known for his pessimism, is too pessimistic—or per-

haps not pessimistic enough. In reality, the actual history of capitalism, as opposed to a stylized neo-Marxian one, shows its stunning
capacity to adapt.

In fact, big corporations have responded to competition by becoming ever more concentrated. If the rate of return is falling, that loss
may affect small investors but not billionaire corporate executives
and hedge fund moguls, who are doing better than ever. Capitalism,
as it has evolved in recent decades, has been corrupted into plutocracy. An analyst for Goldman Sachs, pointing to investment opportunities for elite clients, coined a useful word—"plutonomy"—meaning a
political economy of superconcentrated wealth. Capitalists have kept
high debt levels at bay by having friendly central banks find ways to
expand the money supply to keep capital cheap and plentiful. Even
a financial collapse in 2008 comparable to that of 1929 did not alter
the system in any fundamental way. It's surely true that workers are
squeezed, but today's workers are more inclined to revolt against foreigners and feckless parliamentarians than against capitalists.

One has to be an optimist to believe that a new democratic movement could contain both corporate excess and the neofascist reaction
to it; to believe that there are forms of social economy that would
prove at least as durable, adaptive, and politically anchored as the
one that was achieved during the years after World War II. But then,
one had to be an optimist to imagine anything other than despair in
1940, when Britain stood alone against Hitler and America dithered.

In some respects, a mixed economy is like combining oil and water.
The capitalist parts keep trying to turn everything back into a market commodity. Since money can buy everything else, wealthy people
keep trying to buy political influence. Yet history shows that a mixed
economy works better than either a command economy or an unregulated market. The challenge is for public institutions to be as resil-
ient as commercial ones, and to mobilize the latent power of popular
democracy to keep finance in its proper role as servant of the rest of
the economy. This is difficult, but not impossible.

Today's capitalism is both undemocratic and antidemocratic. Post-
capitalist democracy, with new forms of a social economy, could survive and even thrive. It is admittedly a long shot, but our only shot.

AFTERWORD

ended *Can Democracy Survive Global Capitalism?* on an improbable note of hope. The last chapter identified the United States as the most likely nation to achieve a resurgence both of democracy and of the constructive regulation of capitalism. This seemed wishful, of course. At the time the book appeared, the US was in the first throes of the Trump presidency, and a sickening slide into something like despotism allied with intensified plutocracy.

Trump has combined contempt for democratic norms with an impulsive, autocratic temperament, a thoroughly bogus populism, and a wreckage of the competence of government. He has emulated the blend of personal corruption and alliance with oligarchs, modeled by his ally Vladimir Putin. To an appalling degree, Republicans in Congress, who had little regard for Trump when he ran for their party's nomination, have been his enablers. None of this augured well for American democracy.

But thanks to the durable institutions of the "deep state," Trump's own overreach, and an astonishing mobilization of his opposition in the 2018 midterm elections, democracy has held. And it may even emerge stronger. Turnout in 2018 broke a century-old time record for a midterm election. Nearly 50 percent of the eligible electorate voted, compared to just 37 percent in the previous midterm of 2014. Most of the upsurge was on the Democratic side. Voters aged eighteen to twenty-nine also turned out in record numbers, and voted for the Democrat by better than 2 to 1.

The gains were sufficient for the Democrats to take forty House seats formerly held by Republicans, the best midterm showing since the post-Watergate election of 1974, when they picked up forty-nine seats. And the Democrats achieved these wins despite extreme gerrymandering in nine states controlled by Republicans that gave them a head start of around twenty House seats, according to most estimates. They also succeeded in the face of a variety of voter suppression techniques, including purges of the voter rolls, targeted use of voter ID requirements to hold down minority voting, selective cutbacks in voting hours and polling places, and outright fraud.

In past decades, the Justice Department and the federal courts were counter-forces to efforts by Southern states and other jurisdictions under Republican control to suppress the franchise. But since the 2013 US Supreme Court ruling in *Shelby County v Holder,* overturning the requirement of the Voting Rights Act for Justice Department preclearance of proposed changes in election rules in places with a history of racial discrimination, the federal courts have switched sides. They have become enablers of voter suppression. Under Trump, the Justice Department has also become a force to restrict the right to vote.

Thus, it is all the more remarkable that the great blue wave of 2018 could overcome so many barriers to its success. This took an upsurge of grass roots organizing unseen since the 1960s, one that will only continue to grow. New groups like Indivisible led to thousands of local organizations committed to mobilizing voters. The 2018 midterms were proof that enough strength remained in American democracy that it could make gains, even competing on a tilted playing field.

The book also argued that the deeper cause of Trumpism was the destruction of a social contract that once provided good economic prospects to most Americans. Predatory capitalism was killing democracy, both directly by narrowing the writ of the public realm and indirectly via the neofascist backlash that the ravaging of ordinary people engendered. To redeem democracy, it would also be necessary to build a politics and an ideology of strictly managed capitalism that went at least as far as the postwar social contract in assuring that the economy would deliver for ordinary people once again.

And on this front, one can also discern hopeful tidings. The Democrats who prevailed in 2018 made those gains mainly as progressives. Before the midterms, the press was filled with warnings to Democrats not to run too far to the left. But in the 2018 election, Democrats practiced very astute politics. Most ran not as leftists, but as common-sense progressives, on such kitchen-table issues as defending and expanding Medicare and Social Security, increasing funding for public schools, addressing the student debt crisis, and rebuilding rotting infrastructure. Self-described moderates as well as Bernie Sanders–style radicals embraced these policies and made them winning politics. Progressive became the new moderate, as the entire center of political gravity moved in the direction of containing and complementing capitalism.

Trump attempted to compete for these concerns by posturing tough on trade and making commitments to reclaim American manufacturing that he didn't deliver. But his pose during the 2016 campaign as a great defender of Social Security and a taxer of the rich was soon belied by his actual policies. His one legislative success, a $1.6 trillion tax cut, went overwhelmingly to the rich and became the pretext for a budget that proposed deep cuts in Social Security and Medicare.

As the details of his actual policies sank in, he was increasingly revealed (and reviled) as an ordinary Republican plutocrat trying to disguise his corporate agenda with faux-populist rantings, scapegoating foreigners, and embracing racists. But his act started wearing thin.

In the 2018 midterm, Trump's efforts to racialize pocketbook grievances, as he had done in 2016, largely failed. He went out of his way to make the midterm elections a referendum on himself—and it was, to the great benefit of Democrats. His attempt to portray the Central American refugee caravan as a national security threat backfired. Trump was widely repudiated, especially in the suburbs but also in many working-class districts that had supported him in 2016.

Most encouraging was the broad rejection of Trump's use of dog-whistle racism. Remarkably, eight progressive African American candidates for the House flipped Republican seats in overwhelmingly white districts, some of them deep in Trump territory. In former House Speaker Newt Gingrich's old district, in the Atlanta suburbs, voters elected Lucy McBath, a black woman whose son had been murdered by a racist. She ran—in a Deep South district that was just 13 percent black—on gun control and expanded Medicare. In the Chicago exurbs, in the district of former Republican House Speaker

Denny Hastert, a thirty-two-year-old African American nurse named Lauren Underwood came out of nowhere to take the reliably Republican seat for the Democrats. The district is 3 percent black. These and other gains suggest that the wave of hatred that Trump exacerbated and then rode to victory may be subsiding.

Trump's efforts to turn government police and criminal agencies into his own private government largely failed. Despite Trump's repeated efforts to undermine Special Counsel Robert Mueller's investigation, Mueller survived long enough to deliver several indictments, leaving Trump vulnerable to an eventual impeachment. Trump's appointment of hack loyalist Matt Whitaker to the post of acting attorney general, in the hope of reining in Mueller, also backfired. Whitaker's right to assume a major constitutional office, not having been confirmed by the Senate, was immediately challenged. Mueller continued his work, and ignored Whitaker, who did not dare block him.

Yet it would be woefully premature to celebrate. The policy damage, in areas from taxation to the environment, has been severe. The basic competence of government has been eroded, by both deliberate sabotage and sheer ineptitude. At this writing we have been spared the trumped-up national security crisis that many observers feared. Yet as Trump feels more and more cornered, he becomes ever more unstable and reckless. Until he is removed, resigns, or is defeated for reelection, the republic remains gravely at risk.

As the 2020 election season begins, there are reasons for both optimism and alarm on the Democratic side. The Democrats are clearly riding a progressive tide of activism and a shift of substantive politics to the left. If a progressive is nominated and elected president, the process of regulating capitalism in the broad public interest, largely suspended and reversed in recent decades, could resume.

But the Democrats suffer from an embarrassment of riches. There will likely be more than twenty candidates in the Democratic field. The fact that most of them are progressive, or at least center-left, seems to be good news. But too many progressive candidates could crowd each other out, handing the nomination to yet another corporate Democrat, and reopening disabling divisions in the party.

To govern successfully, the Democrats will also need to win back the Senate, or there will be another four years of Republican obstruction, with no progress on the substantive reform of capitalism and the prospect of a failed, one-term presidency. And that would likely be followed by more Trumpism.

The Republicans now control the Senate, 53-47. Happily, there are seven vulnerable Republicans up in 2020. All Democratic seats seem safe, save that of Alabama Senator Doug Jones. That means, with a strong presidential win and some coattails, the Democrats could have the presidency as well as the House and Senate, and could actually govern.

But given the needed repairs to democracy, and the scale of the deferred reforms of capitalism required to restore broad economic hope and confidence in government, the challenge is monumental. The new administration will need to shore up and expand public systems that are basically popular, including Social Security and Medicare, as well as sponsor a massive public investment and green transition program to create good jobs and rebuilt infrastructure that has been left to rot.

This is the relatively easy part, since such initiatives will have broad public support.

Harder will be a reversal of the Trump tax cuts, and the conventional bipartisan wisdom about the sin of deficits and the need for budget balance. What's needed is a World War II-scale program of social investment to save the planet and to create a lot of new technology and good jobs. That will require public borrowing, as well as higher taxes on the rich. The new president will need to explain that there are good uses of debt and bad ones, and this one is both virtuous and necessary.

By the same token, there are good and bad forms of nationalism. The next president will also need to take back nationalism from the neofascist right. Trump's use of racialized ultranationalism has been so toxic that many commentators have concluded that nationalism itself is to be avoided. This is profoundly wrong.

We value our Constitution and our democratic traditions, as Americans. We value uses of government that deliver broad benefits, such as Social Security, Medicare, and great public universities, as Americans. And we cherish our liberties, as Americans. On occasion, we fight and even die for our country, as Americans.

Trade policy is an area that cries out for constructive nationalism.

Other nations, such as China, have made gains at America's expense, by practicing a predatory form of state-subsidized capitalism. This is a far cry from any version of free trade. Trump, in his clumsy and incoherent way, has done us a favor by blowing up the old trade paradigm. He was just too incompetent and demagogic to put anything in its place. The next president will need to negotiate a *modus vivendi* with Beijing, in which China has the right to its own economic system, and we have the right to defend ours against practices that break rules, such as stealing intellectual property and extracting coercive terms for American-based companies to operate in China at all. And as we embark on a massive program to modernize American infrastructure, financed by American taxes and American debt, there is nothing shameful about including Buy American requirements, so that this effort also produces good American jobs and technology.

Hardest of all will be policies to reregulate finance. It was the extreme license for finance that contributed to the gross concentration of income and wealth that so alienated working-class Americans, and then led to the collapse of 2008 that further paved the way for Trump. We need to go back to a financial system, simple and efficient, that is the economy's servant rather than its master. This will be strenuously opposed not just by Republicans but by corporate Democrats.

Indeed, if a corporate Democrat should win the 2020 election, the deeper unrest that drives support for autocrats like Trump could continue. In short, the test of democracy is not only whether the opposition party can win, but whether it is a true opposition to the license for plutocracy that has been all too common to both parties.

So the road to a successful progressive presidency is narrow, but increasingly thinkable. And the more that the Trump presidency is hobbled by revelations of impeachable forms of corruption, the more the Republican Party is divided and embarrassed, and the wider that road becomes.

The story in Europe is far more worrisome. There, the European Union is paralyzed by a combination of bad economic policies, fragmentation government institutions, and a refugee crisis that only deepens support for the neofascist right. In most of Europe, the far right is either governing (Poland, Hungary, Italy), or is in a coalition government (Norway, Finland), or is now the second largest party (fifteen EU member nations). There is no plausible left opposition to the prevailing policy of austerity combined with license for speculative finance. A stable progressive coalition governs in just one EU member country, Portugal, while politics in France and Germany become more fraught and fragmented.

Britain remains a particularly unfortunate mess. There, the opposition Labour Party could be a progressive alternative to the Conservatives, who sponsored an entirely needless referendum to have Britain leave the EU in 2016, and suffered the consequences as the true costs of Brexit became known. But Labour's leader, Jeremy Corbyn, is a lifelong skeptic of the European Union, and his opposition to Theresa May has been muted and muddled. So while Britain could conceivably elect a progressive government sometime in the next few years, the odds remain long.

Thus, once again, as in World War I, World War II, and the Cold War, the responsibility of defending and advancing liberal democracy falls to the United States of America. As we rebuild our democracy and an economy of broad prosperity at home, we will need to rebuild America's role as a beacon of hope in the world. This will require a foreign policy that defines and defends our vital interests, but that does not attempt to make over the world as an American protectorate. We will need to be resolute without being reckless. If America can turn away from autocracy and oligarchy, the world may begin to turn back to democracy and managed capitalism as well.

All these challenges will require a leader on a par with America's greatest, and a populace that rises to the occasion. This seems a tall order, but so did saving the republic in 1862, or defeating Hitler in 1942, or holding off Soviet communism without starting World War III in 1962.

As we enter a momentous election season, the path to a revived democracy and a decent economy is barely possible—and urgently necessary.

ACKNOWLEDGMENTS

This book began in 2007 as an inquiry into the impact of globalization on the ability of democracies to harness capitalism for the broad public good. Over the ensuing decade, I put this project aside to write two other books on the Obama presidency and one on the financial crisis. I actively returned to it in 2015, as the excesses of global capitalism were increasingly engendering far-right nationalist reaction and threatening democracy itself. The election of Donald Trump provided the exclamation point.

I was able to begin the research for this book while a fellow at Demos, supported in part by the Rockefeller Brothers Fund, and largely to complete it while a visiting scholar at the Russell Sage Foundation in 2015–16. Special thanks to Tom Kruse and Stephen Heintz at the Rockefeller Brothers Fund; to Sheldon Danziger, Suzanne Nichols, Katie Winograd, Claire Gabriel, and David Haproff and colleagues at Sage; and to the leadership team at Demos—Miles Rapoport, Heather McGhee, Tamara Draut, and Amelia Warren Tyagi.

My editors improved the book in numerous ways, large and small—Drake McFeely, Nathaniel Dennett, and Jeff Shreve at W. W. Norton, and copy editor Stephanie Hiebert. Gratitude is also due my agent and friend, Ike Williams.

Thanks, once again, to my colleagues at the *American Prospect*, a venture now approaching its thirtieth year, where many of these ideas originated, especially to Paul Starr, Harold Meyerson, Amy Lambrecht, and Mike Stern; and to my friends and colleagues at the Economic Policy Institute, notably Larry Mishel, Jeff Faux, Thea

Lee, Ross Eisenbrey, Josh Bivens, Heather Boushey, Rob Scott, and
Heidi Shierholz.

I am grateful to colleagues at Brandeis, where I've taught a regular course on globalism and democracy, especially to Lisa Lynch,
Marty Krauss, Mike Doonan, Janet Boguslaw, Tom Shapiro, Deborah Stone, and David Weil, and to my students.

I appreciate the hospitality of the Institute for Advanced Labor
Studies (AIAS) in Amsterdam, where I was a visiting fellow, especially to Wiemer Salverda, Paul de Beer, and Jelle Visser.

Thanks also to the Karl Polanyi Institute of Political Economy in
Montreal, especially Kari Polanyi-Levitt, Marguerite Mendell, and
Ana Gomez.

Special appreciation is due several colleagues and friends who read
part or all of the manuscript: Art Goldhammer, Dani Rodrik, Richard Valelly, Ira Katznelson, Pervenche Berès, Jacob Hacker, Kevin
Gallagher, Richard Parker, and Reuven Avi-Yonah, and to my wife,
Joan Fitzgerald, who read every word of several drafts.

In the decade that I've been gathering material for this book, I've
made a number of reporting and research trips to several countries
and research centers in Europe and Canada. A few people deserve
special thanks for their long-standing friendship and wise counsel, and for directing me to other sources and resources: Pervenche
Berès, John Evans, Allan Larsson, Leif Pagrotsky, George Papandreou, Poul Nyrup Rasmussen, Peter Coldrick, Frans Becker, and
Andreas Botsch.

Among friends and colleagues outside the US, thanks for innumer-
able insights and courtesies to Lars Andersen, Dan Andersson, Gerry
Arsenis, Luisa Bernal, Mark Blyth, Peter Bofinger, Pia Bungarten,
David Cockroft, Jan Cremers, Pierre Defraigne, Dieter Dettke, Gøsta
Esping-Andersen, Jean-Paul Fitoussi, Christoffer Green-Pederson,
Pierre Habard, Hansjorg Herr, Christy Hoffman, Marina Hoffmann,
Gustave Horn, James Howard, Will Hutton, Ronald Janssen, Philip
Jennings, Louka Katseli, Martin Keune, Martin Khor, Verner Sand
Kirk, Katerina Lambrinou, Eloi Laurent, Neal Lawson, Roger Lid-
dle, Mogens Lykketoft, Denis MacShane, Per Kongsjo Madsen, Hen-
ning Meyer, John Monks, Henrik Bach Mortensen, Sture Nordh,
Paul Nowak, Per Nuder, Yannis Palailogos, Bruno Palier, Joakim
Palme, Vassilis Papadimitriou, Catelene Passchier, Kaj Ove Peder-

sen, Norma Percy, Thierry Philipponnat, Jean Pisani-Ferry, Stephen Pursey, Nuria Ramos-Martin, Yaga Reddy, Lars Rohde, André Sapir, Penny Schantz, Jørgen Søndergaard, Peter Birch Sørensen, Roland Spont, Ernst Stetter, Wolfgang Streeck, Paul Swaim, Owen Tudor, the late Ieke van den Burg, Nicolas Véron, Andy Watt, Tommy Weidelech, and Martha Zuber.

At home, special thanks to Elizabeth Warren, Joseph Stiglitz, Damon Silvers, and to Sheila Bair, Dean Baker, Ben Beachy, David Bensman, Suzanne Berger, Jared Bernstein, Marc Blecher, Alan Blinder, Fred Block, Tim Canova, Celeste Drake, Peter Dreier, Kevin Gallagher, Teresa Ghilarducci, Janet Gornick, Peter Gourevitch, Andy Green, Michael Greenberger, Steven Greenhouse, Peter Hall, Owen Herrnstadt, David Howell, Deborah James, Rob Johnson, Simon Johnson, Dennis Kelleher, Bruce Kogut, Mike Konczal, Mark Levinson, Robert Litan, Andrew Martin, Kathie Jo Martin, Rick McGahey, John Mollenkopf, Pat Mulloy, David Orr, Bill Parks, Scott Paul, Frank Portney, Clyde Prestowitz, Carmen Reinhart, George Ross, Anya Schiffrin, John Shattuck, Peggy Somers, Deborah Stone, Katherine V. W. Stone, Michael Stumo, Dan Tarullo, Kathy Thelen, Mark Weisbrod, and Mike Wessel.

I appreciate research help from Emma Stokking and Caite Eilenberg.

I've treated these topics in several magazine and journal pieces in the *American Prospect*, the *New York Review of Books*, and *Foreign Affairs*. Thank you to the editors.

Last and far from least, I appreciate all the help of innumerable people who've saved me from a variety of errors. And, once more, I could not do this work or much else without the wisdom, love, and patience of my wife, Joan Fitzgerald.

NOTES

EPIGRAPHS

xi **"Misery generates hate"**: Charlotte Brontë, *Shirley* (London: J. P. Dent, 1849), 31.

xi **"A polity with extremes of wealth and poverty"**: Aristotle, *The Politics*, trans. C. D. C. Reeve (Indianapolis, IN: Hackett, 1998), 1295b17.

xi **"The victory of fascism was made practically unavoidable"**: Karl Polanyi, *The Great Transformation: The Political and Economic Origins of Our Times* (1944; repr. Boston: Beacon Press, 1957), 257.

xi **"Ideas, knowledge, art, hospitality, travel"**: John Maynard Keynes, "National Self Sufficiency," *Yale Review*, Summer 1933.

xi **"Democracy, national sovereignty and global"**: Dani Rodrik, "The Inescapable Trilemma of the World Economy," June 27, 2007, http://rodrik .typepad.com/dani_rodriks_weblog/2007/06/the-inescapable.html.

PREFACE

xv **Instead, we are witnessing**: See Francis Fukuyama, "The End of History?" *National Interest*, Summer 1989.

xvii **some commentators declared a "clash of civilizations"**: Samuel P. Huntington, *The Clash of Civilizations and the Remaking of World Order* (New York: Simon & Schuster, 1996).

xvii *Jihad versus McWorld:* Benjamin Barber, *Jihad versus McWorld* (New York: Random House, 1996).

xxi **Some have argued**: See Kenichi Ohmae, *The End of the Nation State: The Rise of Regional Economies* (New York: Free Press, 1995); Thomas L. Friedman, *The Lexus and the Olive Tree: Understanding Globalization* (New York: Farrar, Straus and Giroux, 1999).

xxi **Vladimir Putin presides over**: See Joshua Yaffa, "Oligarchy 2.0," *New Yorker*, May 20, 2017, 46–55. Yaffa quotes a source describing Russian oligarchic capitalism as having "switched from a principle of maximizing shareholder profits to one of maximizing contractor profits." The favored contractors are political allies of President Vladimir Putin.

xxii   **As Polanyi demonstrated in his 1944 masterwork:** Karl Polanyi, *The Great Transformation: The Political and Economic Origins of Our Times* (1944; repr., Boston: Beacon Press, 1957).

xxii   **"The fascist solution to the impasse of liberal capitalism":** Ibid., 28.

xxii   **"The origins of the cataclysm":** Ibid., 31.

xxiii **Ideologically, the neoliberal view:** As I wrote in *Everything for Sale: The Virtues and Limits of Markets* (New York: Knopf, 1997), the free marketplace of ideas is one more market that doesn't work like the model.

1. A SONG OF ANGRY MEN

1   **"There's never been a better time to be alive":** Peter S. Goodman, "Davos Elite Fret about Inequality over Vintage Wine and Canapés," *New York Times*, January 19, 2017, https://www.nytimes.com/2017/01/18/business/dealbook/world-economic-forum-davos-backlash.html.

3   **"Technological innovation is not":** Thomas Frank, *Listen, Liberal, or, What Ever Happened to the Party of the People?* (New York: Metropolitan Books, 2016), 215.

3   **mainly because of "deaths of despair":** Anne Case and Angus Deaton, "Rising Morbidity and Mortality in Midlife among White Non-Hispanic Americans in the 21st Century," *Proceedings of the National Academy of Sciences*, 112, no. 49 (2015): 15078–83, www.pnas.org/content/112/49/15078.full.

4   **"shake up the political establishment":** Robert Griffin, John Halpin, and Ruy Teixeira, "Democrats Need to Be the Party of All Working People— of All Races," *American Prospect*, June 1, 2017, http://prospect.org/article/democrats-need-be-party-and-working-people%E2%80%94-all-races.

4   **Working-class white voters:** Alec Tyson and Shiva Maniam, "Behind Trump's Victory: Divisions by Race, Gender, Education," Pew Research Center, November 9, 2016, http://www.pewresearch.org/fact-tank/2016/11/09/behind-trumps-victory-divisions-by-race-gender-education.

4   **As recently as the 1996 presidential election:** Justin Gest, "Can the Democratic Party Be White Working Class, Too?" *American Prospect*, April 3, 2017, http://prospect.org/article/can-democratic-party-be-white-working-class-too.

5   **The white working class declined:** Griffin et al., "Democrats Need to Be the Party."

5   **In key counties of western Pennsylvania:** Ibid.

5   **The recovery that had begun in 2010:** "The New Map of Economic Growth and Recovery," Economic Innovation Group, 2016, http://eig.org/wp-content/uploads/2016/05/recoverygrowthreport.pdf.

5   **A Brookings Institution study found:** Mark Muro and Sifan Liu, "Another Clinton-Trump Divide: High-Output America vs. Low-Output America," Brookings Institution, November 29, 2016, https://www.brookings.edu/blog/the-avenue/2016/11/29/another-clinton-trump-divide-high-output-america-vs-low-output-america.

6 **"embraced the liberal values":** Stanley B. Greenberg, "The Democrats' 'Working Class Problem,'" *American Prospect*, June 1, 2017, http://prospect .org/article/democrats%E2%80%99-%E2%80%98working-class-problem %E2%80%99.

6 **"In areas like Jutland":** Julian Coman, "How the Nordic Far Right Has Stolen the Left's Ground on Welfare," *Guardian*, July 25, 2015, https:// www.theguardian.com/world/2015/jul/26/scandinavia-far-right-stolen -left-ground-welfare.

7 **"The state always seems":** Arlie Russell Hochschild, *Strangers in Their Own Land* (New York: New Press, 2016), 52.

7 **Left-wing populism is binary:** John Judis, *The Populist Explosion* (New York: Columbia Global Reports, 2016).

8 **"They hate me and I welcome their hatred":** Franklin D. Roosevelt, "We Have Only Just Begun to Fight" (campaign address, Madison Square Garden, New York, October 31, 1936).

8 **"dueling injuries" of class, race, gender, and culture:** Robert Kuttner, "Hidden Injuries of Class, Race, and Culture," *American Prospect*, October 3, 2016, http://prospect.org/article/hidden-injuries-0.

9 **Remarkably, in the two decades *before*:** Lawrence Mishel et al., *The State of Working America*, 12th ed. (Washington, DC: Economic Policy Institute, 2015), 68–69.

10 **In Ta-Nehisi Coates's best-selling book:** Ta-Nehisi Coates, *Between the World and Me* (New York: Spiegel & Grau, 2015).

10 **The gap between male and female:** Elise Gould, Jessica Scheider, and Kathleen Geier, "What Is the Gender Gap and Is It Real?" Economic Policy Institute, October 20, 2016, http://www.epi.org/publication/what-is-the -gender-pay-gap-and-is-it-real.

11 **"If we broke up the big banks tomorrow":** Hillary Clinton, [Campaign rally speech] (Henderson, NV, February 12, 2016), https://www.youtube.com/ watch?v=QwBai_U_w0o.

12 **Exit polls showed that he gained the vote:** David Paul Kuhn, "Exit Polls: How Obama Won," Politico, May 11, 2008, http://www.politico.com/story /2008/11/exit-polls-how-obama-won-015297.

12 **In North Carolina, fully 35 percent:** "Election Results 2008: North Carolina Exit Polls," *New York Times*, December 9, 2008, https://www.nytimes .com/elections/2008/results/states/exitpolls/north-carolina.html.

12 **"We're voting for the nigger":** James Hannaham, "Racists for Obama," *Salon*, November 3, 2008, http://www.salon.com/2008/11/03/racists_for_ obama; original source: Sean Quinn, "On the Road: Western Pennsylvania," *FiveThirtyEight*, October 18, 2008, https://fivethirtyeight.com/features/on -road-western-pennsylvania.

12 **As the AFL-CIO's chief economist:** William E. Spriggs, "Why the White Worker Theme Is Harmful," *American Prospect*, June 21, 2017, http:// prospect.org/article/why-white-worker-theme-harmful.

13 **The white working-class vote for Obama:** Nate Cohn, "A Closer Look at Voters Who Backed Obama, Then Trump," *New York Times*, August 17, 2017.

13   **At Breitbart, Bannon had grasped:** For details on Bannon's relationship with Trump, see Joshua Green, *Devil's Bargain: Steven Bannon, Donald Trump, and the Storming of the Presidency* (New York: Penguin Books, 2017).

14   **"The Democrats," he told me:** Robert Kuttner, "Steven Bannon, Unrepentant," *American Prospect*, August 16, 2017, http://prospect.org/article/steve-bannon-unrepentant.

15   **Coelho dramatically increased the Democrats' funds:** Jeffrey H. Birnbaum and Alan S. Murray, *Showdown at Gucci Gulch* (New York: Random House, 1987); Robert Kuttner, *The Life of the Party: Democratic Prospects in 1988* (New York: Viking, 1987).

16   **Only one quasi-liberal group, the AARP:** OpenSecrets.org, "Top Spenders," accessed June 11, 2017, https://www.opensecrets.org/lobby/top.php?indexType=s.

17   **"Americans of all ages, all stations of life":** Alexis de Tocqueville, *Democracy in America* (1840, repr. New York: Vintage, 1945), 2:114.

17   **"mass participation tends to be irrational and unrestrained":** William Kornhauser, *The Politics of Mass Society* (New York: Free Press, 1959), 37.

17   **Their study found that 86 percent:** Sidney Verba, Kay Lehman Schlozman, and Henry E. Brady, *Voice and Equality: Civic Voluntarism in American Politics* (Cambridge, MA: Harvard University Press, 1995), 190.

17   **A 2012 sequel by the same authors:** Kay Lehman Schlozman, Sidney Verba, and Henry E. Brady, *The Unheavenly Chorus: Unequal Political Voice and the Broken Promise of American Democracy* (Princeton, NJ: Princeton University Press, 2012).

18   *Voice and Equality* **concluded:** Verba et al., *Voice and Equality*, 269.

18   **When the American National Election Study first asked:** Pew Research Center, "1. Trust in Government: 1958–2015," November 23, 2015, http://www.people-press.org/2015/11/23/1-trust-in-government-1958-2015.

18   **The military retains the highest degree of trust:** Jim Norman, "Americans' Confidence in Institutions Stays Low," Gallup, June 13, 2016, http://www.gallup.com/poll/192581/americans-confidence-institutions-stays-low.aspx.

19   **"the politics of excluded alternatives":** Walter Dean Burnham, *The Current Crisis in American Politics* (Oxford: Oxford University Press, 1982), 19.

19   **Social scientists Roberto Foa and Yascha Mounk:** Roberto Stefan Foa and Yascha Mounk, "The Democratic Disconnect," *Journal of Democracy* 27, no. 3 (July 2016): 5–17, http://pscourses.ucsd.edu/ps200b/Foa%20Mounk%20Democratic%20Disconnect.pdf.

19   *Affluence and Influence*: Martin Gilens, *Affluence and Influence: Economic Inequality and Political Power in America* (Princeton, NJ: Princeton University Press, 2012).

20   **As Harvard's Theda Skocpol demonstrated:** Theda Skocpol, *Diminished Democracy: From Membership to Management in American Civic Life* (Norman: University of Oklahoma, 2002).

20 **"8 Hours for Work!":** Theda Skocpol, *Protecting Mothers and Soldiers: The Political Origins of Social Policy in the United States* (Cambridge, MA: Belknap Press of Harvard University, 1996), 316.

21 **"as a movement, not an industry":** David L. Mason, *From Buildings and Loans to Bailouts* (Cambridge: Cambridge University Press, 2004), 22.

22 **Reagan's regulators changed the rules:** Ibid., 221.

25 **So, the true gridlock of Washington:** See discussion in Jacob S. Hacker and Paul Pierson, *Off Center: The Republican Revolution and the Erosion of American Democracy* (New Haven, CT: Yale University Press, 2005). See also Thomas E. Mann and Norman J. Ornstein, *It's Even Worse than It Looks: How the American Constitutional System Collided with the New Politics of Extremism* (New York: Basic Books, 2012).

2. A VULNERABLE MIRACLE

28 **"the great exception":** Jefferson Cowie, *The Great Exception* (Princeton, NJ: Princeton University Press, 2016).

31 **In 1941, Roosevelt named Sidney Hillman:** Steve Fraser, *Labor Will Rule: Sidney Hillman and the Rise of American Labor* (New York: Free Press, 1991).

32 **The United Auto Workers' membership rose:** Nelson Lichtenstein, *Labor's War and Home: The CIO in World War II* (New York: Cambridge University Press, 1982), 80.

32 **"The home-front pressures":** Ibid., 5–6.

33 **The Reconstruction Finance Corporation:** Jesse H. Jones, *Fifty Billion Dollars: My Thirteen Years with the RFC, 1932–1945* (New York: MacMillan, 1951).

33 **The war was an accidental full-employment program:** See discussion in Alvin H. Hansen, "Economic Progress and Declining Population Growth," *American Economic Review* 29, no. 1 (March 1939): 1–15.

34 **During World War I, by contrast:** Ibid., 315.

35 **Roosevelt was able to expand:** Ira Katznelson, *Fear Itself: The New Deal and the Origins of Our Time* (New York: Liveright, 2013).

35 **Harold Ickes, former chairman:** Richard Rothstein, *The Color of Law: A Forgotten History of How Our Government Segregated America* (New York: Liveright, 2017).

37 **By 1901, the last post-Reconstruction members:** Richard Valelly, *The Two Reconstructions: The Struggle for Black Enfranchisement* (Chicago: University of Chicago Press, 2004).

37 **"The Southern aristocracy took the world":** Martin Luther King Jr., address at the march from Selma to Montgomery, AL, March 25, 1965.

38 **It used direct Treasury borrowing:** James R. Hagerty, *The Fateful History of Fannie Mae: New Deal Birth to Financial Crisis Fall* (Charleston, SC: History Press, 2012).

38 **Rather than going through private bankers:** C. Lowell Harriss, *History and Policies of the Home Owners' Loan Corporation* (New York: National

Bureau of Economic Research, 1951); Home Loan Bank Board, *Final Report to the Congress of the United States Relating to the Home Owners' Loan Corporation*, 1952.

39 **Once the Depression ended:** US Census Bureau, "Historical Census of Housing Tables: Homeownership," last revised April 23, 2002, http://eadiv. state.wy.us/housing/Owner_0000.html.

40 **But there is a whole other category:** Frank Knight, *Risk, Uncertainty and Profit* (Boston: Houghton Mifflin, 1921).

41 **"the annual liquidation of debt":** Carmen M. Reinhart and S. Belem Sbrancia, *The Liquidation of Government Debt*, NBER Working Paper 16983 (Cambridge, MA: National Bureau of Economic Research, 2011).

42 **War bond sales totaled about $167.2 billion:** Christopher Tassava, "The American Economy during World War II," EH.net, accessed September 14, 2016, https://eh.net/encyclopedia/the-american-economy-during-world-war-ii.

42 **This was the case in World War I:** Steve Fraser, *Every Man a Speculator: A History of Wall Street in American Life* (New York: HarperCollins, 2005).

42 **The policy was formalized:** Timothy Canova, "Public Finance, Agency Capture, and Structural Limits on Fiscal Policy" (unpublished manuscript, 2010), cited with permission of the author.

43 **With low interest costs:** Congressional Budget Office, "Historical Data on Federal Debt Held by the Public," August 5, 2010, https://www.cbo.gov/publication/21728.

43 **For Britain, the ratio dropped:** Christopher Chantrill, *UK Public Spending* (blog), accessed February 17, 2017, http://www.ukpublicspending.co.uk/uk_debt.

43 **"the euthanasia of the rentier":** John Maynard Keynes, *The General Theory of Employment, Interest and Money* (London: Palgrave MacMillan, 1936), 345.

45 **As a young man, Keynes:** John Maynard Keynes, *The Economic Consequences of the Peace* (New York: Harcourt, Brace and Howe, 1920).

46 **In the context of 1944:** Richard N. Gardner, *Sterling-Dollar Diplomacy in Current Perspective: The Origins and Prospects of Our International Economic Order* (New York: Columbia University Press, 1980), 371–78.

46 **To that end, discrimination against imports:** United Nations, Economic and Social Council, *Draft Charter for the International Trade Organization of the United Nations* (Washington, DC: US Government Printing Office, 1947). See Article 6, "Fair Labor Standards."

47 **They finally stabilized:** John Gimbel, *The Origins of the Marshall Plan* (Stanford, CA: Stanford University Press, 1976).

48 **New York bankers had lobbied mightily:** Eric Helleiner, *States and the Emergence of Global Finance* (Ithaca: Cornell University Press, 1994), 39–44.

48 **"Initially, Europe could grow rapidly":** Barry Eichengreen, *The European Economy since 1945: Coordinated Capitalism and Beyond* (Princeton, NJ: Princeton University Press, 2007), 2.

3. THE RISE AND FALL OF DEMOCRATIC GLOBALISM

49   **By war's end, at least 20 million *civilians* had died:** Tony Judt, *Postwar: A History of Europe since 1945* (New York: Penguin Press, 2005), 17.

49   **Not until 1948 did West Germany get a new currency:** See Robert Kuttner, *Debtors' Prison: The Politics of Austerity versus Possibility* (New York: Knopf, 2014), 95–98.

50   **"Europe is steadily deteriorating":** Alan Milward, *The Reconstruction of Western Europe 1945–51* (Berkeley: University of California Press, 1984), 2.

50   **And in June, Secretary of State George Marshall:** Richard N. Gardner, *Sterling-Dollar Diplomacy in Current Perspective: The Origins and Prospects of Our International Economic Order* (New York: Columbia University Press, 1980), 300–301.

50   **George Kennan's "long telegram":** George Frost Kennan, "The Sources of Soviet Conduct," *Foreign Affairs*, July 1947, 566.

51   **In March 1947 he resigned under fire:** Benn Steil, *The Battle of Bretton Woods: John Maynard Keynes, Harry Dexter White and the Making of a New World Order* (Princeton, NJ: Princeton University Press, 2013), 316.

52   **The United States, further marginalizing:** Fred Block, *The Origins of International Economic Disorder* (Berkeley: University of California Press, 1978).

53   **Unions played a particularly strong role:** Gøsta Esping-Andersen, *Politics against Markets: The Social Democratic Road to Power* (Princeton, NJ: Princeton University Press, 1985).

54   **The reality on the ground:** See Dean Acheson, *Present at the Creation* (New York: Norton, 1969).

55   **All six of the foreign ministers:** Tony Judt, *Postwar: A History of Europe since 1945* (New York: Penguin Press, 2005), 156–57.

55   **The social encyclicals of Pope Leo XIII:** John A. Coleman, ed., *One Hundred Years of Catholic Social Thought* (Ossining, NY: Orbis, 1991).

56   **By contrast, democratic corporatism:** See Peter Hall and David Soskice, *Varieties of Capitalism* (New York: Oxford University Press, 2001); Walter Korpi, *The Democratic Class Struggle* (London: Routledge, Kegan and Paul, 1983).

56   **The continental version involved:** See Gøsta Esping-Andersen, *Three Worlds of Welfare Capitalism* (Princeton, NJ: Princeton University Press, 1990).

57   **"Not merely as a feature of the transition":** Rawi Abdelal, *Capital Rules: The Construction of Global Finance* (Cambridge, MA: Harvard University Press, 2009), 7.

58   **"embedded liberalism":** John G. Ruggie, "International Regimes, Transactions, and Change: Embedded Liberalism in the Postwar Economic System," *International Organization* 36, no. 2 (Spring 1982): 379–415.

58   **"Governments would be permitted":** Quoted in Abdelal, *Capital Rules*, 47.

58   **American military aid to NATO countries:** Block, *Origins of International Economic Disorder*, 244n.

58   **US private investment increased:** Robert Kuttner, *The End of Laissez-Faire: National Purpose and the Global Economy after the Cold War* (New York: Knopf, 1991).

59   **The right to regulate cross-border movements:** Abdelal, *Capital Rules*, 6–7.

60   **In Germany, virtually all of the Hitler-era debt:** Timothy W. Guinnane, *Financial Vergangenheitsbewältigung: The 1953 London Debt Agreement*, Center Discussion Paper 880 (New Haven, CT: Economic Growth Center, Yale University, 2004), 8, http://www.econ.yale.edu/growth_pdf/cdp880.pdf.

60   **In one generation after 1945:** Kuttner, *End of Laissez-Faire*, 58.

61   **Even so, the share of US income:** Anthony B. Atkinson, *Inequality: What Can Be Done?* (Cambridge, MA: Harvard University Press, 2015), 60.

61   **In his authoritative 2015 study:** Ibid., 68.

61   ***Full Employment in a Free Society***: William Beveridge, *Full Employment in a Free Society* (London: Allen & Unwin, 1944).

62   ***Capital in the Twenty-First Century***: Thomas Piketty, *Capital in the Twenty-First Century*, trans. Arthur Goldhammer (Cambridge, MA: Belknap Press of Harvard University Press, 2014).

64   **"Triffin dilemma":** Robert Triffin, *Gold and the Dollar Crisis* (New Haven, CT: Yale University Press, 1960).

64   **By 1960, the value of dollars held offshore:** Kuttner, *End of Laissez-Faire*, 61.

66   **The tape from June 23, 1973:** Nixon Library and Museum, "Transcript of a Recording of a Meeting between the President and H. R. Haldeman in the Oval Office on June 23, 1972 from 10:04 to 11:39 AM," http://www.nixonlibrary.gov/forresearchers/find/tapes/watergate/wspf/741-002.pdf.

69   **The Bank of England was torn:** Denis MacShane, *Brexit: How Britain Will Leave Europe* (London: Tauris, 2015).

69   **"Ladies and gentlemen":** John Eatwell, interview with the author, 2007.

71   **Many Marxian scholars have insisted:** See Wolfgang Streeck, *How Will Capitalism End?: Essays on a Failing System* (London: Verso, 2016).

71   **As early as 1972:** Mahbub ul Haq, Inge Kaul, and Isabelle Grunberg, eds., *The Tobin Tax: Coping with Financial Volatility* (New York: Oxford University Press, 1996), 135.

72   **"Speculators," he explained, "invest their money":** "James Tobin: 'The Antiglobalisation Movement Has Highjacked My Name,'" *Der Spiegel*, September 3, 2001, https://web.archive.org/web/20050306201839/http://www.jubilee2000uk.org/worldnews/lamerica/james_tobin_030901_english.htm.

72   **"always and everywhere a monetary phenomenon":** Milton Friedman, *An Economist's Protest* (Glen Ridge, NJ: Horton, 1972), 56.

73   **It would have been far better policy:** Gar Alperovitz and Jeff Faux, "Controls and the Basic Necessities," *Challenge* 23, no. 2 (May–June 1980): 20–22, http://www.tandfonline.com/doi/abs/10.1080/05775132.1980.11470606.

73   **Unions in Scandinavia:** Michael Bruno and Jeffery Sachs, *The Economics of Worldwide Stagflation* (Cambridge, MA: Harvard University Press, 1985).

4. THE LIBERATION OF FINANCE

74   **Now, all capital movements had to be liberalized:** Dani Rodrik, *The Globalization Paradox: Democracy and the Future of the World Economy* (New York: Norton, 2011), 103.

75   **To attract private capital:** John Williamson, "The Washington Consensus as a Policy Prescription for Development" (lecture, World Bank, January 13, 2004), Institute for International Economics, https://piie.com/publications/papers/williamson0204.pdf.

75   **In 1997, Michel Camdessus:** Rawi Abdelal, "The IMF and the Capital Account," in *Reforming the IMF for the 21st Century*, ed. Edwin M. Truman (Washington, DC: Institute for International Economics, 2006).

75   **The Washington Consensus was routinely incorporated:** Joseph E. Stiglitz, *The Roaring Nineties: A New History of the World's Most Prosperous Decade* (New York: Norton, 2003).

75   **In Latin America, which had been encouraged:** Luis Bertola and Jose Antonio Ocampo, *The Economic Development of Latin America since Independence* (Oxford: Oxford University Press, 2013); Paul Blustein, *And the Money Kept Rolling In (and Out): Wall Street, the IMF, and the Bankrupting of Argentina* (New York: Public Affairs, 2005).

75   **The East Asian financial crisis:** Stiglitz, *Roaring Nineties*, 219–21.

76   **(For more details, see my account in *Debtors' Prison*):** Robert Kuttner, *Debtors' Prison: The Politics of Austerity versus Possibility* (New York: Knopf, 2014), 248–60.

76   **The authoritative study on the subject:** Carmen M. Reinhart and Kenneth S. Rogoff, *This Time Is Different: Eight Centuries of Financial Folly* (Princeton, NJ: Princeton University Press, 2009).

77   **The franc had already been devalued:** Arthur Goldhammer and George Ross, "Reluctantly Center-Left? The French Case," in *What's Left of the Left: Democrats and Social Democrats in Challenging Times*, ed. James Cronin, George Ross, and James Shoch (Durham, NC: Duke University Press, 2011), 141–61.

79   **The government also nationalized the "commanding heights":** John Bew, *Citizen Clem: A Biography of Attlee* (Oxford: Oxford University Press, 2016); James Cronin, *New Labour's Pasts: The Labour Party and Its Discontents* (Harlow, UK: Pearson/Longman, 2004); Richard N. Gardner, *Sterling-Dollar Diplomacy in Current Perspective: The Origins and Prospects of Our International Economic Order* (New York: Columbia University Press, 1980).

80   **The British unemployment rate:** James Dennan and Paul McDonald, "Unemployment Statistics from 1881 to the Present Day," in *Labour Market Trends* (London: UK Government Statistical Office, January 1996), chart on p. 7.

83 **This process was given the grandiose euphemism:** Denis MacShane, *Brexit: How Britain Will Leave Europe* (London: Tauris, 2015).

83 **Later, enforcement measures and penalties were stiffened:** David Marsh, *The Euro: The Politics of the New Global Currency* (New Haven, CT: Yale University Press, 2009).

85 **The agreements sponsored by all three institutions:** Organisation for Economic Co-operation and Development, *The OECD Jobs Study: Facts, Analysis, Strategies* (Paris: OECD, 1994).

87 **Fortunes were not made:** Dan Immergluck, *Foreclosed: High-Risk Lending, Deregulation, and the Undermining of America's Mortgage Market* (Ithaca, NY: Cornell University Press, 2009).

87 **The private bond-rating firms:** Financial Crisis Inquiry Commission, "The Financial Crisis Inquiry Report: Final Report of the National Commission on the Causes of the Financial and Economic Crisis in the United States," January 2011, https://fcic-static.law.stanford.edu/cdn_media/fcic-reports/fcic_final_report_full.pdf.

88 **The same claims of maximizing:** Eileen Appelbaum and Rosemary Batt, *Private Equity at Work: When Wall Street Manages Main Street* (New York: Russell Sage Foundation, 2014).

88 **It took a heroic and extralegal:** Roger Lowenstein, *When Genius Failed: The Rise and Fall of Long-Term Capital Management* (New York: Random House, 2000).

89 **Thatcher's chancellor of the exchequer:** "Glass-Steagall: A Price Worth Paying?" *Analysis* (radio program), February 1, 2010, BBC Radio 4, 0:00–13:00, http://www.bbc.co.uk/radio/player/b00qbxwj.

89 **"The U.S. banks set up offshore offices":** Robert Z. Aliber, quoted in Federal Reserve Bank of Boston, *Key Issues in International Banking: Proceedings of a Conference Held in October 1977*, Conference Series no. 18, 48, https://www.bostonfed.org/-/media/Documents/conference/18/conf18.pdf?la=en.

90 **For instance, in 1981:** Daniel K. Tarullo, *Banking on Basel: The Future of International Financial Regulation* (New York: Columbia University Press, 2008), 48.

92 **"Opportunities for manifold forms":** Ibid., 79–80.

93 **"would be competitively disadvantaged":** Ibid., 52.

95 **"The proposed rule would isolate":** MarketsReformWiki, "Volcker Rule—Comment Letters," accessed March 8, 2017, http://www.marketsreformwiki.com/mktreformwiki/index.php/Volcker_Rule_-_Comment_Letters#Goldman_Sachs_-_February_13.2C_2012.

95 **"The Proposed Rule may push":** Ibid.

96 **"In order to avoid the territorial jurisdiction":** US Chamber of Commerce, "Statement of the U.S. Chamber of Commerce, on: Discussion of the Volcker Rule on Markets, Businesses, Investors and Job Creation," May 31, 2012, http://www.centerforcapitalmarkets.com/wp-content/uploads/2010/04/2012-5-31-CFTC-Roundtable-Volcker-Rule.pdf.

5. THE GLOBAL ASSAULT ON LABOR

99 **In one report after another:** Organisation for Economic Co-operation and Development, *The OECD Jobs Study: Facts, Analysis, Strategies* (Paris: OECD, 1994), esp. 34–35.

100 **Total US employment during that decade:** Lawrence Katz and Alan Krueger, *The Rise and Nature of Alternative Work Arrangements in the United States, 1995–2015*, NBER Working Paper 22667 (Cambridge: National Bureau of Economic Research, 2016).

101 **Instacart, mostly for grocery deliveries:** See Robert Kuttner, "The Task Rabbit Economy," *American Prospect*, October 10, 2013, http://prospect.org/article/task-rabbit-economy.

102 **Economist George Akerlof:** George Akerlof and Janet Yellen, *Efficiency Wage Models of the Labor Market* (Cambridge: Cambridge University Press, 1986).

102 **A light bulb went off:** Binyamin Appelbaum, "Yellen's Path from Liberal Theorist to Fed Voice for Jobs," *New York Times*, October 9, 2013, http://www.nytimes.com/2013/10/10/business/economy/for-yellen-a-focus-on-reducing-unemployment.html?pagewanted=all&_r=0.

102 **The workers, savvy about the dynamics:** David Weil, *The Fissured Workplace: Why Work Became So Bad for So Many* (Cambridge, MA: Harvard University Press, 2014), 179.

103 **The subcontracting forced workers:** Robert J. S. Ross, *Slaves to Fashion* (Ann Arbor: University of Michigan Press, 2004).

103 **Only a minority, typically those:** Robert Kuttner, "A More Perfect Union," *American Prospect*, November 28, 2011, http://prospect.org/article/more-perfect-union-1.

104 **Workers are protected:** Katherine V. W. Stone, "Unions in the Precarious Economy: How Collective Bargaining Can Help Gig and On-Demand Workers," *American Prospect*, February 21, 2017, http://prospect.org/article/unions-precarious-economy.

105 **When NYU was embarrassed:** Ariel Kaminer and Sean O'Driscoll, "Workers at NYU's Abu Dhabi Site Faced Harsh Conditions," *New York Times*, May 18, 2014, https://www.nytimes.com/2014/05/19/nyregion/workers-at-nyus-abu-dhabi-site-face-harsh-conditions.html.

105 **Large corporations "have it both ways":** Weil, *Fissured Workplace*.

106 **Such workers are more likely:** Annette Bernhardt, Siobhán McGrath, and James DeFillipis, "Unregulated Work in the Global City: Employment and Labor Law Violations in New York City," Brennan Center for Justice at New York University School of Law, 2007, https://www.brennancenter.org/publication/unregulated-work-global-city-full-report-chapter-downloads.

107 **In cities where Uber drivers have organized:** Steven Greenhouse, "On Demand, and Demanding Their Rights," *American Prospect*, June 28, 2016, http://prospect.org/article/demand-and-demanding-their-rights.

108 **According to Professor Katherine Stone:** Katherine V. W. Stone and Alexander J. S. Colvin, "The Arbitration Epidemic: Mandatory Arbitration

Deprives Workers and Consumers of Their Rights," Economic Policy Institute, December 7, 2015, http://www.epi.org/publication/the-arbitration-epidemic.

111   **The private-equity industry now owns:** Danielle Ivory, Ben Protess, and Kitty Bennett, "When You Dial 911 and Wall Street Answers," *New York Times*, June 25, 2016, https://www.nytimes.com/2016/06/26/business/dealbook/when-you-dial-911-and-wall-street-answers.html.

111   **Before KB went bankrupt:** Eileen Appelbaum and Rosemary Batt, *Private Equity at Work: When Wall Street Manages Main Street* (New York: Russell Sage Foundation, 2014), 157.

111   **Such maneuvers enabled Sun to strip assets:** Eileen Appelbaum and Rosemary Batt, *Private Equity at Work*.

112   **Actually, Elizabeth Warren said it first:** Elizabeth Warren, [Speech] (2012 Democratic National Convention, Charlotte, NC, September 2012).

112   **"his three year investment netted him $4.5 billion":** Appelbaum and Batt, *Private Equity at Work*, 195.

114   **"Harold, a former member and shop steward":** Katherine J. Cramer, *The Politics of Resentment: Rural Consciousness in Wisconsin and the Rise of Scott Walker* (Chicago: University of Chicago Press, 2016), 187.

116   **As the economist Ha-Joon Chang:** Ha-Joon Chang, *23 Things They Don't Tell You about Capitalism* (New York: Bloomsbury Press, 2011), 109.

116   **"The decades-long decline":** David H. Autor, "Skills, Education, and the Rise of Earnings Inequality among the 'Other 99 Percent,'" *Science* 344, no. 6186 (May 23, 2014): 843–51, doi:10.1126/science.1251868.

117   **Earnings for young college graduates:** Lawrence Mishel, Elise Gould, and Josh Bivens, "Wage Stagnation in Nine Charts," Economic Policy Institute, January 26, 2015, fig. 5, http://www.epi.org/publication/charting-wage-stagnation.

117   **At Washington University in St. Louis:** "Some Colleges Have More Students from the Top 1 Percent than the Bottom 60. Find Yours," January 18, 2017, https://www.nytimes.com/interactive/2017/01/18/upshot/some-colleges-have-more-students-from-the-top-1-percent-than-the-bottom-60.html.

117   **Children whose parents are in the top 1 percent:** Raj Chetty et al., *Mobility Report Cards: The Role of Colleges in Intergenerational Mobility*, NBER Working Paper 23618 (Cambridge, MA: National Bureau of Economic Research, 2017), http://papers.nber.org/papers/w23618?utm_campaign=ntw&utm_medium=email&utm_source=ntw.

118   **Contrary to conventional economic wisdom:** Raj Chetty et al., *The Fading American Dream: Trends in Absolute Income Mobility since 1940*, NBER Working Paper 22910 (Cambridge, MA: National Bureau of Economic Research, 2016), 2, http://www.equality-of-opportunity.org/papers/abs_mobility_paper.pdf.

119   **No such family welfare state:** See discussion in Chuck Collins, "The Wealthy Kids Are All Right," *American Prospect*, May 28, 2013, http://prospect.org/article/wealthy-kids-are-all-right.

119   **Not surprisingly, the proportion receiving help:** Quoctrung Bui,

"Almost Half of Young Adults Get Rent Help from Parents," *New York Times*, February 9, 2017.

119 **In his great blueprint for the postwar welfare state:** William Beveridge, "Social Insurance and Allied Services" (London: HMSO, 1942), repr. *Bulletin of the World Health Organization* 78, no. 6 (2000): 847–55, https://www.ncbi .nlm.nih.gov/pmc/articles/PMC2560775/pdf/10916922.pdf.

119 **FDR captured much of the same spirit:** Franklin D. Roosevelt, "Annual Message to Congress on the State of the Union" (Four Freedoms speech, January 6, 1941), http://www.presidency.ucsb.edu/ws/?pid=16092.

119 **Political scientist Jacob Hacker:** Jacob S. Hacker, *The Great Risk Shift* (Oxford: Oxford University Press, 2006).

120 **It wasn't credit card spending binges:** Elizabeth Warren and Amelia Warren Tyagi, *The Two Income Trap: Why Middle Class Parents Are Going Broke* (New York: Basic Books, 2004).

120 **The mortgage collapse of 2008:** Demos, "Homeownership Rate of Young Adults," accessed April 12, 2016, http://www.demos.org/data-byte/home ownership-rate-young-adults.

6. EUROPE'S BROKEN SOCIAL CONTRACT

121 **Overall growth rates roughly tracked:** David Leonhardt and Kevin Quealey, "The American Middle Class Is No Longer the World's Richest," *New York Times*, April 22, 2014, https://www.nytimes.com/2014/04/23/ upshot/the-american-middle-class-is-no-longer-the-worlds-richest.html.

123 **"This Treaty shall in no way prejudice":** Therese Blanchette, Risto Piponnen, and Maria Westman-Clement, *The Agreement on the European Economic Area* (Oxford: Clarendon, 1994), 106.

123 **"certain economic powers which are now":** Friedrich A. von Hayek, "The Economic Conditions of Interstate Federalism," in *Individualism and Economic Order* (Chicago: University of Chicago Press, 1948), 264–65.

123 **"No Socialist Party with the prospect":** Denis MacShane, *Brexit: How Britain Will Leave Europe* (London: Tauris, 2015), 40.

124 **A key constitutional provision of the Maastricht Treaty:** *Treaty on European Union* (Luxembourg: Office for Official Publications of the European Communities, 1992), https://europa.eu/european-union/sites/europaeu/ files/docs/body/treaty_on_european_union_en.pdf.

125 **"Posting is framed as an expression":** "Posting of Workers Directive: Current Situation and Challenges," European Parliament, Directorate General for Internal Policies, July 2016, http://www.europarl.europa.eu/RegData/ etudes/STUD/2016/579001/IPOL_STU(2016)579001_EN.pdf.

126 **Under the rules, a contractor need pay:** Jan Cremers, *In Search of Cheap Labour in Europe: Working and Living Conditions of Posted Workers* (Brussels: CLR/EFBW/International Books, 2011).

126 **These workers, as EU citizens:** Ibid., 26.

127 **So, the posting directive serves:** Line Eldring and Thorsten Schulten, "Migrant Workers and Wage-Setting Institutions: Experiences from Germany, Norway, Switzerland and United Kingdom," in *EU Labour Migration in Trou-*

bled Times: Skills Mismatch, Return and Policy Responses, ed. Bela Galgóczi, Janine Leschke, and Andrew Watt (Abingdon, UK: Routledge, 2016).

127 **On one UK construction project:** Cremers, *In Search of Cheap Labour in Europe*, 40–41.

127 **The contractor was paying these drivers:** Jan Cremers, "Letter-Box Companies and the Abuse of Posting Rules: How the Primacy of Economic Freedoms and Weak Enforcement Give Rise to Social Dumping," ETUI Policy Brief no. 5, 2014, http://www.eurodetachement-travail.eu/datas/files/EUR/Policy_Brief_J._Cremers2014-05.pdf.

128 **This rule, the so-called Bolkestein directive:** "Directive 2006/123/EC of the European Parliament and of the Council of 12 December 2006 on Services in the Internal Market," December 12, 2006, http://eur-lex.europa.eu/legal-content/EN/TXT/?uri=celex:32006L0123.

128 **After extensive public outcry:** Jon Erik Dølvik and Anna Mette Ødegård, "The Struggle over the Services Directive: The Role of the European Parliament and the ETUC," *Labor History*, March 16, 2012, http://www.tandfonline.com/doi/abs/10.1080/0023656X.2012.650433.

129 **The union was liable for financial damages:** Andreas Bücher and Wiebke Warneck, eds., *Viking–Laval–Rüffert: Consequences and Policy Perspectives*, ETUI Report 111 (Brussels: European Trade Union Institute, 2010).

129 **Adding insult to injury:** Ibid.

131 **But the coverage rate is declining:** Jelle Visser, Susan Hayter, and Rosina Gammarano, "Trends in Collective Bargaining Coverage: Stability, Erosion, or Decline," International Labour Office, September 29, 2015, http://www.ilo.org/global/topics/collective-bargaining-labour-relations/publications/WCMS_409422/lang--en/index.htm.

132 **Between 1980 and 2012, the labor share:** "The Labour Share in G20 Economies," International Labour Organization, Organisation for Economic Co-operation and Development (report prepared for the G20 Employment Working Group, Antalya, Turkey, February 26–27, 2015), https://www.oecd.org/g20/topics/employment-and-social-policy/The-Labour-Share-in-G20-Economies.pdf.

132 **Low-wage work, defined as:** Claus Schnabel, "Low-Wage Employment," IZA World of Labor, July 2016, https://wol.iza.org/articles/low-wage-employment/long.

132 **There is a close correlation:** Jérôme Gautié and John Schmitt, eds., *Low-Wage Work in the Wealthy World* (New York: Russell Sage Foundation, 2009).

132 **In the US, where collective bargaining:** Gerhard Bosch and Jérôme Gautié, "Low Wage Work in Five European Countries and the USA: The Role of National Institutions," *Cuadernos de Relaciones Laborales* 29, no. 2 (2011): 303–35, http://revistas.ucm.es/index.php/CRLA/article/viewFile/38018/36773.

133 **Studies have found that the gains:** "Public and Private Sector Efficiency," Public Services and the EU, no. 3 (European Federation of Public Services Unions, May 2014), http://www.psiru.org/sites/default/files/2014-07-EWGHT-efficiency.pdf.

134 **When the system was again privatized:** Owen Jones, "Why Britain's Trains Don't Run on Time: Capitalism," *New York Times*, April 4, 2017, https://www.nytimes.com/2017/04/04/opinion/why-britains-trains-dont-run-on-time-capitalism.html.

135 **Where traditional post offices invested heavily:** Christophe Hermann, "Deregulating and Privatizing Postal Services in Europe," Centre for Research on Globalisation, January 1, 2014, http://www.globalresearch.ca/deregulating-and-privatizing-postal-services-in-europe/5363277.

135 **According to the then prime minister:** Robert Kuttner, "The Copenhagen Consensus," *Foreign Affairs*, March-April 2008, https://www.foreignaffairs.com/articles/europe/2008-03-01/copenhagen-consensus.

135 **"It is hard to imagine a worse match":** Ibid.

136 **So, in less than three years:** Vilhelm Carlström, "Biggest IPO in Danish History Reveals Goldman Sachs Got a Huge Discount in Government Deal," *Business Insider Nordic*, June 1, 2016, http://nordic.businessinsider.com/biggest-ipo-in-danish-history-reveals-goldman-sachs-got-a-$10-billion-discount-on-the-worlds-largest-offshore-wind-operator-2016-5.

138 **The three even jointly wrote a book:** Gösta Edgren, Karl Olof Faxén, and Clas-Erik Odhner, *Wage Formation and the Economy* (London: Allen & Unwin, 1973).

139 **This premise has been strongly supported:** Kuttner, "Copenhagen Consensus."

140 **Some contended that the social buffers:** Peter Katzenstein, *Small States in World Markets: Industrial Policy in Europe* (Ithaca, NY: Cornell University Press, 1985).

144 **But this remarkable act of macroeconomic mercy:** Robert Kuttner, *Debtors' Prison: The Politics of Austerity versus Possibility* (New York: Knopf, 2014), 95.

145 **"the Troika's grasp of the underlying economics":** Joseph E. Stiglitz, *The Euro: How a Common Currency Threatens the Future of Europe* (New York: Norton, 2016), 182–83.

146 **The decline of Greek GDP:** Trading Economics, "Greece GDP," accessed March 21, 2017, http://www.tradingeconomics.com/greece/gdp; Elena Holodny, "History Has Seen Worse Economic Collapses than the Depression Greece Is Now Experiencing," *Business Insider*, July 6, 2015, http://www.businessinsider.com/the-worst-gdp-collapses-since-1870-2015-7.

146 **"undertake rigorous reviews and modernization":** Stiglitz, *Euro*, 221.

147 **"a 16 percent cumulative fiscal adjustment":** Yiannis Mouzakis, "Seven Years of Demanding the Impossible in Greece," MacroPolis, February 16, 2017, http://www.macropolis.gr/?i=portal.en.the-agora.5256.

147 **Even the then-head of the IMF:** "IMF Chief Economist Blanchard Warned in May 2010 Greece Program Was Not Going to Work," Keep Talking Greece, February 15, 2017, http://www.keeptalkinggreece.com/2017/02/15/imf-chief-economist-blanchard-warned-in-may-2010-greece-program-was-not-going-to-work.

147 **Most of the money:** Stiglitz, *Euro*, 203.

147 **The most recent EU Council report on France:** Council of the European Union, "Council Recommendation of . . . on the 2016 National Reform Programme of France and Delivering a Council Opinion on the 2016 Stability Programme of France," June 13, 2016, http://data.consilium.europa.eu/doc/document/ST-9200-2016-INIT/en/pdf.

7. THE DISGRACE OF THE CENTER LEFT

150 **Clinton also calculated that Democrats:** Bob Woodward, *The Agenda: Inside the Clinton White House* (New York: Simon & Schuster, 1994).

151 **"The era of big government is over":** William J. Clinton, "Address before a Joint Session of the Congress on the State of the Union," January 23, 1996, American Presidency Project, http://www.presidency.ucsb.edu/ws/?pid =53091.

151 **He launched an initiative:** National Performance Review, "A Brief History of the National Performance Review," accessed February 23, 2017, https://govinfo.library.unt.edu/npr/library/papers/bkgrd/brief.html.

151 **Its predecessor, Aid to Families with Dependent Children:** David Ellwood, "Welfare Reform as I Knew It: When Bad Things Happen to Good Policies," *American Prospect*, May–June 1996, http://prospect.org/article/welfare-reform-i-knew-it-when-bad-things-happen-good-policies.

151 **It was a complex system of "managed competition":** Paul Starr, *The Logic of Healthcare Reform* (Knoxville, TN: Whittle Direct Books, 1992).

152 **In 1989, two New Democrat intellectuals:** William Galston and Elaine Ciulla Kamarck, "The Politics of Evasion: Democrats and the Presidency," Progressive Policy Institute, September 1989.

152 **The first of these issues:** See Robert Kuttner, "Friendly Takeover," *American Prospect*, March–April 2007.

153 **It passed the House by two votes:** Woodward, *Agenda*.

153 **After initially supporting what turned out to be:** Robert Kuttner, *A Presidency in Peril: The Inside Story of Obama's Promise, Wall Street's Power, and the Struggle to Control Our Economic Future* (White River Junction, VT: Chelsea Green, 2010).

155 **In 1969, the government of Labour prime minister:** Barbara Castle, "In Place of Strife: A Policy for Industrial Relations" (UK government white paper), January 1969.

157 **"The Clinton experience was seminal":** James E. Cronin, *New Labour's Pasts: The Labour Party and Its Discontents* (Harlow, UK: Pearson/Longman, 2004), 364.

157 **"supply side of the left":** See Anthony Giddens, *The Third Way: The Renewal of Social Democracy* (Cambridge, UK: Polity Press, 1998).

158 **It meant deregulation of capital:** See "The Turner Review: A Regulatory Response to the Global Banking Crisis," Financial Services Authority, March 2009, http://www.fsa.gov.uk/pubs/other/turner_review.pdf.

158 **The earnings ratio of the top 10 percent:** Office for National Statistics, "Annual Survey of Hours and Earnings: 2015 Provisional Results,"

Statistical Bulletin, accessed March 18, 2017, https://www.ons.gov.uk/employmentandlabourmarket/peopleinwork/earningsandworkinghours/bulletins/annualsurveyofhoursandearnings/2015provisionalresults.

159   **"It's a monumental farce":** *I, Daniel Blake* (film), directed by Ken Loach, BBC Films, 2016, http://www.bbc.co.uk/bbcfilms/film/i_daniel_blake.

159   **Under Blair and Brown the decline continued:** William Brown, "Industrial Relations in Britain under New Labour, 1997–2010: A Post Mortem," CWPE 1121, January 2011, http://www.econ.cam.ac.uk/dae/repec/cam/pdf/cwpe1121.pdf.

159   **"Is that your trophy gallery?":** John Monks, interview with the author, May 22, 2017.

160   **Blair also retained Thatcher's legal restraints:** Brown, "Industrial Relations in Britain."

160   **Margaret Thatcher once remarked:** Conservative Home, "Margaret Thatcher's Greatest Achievement: New Labour," *CentreRight* (blog), November 24, 2010, http://conservativehome.blogs.com/centreright/2008/04/making-history.html.

162   **"The center needs to develop":** Tony Blair, "How to Stop Populism's Carnage," *New York Times*, March 4, 2017.

164   **German banks traditionally had:** Peter Hall and David Soskice, *Varieties of Capitalism* (New York: Oxford University Press, 2001). See also Jan Fichtner, "Rhenish Capitalism Meets Activist Hedge Funds: Blockholders and the Impact of Impatient Capital," *Competition and Change* 19, no. 4 (August 2015).

164   **"maximize shareholder value":** See Michael C. Jensen and William H. Meckling, "Theory of the Firm: Managerial Behavior, Agency Costs, and Ownership Structure," *Journal of Financial Economics* 3, no. 4 (October 1976): 305–60.

164   **In the view of Joseph Schumpeter:** Joseph A. Schumpeter, *Capitalism, Socialism and Democracy* (1944; repr., London: Allen & Unwin, 1962).

165   **To win East German consent:** David Marsh, *The Euro: The Politics of the New Global Currency* (New Haven, CT: Yale University Press, 2009), 144–45.

166   **These were not replaced by economic growth:** Gerhard Bosch and Claudia Weinkopf, eds., *Low-Wage Work in Germany* (New York: Russell Sage Foundation, 2008), 55.

166   **GDP growth was close to zero:** Christian Dustmann et al., "From Sick Man of Europe to Economic Superstar: Germany's Resurgent Economy," *Journal of Economic Perspectives* 28, no. 1 (Winter 2014): 167–88.

167   **Two aspects of Schröder's policy shift:** Wendy Carlin and David Soskice, "Disentangling the Role of Supply-Side Reforms, Macroeconomic Policy and Coordinated Economy Institutions," *Socio-Economic Review* 7, no. 1 (January 2009), https://academic.oup.com/ser/article-abstract/7/1/67/1693070/German-economic-performance-disentangling-the-role?redirectedFrom=fulltext.

167   **"a type of financial deregulation":** Claus Christian Malzahn, "Taking Stock of Gerhard Schröder," *Der Spiegel*, October 14, 2005, http://www.spiegel

.de/international/the-modern-chancellor-taking-stock-of-gerhard-schroeder-a-379600.html.

167 **The most controversial of these:** Bosch and Weinkopf, eds., *Low-Wage Work in Germany*, 50–52.

169 **"Be it television stations":** "The Locusts: Privaty Equity Firms Strip Mine German Firms," *Der Spiegel*, December 22, 2006, http://www.spiegel.de/international/the-locusts-privaty-equity-firms-strip-mine-german-firms-a-456272.html.

170 **Unemployment did eventually abate:** David Böcking, "Preparing for the Worst: The High Price of Abandoning the Euro," *Der Spiegel*, November 29, 2011, http://www.spiegel.de/international/europe/preparing-for-the-worst-the-high-price-of-abandoning-the-euro-a-800700-4.html.

170 **Many German critics contend:** Sebastien Dullien, Hansjorg Herr, and Christian Kellerman, *Decent Capitalism: A Blueprint for Reforming Our Economies* (London: Pluto Press, 2011). See also Claus Offe, *Europe Entrapped* (Cambridge: Polity Press, 2015); and Hans-Werner Sinn, *The Euro Trap: On Bursting Bubbles, Budgets, and Beliefs* (Oxford: Oxford University Press, 2014).

171 **Blair became even richer:** Luke Heighton, "Revealed: Tony Blair Worth a Staggering £60m," *Telegraph*, June 12, 2015, http://www.telegraph.co.uk/news/politics/tony-blair/11670425/Revealed-Tony-Blair-worth-a-staggering-60m.html.

172 **"The promotion of social justice":** Tony Blair and Gerhard Schroeder, "Europe: The Third Way/Die Neue Mitte," Working Documents, no. 2, Friedrich Ebert Foundation, June 1998, http://library.fes.de/pdf-files/bueros/suedafrika/02828.pdf.

173 **The reference, of course:** Marquis William Childs, *Sweden: The Middle Way* (New Haven, CT: Yale University Press, 1947).

174 **As the Swedish scholar Lars Trägårdh observes:** Lars Trägårdh, "Welfare State Nationalism and the Crisis of European Social Democracy" (unpublished manuscript, 2015), quoted with permission of the author. See also Lene Hansen and Ole Waever, eds., *European Integration and National Identity: The Challenge of the Nordic States* (London: Routledge, 2002), http://www.larstragardh.se/wp-content/uploads/european-integration.pdf.

176 **"Two thirds take part":** "Last Word: Fredrik Reinfeldt," *Newsweek*, December 17, 2006, http://www.newsweek.com/last-word-fredrik-reinfeldt-105811.

177 **"These cumulative policy shifts undermine":** Robert Kuttner, "History's Missed Moment," *American Prospect*, September 22, 2011, http://prospect.org/article/historys-missed-moment.

178 **By 2002, the incidence of low-wage work:** Bosch and Weinkopf, eds., *Low-Wage Work in Germany*, 14.

8. TRADING AWAY A DECENT ECONOMY

180 **"All problems of local [US] industry":** Dwight D. Eisenhower public

papers, quoted in William A. Lovett, Alfred E. Eckes Jr., and Richard L. Brinkman, *U.S. Trade Policy: History, Theory, and the WTO* (Armonk, NY: Sharpe, 1999), 79. See also Michael Schaller, *Altered States: The United States and Japan since the Occupation* (New York: Oxford University Press, 1997), 100.

182 **Under the original 1947 agreement:** Lovett, Eckes, and Brinkman, *U.S. Trade Policy*, 5.

182 **The stillborn International Trade Organization:** Susan Aaronson, *Taking Trade to the Streets: The Lost History of Public Efforts to Shape Globalization* (Ann Arbor: University of Michigan Press, 2001), 52–57.

182 **Over time, these industries came to include:** Chalmers Johnson, *MITI and the Japanese Miracle: The Growth of Industrial Policy 1925–1975* (Stanford, CA: Stanford University Press, 1982).

183 **"Take off those taxes and tariffs":** Robert Kuttner, *The End of Laissez-Faire: National Purpose and the Global Economy after the Cold War* (New York: Knopf, 1991), 176.

184 **Four decades later, a Jeep Wrangler:** Keith Bradsher, "One Rub in Trade Negotiations: Why a Jeep Costs More in China," *New York Times*, March 20, 2017.

185 **Under Robert Lighthizer:** Daniel Marans, "Trump's NAFTA Letter Echoes Obama Administration's Language on TPP," *Huffington Post*, May 18, 2017, http://www.huffingtonpost.com/entry/trump-nafta-obama-tpp_us_591de665e4b094cdba523d00.

187 **"In 1870, Britain accounted for":** Clyde Prestowitz, *The Betrayal of American Prosperity* (New York: Free Press, 2010), 60.

188 **And if other nations subsidized US industries:** Jagdish Bhagwati, *In Defense of Globalization* (Oxford: Oxford University Press, 2007).

188 **the German Friedrich List:** Friedrich List, *The Natural System of Political Economy*, trans. and ed. W. O. Henderson (London: F. Cass, 1983). Originally published as *Système naturel d'économie politique* (1837).

188 **the Americans Paul Krugman and Dani Rodrik:** Dani Rodrik, *The Globalization Paradox: Democracy and the Future of the World Economy* (New York: Norton, 2011).

189 **Advantage can be deliberately created:** Paul Krugman, ed., *Strategic Trade Policy and the New International Economics* (Cambridge, MA: MIT Press, 1986).

190 **After the war, the Kelly Air Mail Act:** See discussion in Robert Kuttner, *Everything for Sale: The Virtues and Limits of Markets* (New York: Knopf, 1997), 212–15.

190 **Between 1929 and 1933:** Lovett, Eckes, and Brinkman, *U.S. Trade Policy*, 68–70.

191 **Between the 1960s and the current era:** Martin Neil Baily and Barry P. Bosworth, "U.S. Manufacturing: Understanding Its Past and Its Potential Future," *Journal of Economic Perspectives* 28, no. 1 (Winter 2014): 3–26, https://www.brookings.edu/wp-content/uploads/2016/06/us-manufacturing-past-and-potential-future-baily-bosworth.pdf.

191   **Manufacturing lost 5 million jobs:** Robert E. Scott, "Manufacturing Job Loss: Trade, Not Productivity, Is the Culprit," Issue Brief no. 402, Economic Policy Institute, August 11, 2015, http://www.epi.org/files/2015/ib402-manufacturing-job-loss.pdf.

191   **In January 1979, the average:** US Bureau of Labor Statistics, "Economic News Release: Table B-8," accessed August 9, 2017, https://www.bls.gov/news .release/empsit.t24.htm.

192   **In other nations that have made a commitment:** Marc Levinson, "US Manufacturing in International Perspective," Congressional Research Service, January 18, 2017, 4, https://fas.org/sgp/crs/misc/R42135.pdf.

192   **The trade deficit in goods in 2016 was $347 billion:** US Census Bureau, "Trade in Goods with China," accessed August 9, 2017, https://www.census .gov/foreign-trade/balance/c5700.html.

192   **On average, jobs in these import-competing industries:** Robert E. Scott, "Unfair Trade Deals Lower the Wages of US Workers," Economic Policy Institute, March 13, 2015, http://www.epi.org/publication/ unfair-trade-deals-lower-the-wages-of-u-s-workers.

193   **"The 'aha' moment":** David Autor, David Dorn, and Gordon H. Hanson, "The China Syndrome: Local Labor Market Effects of Import Competition in the United States," *American Economic Review* 103, no. 6 (2013): 2121–68, http://economics.mit.edu/files/6613.

194   **All told, the Chinese government:** "Plan for $10 Billion Chip Plant in China Shows Strong Pull across the Pacific," *New York Times*, February 11, 2017.

195   **In 1982, Freeman's successor:** Harry L. Freeman, "A Pioneer's View of Financial Services Negotiations in the GATT and the World Trade Organization: 17 Years of Work for Something or Nothing?" *Geneva Papers on Risk and Insurance. Issues and Practice* 22, no. 84 (July 1997): 392–99.

195   **President Reagan's chief of the USTR:** Brian Ahlberg, "American Express: The Stateless Corporation," *Multinational Monitor* 11, no. 11 (November 1990), http://multinationalmonitor.org/hyper/issues/1990/11/ahl berg.html.

196   **"The United States, with the most advanced":** Clyde Farnsworth, "New Trade Struggle: Services," *New York Times*, November 23, 1982, http://www .nytimes.com/1982/11/23/business/new-trade-struggle-services.html.

197   **When Zhu later sweetened the terms:** Joseph E. Stiglitz, *The Roaring Nineties: A New History of the World's Most Prosperous Decade* (New York: Norton, 2003), 214.

199   **Another $500 million suit:** Maude Barlow, "NAFTA's ISDS: Why Canada Is One of the Most Sued Countries in the World," Common Dreams, October 23, 2015, http://www.commondreams.org/views/2015/10/23/naftas -isds-why-canada-one-most-sued-countries-world.

200   **Absurd claims were made:** Jeronim Capaldo, *The Trans-Atlantic Trade and Investment Partnership: European Disintegration, Unemployment and Instability*, Global Development and Environment Institute Working Paper

14-03 (Medford, MA: Tufts University, 2014), https://ase.tufts.edu/gdae/Pubs/wp/14-03CapaldoTTIP.pdf.

201 **"If ever there was a time":** James Mann, *The China Fantasy: How Our Leaders Explain Away Chinese Repression* (New York: Penguin Group, 2007), 80.

203 **"Almost 15 years after China joined":** Stephen J. Ezell and Robert D. Atkinson, "False Promises: The Yawning Gap between China's WTO Commitments and Practices," Information Technology & Innovation Foundation, September 2015, http://www2.itif.org/2015-false-promises-china.pdf.

204 **"Economic freedom creates habits of liberty":** Mann, *China Fantasy*, 2.

204 **"China's going to have a free press":** Thomas L. Friedman, *The Lexus and the Olive Tree: Understanding Globalization* (New York: Farrar, Straus and Giroux, 1999), 183.

205 **"The fundamental problem with this strategy":** Mann, *China Fantasy*, 105.

205 **After the 2016 election:** Timothy B. Lee, "What Donald Trump Got Right and Many Economists Got Wrong about the Costs of Trade," *Vox*, November 30, 2016, https://www.vox.com/new-money/2016/11/30/13764146/china-imports-trump-sad. See also David H. Autor, David Dorn, and Gordon H. Hanson, "The China Syndrome: Local Labor Market Effects of Import Competition in the United States," *American Economic Review* 103, no. 6 (2013): 2121–68.

206 **This claim was preposterous on its face:** Clyde Prestowitz, "Our Incoherent China Policy," *American Prospect*, September 21, 2015, http://prospect.org/article/our-incoherent-china-policy-fall-preview.

206 **"They've already started putting out feelers":** Sarah Wheaton, "Obama: China Might Join Trade Deal—Eventually," Politico, June 3, 2015, http://www.politico.com/story/2015/06/barack-obama-china-join-trade-deal-tpp-118598.

207 **In 2013, the Export-Import Bank of China:** Jing Gu et al., "Chinese State Capitalism? Rethinking the Role of the State and Business in Chinese Development Cooperation in Africa," *World Development* 81 (May 2016): 24–34.

207 **China has also spent some $50 billion:** Norimitsu Onishi, "China Pledges $60 Billion to Aid Africa's Development," *New York Times*, December 4, 2015, https://www.nytimes.com/2015/12/05/world/africa/china-pledges-60-billion-to-aid-africas-development.html?_r=0.

207 **Chinese companies poured about $50 billion:** Kevin P. Gallagher, *The China Triangle* (Oxford: Oxford University Press, 2016), 42.

207 **In 2015, Beijing committed $250 billion:** Ibid., 11.

209 **And while the planned capitalism:** Branko Milanović, *Global Inequality: A New Approach for the Age of Globalization* (Cambridge, MA: Belknap Press of Harvard University Press, 2016), 220.

209 **Rich people in the rich countries:** Ibid., 22–23.

9. TAXES AND THE CORPORATE STATE

212 **In the US and the UK, wartime income tax rates:** W. Elliott Brownlee, *Federal Taxation in America: A Short History* (Cambridge: Cambridge University Press, 2004). For the UK rate, see Thomas Piketty, *Capital in the Twenty-First Century*, trans. Arthur Goldhammer (Cambridge, MA: Belknap Press of Harvard University Press, 2014), 507.

212 **The top rate on labor income:** Ibid., 507, 638n33.

213 **Germany's was the lowest:** "OECD Corporate Income Tax Rates, 1981–2013," Tax Foundation, December 18, 2013, http://taxfoundation.org/article/oecd-corporate-income-tax-rates-1981-2013.

214 **By 2016, for comparison:** "The Sorry State of Corporate Taxes," Citizens for Tax Justice, accessed January 17, 2017, http://www.ctj.org/corporatetaxdodgers/sorrystateofcorptaxes.php.

214 **"Tax and tax, spend and spend, *elect and elect*":** This quote was reported by Arthur Krock in the *New York Times* in 1938 and later challenged by Hopkins: Arthur Krock, "Win Back 10 States; Republicans Take Ohio, Wisconsin, Kansas and Massachusetts," *New York Times*, November 9, 1938.

217 **Voter anger gave legitimacy:** See Robert Kuttner, *Revolt of the Haves* (New York: Simon and Schuster, 1980).

218 **"Whoever is inaugurated in January":** "Mondale's Acceptance Speech, 1984," AllPolitics, accessed February 4, 2017, http://www.cnn.com/ALLPOLITICS/1996/conventions/chicago/facts/famous.speeches/mondale.84.shtml.

220 **Upon taking office in 1979:** Anthony B. Atkinson, *Inequality: What Can Be Done?* (Cambridge, MA: Harvard University Press, 2015), 181.

222 **Between 1981 and 2013:** "OECD Corporate Income Tax Rates, 1981–2013."

222 **Individual income tax rates were also cut:** Chris Edwards and Daniel J. Mitchell, *Global Tax Revolution* (Washington, DC: Cato Institute, 2008), 32.

222 **On capital gains income:** Ibid., 36–38.

223 **"Globalization and tax competition lead to":** Reuven S. Avi-Yonah, "Globalization, Tax Competition and the Fiscal Crisis of the Welfare State," *Harvard Law Review* 113 (May 2000): 1.

223 **"In a modern global economy":** Atkinson, *Inequality*, 103.

223 **In recent years, seven major European countries:** Avi-Yonah, "Globalization, Tax Competition," 6.

224 **"Starving the beast by avoiding":** Tim Worstall, "Tax Avoidance and Tax Evasion Are to the Benefit of Us All," *Forbes*, January 7, 2015, http://www.forbes.com/sites/timworstall/2015/01/07/tax-avoidance-and-tax-evasion-are-to-the-benefit-of-us-all/#4139e327c367.

224 **In the 1920s, foreign funds held:** Gabriel Zucman, *The Hidden Wealth of Nations: The Scourge of Tax Havens* (Chicago: University of Chicago Press), 14.

226 **Juncker was selected to lead the EC:** Simon Bowers, "Jean-Claude Juncker Can't Shake Off Luxembourg's Tax Controversy," *Guardian*,

December 14, 2004, https://www.theguardian.com/world/2014/dec/14/jean-claude-juncker-luxembourg-tax-deals-controversy.

226 **The finance ministers of France, Germany, and Italy:** Gernot Heller, "Germany, France and Italy Urge EU to Write Common Corporate Tax Laws," Reuters, December 1, 2014, http://www.reuters.com/article/us-eurozone-tax-letter-idUSKCN0JF2WN20141201.

227 **Critics of the TTIP have warned:** Jon Stone, "TTIP Could Block Governments from Cracking Down on Tax Avoidance, Study Warns," *Independent*, February 15, 2016, http://www.independent.co.uk/news/uk/politics/ttip-tax-avoidance-corporations-sue-governments-tax-evasion-isds-a6875061.html.

228 **Intel, which builds an average:** Avi-Yonah, "Globalization, Tax Competition," 13.

228 **The study reported that profits:** Jane Gravelle, "Tax Havens: International Tax Avoidance and Evasion," Congressional Research Service, January 2015.

229 **If taxes on those profits were paid in the US:** "Offshore Shell Games 2016," Citizens for Tax Justice, October 4, 2016, http://ctj.org/ctj reports/2016/10/offshore_shell_games_2016.php.

229 **Pfizer, the world's largest drugmaker, ranks second:** https://americansfortaxfairness.org/files/Pfizer-Fact-Sheet-FINAL.pdf; http://www.huffingtonpost.com/martin-sullivan/pfizer-taxes_b_3490510.html.

229 **Some 55 percent of foreign US corporate profits:** Zucman, *Hidden Wealth of Nations*, 105.

229 **In the absence of a whistle-blower:** https://www.forbes.com/sites/nathanvardi/2017/03/02/how-a-swiss-affiliate-led-to-thursdays-federal-raid-of-caterpillars-headquarters/#63a771c76832.

230 **The economist Gabriel Zucman:** Ibid., 35–36.

230 **James Henry, former chief economist:** James S. Henry, "The Price of Offshore Revisited," Tax Justice Network, July 2012, http://www.taxjustice.net/wp-content/uploads/2014/04/Price_of_Offshore_Revisited_120722.pdf.

231 **The entire game of booking assets:** Ronen Palan, Richard Murphy, and Christian Chavagneux, *Tax Havens: How Globalization Really Works* (Ithaca, NY: Cornell University Press, 2010).

231 **By the time Trump took office:** Nicholas Confessore, "How to Hide $400 Million," *New York Times*, November 30, 2016.

232 **"erode the tax bases of other countries":** Organisation for Economic Cooperation and Development, *Harmful Tax Competition: An Emerging Global Issue* (Paris: OECD, 1998), https://www.oecd.org/tax/transparency/44430243.pdf.

233 **A front group was created by Daniel Mitchell:** Edwards and Mitchell, *Global Tax Revolution*, 196.

233 **"Tax competition is greatly beneficial":** Ibid., *Global Tax Revolution*, 177.

233 **Cracking down on tax havens:** Nicholas Shaxson, *Treasure Islands: Uncovering the Damage of Offshore Banking and Tax Havens* (New York: St.

Martin's Press, 2014), 156. Edwards and Mitchell, *Global Tax Revolution*, 165–67.

233 **In May, the Bush administration:** Dana Milbank, "U.S. to Abandon Crackdown on Tax Havens," *Washington Post*, May 11, 2001.

233 **"I am troubled by the underlying premise":** "Treasury Secretary O'Neill Statement on OECD Tax Havens," US Department of the Treasury, May 10, 2001, https://www.treasury.gov/press-center/press-releases/Pages/po366.aspx.

235 **Rubin, after leaving the Treasury:** "Private Banking: Raul Salinas, Citibank, and Alleged Money Laundering," US Government Accountability Office, October 30, 1998, http://www.gao.gov/products/OSI-99-1.

235 **That was business as usual, not terrorism:** Kathleen A. Lacey and Barbara Crutchfield George, "Crackdown on Money Laundering: A Comparative Analysis of the Feasibility and Effectiveness of Domestic and Multilateral Policy Reforms," *Northwestern Journal of International Law & Business* 23, no. 2 (Winter 2003). See also George A. Lyden, "International Money Laundering Abatement and Anti-terrorist Financing Act of 2001: Congress Wears a Blindfold While Giving Money Laundering Legislation a Facelift," *Fordham Journal of Corporate and Financial Law* 8, no. 1 (2003): 201–43.

235 **The fine was a cost of doing business:** Zucman, *Hidden Wealth of Nations*, 68.

235 **"You can't prove criminality":** Shaxson, *Treasure Islands*, 168.

236 **Not surprisingly, everyone complied:** Ibid., 169.

236 **For notorious havens like the Cayman Islands:** "The Case of the Disappearing Tax Havens," Tax Justice Network, November 12, 2010, http://taxjustice.blogspot.com/2010/11/case-of-disappearing-tax-havens.html.

237 **The complex games of booking costs and sales:** Michael Stumo, "The Progressive Tax Reform You've Never Heard Of," *American Prospect*, October 27, 2016, http://prospect.org/article/progressive-tax-reform-you%E2%80%99ve-never-heard.

10. GOVERNING GLOBAL CAPITALISM

238 **In January 2001, while the global:** World Social Forum 2016, "About the World Social Forum," accessed December 8, 2016, https://fsm2016.org/en/sinformer/a-propos-du-forum-social-mondial.

240 **Many standards for business conduct:** See discussion in Tim Buthe and Walter Mattli, *The New Global Rulers: The Privatization of Regulation in the World Economy* (Princeton, NJ: Princeton University Press, 2011), esp. chap. 2.

241 **In some places, such as England:** John Braithwaite and Peter Drahos, "Property and Contract," in *Global Business Regulation* (Cambridge: Cambridge University Press, 2000), 39–84.

242 **I had firsthand experience with this dynamic:** Mike Koehler, "The Story of the Foreign Corrupt Practices Act," *Ohio State Law Journal* 73, no. 5 (2012): 930–1013, http://moritzlaw.osu.edu/students/groups/oslj/files/2013/02/73.5.Koehler.pdf.

243 **Eventually, by the late 1980s:** "General Motors in South Africa: Secret Contingency Plans 'in the Event of Civil Unrest,'" Michigan in the World, accessed January 9, 2017, http://michganintheworld.history.lsa.umich.edu/ antiapartheid/exhibits/show/exhibit/origins/sullivan-principles.

244 **"non-state, market-driven" strategies:** Michael E. Conroy, *Branded! How the Certification Revolution Is Transforming Global Corporations* (Gabriola, BC: New Society, 2007).

244 **As these corporate social responsibility efforts:** See Raymond W. Baker, *Capitalism's Achilles Heel: Dirty Money and How to Renew the Free-Market System* (New York: Wiley, 2005).

245 **However, more than twenty years:** Daniel Jaffee, "Weak Coffee: Certification and Co-optation in the Fair Trade Movement," *Social Problems* 59, no. 1 (February 2012): 94–116, https://www.pdx.edu/sociology/sites/www.pdx .edu.sociology/files/Soc%20Probs%202012--Weak%20Coffee--Jaffee%20.pdf.

246 **The FSC claims 440 million hectares:** Global Forest Atlas, "Forest Certification," accessed January 19, 2017, http://globalforestatlas.yale.edu/ conservation/forest-certification.

246 **However, that number should be placed:** *State of the World's Forests, 2012* (Rome: Food and Agriculture Organization of the United Nations, 2012), 24, http://www.fao.org/docrep/016/i3010e/i3010e.pdf.

246 **While the FSC claims that about 15 percent:** Forest Stewardship Council, "Facts and Figures," accessed August 19, 2017, https://ic.fsc.org/en/ facts-and-figures.

247 **But successes such as these are rare:** http://www.nytimes.com/2009/11/ 18/business/18labor.html

248 **Reports by monitoring teams in 2016 and 2017:** Robert J. S. Ross, "Bringing Labor Rights Back to Bangladesh," *American Prospect*, July 12, 2015, http://prospect.org/article/bringing-labor-rights-back-bangladesh.

248 **The result is that countries with few:** Jeffrey D. Sachs and Andrew M. Warner, *Natural Resource Abundance and Economic Growth*, NBER Working Paper 5398 (National Bureau of Economic Research, Cambridge, MA, 1995).

249 **"A Crude Awakening":** "A Crude Awakening," Global Witness, December 1, 1999, https://www.globalwitness.org/en/archive/crude-awakening.

249 **In 2003, organizers created:** Mabel van Oranje and Henry Parham, "Publishing What We Learned: An Assessment of the Publish What You Pay Coalition," Publish What You Pay, 2009, http://www.publishwhatyoupay.org/ wp-content/uploads/2015/06/Publishing-What-We-Learned.pdf.

251 **The European Union, for example:** "The European Union's Generalized System of Preferences," European Commission Directorate-General for Trade, 2004, http://trade.ec.europa.eu/doclib/docs/2004/march/ tradoc_116448.pdf.

251 **More than 244 million people:** "244 Million International Migrants Living Abroad Worldwide, New UN Statistics Reveal," *Sustainable Development Goals* (blog), January 12, 2016, http://www.un.org/sustainabledevelopment/ blog/2016/01/244-million-international-migrants-living-abroad-worldwide-new-un-statistics-reveal.

252 **Nepalis regularly travel to India:** Seema Rajouria, "World Cup Corruption: The Bigger Scandal," *American Prospect*, July 6, 2015, http://prospect.org/article/world-cup-corruption-bigger-scandal.

253 **"a well-founded fear of being persecuted":** *Convention and Protocol Relating to the Status of Refugees* (Geneva, Switzerland: United Nations High Commissioner for Refugees, 2010), http://www.unhcr.org/protect/PROTECTION/3b66c2aa10.pdf.

253 **Gara LaMarche, a longtime human-rights activist:** Gara LaMarche, "Is Anyone Alien from the Social Contract?" in *What Do We Owe Each Other?*, eds. Howard L. Rosenthal and David J. Rothman (New Brunswick, NJ: Transaction, 2008), 91–100.

254 **The ozone layer is expected to heal:** James Gustave Speth, *Red Sky at Morning* (New Haven, CT: Yale University Press, 2005), esp. chap. 4.

255 **Those not even signed by the US:** See Robert Kuttner, "Global Governance of Capital: A Challenge for Democracy," Demos, October 7, 2014, http://www.demos.org/publication/global-governance-capital-challenge-democracy.

257 **"make the world safe for diversity":** John F. Kennedy, "Commencement Address at American University in Washington," June 10, 1963, American Presidency Project, http://www.presidency.ucsb.edu/ws/?pid=9266.

11. LIBERALISM, POPULISM, FASCISM

258 **Along the way, theorists such as John Locke:** Jonathan Bennett, "Second Treatise on Government, John Locke," EarlyModernTexts.com, accessed March 22, 2017, http://www.earlymoderntexts.com/assets/pdfs/locke1689a.pdf.

259 **For centuries, there have been plenty:** Isaiah Berlin, "Two Concepts of Liberty," in *Four Essays on Liberty* (Oxford: Oxford University Press, 1969), 166–217.

259 **As the economist and political philosopher Joseph Schumpeter:** Joseph A. Schumpeter, *Capitalism, Socialism and Democracy* (1944; repr., London: Allen & Unwin, 1962).

260 **"Its truth rested not upon the truth":** Robert O. Paxton, *The Anatomy of Fascism* (New York: Vintage, 2005), 17.

260 **"The democrats of *Il Mondo* want to know":** Ibid.

261 **In his synthesis of core principles:** Ibid., 41.

262 **Germany and Italy, divided among several:** Amos Elon, *The Pity of It All: A Portrait of the German-Jewish Epoch 1743–1933* (New York: Picador, 2002).

262 **"reached a turning point, but failed to turn":** A. J. P. Taylor, *The Course of German History: A Survey of the Development of German History since 1815* (1945; repr., London: Routledge, 2001), 71.

263 **"a substitute for national emancipation":** Hannah Arendt, *The Origins of Totalitarianism* (Cleveland, OH: Meridian, 1958), 170.

264 **"The liberal state is destined to perish":** Ira Katznelson, *Fear Itself: The New Deal and the Origins of Our Time* (New York: Liveright, 2013), 5.

265 **"The Fascist conception of the State":** "The Doctrine of Fascism: Benito

Mussolini (1932)," World Future Fund, accessed December 13, 2016, http://www.worldfuturefund.org/wffmaster/Reading/Germany/mussolini.htm.

265 **"In our time it may be shrewdly forecast":** Richard Washburn Child, foreword to *My Autobiography*, by Benito Mussolini (New York: Scribner, 1928), viii.

266 **"In essence, the populist surge":** Cas Mudde, "The Problem with Populism," *Guardian*, February 17, 2015, https://www.theguardian.com/commentis free/2015/feb/17/problem-populism-syriza-podemos-dark-side-europe.

266 **"escape from freedom":** Erich Fromm, *Escape from Freedom* (New York: Henry Holt, 1941).

266 **These followers were said to have:** Theodore W. Adorno et al., *The Authoritarian Personality* (New York: Harper & Brothers, 1951).

267 **"We have to abandon liberal methods":** Csaba Tóth, "Full Text of Viktor Orbán's Speech at Băile Tușnad (Tusnádfürdő) of 26 July 2014," *Budapest Beacon*, July 29, 2014, http://budapestbeacon.com/public-policy/full-text-of-viktor-orbans-speech-at-baile-tusnad-tusnadfurdo-of-26-july-2014/10592.

267 **"Democratically elected regimes":** Fareed Zakaria, "The Rise of Illiberal Democracy," *Foreign Affairs*, November–December 1997, 22–23, https://www.foreignaffairs.com/articles/1997-11-01/rise-illiberal-democracy.

267 **"are not just about liberalism (or the rule of law)":** Jan-Werner Müller, *What Is Populism?* (Philadelphia: University of Pennsylvania Press, 2016), 55.

269 **In case the message was not clear enough:** Krisztina Than, "Hungary's Anti-Soros Posters 'Recall Europe's Darkest Hours': Soros Spokesman," Reuters, July 14, 2017, https://www.reuters.com/article/us-hungary-soros-idUSKBN19W0XU.

270 **The Orbán government also acted:** Benjamin Novak, "Princeton's Kim Scheppele on Viktor Orban and His Fidesz Supermajority," *Budapest Beacon*, November 27, 2014, http://budapestbeacon.com/politics/princetons-kim-scheppele-on-viktor-orban-and-his-fidesz-supermajority/15617.

271 **"There were no disagreements in Stalin's universe":** Tony Judt, *Postwar: A History of Europe Since 1945* (New York: Penguin Press, 2005), 188.

272 **The rise of far-right parties was abrupt:** Dani Rodrik, *Populism and the Economics of Globalization*, NBER Working Paper 23559 (Cambridge, MA: National Bureau of Economic Research, July 2017).

272 **Ominously, neofascism has more popular appeal:** See discussion in Agnes Cornell, Jørgen Møller, and Svend-Erik Skaaning, "The Real Lessons of the Interwar Years," *Journal of Democracy* 28, no. 3 (July 2017): 14–28.

273 **Jan-Werner Müller has observed:** Jan-Werner Müller, "How Populists Win When They Lose," Social Europe, June 29, 2017, https://www.socialeurope.eu/2017/06/populists-win-lose.

273 **In several former Soviet satellites:** Rick Lyman, "In Bulgaria, a Businessman Who Talks (and Acts) like Trump," *New York Times*, February 24, 2017, https://www.nytimes.com/2017/02/24/world/europe/in-bulgaria-a-businessman-who-talks-like-trump-acts-like-trump.html.

273 **In Bulgaria, Veselin Mareshki:** https://www.nytimes.com/2017/02/24/world/europe/in-bulgaria-a-businessman-who-talks-like-trump-acts-like-trump.html.

273 **In the Czech Republic, Andrej Babiš:** http://www.reuters.com/article/us-czech-government-babis/billionaire-businessman-babis-is-at-heart-of-czech-political-crisis-idUSKBN1800ZH.

273 **And in neighboring Slovakia, Boris Kollár:** https://www.nytimes.com/2017/02/24/world/europe/zbigniew-stonoga-andrej-babis.html?mcubz=3.

274 **Hitler, once in office:** Gotz Aly, *Hitler's Beneficiaries: Plunder, Racial War and the Nazi Welfare State* (New York: Metropolitan Books, 2006).

277 **Abraham Lincoln, as Doris Kearns Goodwin wrote:** Doris Kearns Goodwin, *Team of Rivals: The Political Genius of Abraham Lincoln* (New York: Simon & Schuster, 2005).

282 **The new American leader:** Robert Kuttner, *Obama's Challenge: America's Economic Crisis and the Power of a Transformative Presidency* (White River Junction, VT: Chelsea Green, 2008).

12. THE ROAD FROM HERE

283 **In the 1990s, a formulation popularized:** George Soros, *The Alchemy of Finance* (Hoboken, NJ: Wiley, 1987).

283 **A more pointed distinction:** George Soros, *The Crisis of Global Capitalism: The Open Society Endangered* (New York: Public Affairs, 1998).

284 **Some twenty-five democracies:** Edward Luce, *The Retreat of Western Liberalism* (New York: Atlantic Monthly Press, 2017), 12.

284 **As James Mann prophetically warned:** James Mann, *The China Fantasy: How Our Leaders Explain Away Chinese Repression* (New York: Penguin Group, 2007).

285 **"Political Aspects of Full Employment":** M. Kalecki, "Political Aspects of Full Employment," *Political Quarterly* 14, no. 4 (1943): 322–31.

286 **But Kalecki's insight:** See also Charles E. Lindblom's classic discussion on the residual power of business in a market economy: *Politics and Markets: The World's Political Economic Systems* (New York: Basic Books, 1977).

286 **"countervailing" forces:** John Kenneth Galbraith, *American Capitalism: The Concept of Countervailing Power* (Boston: Houghton Mifflin, 1952).

287 **"The 'populist' whose politics you abhor":** Michael Kazin, "How Can Donald Trump and Bernie Sanders Both Be 'Populist'?" *New York Times Magazine*, March 22, 2016, https://www.nytimes.com/2016/03/27/magazine/how-can-donald-trump-and-bernie-sanders-both-be-populist.html.

287 **"demagoguing" the trade issue:** Paul Krugman, "Trade and Tribulation," *New York Times*, March 11, 2016, https://www.nytimes.com/2016/03/11/opinion/trade-and-tribulation.html?_r=0.

288 **The current abuses and Warren's efforts:** Lawrence Goodwyn, *Democratic Promise: The Populist Moment in America* (New York: Oxford University Press, 1976).

291 **Most immigrants to the US:** Douglas S. Massey, ed., *New Faces in New*

Places: The Changing Geography of American Immigration (New York: Russell Sage Foundation, 2008), 343–54.

291 **The strongest bases of resurgent:** See Harold Meyerson, "Dan Cantor's Machine," *American Prospect*, January 6, 2014, http://prospect.org/article/dan-cantors-machine; Harold Meyerson, "How California Hopes to Undo Trump," *American Prospect*, March 29, 2017, http://prospect.org/article/how-california-hopes-undo-trump.

293 **Bullock's two-term predecessor:** Justin Gest, "Can the Democratic Party Be White Working Class, Too?" *American Prospect*, April 3, 2017, http://prospect.org/article/can-democratic-party-be-white-working-class-too.

294 **"As long as egalitarians assume":** Christopher Jencks, *Inequality: A Reassessment of the Effect of Family and Schooling in America* (New York: Basic Books, 1972), 265.

295 **Indeed, long before the Sanders campaign:** Harold Meyerson, "The Long March of Bernie's Army," *American Prospect*, March 23, 2016, http://prospect.org/article/long-march-bernie%E2%80%99s-army.

295 **A lesson of that era:** Lindblom, *Politics and Markets*.

296 **The Meidner plan never became law:** Rudolf Meidner, "Why Did the Swedish Model Fail?" *Socialist Register*, 1993, 211–28, http://socialistregister.com/index.php/srv/article/view/5630/2528.

296 **"decommodified":** Gøsta Esping-Andersen, *The Three Worlds of Welfare Capitalism* (Princeton, NJ: Princeton University Press, 1990).

298 **The American Society of Civil Engineers:** American Society of Civil Engineers, "2017 Infrastructure Report Card," accessed February 21, 2017, http://www.infrastructurereportcard.org/the-impact/economic-impact.

299 **"Democracies have the right to protect":** Dani Rodrik, *The Globalization Paradox: Democracy and the Future of the World Economy* (New York: Norton, 2011), xviii.

301 **They have employed techniques:** See discussion in Gary L. Reback, *Free the Market! Why Only Government Can Keep the Marketplace Competitive* (New York: Portfolio, 2009); and Robert B. Reich, *Saving Capitalism for the Many, Not the Few* (New York: Knopf, 2016).

302 **A more promising version has been proposed:** Peter Barnes, *With Liberty and Dividends for All: How to Save Our Middle Class When Jobs Don't Pay Enough* (San Francisco: Barrett-Koehler, 2014).

303 **Alternatively, my colleague Paul Starr:** Paul Starr, "The Next Progressive Health Agenda: Part Two of the Republican Health-Care Unraveling," *American Prospect*, March 23, 2017, http://prospect.org/article/next-progressive-health-agenda.

305 *policy is frozen politics*: "David Rolf, president, Workers Lab, Service Employees International Union, Local 775" (Albert Shanker Institute), YouTube, January 19, 2015, https://www.youtube.com/watch?v=005d8e5Swec.

305 **"It doesn't matter, Republican, Democrat":** Julia Preston and Lizette Alvarez, "Florida's Changing Latino Population Veers from G.O.P.," *New York Times*, October 3, 2016, https://www.nytimes.com/2016/10/03/us/hispanic-voters-florida-republicans.html.

306 **"32 percent chose":** Guy Molyneux, "A Tale of Two Populisms: The Elite the White Working Class Loathes Is Politicians," *American Prospect*, June 1, 2017, http://prospect.org/article/tale-two-populisms.

307 **"Brexit advocates in Britain presented":** Dani Rodrik, *Populism and the Economics of Globalization*, NBER Working Paper 23559 (Cambridge, MA: National Bureau of Economic Research, July 2017).

308 **Wolfgang Streeck:** Wolfgang Streeck, *How Will Capitalism End?: Essays on a Failing System* (London: Verso, 2016).

309 **"plutonomy":** Ajay Kapur, Niall Macleod, and Narendra Singh, "Plutonomy: Buying Luxury, Explaining Global Imbalances," Citigroup, October 16, 2005, https://delong.typepad.com/plutonomy-1.pdf.

INDEX

ABOUT THE AUTHOR

Robert Kuttner is cofounder and coeditor of *The American Prospect* magazine, and the Ida and Meyer Kirstein chair at the Heller School for Social Policy and Management at Brandeis University. He was a founder of the Economic Policy Institute, and serves on its executive committee.

Kuttner is the author of eleven books, including the 2008 New York Times best seller *Obama's Challenge*. His other writing has appeared in *The Atlantic*, *The New Yorker*, *Harper's Magazine*, *New York Review of Books*, *New Republic*, *Foreign Affairs*, *Dissent*, *New Statesman*, *Harvard Business Review*, *Columbia Journalism Review*, *Political Science Quarterly*, and the *New York Times Magazine* and *New York Times Book Review*. He has contributed major articles for the *New England Journal of Medicine* as a national policy correspondent. He is a weekly columnist for HuffPost.

He previously served as a national staff writer on the *Washington Post*, chief investigator of the U.S. Senate Banking Committee, economics editor of *New Republic*, and was a longtime columnist for *Business Week* and for the *Boston Globe*, syndicated by the *Washington Post*. He is the two-time winner of the Sidney Hillman Journalism Award. He is the recipient of the John Hancock Award for Excellence in Business and Financial Journalism, the Jack London Award for Labor Writing, and the Paul G. Hoffman Award of the United Nations Development Program for his lifetime work on economic efficiency and social justice. He has been a Guggenheim Fellow, Woodrow Wilson Fellow, German Marshall Fund Fellow, and John F. Kennedy Fellow.

Educated at Oberlin College, The London School of Economics, and the University of California at Berkeley, Kuttner is the recipient of honorary degrees from Swarthmore College and Oberlin. In addition to Brandeis, he has also taught at the University of Massachusetts, the University of Oregon, Boston University, and Harvard's Institute of Politics. He lives in Boston with his wife, Joan Fitzgerald, a professor of public policy at Northeastern. He is the father of two grown children and has six grandchildren.